Making a Middle Landscape

Making a Middle Landscape

Peter G. Rowe

The MIT Press

Cambridge, Massachusetts

London, England

This book was set in Times Roman by DEKR Corporation and printed and bound in the United States of America.

Library of Congress Cataloging-in-Publication Data

Rowe, Peter G.
Making a middle landscape / Peter G. Rowe
p.   cm.
Includes bibliographical references.
ISBN 0-262-18138-X
1. Suburbs—United States. 2. City planning—United States. 3. Public spaces—United States—Planning.
4. Land use, Urban— United States. I. Title.
HT352.U6R68   1991
307.74′0973—dc20   90-6674
                                                                                 CIP

To my family, all of them suburbanites

Contents

Acknowledgments

Books of this sort are seldom written without the assistance and encouragement of others. Three persons were particularly influential. Laurie Olin's constant encouragement, incomparable insights, and tireless consultation provided the backbone of support. My teacher, former colleague, and friend, O. Jack Mitchell, was responsible for my introduction to American urban development and continued to give me his forthright counsel. Finally, through the eyes of "me mate," Jim Blackburn, I saw the contemporary metropolitan terrain so much more clearly.

I must also acknowledge the encouragement and support of Tony Gomez-Ibanez, Rodolfo Machado, Ed Robbins, Jorge Silvetti, Dan Schodek, and Ellen Whittemore, my colleagues at Harvard, as well as Alex von Hoffman, Alex Krieger, and John Stilgoe, with whom I share a special interest in American environments. I remain grateful to John Whiteman, my former colleague, for his design studio collaboration and early advice, together with David Dillon of the Dallas Morning News *for his enthusiastic encouragement. To my dean at the Graduate School of Design, Jerry McCue, I extend special thanks for his understanding, constant encouragement, and help. In this light I am also grateful for the support of the late Michael Spear, chairman of the Graduate School of Design's Visiting Committee and president of the Rouse Company.*

Graduate students often form a cadre of willing assistants, and this project was no exception. To John Michael Desmond, Glenn Forley, Bill McIlroy, Donna Paley, Riccardo Tossani, and Vasilios Tsakalos, I owe a special debt of gratitude. Several classes of first-year urban design students at Harvard struggled tirelessly with the conditions of American urbanism that we set them. Their insights clearly helped shape mine.

This enterprise received financial assistance over the years from a number of foundations and granting agencies. Much of the work was made possible by a grant from the Design Arts Program of the National Endowment for the Arts and matching grants from the Milton Fund and from a gift to the Graduate School of Design by Joseph Wasserman. The Joint Center for Housing Studies at MIT and Harvard University provided support for research on residential development. Without these generous grants, this book would never have been written.

Support in preparing manuscripts and administering research is a crucial part of any scholarly undertaking. My special thanks go to Carmen Hurwitz-Morales for her understanding and tireless oganizational contributions; to Linda Coe and Polly Price for their help in administering the research; and, perhaps foremost, to Jennifer Frey, Richard Aguilar, and especially Lilia Garcia-Leyva for their work in preparing the manuscript.

Finally, I wish to express my affection and esteem for my wife, Marianne, for her constant encouragement, proofing, and critical commentary, and for my son Anthony, for his tolerance and forbearance.

Sub-Urbs in Rure

This book is about the physical character of American suburban and ex-urban development that has occurred during the modern era. In essence, it is about the making of a middle landscape between city and countryside.

The orientation is threefold. The first concerns what has actually been built since about 1920, when relatively simple arrangements of land, buildings, and infrastructure swiftly became transformed into complex multiuse centers and heterogeneous living environments. The second probes behind these physical manifestations of the middle landscape to uncover mythic themes, root metaphors, and attitudes of mind that seem to be at play. In large measure, this is an attempt to describe and dissect the symbolic landscape and some of its important cultural artifacts. The third focus concerns the problem of finding an appropriate poetic for the middle landscape and, in short, of defining proper design principles for its making.

Part One examines the territorial transformations made as a consequence of suburban metropolitan expansion. At first, decentralization and deconcentration of population and land use were the trends, followed by reconcentration and specialization. The result was a sprawling metropolitan cultural and spatial mosaic.

Part One also deals with simultaneous changes that have occurred in the way in which we have perceived cities. Shunned at first for its monotony and conformity, being "suburban" for most Americans quickly took the place of being "urban." In the process the historical rise of pluralism in society, whose beginnings coincided with early suburbanization in the nineteenth century, was more fully institutionalized and geographically inscribed on the metropolitan landscape. In short, "urbs et rus" gave way to "sub-urbs in rure."

1   *Territorial   Transformations*

During the modern era of American life there have been two intense episodes of suburban expansion. The first took place after the armistice in 1918, terminating in the aftermath of the Wall Street crash of 1929, a period spanning roughly 1920 to 1930. The second began after World War II and the subsequent demobilizations of servicemen and women, a period spanning approximately 1950 to the present. During both episodes, and particularly during the latter, Americans saw extensive deconcentrations of urban populations and substantial transformation of the landscape around their metropolitan areas. Any sharp distinction between city and country remaining from prior urban settlement was quickly obliterated and replaced by a middle landscape of suburban and exurban development.

FROM CITY TO SUBURB

The year 1920, or thereabouts, marks something of a watershed in domestic American circumstances. It was the time when most Americans crossed over into the modern era. For the first time in history a majority of Americans were urban dwellers (figure 1). The urban population, which was 39 percent of the total only two decades earlier in 1900, now stood at 51

percent (U.S. Bureau of the Census 1900–1920). The pace of house building, in decline during World War I, suddenly intensified, reaching a new benchmark of about 1 million starts annually by 1925 (U.S. Department of Commerce 1955). In the immediate wake of the progressive era's revolt against Victorian excesses, the pattern of small, simple cottages on modest individual plots of land was quite firmly established (Wright 1981, Clark 1986). Domestic electrification, with all its significant side effects on household appliances and social communications, also became a reality in most American homes. Indeed the rapidity with which the American home was transformed in this manner was startling. In 1917 only 24.3 percent of all homes in the United States were electrified. By 1920 electrification reached 47.7 percent, subsequently rising to 85 percent by 1930 (Cowan 1982).

During the 1920s the decentralization and deconcentration of urban development began to intensify. From the advent of the Victorian streetcar suburb there had always been a tendency in that direction. Even earlier, the first American suburbs— around eighteenth-century Philadelphia—had represented decentralized pockets of urban concentrations although on a much more local scale (Warner 1968, Jackson and Shultz 1972, Jackson 1985). Now, how-

Figure 1   The progress of urbanization: triple-decker development in the Boston area. Copyright 1985 David King Gleason from "Over Boston"

ever, following an intensive period of city building stretching from the end of the Civil War to 1920, some sixty cities began to decentralize, principally as a result of improved public transportation and widespread private automobile use (Wilbur Smith and Associates 1961). Motor vehicle registrations, mainly of automobiles, rose from a paltry 2 million in 1912 to over 26 million by 1930, subsequently remaining relatively stable until another period of sharp increase following World War II (U.S. Bureau of Public Roads 1965). Domestically the radical restructuring of households that had taken place during the progressive era (1890–1920) now began to stabilize. For instance, the rate of decline in household size, which had been quite dramatic during the first decades of the twentieth century, almost halved during the twenties.

The large and extended family structure of the Victorian era was replaced by the now-familiar nuclear family of considerably smaller size and hierarchical complexity. (U.S. Bureau of the Census 1900–1980, Masnick and Bane 1980). All of these changes coincided with the rise of the automobile suburb with its characteristic array of residential streets lined with single-family detached houses.

Later, following the tragic interlude of the Great Depression and World War II, the 1950s bore witness to another watershed in American life. Between 1950 and 1960, America became a nation of predominantly suburban dwellers. The decentralization of urban populations, which was so pronounced during the 1920s and had become even more intense in the decade after World War II, now pushed the suburban proportion of metropolitan development within the United States beyond 50 percent. This proportion continued to rise, reaching about 65 percent by 1980 (U.S. Bureau of the Census 1900–1980).

During certain periods the rate of population growth in suburban locales was astounding. Between 1950 and 1960, for example, large metropolitan areas on the average experienced a 53.9 percent increase in suburban population, compared to only a 1.5 percent increase within central cities, for a total gain of 33.1 percent overall. In Miami, suburban population expansion was as high as 72 percent, and almost all long-established cities on the eastern seaboard saw suburban expansion of 20 percent or more (U.S. Bureau of the Census 1900—1980, Wilbur Smith and Associates 1961). The process of urbanization that was so intense, particularly toward the end of the nineteenth century, was now unraveling and moving back out into the countryside (figure 2). In fact, most recent small to moderate-sized metropolitan areas expanded more rapidly than their larger, more traditional counterparts, and nonmetropolitan regions grew substantially faster than metropolitan areas as a whole (Long 1981, Rothblatt and Garr 1986).

By 1950 the United States had become a nation of homeowners. The percentage of those owning homes compared to those renting, which had hovered between 40 and 50 percent during the first four de-cades of the century, now stood at 55 percent. This proportion climbed to 66 percent by 1970 (U.S. Bureau of the Census 1900–1980). Housing starts, by 1949, returned to just above the predepression years' high of 1 million, never to go below during the following almost forty years (U.S. Department of Commerce 1955 and 1955–1987). Automobile ownership, once more on the rise, reached three out of every four American families during the 1950s, passing the ratio of one car per family overall by 1955 for

Figure 2   Patterns of rural settlement: Worcester Turnpike near Framingham, Massachusetts, 1947

the first time in history (Gakenheimer 1978). The era of freeways and dispersed development was truly in effect.

The territorial transformations that accompanied these suburban expansions were considerable. The rural landscape, once only crisscrossed by railroads and farm-to-market roads, now was ribboned by turnpikes and interstate highways (figure 3). Highway legislation enacted by the U.S. Congress in 1956 alone had as a target 41,000 miles of high-speed limited-access roadway (Wilbur Smith and Associates 1961). With widespread improvements in transportation accessibility came changes in land use. People no longer had to live close to where they worked, and the conveniences of one-stop shopping and accessible cheap land radically altered patterns of retail commercial development (Baker and Funaro 1951, Gillette 1985). Industry and office establishments took advantage of new locational patterns, moving into the suburbs and countryside around and between larger metropolitan areas (Jackson 1985). In both instances the scale and land area of commercial facilities increased appreciably, transcending earlier urban building types. According to Homer Hoyt's landmark study of 1960, nearly sixty shopping centers, with in excess of half a million square feet of floor area each, stood where there had been practically none only half a decade earlier (Hoyt 1960). Decentralized industrial parks replaced the multistoried loft buildings of older cities. Firms began to follow their workers into the suburbs, taking advantage of bucolic settings and relatively less expensive land to create a new image for the office, the workplace for a majority of America's work force (Kostof 1987). To cite but

Figure 3   The portents of things to come: construction of Route 128 and the Massachusetts Turnpike, 1955

one example, by 1957 some ninety-nine new industrial and commercial facilities were located along Boston's Route 128, one of the nation's first perimeter circumferential freeways. Of these facilities more than seventy were formerly located within a 4-mile radius close in toward the center of Boston (Bone and Wohl 1959).

The migrations that characterize modern urban growth dynamics began to change in yet another way. From the end of World War II until about 1960 or 1965, most of the movement was generally from the central city to the suburbs. Furthermore, housing starts, a reasonable measure of where development is occurring, were relatively evenly distributed among the major regions of the United States (U.S. Department of Commerce 1955–1987). After this period, however, interregional shifts in development emphasis suddenly became prominent. The South, which had had only 29 percent of total housing starts in 1955, jumped to close to 50 percent by 1980. By contrast, starts in the Northeast declined from 21 percent to under 10 percent in the same period. No doubt these fluctuations were closely associated with the dramatic rise of the so-called sunbelt cities (Abbott 1981, 1987). Net changes in rate of regional development were most noticeable during the 1970s and 1980s and suggest another kind of urban migration altogether (Morrison 1979). Now movement occurred not in a trajectory from city to suburb but from one metropolitan region to another, often in completely different parts of the country. Local suburban metropolitan development was being driven rather strongly by economic fortunes nationwide.

A TALE OF TWO TOWNS

Beyond the abstractions of this kind of general account, we find numerous tangible examples of the suburbanization process that have touched the lives of most Americans. Although separated by both time and space, the township of Framingham in the metropolitan region of Boston and the suburb of Sharpstown in Houston, Texas, have a number of commonalities and illustrate some of the surprising contemporary turns America's suburbs have taken.

At first glance, the differences between the two places seem to be enormous. Settlement began in Framingham in the seventeenth century. By contrast, urban development in the Sharpstown area was sparse until the 1950s and, at least initially, it was the vision of one man. The topography of Framingham is typical of the verdant New England rolling countryside. Sharpstown is flat and, in its natural state, a grassy prairie. Framingham has a temperate climate, whereas Sharpstown is semitropical. Framingham

has a strong institutional tradition in public sector land use controls and planning, typical of the Boston region. Sharpstown and Houston, lacking such land use controls, reflect almost the opposite kind of entrepreneurial spirit.

But there are also similarities between these two areas. Both have regional locations between the inner and outer circumferential metropolitan loop roads that have so strongly influenced postwar suburban development. Both contain large metropolitan shopping centers and enjoy the status of being subregional centers of employment. Both have experienced boom periods of development during the last twenty years. There was intense development during the 1970s in Houston and a similar period of intense development in Boston during the 1980s. Both are relatively mature suburban developments, dating back to the halycon days of the 1950s. In both their common and contrastive characteristics, these towns represent much of modern suburban America.

Framingham and the Suburbanization of the Boston Region

In 1930 the population of the Boston metropolitan region was close to 2.3 million and remained at that level through much of World War II (U.S. Bureau of the Census 1930–1980a). The spatial distribution of this population was largely concentrated in the city of Boston and the older surrounding streetcar suburbs. But there were small concentrations of population in outlying towns served by the railroad, although linkages here to central areas of the metropolitan region were primarily based on industrial production and the transfer of goods. Overall the shape of the region conformed to a traditional monocentric or core-periphery model of the city, where employment is concentrated toward the center, with residential development in suburban rings of descending density on the periphery. Seventy-three percent of the region's population fell within commuting distance of Boston proper, or the area now described as lying inside Route 128, the ringroad shown in figure 4 that began construction in 1949 as part of a new expressway system (Metropolitan Area Planning Council 1982). In spite of their proximity to Boston, a number of towns that formed part of this inner area of the region, among them Lexington, Dedham, and Burlington, were sparsely settled and little different from other small communities farther out in the countryside (U.S. Geological Survey 1950).

The structure of these urbanizing areas was dominated by a conjunction between land use and transportation in which fixed rail and trolley systems defined either the corridors along which the most intensive residential and commercial development was located or the transit stops that formed the nucleus for similar activities (Schaeffer and Sclar 1975, Sutcliffe 1984). Beyond both lay residential development in suburban tracts of varying density. Usually the closer the site was to the local commercial center or the closer the town was to the center of the region, the higher was the residential density. Gradually several roads, including the Worcester Turnpike, took on more significance than simply an upgrading of traditional routes for automobile use; they became commercial highways with widespread recreational driving on weekends (Merriam 1948). Natural terrain also shaped the direction and layout of settlements.

Typically they were built not on steeper hillsides but on relatively flat ground, especially adjacent to well-traveled arterial roads. Similarly, low-lying, flood-prone, or marshy areas were skirted in favor of less costly and less troublesome building sites.

Located in the western portion of the Boston metropolitan area, about halfway to the central Massachusetts city of Worcester, the town of Framingham largely conformed to this pattern of development and to its role as a regional industrial town (figure 4). Considerably larger than neighboring Natick, Ashland, and Wellesley farther to the east, Framingham was the local center, the most prominent stop on the rail line leading west from Boston, and a frequent destination of travelers from the city (Merriam 1948). Its residential population of 22,210 persons in 1930 primarily lived in single-family detached houses, some dating back as far as the Victorian era (Traylor 1983). Although settlers had come to this area as early as 1647, it was only in the nineteenth century that Framingham had become established (Leavitt and Ryder 1947), primarily as a consequence of the Sudbury River, which flowed through the town on its northerly course toward the Merrimack. In typical New England fashion, urbanizing areas within the township, like Saxonville to the northeast of Framingham center (figure 5), made use of the Sudbury to power the industrial mills located on the river bank. The Roxbury Carpet Company, for instance, employing something on the order of 500 people, was firmly established there in 1860 (Row, Dolbeare, and Tannenbaum 1948).

By 1940 Framingham's population, at 23,214, was little changed, a rise of just 4.5 percent during the

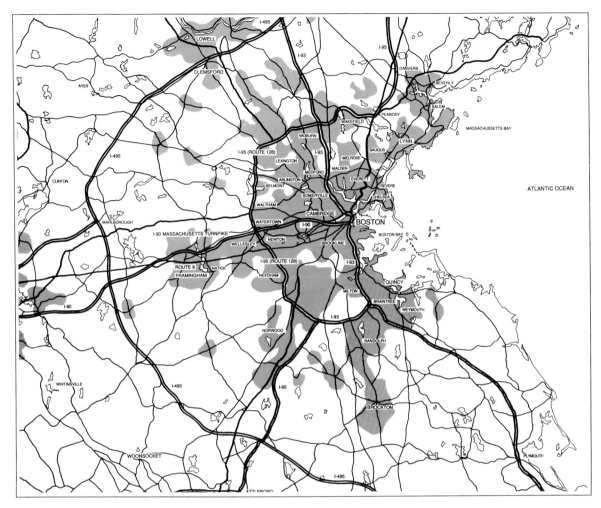

*Figure 4   The Boston Metropolitan Region today,
showing major thoroughfares and urbanized areas*

intervening decade (Metropolitan Area Planning Council 1982). The landscape of the town was primarily made up of single-family detached houses, with single- and double-storied storefronts lining the main streets toward the heart of the town, some with small skylit arcades (Taylor 1983). Here there was a convergence of roads and commercial establishments around the train stop, a handsome Victorian neoromantic structure designed by the architect H. H. Richardson, on the north side of the train tracks as they ran east-west through the town (Ochsner 1982).

Industry lay on both sides along the railroad, with sidings providing immediate access for incoming and outgoing goods. Of particular prominence was the Dennison's paper goods manufacturing plant, with over 2,700 employees (Row, Dolbeare, and Tannenbaum 1948). In short, the layout of the township of Framingham pivoted around the rail line. As something of a barrier to development, it also incorporated unfortunate yet commonplace socioeconomic distinctions between those who lived to the north, on the right side of the tracks, and those who did not—a social distinction that has persisted throughout most of Framingham's history.

The other prominent feature on the landscape was Route 9, also known as the Worcester Turnpike. Firmly established by 1940 as one of the few high-capacity thoroughfares running between regions, the turnpike not only provided for commerce between Boston and Worcester but opened up the western portion of the region for recreational use. Again in rather typical fashion for the day, the turnpike bypassed the town of Framingham proper in the interests of less congestion, higher speeds, and the economics of road building. Road rights-of-way, always difficult to secure even at the best of times, were relatively unencumbered away from denser urban areas, particularly across less desirable, occasionally marshy land. No doubt natural breaks in the Cochituate chain of lakes, running north-south between Natick and Framingham, also had something to do with the alignment (figure 5). This thoroughfare played an impor-

Figure 5   Prominent features of Framingham's natural and manmade landscape

tant role in the radical restructuring of Framingham during the 1950s and 1960s. One of the consequences of the improved accessibility was a small yet significant and systematic decline in Framingham's share of the western subregion's total population. During 1930, with 38 percent, Framingham had the lion's share of population in what is now the Metrowest subregion. This share consistently diminished to about 32 percent in 1950, while other towns in the subregion, and particularly Wellesley and later Weston to the east nearer Boston, grew at slightly faster rates (Metropolitan Area Planning Council 1985a). In short, as a shift was made toward vastly improved road transportation, accessibility to the area was more widespread and less dependent on the fixed routes of the train system. At the same time commuter suburbs were spreading slowly westward from Boston as part of a general expansion of the metropolitan region.

This growth on the fringes beyond Route 128 accelerated appreciably during the 1950s and the 1960s, registering a 36.4 percent and 25.7 percent increase in population, respectively, during those decades. By contrast, the inner regional area grew modestly during the 1950s, posting little under a 3 percent gain in population, and actually declining during the 1960s, with a 1.5 percent overall loss of population (Metropolitan Area Planning Council 1982 and U.S. Census Bureau 1930–1980a).

Given the reasonably robust boom in the same area shortly after World War II, these trends are significant. Population growth in the entire metropolitan region was relatively constant over the period from 1940 to 1970 at around 8 to 9 percent each decade,

and yet peripheral areas were growing at a much faster rate (Metropolitan Area Planning Council 1982). Clearly Boston was suburbanizing as automobile-oriented lower-density residential areas filled in available land closer to the city and expanded outward toward the periphery. The white middle class became more affluent once again after the tribulations of the depression and the war, and with this affluence many sought the relative comfort and security of their own home and land beyond the city and its inner suburbs.

The urban morphology of the region also changed substantially, largely under the aegis of the private automobile and accommodations that were made to this broadly based form of personal transportation. Perhaps the most significant among these was the interstate highway system, which secured congressional approval in 1956, together with the metropolitan freeways that supported these cross-country links, bypassing congested inner city streets. The resulting loop and radial, limited-access, high-capacity roadway design was superimposed, terrain permitting, on practically every American city (Wilbur Smith and Associates 1961). In fact, with the construction of Route 128 in 1949, the nation's earliest loop road, and the Massachusetts Turnpike during the mid-1950s, Boston was one of the first metropolitan areas to move into this new freeway era. Instead of residential neighborhoods adhering to corridors of commercial development that moved out from the city center along principal transportation routes, a much looser and less continuous mosaic of urban development occurred, made possible by increasing levels of private automobile ownership and use. The practice of wives chauffeuring their husbands to transit stops emerged, conveniently accommodating outlying low-density single-family residential development to the dictates of the daily routine of commuting.

A closely related feature of automobile-oriented residential development was the relatively low cost of land (Sutcliffe 1984). Although land rent generally continued to be directly related to transportation accessibility, the ubiquity and relative uniformity of patterns of convenient access provided by widespread use of the private automobile brought more land within affordable reach of homeowners without requiring increases in residential density (Clawson 1971). The combination of radial and circumferential high-capacity freeways also changed the overall pattern of metropolitan accessibility, making it less dependent on a traditional center supported by traditional modes of fixed transportation (Gruen 1973).

In 1950 the township of Framingham was quite sparsely populated except in established areas like Framingham center (figures 6 and 7) and nearby Saxonville. The population had jumped about 21 percent since 1940, mainly during the post–World War II era, reaching 28,086 (U.S. Bureau of the Census 1930–1980a). Like the region as a whole, Framingham was beginning to feel the effects of the impending urban boom. General Motors established a huge plant on the southern outskirts of the town in 1947, which employed over 2,000 people (Row, Dolbeare, and Tannenbaum 1948). The township remained relatively stable, middle class, and prosperous. Household size was 3.45 persons on the average, well in keeping with national trends, and there was not much fluctuation among areas within the township. Most people lived in traditional family settings, with slightly higher proportions living in neighborhoods out around local commercial areas than closer in to the centers. Median family incomes were relatively evenly distributed, again with slightly higher levels among households outside the local centers. Unemployment was moderate, with an overall average of 3.8 percent, although much higher levels, at 5.3 percent, characterized households south of the main rail line in and around Framingham proper. There were no minority populations to speak of, and the population's median age, at 31 years, was fairly typical for the early years of the baby boom. All in all, one might say past patterns of middle-class life had largely continued to flourish (U.S. Bureau of the Census 1930–1980a, Metropolitan Area Planning Council 1982).

During the next two decades this trend changed dramatically and even radically. First, population increased substantially by close to 59 percent between 1950 and 1960, continuing the post–World War II boom, followed by only a slightly lesser rate during the 1960s. By 1970 the population had reached 64,040. Caught in the grips of postwar prosperity and the baby boom, the population, not unexpectedly, became younger, even more family oriented, and considerably better off economically. Unemployment dropped to as low as 1.8 percent in 1960 before rising to 2.6 percent in 1970. The population per household increased in 1960 with a corresponding decrease in the number of single persons living alone. (This trend was to reverse in the subsequent decade, again in keeping with urbanizing areas in many other parts of the country.) The median age fell to 24 years by 1970

*Figure 6   Commerce and transit: aerial view of
Framingham Center in the 1950s*

before rising again. Most people continued to own
their own homes, with the amount of renter-occupied
housing remaining near 1950 levels of about 40 percent. The number of minorities increased, although
still remaining a very small proportion of the total
population, and spatially the township began to assume a more heterogeneous social complexion. By
1970 most socioeconomic indicators like household
size, median income, median age, and occupation
showed a much greater diversity across the popula-

tion than they exhibited in 1950 (U.S. Bureau of the
Census 1930–1980a, Metropolitan Area Planning
Council 1982, 1985b). Migration into the area, as
part of the general metropolitan expansion of Boston,
was bringing with it a diversity of people. Furthermore, established neighborhoods were already stratified by longer-term residents who remained. Looked
at from a slightly different perspective, with a more
than doubling of population in the relatively scant
space of twenty years, Framingham was beginning to

Figure 7   Postwar prosperity: commercial heart of Framingham Center

assume the characteristics of a much larger urban area, a trend that has continued. This former rural industrial town was clearly undergoing changes in structure and status. For instance, the declining share of subregional population turned around by 1970, and the share of subregional employment grew steadily in small increments to about 40 percent during the same period (Metropolitan Area Planning Council 1985a).

In keeping with both metropolitan growth and the higher degree of integration of Framingham into the affairs of the region, the physical pattern of ur-

banization within the township altered appreciably. Shoppers World, one of the first large centralized pedestrian malls in the country, was built in 1951 (figure 8) adjacent to the Worcester Turnpike on a vacant site remote from any previous urban development (Architectural Forum 1951, Baker and Funaro 1951). The location took considerable advantage of the restructured patterns of accessibility that would be associated with completion of the Massachusetts Turnpike, or Interstate Highway 90, and Route 128 to the east. In fact, Shoppers World was ideally situated to capture the retail market of a very large proportion of metropolitan Boston's suburban growth—precisely the point of the development. By moving out beyond the growing yet exclusive residential areas of Wellesley and Weston, where a site would probably have been difficult to obtain for local political reasons, Shoppers World was poised to take full advantage of a metropolitan growth corridor.

Such a locational strategy was not entirely new. As early as the late 1930s and early 1940s larger automobile-oriented shopping centers in California usually located toward the outskirts of town, near major regional roads (Gillette 1985). Nevertheless, both the size and type of the mall development was something very new and a truly radical departure from the merchandising that took place along the town's main street and scattered strip developments that had grown up along the Worcester Turnpike (Liebs 1985). First, Shoppers World was very large—500,000 square feet—and concentrated in one place. Second, the facility turned away from the highway, surrounded by huge parking lots on all

Figure 8   A new commercial venue: Shoppers World on the Worcester Turnpike shortly after opening in 1951

sides. Once out of the parking lot and into the mall proper, shoppers found themselves in an entirely pedestrian environment, centered around a carefully designed garden setting. Finally, a new style of merchandising conveniently brought together a variety of stores and entertainment facilities that previously could be found only in the city. All in all, it was an attractive invitation to make a special trip with the family and spend.

During the next two decades, other similar regional facilities located near Shoppers World. Gradually the area roughly bounded by Route 9, Route 30, and the Cochituate lakes was transformed from wooded and open sites into a thriving yet uncoordinated commercial center (figure 9). Natick Mall was built to the east, alongside Shoppers World, across the line in the neighboring township of Natick. Strip retail commercial establishments flourished along the Worcester Turnpike, and a small number of office buildings, apartments, and motels were constructed.

From the outset, direct connections between this commercial development and the communities of Framingham and Natick were largely circumstantial. Certainly these facilities provided additional employment in the area at a time in which traditional industrial bases were eroding. It was also the case, however, that Framingham was the right place at the right time for regional rather than local interests. In fact, there continue to exist feelings of superimposition and estrangement toward the commercial complex by many Framingham and Natick residents. Located out on the turnpikes, it is as if the complex was out of sight and out of mind, although clearly on matters of traffic congestion and visual encroachment it is not.

Figure 9   Uncoordinated development and commerce: Shoppers World and adjacent development in Framingham, Massachusetts, 1987

Taken together with the political complexities produced by the lack of neat and tidy jurisdictional boundaries, it is small wonder that little coordination and planning has taken place.

Between 1970 and 1980 the population of metropolitan Boston declined for the first time in two centuries, dropping 4 percent from 3,013,912 to 2,884,712 (U.S. Bureau of the Census 1930–1980a). Higher costs of living associated with the energy crisis and changing economic fortunes among different areas of the country, particularly between the North and the South, caused substantial net migration out of the region. The end of the baby boom and concomitant changes in patterns of family structure saw a rather dramatic decline in natural population growth. In fact, net migration went up something like tenfold, and the natural increase in population was about 69 percent less than for the previous decade ending in 1970. Most of this population decline, however, took place within the inner regional areas as suburbanization continued out beyond Route 128, although at a

much slower pace. Between 1970 and 1980 the inner region declined in population by 9 percent, whereas the outer region increased by 2 percent. For the first time the number of people in the metropolitan area living outside Route 128 began to approach the number residing inside the loop in more traditional inner suburban and city settings. In Boston's economic revival of the 1980s, the proportion finally tipped toward outer suburban areas (Metropolitan Planning Council 1985b).

Some measure of this revival is evident within the Metrowest region, essentially the western suburbs of Boston, where employment between 1970 and 1980 jumped appreciably by 34 percent to close to 100,000 jobs. Of this total Framingham increased its share from 38 percent to 44 percent, and Framingham and Natick together amounted to 60 percent of this total, forming a clear center for the region (U.S. Bureau of the Census 1984a). A recent transportation survey of residence and workplace origins and destinations showed that about 58 percent of Metrowest's population work in Metrowest. Further, 50 percent of all Metrowest employees originate in the same region, indicating a slight net draw in employment from the outside (Metropolitan Area Planning Council 1985a). In almost all categories of proposed commercial development, Framingham is expected to garner over 60 percent of the Metrowest total (U.S. Bureau of the Census 1983). Together with the Natick portion of the turnpike complex (figure 10), this proportion rises to above 80 percent, or something like 5.1 million square feet of commercial facilities (Metropolitan Area Planning Council 1985a, U.S. Bureau of the Census 1985). Framingham has shifted from a small rural industrial town, linked with Boston, to a substantial regional trade and service center, all in fifty years. Ironically the lessening of a dependence on Boston is now returning to the levels of a much earlier time when the township was small and relatively isolated.

In keeping with the region as a whole, population growth in Framingham between 1970 and 1980 slowed considerably, with only a 1.7 percent increase to 65,113 people. Nevertheless, the township did increase slightly its proportional share of the Metrowest population, continuing the trend observed in 1970 (Metropolitan Area Planning Council 1985b). Compared to the dramatic increase in employment, this relatively slow population growth suggests a substantial change in both the subregion's and Framingham's

role in the metropolitan area. Any tendency for the area to be just a bedroom community had passed. Framingham was on its way to becoming the functionally diversified center of its region.

Socioeconomic characteristics of the township also reflect this difference in function and status, as well as those of the changing times in general. The average population per household declined substantially from 3.37 in 1970 to 2.60 in 1980, slightly below the metropolitan average. Not only did this change reflect national shifts in family structure but also Framingham's more significant role as an employment center, attracting single members of the metropolitan labor force. The median age of the population rose to around 32 years, again reflecting national demographic trends and an end to the baby

Figure 10   The commercial center of the Metrowest region: Framingham and Natick, Massachusetts

boom. Median family income declined in real terms from 1970 levels after posting increases in the previous two decades. The same indicator also showed an increased disparity from one part of town to another. The proportion of households below the poverty line increased to above 10 percent in some older areas of town, though the overall average increased only a little, to slightly above 4 percent. In addition, the proportion of minority populations increased to around 6 percent (Metropolitan Area Planning Council 1982, 1985a, 1985b).

Compared to similar statistics for surrounding towns, Framingham was conspicuous on numerous counts. The age distribution of its population was more diverse; its settlement patterns were denser although still not very high; and there were higher levels of service industry employment, minorities, and poor people. In short, Framingham's population was now beginning to resemble much more closely the populations of central city areas, in both absolute terms and especially in comparison to neighboring areas of the subregion. Socioeconomic circumstances of residents were certainly more heterogeneous, and probably the community's tendency to become more segregated in attitudes, values and lifestyles had also become stronger (U.S. Bureau of the Census 1930–1980a).

The construction of a significant number of office buildings in the commercial areas adjacent to the highway accounts for the dramatic increase in subregional employment. Built either speculatively or for specific business and electronics enterprises, most were concentrated between the Massachusetts Turnpike and the retail areas of Shoppers World and Na-

tick Mall to the south. Now covering roughly a 2-square-mile area, extending from the Turnpike to Route 9 in the north-south direction and about 2 miles westward from the Cochituate State Park, the commercial complex had become sufficiently diversified and intensive in development to warrant special planning and urban design consideration. It is no longer simply a commercial strip on the outskirts of a residential neighborhood. Furthermore, a lot has happened since Shoppers World's dramatic arrival in 1951, even to the point that the old mall, now almost a historically significant site, may soon undergo a major alteration and expansion.

Sharpstown and Houston's Sprawl

In stark contrast to Boston, by 1930 the population of Houston, Texas, stood at a scant 300,000 people (U.S. Bureau of the Census 1930–1980b). Only well after World War II did the city begin to grow and develop with the rapidity that was to win it such recent notoriety (figure 11) (McComb 1981, Abbott 1987).

From 1940 to 1945, Houston became strongly involved in the war effort. Commerce was replaced by manufacturing as the most important industry, with special emphasis on traditionally strong sectors for the region such as petroleum, chemical, and metal industries. After the war these industries, easily converted to peacetime purposes, continued to flourish, creating a significant part of the economic base on which Houston was to prosper and even boom for the next thirty-five years (Hutton and Henderson 1976, McComb 1981, Hadley 1983).

Between 1945 and 1950, several major oil companies, among them Shell, Humble, and Continental

Oil, began sending large segments of their corporate operations to Houston (Hutton and Henderson 1976). And in the 1970s most of them located research and headquarter facilities on the city's western suburban fringe. By 1950 the metropolitan population stood at 806,701, having posted a sizable 52.51 percent gain during the preceding decade (U.S. Bureau of the Census 1930–1980b).

Like many other cities in the Midwest and Southwest, Houston had a modest downtown area containing, at 95.5 percent, practically all of the city's office commercial activity (Rice Center for Community Design and Research 1978a). The layout of the downtown took the form of a rectilinear street grid, first established by the Allen brothers when they paddled up Buffalo Bayou from Trinity Bay and the Gulf of Mexico to found the city as an entrepreneurial venture in 1835. The pattern of settlement and structure of the city in the 1940s conformed to the monocentric model, where a major downtown employment center is surrounded by a roughly annular mosaic of residential areas of decreasing density (figure 12). On the flat coastal prairie the only features that interfered with this regular pattern were the systems of creeks and rivers, locally termed bayous, several large parks like Memorial Park on the west, formerly an army post, and the large port facilities to the east. Elsewhere the suburban gridiron prevailed, its continuity broken here and there by changes of direction and adjustment to local circumstances (McComb 1981, Davis 1982). Most of the residential development in the 1940s occurred on the northern side of the city, where developers and residents alike could take advantage of less flood-prone land and the higher natural amenity of

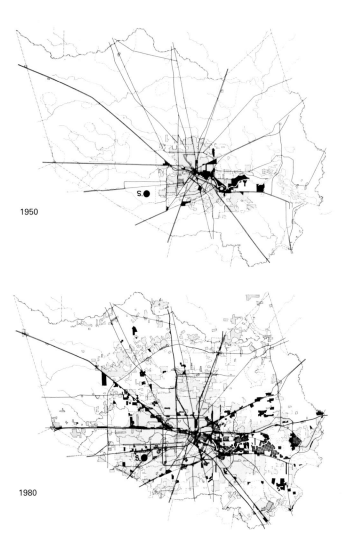

1950

1980

Figure 11   Rapid urban growth: Houston metropolitan area in 1950 and 1980. Map shows Sharpstown's location as (s)

pine forests as they emerged southward into the coastal prairie (Houston City Planning Commission 1942).

A major street plan was undertaken in 1942 as one of the first real efforts at planning the city. Although the City Planning Commission had been established in 1924, it had done little, and by the 1940s, Houston had become one of the largest cities in the United States without a land use zoning ordinance

Figure 12   A monocentric city: Houston central business district in 1953, with Memorial Park to the west

(Houston City Planning Commission 1940, 1942). Nevertheless, encouraged by provisions in the Texas state constitution, it did manage to resist the balkanization that overtook most other cities in Texas and elsewhere, by pursuing a vigorous process of annexation. Consequently Houston annexed enough land area to double its size in 1948 and again in 1956, when it became the nation's second largest city in terms of land area (McComb 1981). Meanwhile, the long-overdue thoroughfare plan was completed in 1953, calling for quick adoption of the latest in radial and circumferential freeways. By 1957, only about a year after passage of the federal highway provisions, $60 million had been expended on 85 miles of a projected 237-mile system of new roadways (Hutton and Henderson 1976, McComb 1981, Hadley 1983).

Unlike the more piecemeal and incremental kind of suburban development of areas in the Northeast, like Framingham, Sharpstown was the the brainchild of one developer. Frank W. Sharp came to Houston to work his way through business school from the small town of Crockett, Texas. In one of those careers that adds to the lore of the American entrepreneur, Sharp reputedly borrowed $150 in 1936 to build his first home, to be quickly followed by increasingly more lucrative ventures. During the war years he refined the tools of his trade building war worker housing and other needed facilities around the Port of Houston and Texas City (Newsweek 1955, Papademetriou 1972). At the end of hostilities in 1946, he developed the 4,000-home Oak Forest subdivision on Houston's northwest side, (figure 13), the largest residential subdivision in the United States until William Levitt came along in 1949 and 1950 to build his 5,000-home Levittowns in Pennsylvania and on Long Island, New York (Papademetriou 1972). In 1954, Frank Sharp was back again with Sharpstown, regaining the sobriquet as the builder of the largest single residential subdivision in the country (McComb 1981).

Built on the prairie on the outskirts of town in southwest Houston, Sharpstown was to provide the site for some 25,000 residences, a large shopping complex, office space, and a considerable amount of recreational space and facilities. Covering some 6,500 acres, the subdivision consisted mainly of speculatively built three-bedroom brick-veneer single-family detached houses, valued in 1956 at an average price of about $14,500 (Papademetriou 1972). Reporting the opening of the project, *Newsweek* noted that "Sharp still doesn't know how many country clubs he will need, but every family will be a member of one. . . . Land has been set aside for churches, schools and libraries" (*Newsweek* 1955).

Figure 13   A postwar suburban street: Oak Forest subdivision, 1946

Sharp had drawn upon his prior experiences as the developer of Oak Forest in order to create a reasonably attractive, moderately priced subdevelopment, shrewdly located in front of the new wave of suburban expansion now moving out in a southwesterly direction from the center of Houston.

The spatial organization of the subdivision borrowed from both prevailing neighborhood planning concepts and the Garden City movement. (The latter influence is also to be found in Oak Forest, Sharp's first major effort, and is strongly reminiscent in its pattern of curvilinear streets and landscaping of River Oaks, the expensive and exclusive Houston subdivision from the 1920s by Potter, Unwin and company [Mason 1982, Stern 1986a]). The subdivision is roughly square and divided into quadrants by Bellaire Boulevard running in a northwest direction and by Fondren Road running in a north-south direction (figure 14). Near the center of each quadrant so formed

was located a major amenity or nonresidential use. For instance, the northwest quadrant was occupied by the Sharpstown Country Club an eighteen-hole golf course with clubhouse facilities for local residents, and the southwest quadrant was occupied near its center by a high school. Other facilities like the Houston Baptist College were located completely within the ambit of the subdivision. The residential streets tended to meander in a curvilinear fashion. Besides their picturesque appearance, they also had an engineering cross-section whereby the residential lots on either side were raised at the building line 2 to 3 feet above the crown of the road, thus providing a conduit for flood waters. Sharp was familiar with Houston's perennial flooding problems, especially the disastrous flood in 1935 (Hadley 1983), and he was also well aware of the relatively close proximity of and potential flood danger posed by Brays Bayou nearby to the south of the subdivision. Like Levittown, houses were located on floor slabs at grade, although they tended in style toward informal ranches rather than traditional colonial styling. There was an element of self-containment to Sharpstown both for the purpose of minimizing uncertain speculative contact with adjacent developments and for the purpose of creating a strong sense of community identity. Sharp called the project "a new experiment in our way of life" (*Newsweek* 1955, p. 40).

Sharp and others quickly appreciated the significance of the federal highway plan and the regional access provided by urban freeways, so much so that in 1957 they donated 10 miles of 300-foot right-of-way for the construction of the Southwest Freeway, scheduled to come out of central Houston and the in-

Figure 14 Large-scale planned subdevelopment: aerial view of Sharpstown in the 1970s

ner 610 loop road (figure 15), in a southwesterly direction (McComb 1981). Although the right-of-way was not the one originally chosen by the highway engineers, it was close enough, reasoned the city and state. The developers were only too happy to give up some land, which was abundant anyway, on the condition that haste be made with the project. And so it was that when construction of the freeway began in 1958, the adjacent developers' land values skyrocketed accordingly (McComb 1981).

By 1960 metropolitan Houston had increased its population since 1950 by 54.1 percent to 1,243,158 (U.S. Bureau of the Census 1930–1980b). The city of Houston had grown a little more modestly at 31.4 percent to close to a million people. However, given the vigorous annexation policy it pursued, this does not give an accurate measure of suburban growth. On the contrary, most of Houston was by now suburban in character, and suburban expansion was burgeoning.

Sharpstown in 1960 was still a fledgling community with a population of only some 8,000, primarily located in the southeast quadrant. Surrounding areas forming a more or less contiguous link closer in toward the city were also growing, especially the residential subdivisions toward the south and southeast,

Figure 15   The intersection of Highway Loop 610 and the Southwest Freeway in Houston

attracted by the amenity beside Brays Bayou. The predominant character of this growth was single-family detached housing for young, white, middle-class families (figure 16). Fully 94 percent of the units were owned or on their way to being owned under Federal Housing Administration–insured mortgages. The population per household was around 3.8 persons, much higher than the national average of 3.4. There were very few single householders—only about 4 percent—and the median age of the community was quite young, around 25 years (U.S. Bureau of the Census 1930–1980b).

The pace of Houston's metropolitan growth quickened between 1960 and 1970. The population rose to just under 2 million people, an astonishing increase of almost 60 percent for the decade (U.S. Bureau of the Census 1930–1980b). By 1970, Houston was one of the fastest-growing regions of the United States. Some diversification of the economic base occurred with the introduction of the Johnson Manned Space Craft Center and other technical and service industries. The spatial distribution of commercial offices continued to decentralize. The downtown's share of office space declined further, from 77 percent in 1960 to 62 percent in 1970 (Houston City Planning Department 1980).

Construction of the Southwest Freeway, or Interstate Highway 59, and the opening of the Sharpstown Center in 1961, a large, enclosed, air-conditioned regional mall complex (figure 17), began to change Sharpstown's suburban idyll (Papademetriou 1972). Located on 70 acres of land immediately adjacent to the Southwest Freeway and Bellaire Boulevard, a major at-grade traffic arterial, the Sharpstown Shopping Center was ideally located to take advantage of almost all the retail trade in the rapidly expanding markets of Houston's southwest region, so much so that Foleys, the city's major department store, made its first suburban move to the center as it opened (McComb 1981). Accessibility to many of the older, established suburban communities within the Highway 610 loop road was also high, adding to the center's competitive advantage (Rice Center 1979). Surrounding land parcels subsequently became

Figure 16   Residential development on the prairie: Sharpstown in the 1960s

Figure 17 Large-scale mixed-use commercial development: Sharpstown Center

developed for other commercial activities, including some high-rise offices and residential condominium towers. The frontage roads along the Southwest Freeway assumed the character of the ubiquitous commercial strip with fast-food establishments, car dealerships, and small office buildings running their length. Medium-density garden apartment complexes were constructed around this commercial activity, especially close to the mall complex and offices in the northeast quadrant of the Sharpstown area.

These local trends in land use began to be reflected in the demographic character of Sharpstown. Population in the area as a whole rose dramatically between 1960 and 1970, increasing by over 80 percent. The single-family neighborhoods continued to remain predominantly white and middle class; however, the level of homeownership started to decline to

around 65 percent by 1970. Most of the newcomers to the area appeared to be younger, more likely than before to be single, and mostly apartment dwellers. In short, the population was becoming more heterogeneous and more reflective of demographic and other social trends within the city of Houston as a whole (U.S. Bureau of the Census 1930–1980b, Bank of the Southwest 1971).

The decade from 1970 to 1980 saw even more explosive growth in the Houston metropolitan region, with population expanding by almost 1 million people to around 2.9 million. If other adjacent outlying areas are included, this figure is probably closer to 3.1 million people, or roughly the same size as metropolitan Boston (Houston-Galveston Area Council 1981). The effect of this growth was a continuation of past trends toward decentralization and deconcentration of activities, culminating in a radical restructuring of the city. Office space continued to collect in multiple centers, located around the city, mostly in the western half. The downtown, for instance, continued to decline to less than 50 percent of the region's total share of office space in spite of impressive new construction (Rice Center 1979, Houston City Planning Department 1980). Mixed-use areas, often centered on shopping malls, formed other adjacent centers of activity. Perhaps the best known and most extensive of these centers was the City Post Oak area, built around Gerald Hines's Galleria complex and an extensive array of multistory office buildings on the west side of Houston, just beyond Loop 610 (figure 18). For many this became the center of Houston, replacing the traditional role of the downtown (Rice Center 1979). The dominant role of the automobile and automobile access became almost absolute. In spite of efforts to create a rapid mass transit system tying some of these mixed-use centers together, the idea was soundly defeated at the ballot box. Houston today remains largely an automobile precinct, particularly in areas between the small private preserves and enclaves of business, shopping, and residence.

In a manner not dissimilar from Framingham, the Sharpstown area during the 1970s continued to diversify in land use and became far more heterogeneous in its population. Overall growth slowed, although the area still registered a 55 percent increase in population, as available residential building sites were more fully developed. With the apartment building boom, also rife in other parts of the country, the population per household continued to decline to an overall average of about 2 persons per household,

well below the national average of 2.7 persons. In the northwest quadrant of the Sharpstown area, a neighborhood previously planned to accommodate more affluent single-family homes around the country club, population per household plummeted from 3.9 persons in 1960 to 1.73 persons by 1980 (U.S. Bureau of the Census 1930–1980b). Apartment buildings began to be constructed beside the open space of the country club, expanding westward in a linear fashion along bellaire Boulevard. Finally, the country club, a major component in Sharp's original design, fell into receivership and was picked up by the City of Houston as a municipal facility. By now, however, the open space of the golf course was con-

Figure 18   A major suburban center: City Post Oak adjacent to Highway Loop 610, Houston

siderably reduced in size due to encroachment by surrounding higher-density development. Gone was the dream of local community good life in the clubhouse by the eighteenth hole.

Not all areas changed quite so dramatically. Certain pockets of residential development retained their original comfortable character. Sharp's dream of curving tree-lined streets amid the barren prairie had become a reality (figure 19). But the continuity and planned community ambience had vanished. In their place was created a mosaic of much more specific and diversified subdevelopments, each responding to local exigencies of market forces. The Sharpstown that had boldly attempted to chart the course of Houston's future some twenty-five years earlier had become just another piece of the general landscape (Rice Center 1978a). In fact, it had become many rather different pieces.

As a footnote in this story, brief mention should be made of the so-called Sharpstown scandal, which allegedly involved Frank Sharp with several high-ranking members of the Texas House of Representatives in collusion over utility districts. The facile creation of municipal utility districts (MUDs) had long been a driving force behind the land development boom in Houston and other parts of Texas. Under state law they could rather easily be created to bear almost the full burden of development costs for utilities such as water, drainage, and other site improvements. What usually transpired was the creation of the utility district, followed by a municipal bond election among the almost nonexistent population of the subdivision, the proceeds of which were immediately put to work in constructing the subdevelop-

Figure 19   A tree-lined residential neighborhood: Sharpstown, Texas

ment. As long as this process unfolded in an orderly and timely manner, sufficient fees could be garnered from homeowners to begin refunding the debt while maintaining services. When it did not unfold quite so neatly, the process, as at Sharpstown, could have disastrous effects, plunging many poor, unsuspecting homeowners into a posture of considerable municipal debt and even bankruptcy. In one of those ironic events, it was Sharp in his moment of disgrace who once again pointed the way toward the future. This time, however, the response was legislative, with enactment during the mid-1970s of the so-called 30 percent rule, whereby a developer had to contribute, up front, 30 percent of the total subdevelopment costs (Rice Center 1978b).

The profound role of MUDs in shaping the direction and extent of Houston's growth also requires comment. Without a doubt they are the legal and financial mechanisms that lay at the heart of the land development process known as leapfrogging that gave Houston and several other metropolitan regions in the country a characteristically extensive and discontinuous pattern of suburbanization. MUDs enabled subdivisions to be created readily on the fringes of a metropolitan region beyond the incorporated limits of the nearest city or town. With nearness to and continuity with other urbanizing areas no longer a concern for reasons of service provisions, the locations of subdivisions became highly sensitive to land prices and the vagaries of market predictions about the direction and rate of urban growth demands. Developers trying to outguess one another and improve their profit margins moved geographically farther outward in advance of this demand. In so doing they leapfrogged over each other's subdivisions, creating a patchy landscape of a subdivision here, vacant land there, a roadway improvement over here, and so on. At least during the 1960s and 1970s in the Houston metropolitan region, this process proved to be highly efficient for the private developers, especially considering the cheap sources of water supply to be provided from nearby underground aquifers. In the long run, however, the broader social costs of this form of scattered development are proving to be quite high. As subdivisions mature and become more fully developed, maintenance of relatively extensive roadway infrastructure has become an issue. Excessive groundwater withdrawal from the underlying aquifers has resulted in land subsidence, with dire consequences for drainage and flooding. Finally, with recent substantial and sudden declines in the rate of urban growth, many residents of subdivisions have suffered similar fates to earlier Sharpstown residents who could not afford the utilities on which they were so dependent (Real Estate Research Corporation 1974, Rice Center 1980).

Unless a process of gentrification subsequently reshapes its future, perhaps the final epitaph to Frank Sharp's dream of a white, middle-class community idyll has come at the hands of ethnic minorities. In the Sharpstown area as a whole, the nonwhite population, which was negligible in 1960, reached about 7 percent in 1970 and then rose dramatically to 20 percent by 1980. This phenomenon was relatively widespread and not necessarily confined to one specific subarea. Desegregation certainly did occur, but the mosaic of separate subdevelopments, so marked in Houston, probably also contributed to this aggregate heterogeneity while maintaining local ethnic separation. Also, the presence in Sharpstown of numerous commercial establishments, not to mention several hospital facilities and schools, provided a diversified base of employment and, during the boom years, one that had to compete strongly for an adequate share of the available metropolitan labor force (Rice Center 1979). Undoubtedly this competition attracted a socially and economically diversified population creating a broad housing market.

In addition to blacks and Hispanics, Houston's traditional minorities, Chinese, Vietnamese, and other recent immigrants from Southeast Asia make up a significant proportion of the Sharpstown area's minority population—so much so that the area along Bellaire Boulevard near Gessner has become a Chinatown, albeit of a suburban variety. Minimalls and strip commercial developments now carry both oriental and occidental signs. Furthermore, most of the new commercial development and redevelopment, like the establishments shown in figure 20, has the unmistakable mark of foreign capital from the Far East. In one of those migratory cycles so common to many other American city neighborhoods, one socio-cultural group replaces another. Just as the Sharpstown area provided a life for young, white families shortly after World War II, now it becomes a port of entry for Asian newcomers to the city as well.

Figure 20   Asian influence on Sharpstown's strip commercial development

FROM SUBURB TO URBAN METROPOLIS

The metropolitan growth of Boston and Houston over the past fifty years and its effects on Framingham and Sharpstown, respectively, illustrate several important developmental trends in the spatial restructuring of American cities. The first and perhaps most obvious aspect of metropolitan growth is the inexorable pattern of suburbanization that has taken place since 1920. Not only has the balance in the spatial distribution of residences between city and suburb become reversed, so that more people now live in the suburbs than in the city, but the spatial structure of other activities has also changed. In 1973 the amount of employment provided in the suburbs overtook the amount provided in the city (Muller 1981). The upshot is a relatively low-density, almost uniform network of urbanization moving out over the landscape, punctuated by agglomerations of a much higher intensity and difference in function (figure 21).

Economic theorists writing as early as the late 1950s expected this evolutionary process of urban growth and change (Myrdal 1957, Hirschman 1958).

Development begins around a few attractive so-called growth poles. This concentration of activity is followed by the growth and subsequent dominance in most activities of suburban rings and subcenters peripheral to the original growth poles and the accompanying decline in importance of central cities. Finally, economic activity and population disperse away from even these second-stage metropolitan growth centers in the direction of new growth poles in outlying less-developed areas. (This highly decentralized evolutionary pattern of urban development is characteristic of economically highly developed nations throughout the world [Long 1981, Rothblatt and Garr 1986].)

The second and closely related characteristic of large contemporary metropolitan areas is that internally they no longer conform to traditional monocentric, core-periphery models of urban spatial structure. As we saw in the two examples, by 1970 multiple centers of nonresidential activity had begun to emerge outside both central Boston and Houston. By 1980 many of these centers and the surrounding mosaic of mixed-use although predominantly residential development had created rather distinct subregions or separate urban realms. According to theorists such as Vance (1962, 1977) and Muller (1981), when people become increasingly dispersed to outer urban locations, interaction across the whole metropolitan region becomes more difficult to sustain, and diseconomies of scale go into effect, such as traffic congestion, high land costs, overcrowding, and pollution. This curtailment strengthens a tendency to decentralize nonresidential activities, such as retail and office commercial enterprises, that are becoming locationally footloose because of the elimination of metropolitan-wide transportation accessibility differences between suburbs and city that accompanied freeway construction. The result is that outlying populations sever their direct ties to the central city, giving rise to "separate and self-sufficient 'urban realms' which soon become self-acting urban systems, independent of the parent city and increasingly duplicative in function" (Muller 1981, p. 8). The extent, character, and internal structure of these urban realms are shaped by four criteria: terrain, especially topography and water bodies; the overall physical size of the metropolis; the amount and type of economic activity contained inside a realm; and the configuration of the regional transportation network, especially the ease of movement within a realm to its local centers or minicities (Vance 1977). We have seen the effect of most of these criteria in shaping the futures of Framingham and Sharpstown.

For some time Los Angeles, a sprawling urban area divided by mountain ranges and centered on multiple commercial centers, has been the paradigm case of this phenomenon. Sometimes these realms are referred to as urban villages (Leinberger and Lockwood 1986), conjuring up the image of a relatively low-density residential life-style served by moderately sized commercial and entertainment centers. During the past ten to twenty years they have grown up in many metropolitan regions of the United States, especially in sunbelt cities like Dallas, Houston, and Atlanta (Abbott 1981, 1987) but also in older, more developed northeastern cities like Philadelphia and Boston.

The Metrowest subregion in metropolitan Boston is now one such urban realm. Framingham, at its center, performs the role of a minicity. So is develop-

Figure 21   Agglomerations of commercial activity within the Houston metropolitan region. The central business district is in the background and the Texas Medical Center in the foreground.

ment in southwest Houston with Sharpstown as its lo-cus. No longer can the metropolitan area be seen as a singular entity across many activities. Instead it has become a social and cultural mosaic of largely auton-omous subregions spread out across the landscape, each more or less duplicating many of the functions of another. It is as if motive and opportunity have conspired, allowing Americans to turn their backs on the city form of the industrial era in favor of at least the aura and convenience of a small town setting. It does not seem to matter that the resulting patterns of metropolitan development are in many respects quite unlike small towns (figure 22). In those features of life that count most, such as travel, work, and recrea-tion, they appear to be sufficiently alike, at least in mythic terms, to hold considerable appeal.

The stereotype image of the American suburb, a vestige of an earlier stage of development, no longer applies. Contemporary suburban life is simply not a case of "white, middle class homeowners, single-family homes, men commuting to city jobs, women at home caring for the children, stable neighborhoods and safety" (Baldassare 1986, p. vii). Within the middle landscape shaped out of the suburban mosaic, society is becoming as heterogeneous and life is be-coming as diversified as they once were in the city. In a remarkable transformation, it is as if the city has gone into the suburbs, just as the suburbs left the city shortly after the turn of this century. Singular con-cepts like core and periphery, city and suburb, are less and less descriptive of contemporary patterns of physical development.

The third general aspect of suburban metropoli-tan development was the strong influence of transpor-

tation technology and its adoption by the general pub-lic. Particular kinds of conjunctions occurred among buildings, land uses, and infrastructure facilities, such as roads, streetcar lines, rail lines, and free-ways. Widespread use of streetcars tended to lead to a radial pattern of highly traveled corridors leading out from an urban center. The immediate edges of the corridor's right-of-way were developed most densely, with a general decrease in this density to-ward the periphery, along the length of the corridor (Warner 1962). These particular conjunctions of land use and transportation were of general and relatively long-lasting import. Each belonged to a broad tech-nological era, and they are a way of defining stages of urban growth. Usually, outward urban development took place until technical and economic limits were approached, and then adjacent undeveloped areas were filled in under the same kinds of sociotechni-cal criteria. Thus new transportation technologies brought with them entirely new limits and predomi-nant forms of development. Far from being a contin-uous progressive or evolutionary process, the pri-mary thrust of urban development in a given period conformed to a fixed set of controlling circum-stances. In short, the overall effect was one of a stage-process model, with transitions occurring from largely separate stages.

In the case of Boston the stages of urban devel-opment, roughly in order of progression, were asso-ciated with a combination of streetcar, pedestrian movement, and commuter rail; recreational and spe-cial use of autos together with the foregoing modes; and the freeway era with a widespread use of auto-mobiles and a concomitant limited use of mass tran-

Figure 22   The suburban spatial mosaic near Radburn,
New Jersey

sit. The three stages are clearly evident in Framingham. First the rail line and station became the armature of urban development, followed by the Worcester Turnpike outside the town proper, with scattered commercial development, and then finally the interstate highway system, together with the emergence of a regional commercial service center. For Sharpstown in Houston, the process was largely confined to the freeway era and to almost exclusive use of the automobile.

As a corollary to this kind of observation, the styles and representational qualities of suburban buildings altered during successive stages of development. Generally the sense of progress usually associated with more radical shifts in development tended to lessen the regard with which the forms of

urban development from the preceding era were held. For example, the confident image of technology and material consumption exuded by cars, shopping centers, and other automobile-oriented cultural artifacts of the 1950s undermined any need for, say, concern about natural resource conservation or the fate of the older local main streets in the center of town (Liebs 1985). By contrast, today some of the artifacts that were produced with such confidence in the 1950s, such as roadside motels, stand deserted and seem to be either pathetic anomalies or, given the right distance of time, objects of nostalgic curiosity. It is probably not so much the building's use that is the subject of attention as its iconography. After all, we are still in an era of cars, shopping centers, and freeways. However, as more and more development occurs and we move deeper into an era, our symbolic needs and aspirations seem to change. Buildings and other artifacts, which were once new and novel but are now commonplace, no longer need the expressive qualities of their novelty, such as, for example, the space-age imagery of Framingham's Shoppers World. The point about progress has been made and the reformation accomplished. Typically it is just the placement of these buildings in the landscape in conjunction with the surrounding infrastructure that gives them their denotative character. A large warehouse-like structure, for instance, surrounded by a parking lot on a main road, now needs little more than a bland sign to conjure up images of shopping mall and the fantasy world that awaits inside.

To speak of continuity with the past in this context is to raise the question: which past? Physical development was a matter of different stages and, perhaps most important, a matter of all the controlling cultural imagery that also helps us define those stages. Development has not occurred in one long, continuous stream. We do not readily arrive at the idea of contemporary shopping malls by examining "Main Street." On the contrary, the urbanized metropolitan landscape is as fragmentary in physical form as it is in socioeconomic circumstances.

Similarly each stage of development appears to have possessed a characteristic scale and sense of belonging to its surrounding landscape, a feature that seems to be entwined with movement and spatial perception. During the pre–World War II period of commuter railroads and recreational use of automobiles, when people walked more and lived closer to the commercial centers of their communities, scale was geared to individual houses, stores, parks, and so on. A sense of fittness was usually accommodated by accretive forms of urban development where one house was simply placed next to the others. By contrast, the postwar use of automobiles brought with it a different sense of scale suited to faster and more continuous movement. As a consequence, the buildings and other urban artifacts of this era tended to be larger in size, often spaced farther apart, and possessive of a much greater sense of being superimposed upon the landscape than fitted in next to it. Consequently natural features such as hills and lakes also took on a different aspect, sometimes becoming close in scale and perception to neighboring buildings and building complexes. In this formal ensemble the natural landscape tends to take on a more domesticated status, closer to a garden than to a wilderness. The modern adoption of natural landscapes as the gardens for heroic large-scaled buildings seems to be quite appropriate. Certainly, when done well, the gestural quality of the man made with the natural in the modern use of highway and highway buildings is in keeping with the scale of surrounding terrain.

Finally, from the standpoints of land use and urban development, Framingham and Sharpstown are very similar, although the overall pattern, grain, scale, and even density of the resulting landscapes differ in important ways. First, in spite of substantial development, Framingham remains very much in contact with its natural circumstances; the natural setting still provides most of the structure and focus for the urbanizing landscape. Sharpstown, by contrast, is denser, more continuous in its urban character, and almost independent of its natural setting, save coping with the exigencies of natural disasters like floods. It is as if Framingham's bucolic environment so complements urban development that it also acts as something of a restraint. Without such appeal, Sharpstown's prairie is almost irrelevant and overwhelmed by development. Second, it is also apparent that there were very real differences in the scope, timing, and rates of urban growth in the two metropolitan regions. From 1930 to 1980 Boston's population grew from 2.3 million to almost 3 million people, whereas Houston's grew to much the same size from only about 300,000 inhabitants in 1930. Consequently the increments of subdevelopment in Houston were generally larger and more instantaneous than those in Boston. Third, ironically perhaps given the disregard of planning in Houston as compared to Boston, Sharpstown appears to be more planned. In fact, from the perspective of suburban development, it is much more planned. It was , after all, the vision, at least initially, of one entrepreneur. Overall there is a rationalism to Sharpstown's urban landscape that makes Framingham's seem almost whimsical. In the end, to describe suburban development as if to cover the phenomenon in one broad sweep is inaccurate. There are many different kinds of suburban and metropolitan development, producing not just one but a variety of middle landscapes.

Depending upon which prism is used, the resulting view of suburban metropolitan development can vary widely. Moreover, like many other evolving and unresolved subjects, it very much depends upon who is doing the looking. Over the past twenty-five years, for instance, the *New York Times,* something of a barometer of public feeling, has published a wide variety of opinions on this matter (Masotti and Hadden 1974). What is certainly clear, however, is that customary distinctions and attitudes that once followed from spatial concepts like town and country no longer seem to apply so easily. The geographical fragmentation of urban life's daily rituals tends to work against the solidarity of image and purpose with which traditional cities were once viewed. Next-door neighbors, for example, may well work miles apart and in different directions. If they do not suffer a certain amount of estrangement as a consequence, then the place-specific references they might once have enjoyed must now be replaced by other references. Usually they have either a more local focus or reach beyond the metropolis to larger jurisdictions like state and nation. Sports teams, for instance, formerly never bore the imprimatur of an entire state or region. Now we have the California Angels and the New England Patriots. The city of old is no longer quite the same center of attention and affection it once used to be.

This change in attitude often runs the risk of hampering metropolitan-wide cooperation, except perhaps on the most dire or common of issues. Not only do sewer plants become difficult to locate and highways hard to build, but common property resources like rivers and bays go largely unattended. Furthermore, ethnic and socioeconomic segregation, always a disturbing part of suburban life, may be exacerbated (Clark 1979, and Jackson 1985).

On the other hand, local pride of place can flourish. Many towns and local communities have recently undertaken projects of civic improvement, typically focusing on some unique historical feature as a point of reference. For example, Framingham has made several efforts in this direction by rehabilitating parts of old commercial areas. After a certain period of neglect, the ideal of the small town appears to have reasserted itself once more, this time in a decidedly suburban context.

The question still remains, however, as to how we should value the suburban metropolitan transformation of traditional categories like city and country. Is it a state of affairs that we should view with alarm, or should we see it as simply another progressive turn of human events? Should we strive to protect a city or country way of life or surrender to what seem to be the inevitable influences of a much larger, sprawling metropolitan urban realm?

For some answers to these questions we can turn in several directions. First, we can inquire further about the suburban metropolitan region as a social entity. Who lives there, and what bearing does the new spatial structure seem to have on the quality of daily life? Second, we can look at the suburban metropolitan political terrain. What kind of influence does the urban structure have on the way people organize, and what issues does it produce? Third, we can narrow our focus and examine some aspects of the role of private property rights. Has the public realm, for instance, been overwhelmed by individual interests? Following that we might ask about the suburban metropolitan life-style itself and ways in which it is territorially molded. Finally, we can begin to examine what kind of place has been made and what sort of relationship we enjoy with it.

MONOLITH OR DIVERSE SOCIAL ENTITY?

The simple answer to an inquiry about the social composition of suburban metropolitan regions is that they are socially diverse entities (Feldman and Thielbor 1975). It may not always have been that way, but certainly by the late 1950s sociologists were discovering signs of considerable social heterogeneity (Berger 1960, Kramer 1972, Fischer 1976). In common with neighborhoods in traditional cities, suburbs have varied with respect to both economic status and social class (Dobriner 1963, Fischer 1976). More-

over, major class differences, when apparent, seem to have little to do with suburban locations per se (Rubin 1967). In addition, the expectations of suburban residents are much the same as those held by similar inhabitants of inner-city areas (Gans 1967).

Suburban populations tended to start out exhibiting a fairly high degree of social homogeneity. They were inhabited mostly by young white families of moderate means (figure 23), almost all adult males gainfully employed and on their way to owning homes. In the space of several decades, however, these demographic circumstances changed abruptly. The family and age structure diversified, particularly as young singles moved into an area in search of emerging employment opportunities (Masotti and Hadden 1973). In addition, suburbs were no longer racially so homogeneous as middle-class minorities also moved away from the central city, although many were left behind in the urban ghettos (Toll 1969, Clark 1979). Overall the proportion of all blacks in central city areas, for instance, is still on the order of 55 percent, compared to just 25 percent for whites (Lake 1981).

In spite of this social diversification, both lay and, at times, scholarly views of the suburban phenomenon have adhered closly to what Robert Wood referred to some time ago as the "looking glass interpretation" (Wood 1958). Under this lens, suburbanites are white, middle class, and extremely self-conscious. They are not, as Wood put it, "the 'inner-directed' man of the nineteenth century . . . nor the sturdy yeoman, nor the hard-working capitalist" (p. 4). Instead they lack personal conviction; are overly concerned about the opinions of others, espe-

Figure 23   The ideal of a postwar suburban way of life

cially so-called experts; and care a great deal about material consumption and security yet without the risks of individual ambition (pp. 4ff.). The suburbanite, or certainly the male of the species, is seen very much as the "organizational man" (Whyte 1956). As another commentator put it, "Suburbia is a white haven . . . [where] one can live among those of similar income, life-style, and complexion, enjoying the neighborliness of persons who think, act and look alike" (Teaford 1986, p. 104). Incidents such as the vicious harassment in 1957 of the first blacks to attempt to integrate Dogwood Hollow in Levittown, Pennsylvania, an early icon of suburbia, reinforced this view of exclusivity and intolerance (Teaford 1986).

A more complicated answer to the question of suburban social complexity is that there is a certain truth to both perceptions. Metropolitan areas on the whole remain racially segregated, and there are few very poor suburban areas, certainly in comparison to their inner city counterparts (Masotti 1975, Clark 1979, Teaford 1986). The white flight from the cities, a constant urban theme during the 1950s and 1960s, has left many inner urban areas as minority ghettos. For instance, the black population of Newark, New Jersey, has risen steadily from 17.1 percent in 1950 to 34.1 percent in 1960 and to 54.2 percent by 1970. Today the proportion of blacks is even higher (U.S. Bureau of the Census 1950–1980).

Nevertheless, households different from young,

white middle-class families with children seem to make their homes readily in suburbia (figure 24). The suburban black population increased by nearly 40 percent during the 1970s, moving much further into the suburban mainstream than the marginal locations they occupied only a decade earlier (Lake 1981). In addition, suburban enclaves have frequently become ports of entry or zones of emergence, to use sociologists' terminology about immigrant concentrations soon after they enter the country (Park and Burgess 1925, Woods and Kennedy 1962). Also modern suburbs of a large metropolitan region usually exhibit considerable variation in their inhabitants' economic well-being. Finally, the label "suburb" is certainly no longer synonymous with "bedroom community." Similar conclusions have been found elsewhere (Lemann 1989). The subregional centers of urban realms are now major employers, providing a continual push toward further socioeconomic diversification.

The apparent resolution of such divergent claims about the social scope and complexity of metropolitan suburban areas is largely a matter of geography. On a metropolitan scale the social composition of particular suburban areas varies widely. Claims about heterogeneity and diversity can be well supported. Not only are the suburbs no longer so distinct from

Figure 24   Newcomers to the suburban way of life

the city, they are also far from monolithic. Land use distributions tend to be more varied than they once were and even more integrated. In a suburban area such as Sharpstown, for instance, it is not unusual to find a variation in residential land use ranging from single-family detached dwellings all the way up the scale of density to high-rise condominiums. Commercial land uses are also typically just as varied and interspersed between residential areas. The resulting grain of the suburban landscape resembles a patchwork quilt, or mosaic of individual subdevelopments, more than it does an endless undifferentiated carpet of land use.

By contrast, on the smaller scale of the subdivisions and subdevelopments themselves, the suburban landscape tends to be quite homogeneous both physically and socially. Likeminded people of the same economic class do tend to reside together in similar houses and commute to work in similar cars to similar offices and other environments. Even specific commercial segments of the suburban mosaic are often homogeneous in use and architectural conformity.

Mixing of different uses is achieved largely through horizontal aggregation of land parcels. Consequently functional integration is largely a matter of being spatially next to, adjacent to, or across from some appropriate clustering. By the same token, the converse condition of separation is just as common, if not a more prevalent feature of these subdevelopments. Each is, in effect, a single-use enclave, well illustrated by figure 25, with an emphasis on minimizing outside influence and maintaining a distinct internal atmosphere. This enclave-like character is particularly apparent in single-family residential sub-

Figure 25   Residential environments as exclusive enclaves

divisions, often surrounded by garden walls or other similar enclosing devices. It is also apparent in garden apartment complexes with their distinctive architectural identities and encirclement of swimming pools and other community facilities. Such an inward, protective, and yet distinctive orientation has a strong real estate rationale. Any significant changes that may befall an adjacent parcel of land due to uncertainty in the marketplace, a lack of adequate land use control, and so on can be screened out. Thus any adverse real estate implications can be effectively minimized. At the same time this planning strategy allows a subdivision to be strongly delimited and differentiated from other surrounding developments. This, according to real estate principles, markedly increases its market profile. Moreover, it is usually a market profile gauged to be most appealing to a specific socioeconomic group of prospective dwellers, almost guaranteeing homogeneity of social circumstances. On a larger geographic scale the result of this process of commodification is an urbanized landscape made up of enclaves and separate land use fragments.

Are these physical and social circumstances any different from those found in older cities? Does this pattern of enclaves matter very much? After all, in many instances segregated neighborhoods, sometimes even more so, are to be found in central city areas. Certainly many of the much earlier streetcar suburbs, which occupy the inner zones of large, older metropolitan regions, have this subdivided character to them. Nevertheless, they also often exhibit a much freer mixing of commercial and residential uses responding to, among other things, the walking-distance constraints of late nineteenth- and early twentieth-century subdevelopments. The lack of continuity from one subdivision to its neighbor is also likely to be much less in earlier examples, although in the use of cul-de-sac and other similar street arrangements, they too could convey a strong sense of being exclusive.

As to the second question of whether enclaves matter, the answer is that they should be of concern. On the face of it, there is nothing wrong with similar people congregating together in a spirit of goodwill and common interest; in large part it is what neighborhoods seem to be about. There is, however, a problem when they band together at the punitive exclusion of others. Less obviously, perhaps, there is the further question as to whether it is actually in the best interests of likeminded citizens themselves to choose to reside together at the exclusion of other members of society. No doubt their day-to-day existence of home, work, commuting, and shopping is made potentially as hassle-free and as harmonious as it might be in an urban circumstance. Almost all social contact, from the moment of awakening to the moment of sleeping, is potentially well under control. There, however, is the rub. It is precisely this predictability and control, quite apart from the monotony it may produce, that precludes the unexpected and even alien confrontation from everyday existence. Further, as Sennett and others have persuasively argued, it is precisely these moments of being pulled up short that cause us to reflect upon ourselves—our lives and our values—and thus increase not only our tolerance for but our understanding of the world (Sennett 1977, Maslow 1968). Social patterns and spatial structures that insulate us to such an extent that we can no longer grow in this manner are not only socially destructive but individually debilitating. Modern suburban subdevelopments run a relatively high risk of this form of exclusion.

WASTEFUL FRAGMENTATION OR PURE DEMOCRACY?

The symbolic power of the center city has not entirely lost its significance. When asked where they are from, residents of Chestnut Hill, Pennsylvania, for instance, are quite likely to say that they are from Philadelphia. This response is strictly inaccurate yet simplifies matters in a country that continues to proliferate separate communities. For example, the Boston metropolitan region alone is made up of some 101 different cities and townships, each incorporated and empowered with a mandate of self-government and home rule (Metropolitan Area Planning Council 1985b). Even the city of Houston, which has managed to avoid the balkanization into separate jurisdictions that befell many other cities, still relies on an extensive system of over 350 deed-restricted subdivisions to protect and nurture the homes of its citizens (Siegan 1972). Under this arrangement neighbors are largely bound to each other through the covenants of private property transactions and form civic associations to help perpetuate and improve their residential environments. Around political matters, or so it would seem, urban metropolitan regions are rarely, if ever, organized as singular entities.

This fragmentation and dispersal of authority may be both irrational and unwise. In fact, in the debates that have surrounded appropriate scales and levels of municipal government, it has been roundly criticized (McKenzie 1933, Jones 1942, Tableman 1951, Real Estate Research Corporation 1974). The coordination of needed infrastructure improvements, such as roads and waste disposal facilities, whose service areas extend well beyond single, local jurisdictions, can be more efficiently accomplished through metropolitan authorities (figure 26). Regional common property resources like rivers, water supply reservoirs, bays, and estuaries transcend local jurisdictions in their geographical scope and socioeconomic significance. The efficient and effective management of pollutants that are damaging to environmental quality—liquid waste from factories, erosion from the land, and others—usually requires broad metropolitan jurisdictions. Generally good governance requires that the geographical extent of the phenomenon under consideration coincide with the jurisdiction of the authority concerned. In other words, whenever possible, all externalities should be internalized.

Even with broader metropolitan governance, efficient functioning presumes knowledge of substantive and administrative issues. After all, an important feature of a technocracy is data and a striving toward

Figure 26   The postwar urban freeway: an example of local cooperation and public works

perfect information. In spite of a willingness of several municipalities to cooperate, a lack of first-hand experience and imperfect information may get in the way of efficient, rational decision making. A potential source of reduced information and even misinformation is the fragmented, nonoverlapping spatial terrain of lives that inevitably accompanies contemporary regional metropolitan expansion. In the past, the central city was a focus of everyone's activities. Now, quite apart from not knowing much about the central city, we may unintentionally misrepresent its condition and needs.

Arguments have been made about certain other economies to be had at the larger scale of metropolitan jurisdictions. Resources can be balanced and allocated more efficiently in order to maximize notions of social welfare, unencumbered by the interruption of special interest groups and their local jurisdictions. For example, industry and commerce, which provide the lion's share of a region's ad valorem tax base, can be allowed to locate rationally and efficiently to take advantage of transportation and other resource needs. These locational decisions would no longer be muddled by several small local jurisdictions competing with one another over the same firms and, in the process, artificially fragmenting the industries' requirements for location and agglomeration. There would be greater flexibility in the expenditure of tax revenues, allowing areas of greatest need to be rationally assigned appropriate priorities. We might even imagine some relaxation of requirements from ironclad zoning ordinances, which, since widespread enactment in the 1920s, have so successfully molded and maintained the suburban landscape in the form of separate zones for residential, commercial, and industrial functions (Babcock 1966). There would be far less of a need, for instance, to balance the tax base

by courting commerce and industry that could not avoid being located near residential areas in the relatively small confines of a local jurisdiction (figure 27). Consequently the need to protect those residential areas from potential contamination and blight would be less pronounced. In fact, the net effect on the distribution and eventual integration of land uses might be quite positive by helping to undermine the rationale for single-use enclaves. Care should be taken, however, in such a relaxation of land use restrictions; otherwise increased uncertainty in the real estate market will exaggerate enclave-like developments in order to minimize risks.

Another closely related argument in favor of large jurisdictions stems from the charge that newer suburbs are parasitic on older, established urban areas. In this view, traditional city centers are the workplaces, recreational areas, and cultural centers

*Figure 27   A jarring juxtaposition of land uses:
commercial encroachment into a residential neighborhood*

for a vast surrounding population, and, as such, they absorb many of the costs for providing these benefits. The suburbs, by contrast, are bedroom communities with little congestion and need for services. Commuting suburbanites then enjoy the best of both worlds: good jobs, civic excitement, and clean living. As property values rise in suburban locations, so do the local tax bases, the proceeds of which can then be spent on better schools and recreational amenities, without the need to worry about more extensive and capital-intensive public services. Under this doctrine, the rich suburbanites remain rich, and the poor become poorer at the expense of the rich. In principle, geographically large municipal jurisdictions would help rectify these inequities, allowing service provision to be placed where it is needed most and for everyone concerned to pay their way in the world fairly and rationally. With the recent emergence of urban realms and multiple suburban centers, this kind of interpretation is less telling. Nevertheless, such an argument could be made (Chinitz 1964, Siegan 1972).

According to Robert Wood in his excellent early account of the political orientation of suburbia, "by ordinary standards of effective, responsible public services, the mosaic of suburban principalities creates governmental havoc" (Wood 1958, p. 10). Spurred on by the virtues of large-scale efficient organization and the blandishments of scale economies, it is hard to imagine that we would organize ourselves and govern ourselves at anything but a comprehensive metropolitan-wide scale. Nothing could be further from the truth. We might be interested in modernity when it comes to products of mass consumption. We are evidently not when it comes to how we make decisions about our daily lives. Here, as Wood points out, we are thoroughly traditional. We "cling persistently to the independence [we] received when [we] were in isolated villages and hamlets in a rustic countryside. . . . [We] insist on retaining the legal form and the public institutions which are relics of a bygone age" (p. 9). He continues, "The [only] justification of legal independence rests on the classic belief in grassroots democracy . . . that small political units represent the purest expression of popular rule, that government closest to home is best" (p. 11).

In spite of the apparent anachronism of suburban local authority, there is something rather appealing in stubborn resistance to the technocratic hegemony that seems so sure to follow big government. Far from being an ostrich act of placing one's head in the sand or an exercise in nostalgic early American sentiment, there is something consistent in the enjoyment of the rights of individual ownership, suffrage, and an insistence upon having a voice that is heard. It is ultimately democratic and, regardless of the inefficiencies and occasional flights of irrationality, a vastly preferred way of managing urban affairs.

Lurking underneath this somewhat virtuous, traditional, small town outlook is also a strong sense of self-preservation, however. Likeminded people banding together may bring with them an independence and an instinct for autonomy (figure 28). However, with rising property values, this instinct may also be very exclusionary as well. Furthermore, turf protection is usually a manifestation of a profound concern with the status quo. Having worked hard and purchased my portion of the good life, I am reluctant to share it, let alone give it up to someone else.

This kind of conservatism in the new suburbia, which has emerged in the last couple of decades, produces a number of substantial issues. Among the challenges facing many suburbanites (Baldassare 1986), growth management and a resistance to change follow from a sense of self-preservation. So too does an apparent mistrust of local government and a concern over the rise of special interest groups. Clearly both are related, and yet both belie a lack of confidence, even frustration, with not being heard as an individual. Ironically a fear is abroad now that there might be too few likeminded people in suburbia.

The relatively recent tax revolt in many parts of the country was led from suburban enclaves, with the reasonably well-to-do and especially those on fixed incomes at its forefront. Nevertheless, it was yet another manifestation of self-preservation, in spite of its portrayal as a desire to make local governments more accountable to their constituencies (Baldassare 1986).

The suburban housing crisis and the problems of dispersed service delivery seem to be cases of disillusionment and broken dreams. As housing prices escalate and the ability to build affordable single-family houses diminishes, more and more households must be satisfied with renting. This is certainly not part of the American dream. A further consequence is the inevitable spatial segregation of the haves from the have-nots between tree-lined tract developments and much higher-density garden apartments (Perin 1977). When it comes to public services and provision of those amenities that made suburbia so attractive in the first place, storm clouds are also gathering

Figure 28   A bucolic suburban setting: common property and exclusive resource

on the horizon. There is clearly a growing gap between reality and expectations (Baldassare 1986). Not only have expectations been rising, perhaps quite unrealistically, but there have been reversals in the quality and extent of public amenities. For instance, in the last chapter we saw the partial abandonment and diminution of the country club golf course facility in Sharpstown, an integral part of the original community concept in the early 1950s. Similar problems have occurred in other parts of the country.

In the case of both housing and public services, however, we might also be simply witnessing the maturation of a suburban area and the decline of its initial mode of life-style. Clearly many older suburbs are in transition, and we are recognizing them, perhaps for the first time, as segments of the city with all the same familiar problems. In the end, with so much decentralization, it is not inefficiency and irrationality that undermine the suburban metropolitan experience. It is the darker underside of the idea of democracy, when people forget that it involves the common good as well as individualism.

PRIVATE COMMODITY OR PUBLIC GOOD?

One of the principal underpinnings of a suburban way of life is preservation of and a belief in private property rights. Although this Enlightenment notion, stemming from John Locke's *Treatise of Government* (1690) and later ideas from William Blackstone, was enshrined in the U.S. Constitution, it was not until recently that society had the means to partake widely of its benefits (Rowe et al. 1978). Soon people in droves

began to escape the dinginess and deterioration of the central city, and everyman's house became his very own home. More recently pursuit of private property has been roundly criticized for transcending simply the realization of the suburban good life and becoming just another example of our consumer society's propensity toward commodification (Hayden 1984).

Shortly before the economically uncertain and inflationary period of the mid-1970s, housing was not something constructed simply to provide shelter for households. It had become an object for speculative investment and, judging by the building boom, an attractive investment at that. In 1971, the total number of housing starts in the United States jumped from around 1.5 million the year before to over 2.0 million, with much of this expansion taking place in second homes and multifamily units. Housing starts reached an all-time annual high of about 2.4 million in 1972 before suddenly declining to 1.1 million in 1975, after the full economic effects of the 1973 oil crisis had set in (U.S. Department of Commerce 1955–1987). Today, for those who can afford to own it, housing is often another commodity to be treated in much the same way as, say, a stock portfolio. Nevertheless, commodification as such is a process that can be associated with practically any product that is in demand and can be effectively traded. Thus real estate—suburban, urban, or rural—is prone to fall into that category.

There is, however, an aspect of the process of commodification in which artifacts, such as the houses in a suburban landscape shown in figure 29, play a significant role. Wherever it is used, money is more or less the same color; there is simply more of it or less of it. By contrast other artifacts, like commodities, have multiple features according to which we make distinctions and value judgments. All paintings of the same size and period are not equal. The tracings of technique and artistic talent across the canvas clearly come into play. Houses of various shapes, sizes, and styles allow similar kinds of distinctions to be made. They represent what urban economists rather illustratively like to call bundles of services (Mieskowski and Straszheim 1979). The extent to which exploitation of these multiple features is a case of commodification or simply a case of genuine self-expression is not only a matter of degree but also one of kind. Is it acceptable, for example, to have a radically different appearance to your house from your neighbors'? The answer has a strong bearing on whether we can regard suburban housing as primarily a commodity or as something with societal value well beyond its potential for private transaction—that is,

Figure 29   Home as house and house as commodity: a tract development in the Southwest

as a public good. Although all housing might be regarded in this manner, suburban single-family houses are particularly susceptible to this kind of analysis. It is exactly because of their singularity in appearance as separate buildings, and their strong iconic correspondence to individual private property rights, that they run the risk of becoming another form of trading token.

Constance Perin's account of housing, property ownership, and land use in suburbia made a strong argument for a linkage between social mobility and status, on the one hand, and homeownership in varying degrees on the other (Perin 1977). Success in what she called the ladder of life was marked by whether one rented or owned one's dwelling, whether it was a house or an apartment, and so on. Higher rungs on the ladder corresponded to large, single-family, detached homes in a garden, in a good neighborhood, served by good schools, and so forth. Others have pursued the matter by taking into account various architectural features of the house, introducing temporal trends of fad and fashion (Marcus, Francis, and Meunier 1980, Langdon 1984). It is the presence of these norms and codes in a widely shared manner that gives the single-family house its public presence (figure 30). Without them it would certainly remain a building but not one of such social significance. The difference, then, between this public presence representing either a public good or a commodity is determined not only by the allowances and encouragements made for genuine self-expression but by the latitude for collective expression as well. If all the markings and expressions of house are calculated solely toward social status, then both individual

*Figure 30   A rung on the ladder of life: the single-family
American home*

and collective expressions of house as home can be called into question. It is not the similarity in appearance of units or the exercise of bad taste, as some critics claim, that commodifies the domestic suburban landscape (Relph 1987); rather, the problem is that the typical suburban single-family house runs those risks, without the intrinsic support to be found in more substantial urban dwellings for giving some semblance of community identity. In short, sameness and unnecessary decoration can have a rationale vested solely in social status and real estate rather than in genuine feelings of either individual or community expression.

Another interesting and related facet of the suburban metropolitan landscape is the lack of consistency in the collective intensity by which various building complexes and land uses are collectively regarded. Close to home, most houses and residential environments commonly receive enormous amounts of care. More distant special places, where one likes to go for recreation or cultural enjoyment, may not be doted upon, but they do receive attention.

Meanwhile, it is precisely in the intermediate commercial realm of a metropolitan region's urban realms that an overall ambivalence in attention is usually most pronounced. As we saw, private entrepreneurial interests surrounding the Framingham-Natick commercial center are likely to be rather narrowly defined and competitive. Moreover, a more widespread community constituency tends to be amorphous and unfocused, particularly when it comes to action. It is not that the commercial facilities and amenities are disliked. On the contrary, in many parts of the country, the malls and surrounding developments, as illustrated in figure 31, have become favorite hangouts and have even replaced more traditional sites as the realm of civic and institutional activities (Muller 1981). What is missing is any real sense of community participation beyond the rather narrow confines of specific uses. First, the complexes are private, often in ways that traditional commercial areas are not. The primary, formal pedestrian areas of a mall, for instance, are internalized and not streets in the public rights sense, in spite of streetlike accoutrements like storefronts and promenades. Second, even

Figure 32   The interior professional world of business: Galleria Post Oak, Houston, 1980

Figure 31   Mall as community facility: Southdale, Minneapolis, by Victor Gruen, 1955

without such juridical distinctions, the inner realms of these complexes appear very much as worlds of their own, often with a futuristic or make-believe quality, invariably detached from the exterior landscape. Certainly the representational and expressive conventions of the inner and outer realms, amply illustrated by figures 32 and 33, are likely to be radically different in both kind and magnitude. However, this may not matter. In fact, some may well regard it as a source of delight. Unfortunately it raises the question of civic authenticity and a sense of appropriateness. Should the space that looks for all the world like a street not be a real street but a private area instead? Can we have a public realm without concomitant concepts like citizenship and public assembly? After all, commerce is an activity allowed by society, not vice versa.

Finally, the privatization of space notwithstanding, in a shopping mall there is an intrinsic absence of

any strong surrounding sentiment of public responsibility. Traditional urban areas are also largely private, yet the civic realm in between seems to exert itself, usually resulting in conventional public fronts to buildings, modes of orientation, entry, egress, and so forth. Paradoxically, in the shopping mall, a passing sense of expressive responsibility is perhaps best exhibited like some perverse sleight of hand on the inside where it is actually most private. In the truly public realm outside, visual blight and placelessness are perpetuated in the domain of roads, parking lots, and billboards.

MONOTONOUS CONFORMITY OR INDIVIDUAL COMFORT?

Although far less prevalent than it was in the 1950s and 1960s, the standard view of suburban life presents a portrait of a monotonous landscape and an unfulfilled existence pervaded by a deep sense of ennui (Whyte 1956, Keats 1957, Dolce 1976). Much of the responsibility for this state of affairs was placed at the feet of big buisness or seen as an unfortunate yet inevitable by-product of a modern way of life so dependent for guidance on management, organization, and technocracy (Whyte 1956, Wood 1958). With allegedly large, faceless corporations as their employers and sometimes quite literally on their doorsteps, how could white-collar suburbanites remain unaffected? These sentiments were propounded in popular literature through works like Wilson's *Man in the Gray Flannel Suit* (1955) and Burdick's biting *Ninth Wave* (1956).

Regimentation and conformity were ubiquitous but most apparent in the endless lines of so-called ticky-tacky little houses that seemed to spring up throughout the urban periphery (figure 34). They were what John Keats, one of the most bellicose antisuburban commentators of the 1950s, referred to as "identical boxes spreading like gangrene" (Keats 1957, p. 23).

Certainly many of the mass-produced subdivisions of the day lent considerable credence to this viewpoint. With master-builders-turned-developers, like Levitt and Sons, Inc., turning out thousands of units a year on single, large tracts of land, the initial result did fit Keats's epithet. Having developed some higher-priced subdivisions in the 1930s and over 2,000 units of low-cost defense housing in Norfolk, Virginia, during the war, the Levitts—Abraham, Alfred, and William—moved their operation in 1949 to Hempstead, Long Island (Wright 1981). There, on several thousand acres that were purchased and optioned, they proceeded to build four-room "Cape Cod" cottages on standard 25-foot by 30-foot concrete slabs (figure 35), which they sold mainly to young families for around $7,990. With Federal Housing Administration and Veterans Administration financing, the family would typically make a $90 down payment and pay off a twenty-five-year mortgage at about $58 per month. These inexpensive units were extremely popular—and profitable. By constructing 150 houses per week, or one every sixteen working minutes once the production process was

Figure 33   The exterior commercial world of billboards, neon, and parking lots

Figure 34   "Little boxes" : Daly City, California

fully operational, the Levitts were able to walk away with something on the order of $1,000 profit per house (Mason 1982, Eichler 1982, Teaford 1986). Other residential subdivisions had similar development profiles, including Sharpstown and Daly City outside San Francisco, reputedly the source of the ballad "Little Boxes," made popular by the Kingston Trio (Kostof 1987).

Nevertheless, there was also an attempt to create a sense of a complete community. Levittown, Pennsylvania, for instance, begun in 1950, was planned to sprawl across 5,000 acres of land, to house 60,000 to 70,000 residents, and to be divided into eight master blocks, each centered on a school or recreation area (Levitt and Sons, Inc. 1951). Each master block was then subdivided into three or four residential neighborhoods. Generally broad and straight arterial roads bounded the master blocks, and the internal streets were organized in a picturesque curvilinear manner. A 250-acre forest reserve was set aside as a recreational area, and some 48,000 blooming fruit trees

were reportedly planted within the urbanizing landscape (Levittown 1951, Mason 1982, Teaford 1986). Frank W. Sharp followed a similar recipe in his Sharpstown project of 1954 and earlier in his Oak Forest subdivision in Houston of 1946. Undoubtedly conformity was a predetermined characteristic of these subdevelopments, as illustrated by the house in figure 36, if for no other purpose than enhancing and maintaining construction efficiencies (Mason 1980, Eichler 1982). It was, however, certainly not a mindless array of blocks, lots, and buildings as Keats and others might suggest. Planning and integration with other facilities, as far as it went anyway, was a key feature of the projects.

Another closely related symptom of regimentation was the alleged reliance of homeowners on experts. According to Blum and others, the 1950s was an era in which technical expertise invaded the home front, from Dr. Spock providing advice on how to raise children to *Harper's Bazaar* on home furnishings (Blum et al. 1963, Hayden 1984). This was not the only period of such paternalism. During the Victorian era, another time of big business, expert advice was dispensed with alacrity (Wright 1981). However, the sheer number and scope of housing-related experts ready to assist private homeowners make their personal choices was probably unprecedented. As Wood observed, there was a strong tendency for the organization man to "build a house which expresses values of real estate experts but never his own" (Wood 1958, p. 5).

The homogeneity of residential areas, the lack of public transportation, and, thus, the spatial displacement of home from work, shops, schools, and other supporting facilities strongly insinuated another kind of regimentation on the lives of suburbanites. The necessity to schedule events pervaded even mundane activites. For instance, chauffeuring became a pastime and, with it, clock watching (Wood 1958). Once again it was as if business life had invaded home life and was working to undermine cherished assumptions about autonomy and having one's own place away from it all.

Yet another guardian of regimentation and conformity was the presumed control, one might say tyranny, of the group (Wood 1958). In this depiction, one "buys the right car, keeps his lawn like his neighbors', eats crunchy breakfast cereal, and votes republican" (Teaford 1986, p. 104). One of the presumed reasons for moving to the suburbs was to congregate inexpensively with likeminded people with similar backgrounds and, further, to take solace and pride in that likemindedness and similarity. As Constance Perin points out, once there, a kind of moral suasion goes into effect starting with trivialities like lawn maintenance and gradually extending over most aspects of the domestic environment until "everything is in its place" (Perin 1977). Stilgoe also points to the

Figure 35   Building the American dream: Levittown, New York, under construction in 1950

"love of shaping space" on the part of suburbanites, in spite of critical derision (Stilgoe 1988, p. 305).

This kind of influence can take another related turn. Maintenance according to neighborly norms is essential to preserve and even advance the economic viability of the home investment. A home can be a commodity and therefore subject to market transactions. Invariably real estate is a fickle market, although one way of diminishing the risks is to present a likable yet familiar appearance. Ironically homeowners residing in a place are also preparing to leave it.

Claims of monotony, conformity, and regimentation are not exclusive to suburban residential environments. Much the same kind of criticism might be leveled at retail commercial establishments, especially chain stores that repeat across the landscape. The sheer physical similarity and predictability of

Figure 36   Levittowners and their one-and-a-half story cape: Levittown, New York, 1948

most shopping malls can be as numbing to the senses as it is symbolically reassuring and convenient. When contact is made, the dispensation of services is polite yet often highly impersonal.

Deeper themes of isolation and alienation course beneath the surface of the suburban metropolitan life-style, more often than not strongly related to senses of monotony and boredom. "Chappaqua is a good address, after all . . . ," said Phyllis Sanders in Linda Greenhouse's short story. "The real estate agent's pitch is that you'll be here in your pretty house surrounded by trees, and nobody will bother you." Yet she hastens to ask, "Does the nice house and green yard make for happiness?" (Greenhouse, 1974, p. 32).

Often, according to social scientists, the answer is no; a tragic outcome of such an existence is pathetic loneliness and eventual alienation (Riesman 1950). It was that great student of alienation, Albert Camus, who reminds us that it is a condition that arises when we act outside ourselves and become distanced (Camus 1955). Certainly a lack of autonomy due to regimentation by others in and around our residential environments could be seen to promote feelings of alienation. The feeling may be active, in the sense of having little or no control, or it may be far more insidious, deriving instead from absurd moments of estrangement produced by sameness and boredom (after Camus 1955). Similar kinds of moments might also be encountered when confronted with the commercial artificiality and lack of depth of many contemporary suburban retail environments, so forcefully described, for instance, in Henry Miller's "Air Conditioned Nightmare" (1945). Suddenly the all-too-familiar seems incomprehensible, foreign, and alien.

Self-indulgence, self-consciousness, and anxiety, brought about by a similar denial of meaningfulness, are constant themes in earlier works of painters like James Rosenquist and by more contemporary artists like Eric Fischl. The strong narrative aspect of many of Fischl's canvases and collages is, as one critic put it, the "hidden life of suburbia" and "the suburb as failed Eden" (Hughes 1988). From the settings of suburban houses we are at once embarrassed and confronted both literally and figuratively with our naked inadequacy to deal with anything much more profound in life than conspicuous consumption and self-gratification. In the painting *The Power of Rock and Roll,* from a suite titled "Rooms of the House," we see the image "of a small pre-pubescent boy dancing naked surrounded by prestige symbols of success. . . . His walkman is held aloft and with his eyes closed he dances to unheard music, isolated in a frenzy of self-induced ecstasy, that ignores the world outside" (Godfrey 1986, p. 151). The technique of the painting is also telling in the same regard, for it is deliberately slick and commercial. In another compelling work, *Barbeque* (1982), an otherwise suburban scene of backyard and swimming pool is interrupted with the literal image of the chef as sideshow-like fire-eater (Whitney 1988).

By the late 1960s and early 1970s however, numerous commentators were willing to admit that the suburban life-style was in transition and certainly was not as conformist and monotonous as the earlier standard view suggested (Donaldson 1969, Masotti and Hadden 1974, Dolce 1976). Furthermore, the senses of loneliness, anxiety, and estrangement that had been epitomized by suburban life were well and truly ascribed to the modern urban condition in general. After all, if we want to compare paintings, Edward Hopper's *Office at Night* (1940) or his masterpiece *Nighthawks* (1942), both set in traditional big city environments, evoke feelings of loneliness and alienation (Fisher 1985). As far as the "ticky-tacky" residential boxes are concerned, in the revisionist words of one historian describing postwar suburban development, "Americans continued to migrate to the suburbs. . . . Even standardized Levittown offered greater opportunity for individual creativity than life in dreary urban apartment blocks. . . . After a decade of ownership, the individual taste of homeowners had tempered the monotony of the streetscape and had produced rows of distinguishable homes" (Teaford 1986, p. 105).

An alternative view praised suburbia for its egalitarianism and the "democratization of comfort" (Blum et al. 1963, p. 798). With rising affluence and product lines within their reach, many families now had access to life-style opportunities formerly available only to the wealthy elite (Galbraith 1958). According to one homeowner, "You can still remember walking up to your new house . . . that day it was legally yours. You didn't see the unlandscaped mud on your lawn, you saw thick green grass and flowers, all kinds of flowers. And when you opened the door . . . you didn't see the emptiness, you saw a cozy furniture arrangement around the fireplace" (Martin 1950, p. 14).

Contrary to the organization man and group man views of the world, Robert Wood argued cogently

that while they might be employed by big business, suburbanites do not bring corporate managerial styles home with them. Instead he finds that they are more inclined toward traditional beliefs in individual autonomy and the virtues of small local governments (Wood 1958). Meanwhile, tendencies to see suburban subdevelopments through the lens of agrarian idealism and nostalgic rusticity were also being strongly challenged (Donaldson 1969).

The more recent transition from city, suburb, and countryside to an urban and suburban metropolitan region underlies, not unenthusiastically, several major contemporary pieces of art and literature. In his numerous pictures of houses, pools, and lawns, like the enigmatic *Big Splash* sequence (1966–1967) and *A Lawn Being Sprinkled* (1967), David Hockney portrays the blank good life and commonplace clichés of his beloved southern California with acuity and unswerving affection (Knight 1988). In contrast to Fischl's disturbing and anxiety-ridden images, Hockney's sunny Eden remains intact and even resplendent. Hockney seems to suggest that compositional interest and visual delight can be found in even mundane pieces of domestic landscape, like his beautifully textured wooden fence in *A Lawn Being Sprinkled* (figure 37).

On a much grander scale, Hockney provides a colorful and delightfully exuberant graphic representation of the metropolitan landscape in two pieces: *Mulholand Drive: The Road to the Studio* (1980) and the more countryfied *Nichols Canyon Road* (1980). Both works draw their narrative strength and pictorial qualities from the open patchwork quilt of development, industry, open space, and recreational facilities

Figure 37   David Hockney, A Lawn Being Sprinkled,
1967

that characterize suburban metropolitan areas. In
Hockney's hands, they are transformed into a bril-
liant, energetic, and intriguing ensemble moving
across the landscape. Hockney's pictorial unfolding
of the roadway scenes emphasizes perhaps the principal expressive dimension of this kind of landscape:
automobile movement.

In *The Crying of Lot 49* (1966), Thomas Pynchon is far less sanguine about suburban metropolitan
regions in general and about Los Angeles in particular. For him the city in any traditionally legible sense
is dead. In its place is a group of concepts, so that an
area such as Los Angeles becomes, like the illustration in figure 38, a "printed circuit" (Sharp and Wal-

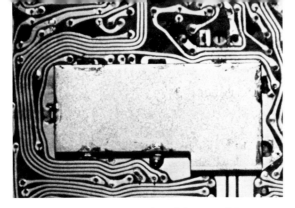

Figure 38 Pynchon's metaphor of the Printed Circuit

lock 1987). In Pynchon's words, "San Narciso . . . like many named places in California . . . was less an identifiable city than a grouping of concepts—census tracts, special purpose bond-issue districts, shopping nuclei, all overlaid with access roads to its own freeway. . . . But if there was any vital difference between it [San Narciso] and the rest of Southern California, it was invisible on first glance. . . . Though she knew even less about radios than about Southern Californians, there were to both outward patterns, a hieroglyphic sense of conceded meaning, of an intent to communicate" (Pynchon 1966, pp. 12–13). Here the functions and spatial domain of the suburban metropolitan area are reduced to information flows, transponders, and responders. Far from being an entirely dystopian view, however, Pynchon then seems to delight in exploiting both the absurdity and the fictional richness of this scheme.

PLACELESSNESS OR PLACE?

Pynchon's metaphorical reference to Los Angeles carries a sense of both chaos and strict predetermination. The chaos derives from the possibility that the printed circuit will become overloaded and so complex that no one knows where bits of information are coming from or going to. The sense of predetermination, by contrast, derives from the inherent structure of the printed circuit as a well-defined, precise, and purposeful artifact, thoroughly committed to the causes of logic and computation.

Similar sentiments surface in discussions about the sense of place conveyed by contemporary suburban metropolitan regions. Sometimes the same piece of geography will even conjure up similar reactions almost from opposite directions. For example, a suburban area may be shunned as being incoherent, cacophonous, and chaotic. References might be made to the seemingly endless commercial strips of neon signs, billboards, and large, permanent-looking structures mixed willy-nilly with small, temporary-looking shacks. No doubt it is also a reaction to the sheer jumble of land uses, the difficulty, much of the time, in telling one building's function apart from another's, and the general unfinished, muddled illegibility of an area.

By contrast, incoherence can also derive from feelings of sameness, predictability, and blandness. Typically this is not only a reference to the little boxes of suburban residential environments but to the lookalike wastelands of parking lots and roadways that make up most suburban commercial districts. This sameness, predictability, and blandness either assaults through blaring signage and light or stealthily confronts through anonymity and blankness. Either way—roar or silence—the landscape appears to be undifferentiated and lacking in any real meaning, let alone profundity.

An environment can be incoherent in yet a third way. There can be discord or a lack of conformance between what we might expect of a place and how that place actually presents itself. This results in a sort of mistrust or disbelief. For example, the suburban metropolitan landscape as a whole is rather complex in its irregular mosaic of different land uses and buildings. In much of its detail, however, it is surprisingly simple. Most single-family residential neighborhoods have a straightforward physical structure: simple houses placed uniformly on lots of much the same dimensions, arranged in an uncomplicated yet pleasing manner. Even large and sophisticated commercial enterprises like shopping centers tend to have clear, rational, and uncomplicated layouts. What the metropolitan landscape seems to convey is an overall complexity yet simplicity in its parts: those points of origin and destination and the places where we spend most of our time (Relph 1976). Again, it is another case of everything in its place, although this time disguising the inherent complexity of many relationships and issues confronting the inhabitants.

Not that there is any necessity for exact conformance between the physical appearance of an environment and, say, its political organization or social structure. Nevertheless, there is usually a rather rough coincidence between these dimensions; large houses, for instance, typically belong to wealthy people. Matters become problematic when the appropriate mirroring effect of form and purpose becomes so totally transgressed as to be entirely misleading. For example, the rusticity and nobility of simple cottage life, one of suburbia's major themes, may not only seem anachronistic but may also be socially costly, especially when the sentiments that stem from that belief are extended to matters of modern, metropolitan service provision and social integration where they no longer apply.

Others can see the selfsame environment as being reasonably coherent, even efficient, and yet lacking in any capacity for commitment or passion (figure 39). Relph in a recent work on the "placedness" or "placelessness" of contemporary urban environments invoked Kierkegaard's lament about our time as being "a reflective and passionless age," one that "leaves everything standing but cunningly empties it of significance" (Kierkegaard 1962, pp. 42, 51). He then struck an equation between this sentiment and what he referred to as "the landscape of reflection and reason," the well-engineered suburban environment we find today (Relph 1976, p. 125). In the end, it is a denial of "deeper experiences" that so disturbs Relph and others about these circumstances. Another slightly different way of expressing reservations about these qualities of coherence and efficiency is by reference to the comforts of suburban existence. Convenience coupled with the sort of

Figure 39   Life in the printed circuit: a modern shopping center

frictionless negotiation that is so often characteristic of better suburban environments can be disengaging.

In the extreme, both incoherence and passionless coherence can converge on the same resultant feelings of disassociation, personal distancing, and disowning. Both can lead to a sense of estrangement and alienation (after Camus 1955). More specifically, we can be made to feel as outsiders (Norberg-Schultz 1971, Relph 1976). First, we can be rebuffed by the unfamiliarity or illegibility of the urban terrain. In other words, either literally or metaphorically, we cannot place ourselves, do not know where we are, and become lost. Second, we can be repelled by disturbing or irritating sights and sounds. Although a place might be quite familiar to us, we may consistently not enjoy being there. Finally, the environment can be entirely incidental to our actions, what Relph describes as an "incidental outsideness" engendering "an unself-conscious attitude in which places are experienced as little more than the background or setting of activities and quite incidental to those activities" (Relph 1976, p. 52).

By contrast, the French intellectual Jean Baudrillard equates the unassuming banality of much of the contemporary American landscape with a sense of expressive freedom. Things are simply the way they are and make no pretense to anything beyond. Moreover, this capacity for being "just that" convincingly demonstrates the ultimate presence of cultural freedom (Baudrillard 1988).

In this general debate about place and placelessness, there are others, like Melvin Webber, who also argue that nothing more, or less, should be expected from modern metropolitan environments (Webber et al. 1964). To them it is an outmoded traditional and culturally ingrained idea that spatial proximity and place are tied so closely to notions of community, a sense of vested common interest, goodness, and caring. In spite of the approbation that is given to, say, medieval towns and their sense of place, in fact travel frictions in those days were very high, resulting in the absolute necessity of geographically centered associations. With modern transportation and communications systems, we find ourselves capable of thriving in what Webber dubbed a "nonplace urban realm," readily maintaining a network of social and business contacts based more on personal and individual affinities than on geography and propinquity (Webber 1964, pp. 74f.). One of the most profound territorial transformations of metropolitan regions is the creation of these realms and a functional state of affairs quite close to a less delirious and more benign, serendipitous version of Pynchon's printed circuit. Some think that we have literally crossed that threshold by placing ourselves into the realm of electronic media (Meyrowitz 1985).

In another, not unrelated, defense of the suburban landscape's inherent fragmentation and general spatial messiness, the positive attributes of increased social accessibility and unexpected yet serendipitous relationships among land uses have been enumerated (de Monchaux 1988). The presence of seams and fissures in the metropolitan spatial mosaic appears to provide needed flexibility for subsequent action and reaction. A remarkable characteristic of many American suburbs is a capacity for adaptation and physical change. Moreover, this is at least partly due to a lack of systematic planning and completion. By contrast, many locales in other suburban nations like Canada and Australia, with strong traditions of hierarchically organized centralized local government, are often far more relentlessly complete in their physical attributes and resistance to change.

During the 1960s, concepts not unlike Webber's nonplace urban realm emerged in architectural circles. The Japanese Metabolists, for instance, and the British group Archigram made proposals for cities as organisms and systems of events rather than as place-centered realms (Cook 1970). One of the most sympathetic proposals came from the direction of pop realism in the form of Archizoom Associati's hypothetical utopian Nonstop City of 1970 (figure 40). Rather than seeing the culture of consumption as the inevitable downfall of modern metropolitan humanity, it was viewed as a way of "fulfilling the highest potential for creativity" (Branzi 1984, p. 54). More specifically, Nonstop City drew attention to the profound changes that cities had undergone. In the words of Archizoom Associati, "The modern metropolis has ceased to be a place and [instead] has become a condition . . . a state of being, uniformly articulated throughout society by consumer goods" (Branzi 1984, p. 63). Further, in a manner somewhat analo-

gous to Pynchon's metaphor of the printed circuit, Archizoom saw a city composed of behavioral modes, consumer products, and, above all, information, "stretching as far as these media's reach" (Branzi 1984, p. 63). In the proposal huge warehouse spaces equipped with artificial lighting and micro-conditioning were inhabited and simply modified amid a littoral of mass-produced articles, according to particular needs and wants. The polemical quality of the proposal was essentially threefold. First, architecture no longer represented society, there being no buildings to speak of, but simply contained it. Second, because of a world now defined primarily by products, design rather than more traditional methods became the fundamental planning instrument. Finally, the reduction of living and working environments to large, comfortable spaces filled with objects provided the freedom necessary for experimentation with, as they put it, "new forms of communal experience" (Branzi 1984, pp. 67, 69).

Removal of special activities to dispersed and remote sites, however, runs the risk of reducing a place-centered sense of community to only those mundane, day-to-day functions that emphasize pragmatism and efficiency. The result may deprive an area of all those vicarious encounters with special places that cause us to pause and truly reflect, if only for a moment. For example, in a traditional town, the main civic square, public buildings, and perhaps a church usually occupied the center and lay in the path of most day-to-day activities. In a normal routine we would pass by and, at least once in a while, be interrupted by what was around us, causing us to look up, contemplate, and reflect for a moment on the higher order of things. As

Figure 40   Archizoom's Nonstop City, 1970

a consequence the townscape provided a certain depth and significance to our daily lives. With highly specialized spaces and so much of an emphasis on purposive efficiency in our contemporary suburban metropolitan environments, we may miss out on this kind of experience altogether. By the same token, we may also take advantage of "accessibility without propinquity" in order to provide a basis for enriching our daily lives (Webber 1964). If, for instance, "vicarious encounters of an uplifting kind" can result in critical reflection upon commonplace existence, then we should deliberately set out to disturb the "frictionless field" of activity to create places that are certainly more meaningful than the kitsch of a shopping mall's fantasy realm. The question remains, though, how do we do it?

A METROPOLITAN SPATIAL SYNTHESIS

With a majority of Americans living in suburban metropolitan areas, it is fair to say that the urban suburban experience reflects much of America itself. It is what some have described as being a segregated, pluralistic society (Dolce 1976). Certainly the state of affairs in suburbia depends on the eye of the beholder. To those inclined toward traditional, nineteenth-century views of city and country, suburbia appears as a monolithic structure bent on arbitrary and wasteful social fragmentation, all for the purpose of protecting private property. The result is monotonous conformity with a sense of placelessness. Others might perceive suburbia as a diverse social unit, operating closer to the principles and reality of a pure democ-

racy for both public good and individual comfort. In this view the resulting sense of place is specific enough to promote feelings of community and convenience, without the necessity of nearness and its inevitable conditions of confrontation, conflict, and nuisance. But probably few of us harbor such extreme opinions. Rather the suburban urban experience is daily life. Its positive attributes are chalked up on one side of the ledger and, when consistent enough, held up as a justification. Negative attributes are reasons to pause, perhaps reflect a little, possibly consider alternatives, but ultimately to work out some form of coping behavior.

The spatial structure and layout of settlements tend to reflect dominant or consensus views of social organization. The conformance is rarely, if ever, exact, because social organizations evolve and change in places where it is sometimes difficult to remake the city accordingly. Urban form is also limited in the means available to represent fully the complexity and nuance of social structures. Furthermore, it has a symbolic logic of its own. Nevertheless, as history repeatedly shows us, there is a relationship between urban society and its signs (Reps 1965).

In many important respects, the suburban urban development that took place in the United States from early in this century reflects the synergism of two broad national commitments toward social organization: majoritarian democracy, the ideal of self-rule by popular majority, and "defense of the rights of individuals and of minorities against the tyranny of the majority, a form of pluralism" (Nelson 1982, pp. 1f.). According to Nelson, a legal historian, republican rule by the majority was the dominant force in

American politics until the Civil War. During Reconstruction concern for the rights of minorities began to intrude upon majoritarian democracy, finally becoming institutionalized in the modern professional bureaucracy we maintain today. In effect bureaucracy became an amalgam of decision makers representing different interests and interest groups, more or less insulated from the vicissitudes of broader popular opinion (Nelson 1982). This trend also coincided with the rise of professional elites and the training and use by these specialists of formal processes of reasoning peculiar to their fields of interest (Weber 1952, Nelson 1982). In addition to the creation of legal associations by 1870, professional societies for medical doctors, engineers, and architects followed shortly after. To this we should add the technological advancement that took place during the last half of the nineteenth century, continuing well into the present period. Scientific management, under the leadership of men like Frederick W. Taylor, began storming into most walks of life prior to World War I (Haber 1964). Further application and refinement, particularly for the purpose of mass-producing consumer goods, followed in the 1920s. On Henry Ford's assembly lines, good management and efficiency were essential, together with a high degree of task specialization (Hounshell 1985). The upshot was an apparent merger, in style anyway, of big business and big government (figure 41). Both affected a roughly neutral moral stance or value-free attitude toward their tasks through objective, scientific reasoning. Both strove toward concepts like formal parsimony and operating efficiency, and both had a penchant for specialization (Bernstein 1976, Nelson 1982).

Figure 41   Early arrival of big business, big government, and bureaucracy

An underlying tension was created by strong parallel commitments toward majority self-rule. At bedrock, Americans still believed strongly in the essential efficacy and fairness of the "republican principle of the supremacy of the will of the majority" and the mandate that should be accorded that majority in making their program effective (Nelson 1982, pp. 156f.). For many, like the framers of the Constitution, this was a natural and enlightened order of things. Moreover, democracy worked best when everyone could be heard, thus forming the right basis on which a majority decision could be taken.

Without diminishing the importance of particular events like the rise of transportation technology, the willingness of local governments to support real estate development, and so on, the emergent suburban landscape effects a spatial synthesis of these two broad themes. The availability of technology and land are not enough. There must be a more specific direction to follow, a way to use the land and harness the technology. In short, a social organizational process must be at work.

As Wood has shown, suburban residential neighborhoods and municipalities have the potential for closely adhering to and embodying republican colonial notions that majority self-rule and democratic purity are best when held closely at home (Wood 1958). On the other hand, an argument can also be made that broadly based majority self-rule has been successfully circumscribed, in the name of individual and minority rights, so as to produce a heterogeneous collection of suburban enclaves, each a variant of the others but with its own particular identity.

Admittedly this and other features are not much different from mixed spatial distributions in traditional cities and the countryside, except for one significant proviso. The mixing of uses and population takes place horizontally in the form of a geographic mosaic. Moreover it is a pattern that gives full rein to the inherent tension in modern democratic life. I might go further and say that this pattern of development is a logical outgrowth of a traditional urban morphology. For instance, on foot, about the same degree of separation of land uses and populations could be obtained within denser and more highly mixed urban areas. Retail on the ground floor and residential above was separate enough; so was the simple separation of residential neighborhoods by a couple of blocks. Widespread automobile movement changed all that. Retail stores with residences above now appeared together at more or less the same destination. Any necessary separation had to be maintained by real horizontal distance, resulting in an aerial mosaic of land uses and neighborhoods. On the

whole there is no such thing as a special social character to suburban metropolitan areas—only a different spatial structure (Dolce 1976). Circumstances changed, we might say, in order to stay the same.

Special uses controlled by special governmental departments and, in fact, the very specialization and separation of suburban uses themselves, conforms to the opposite tendency: a pluralistic and bureaucratic attitude toward people's needs. We constantly see requirements for rationalized and efficient use of space, complete with flexibility for future development, exemplified in suburban office parks, shopping malls, cinema complexes, and so forth. Furthermore, the location of many of these facilities conforms to a rational picture of technical efficiency concerned with movement and accessibility. We also see other notions of social efficiency played out in zoned separation of land uses in the name of public health, safety, and welfare, not to mention protection for individual rights to the "highest and best use" of the land (Babcock 1966, Toll 1969, Mandelker 1971). In addition, parochial interests are to be found at work in the location of special uses. First, they are there because an individual community wants and welcomes them. Second, they are not located where they might logically be expected because, although needed, they are unwelcome. Unfortunately, the actions that often accompany expressions like "not in my back yard" can significantly distort rational bureaucratic plans for public service delivery.

Finally, accessibility, that ubiquitous feature of modern suburban metropolitan regions, allows for a spatial synthesis of both general attitudes toward social organization (figure 42). Pluralism and a distinct

Figure 42   Accessibility in the nonplace urban realm

identity can be spatially maintained without too many adverse effects of physical separation from services, jobs, and entertainment. With mobility, individuals get to pick and choose. Although less directly, accessibility also allows the temperament of majority self-rule to flourish. With their pluralistic values safeguarded, small enclaves and communities can band together and more confidently seek consensus on subregional or metropolitan-wide issues. They are now connected and within relatively easy reach of one another. Consequently the effects of any new urban developments tend to be pervasive and of concern to all. Good examples are the environmental impacts, such as land-surface subsidence and downstream flooding in a city like Houston, that can accompany seemingly remote new developments on the metropolitan periphery. Another example involves additional regional job opportunities at a relatively remote site, like the Framingham-Natick com-

mercial complex, which also produces local traffic congestion. In both instances, local interests alone are not enough to resolve the problem.

The longitudinal record of suburban metropolitan development probably points toward increased bureaucracy and vigilance on matters of individual and minority rights over a more majoritarian form of consensus. Certainly from the earlier prewar and immediate postwar exclusivity of the suburbs as white, middle-class precincts, pluralism has gained more of an upper hand. As we shall see, specialization of the suburban metropolitan landscape has also become a more permanent physical and functional feature. If one follows Nelson's hypothesis, we are witnessing perhaps a logical extension of a broad sociopolitical trend set in motion shortly after the Civil War. Not coincidentally, this trend also parallels the period of early modern and modern American suburban development, roughly from 1870 to the present. The current emphasis, toward pluralism and a mosaic of neighborhoods and land uses, resulting from the spatial synthesis of underlying organizational tensions, follows that trend. What were once far greater distinctions between broad, largely homogeneous areas like city, suburb, and countryside have now diminished to be replaced by the subtler boundaries between urban realms with specific functional and social identities. The resulting patterns of suburban metropolitan settlement represent a different symbolic landscape as well.

PART TWO

Cultural Artifacts

The second part of this book is about the building that took place in the middle landscape, enabling people to live, shop, work and move around. Four typologies are presented, each describing artifacts that have proved central to the cultural enterprise of modern metropolitan development.

The first is the single-family house in its garden, undoubtedly the most prevalent feature of the American middle landscape. In all, six house types are presented, including vernacular bungalows, colonial revivals, ranch houses, and contemporary homes. During its evolution since 1920, the program of the suburban house expanded and became more specialized in order to meet changing social circumstances. Landscape qualities also reflected different cultural preoccupations, involving personal health, physical exercise, and recreation for the mind. Generally the spirit of adventure, equality, informality, and progressive opportunity have been symbolized by allusions to the American West, whereas sentiments of solid respectability and status have drawn upon models from the colonial East.

The second typology describes developments in the retail realm of American suburban life from roadside franchises and strip commercial developments to shopping villages and pedestrian malls. Generally both the size and functional diversity of facilities have increased to match rising development costs and operational economies of scale. Apart from housing retail commercial activities, shopping centers have increasingly become venues for leisure-time and recreational pursuits. Their identity as community centers still remains ambiguous, however, in spite of the persistent efforts of socially minded planners and use of the metaphor of the traditional market town.

The third typology deals with the modern workplace in the guise of office parks and corporate estates. From administrative facilities adjacent to factories located on the outskirts of cities, suburban office complexes have emerged in a variety of forms, ex-

pressive of both business functions and corporate images. Typically abstract modern office buildings and pastoral landscapes combine to make seemingly benign symbols of managerial organization and corporate power.

The fourth typology concentrates on the design and construction of modern roadways, the infrastructure necessary for modern metropolitan development. From a primary concern with simply upgrading existing roads, emphasis shifted toward the provision of higher levels of service. As a consequence the hierarchy of roads and related subdivision layouts became more pronounced. Functional reasoning combined with environmental integration to produce specialized highways and other forms of street layout.

3   *Houses in Gardens*

The dominant feature in the American middle landscape is the single-family home. No other artifact is as pervasive or carries the same emotional charge as the detached house in its suburban garden. It is the building type we most closely associate with suburban metropolitan development and the one that gives this environment its tone.

Since the turn of the century, more and more people have invested their financial futures in modest-sized homes secured by mortgage debt. From 1890 until 1920 the proportion of homes that were mortgaged nationwide rose from 27 to around 40 percent (U.S. Bureau of the Census 1923, Weiss 1987, p. 6). After resuscitation of the housing industry following massive numbers of foreclosures and other cruel effects of the Great Depression, this trend accelerated, widely supported by low-interest, long-term, government-secured loans and local government patronage (Fish 1979, Eichler 1982). Between 1920 and the present there were over 70 million housing starts in the United States, 65 percent of these for single-family homes (U.S. Department of Commerce 1955, 1987).

The prominence of the single-family home in American hearts and minds was established and maintained in several ways. For instance, there were perennial statements by presidents and other high-ranking government officials that struck a strong equation between ideas of family, home, and national welfare. Understandably perhaps, this practice was particularly marked during the rallying calls that accompanied moments of domestic crisis. When convening the President's Conference on Home Building and Homeownership in August 1931, Herbert Hoover emphatically stated," Adequate housing [by which he meant primarily single-family homes] goes to the very roots of the well-being of the family, and the family is the social unit of the nation." He continued, "Nothing contributes more to happiness or sound social stability than the surroundings of [their] homes" (Gries and Ford, 1932, p. xv, Fish 1979, pp. 133ff).

The prominence of single-family housing was institutionalized even earlier, however. In 1928 the U.S. Supreme Court upheld the constitutionality of municipal zoning ordinances for the purpose of separating land uses in the interests of public health, safety, and welfare (American Law Institute 1975, Perin 1977, Weiss 1986). In so doing, they ratified the standing of the single-family residential category at the apogee of the hierarchy of land uses, where it continues to receive protection.

HOUSING TYPES

Over the past sixty or seventy years, the layout and general form of single-family houses has varied. Beyond matters simply of decoration and style, the underlying spatial structure and architecture have differed, giving rise to a number of distinct house types.

In the vernacular realm of single-family housing built since 1920, six house types can be identified: the bungalow, the colonial revival, the ranch, the figured compact plan, the zero-lot-line configuration, and the contemporary home. This terminology is somewhat makeshift, reflecting the merger of a number of characteristics that are often held apart when distinguishing between one type and another. Harrison (1973), for example, describes a classification scheme realtors use in which the plan of the house is described one way and the "look" or so-called style of the home another way. By contrast, the McAlesters concentrate almost solely on style as the distinguishing feature, although with a more systematic reference to particular periods (McAlester and McAlester 1986). Nevertheless, my classification avoids the unnecessary proliferation of house types contained in the earlier documents, without also oversimplifying the matter (Clarke 1986). It clearly recognizes that particular plans and styles are derivatives from one another and should not constitute a distinct type. Most of the categories have the advantage of a commonplace resonance about them that is recognizable to the general public. The terms *ranch* and *colonial* are rather unequivocal in this regard.

The Bungalow

Bungalows first appeared late in the nineteenth century (Lancaster 1985, 1986, Clark 1986), by and large in response to rising demands for modest, affordable housing and the cultural dictates of the progressive movement, with its emphasis on a simple, natural, out-of-doors way of life (Wright 1981, Hayden 1984).

Although predominantly a vernacular house type, the bungalow enjoyed a rich architectural heritage, with direct influences from the prairie school movement emanating from Chicago around the turn of the century (Lancaster 1985). Certainly the Bradley house (1900) and the Hickox house, both by Frank Lloyd Wright, in Kankakee, Illinois, are bungalow-like in their details and overall conformation. Wright's highly influential proposal, "A House in a Prairie Town," which appeared in the *Ladies Home Journal* in 1901, clearly advanced the idea of an organic domestic architecture in which stress was placed on honesty, simplicity, and functional integrity (Wright 1901, Brooks 1975). These were all characteristics that found their way into the bungalow. Only a few years later, between 1907 and 1909, the brothers Greene and Greene built their major California bungalow projects like the well-known David W. Gamble house and the Robert R. Blacker House, both in Pasadena, California (Makinson 1974, Lancaster 1985). Here we find distinctive rooflines with broad overhanging eaves, extensive functional use of woodwork as the sole decorative element, and a strong orientation of the house toward the out-of-doors, including numerous sleeping porches. Finally, Gustav Stickley's publication, *Craftsman Homes* (1909), popularized the architectural program of the progressive movement, echoing many of the same sentiments as Frank Lloyd Wright nearly ten years earlier. On matters like function and the use of material, Stickley insisted upon the parsimonious principle of doing the most with the least (Stickley 1909).

Key features of the commonplace bungalow were a compact single-story plan; a prominent hipped roof, usually with a sloping segment presented to the street; a spacious porch across the front of the house; and a simple, direct, perpendicular arrangement of the building on a modest rectangular lot. Most of these houses, built during the 1920s, ranged in floor area from about 1,200 to 1,800 square feet, with an average area around 1,300 to 1,400 square feet (Rowe and Desmond 1986).

The floor plan was strictly arranged into two zones placed roughly side by side across the site, with increasing levels of privacy away from the street at the front of the house (figure 43). The two-zone arrangement was divided between the private realm of bedrooms and the family entertainment area, consisting of living room, dining room, and front porch. The kitchen, usually located to the rear of the dining room with a separate outdoor back entrance, was used for both food preparation and informal eating. An unusual feature of most examples of the type was the formal character of the dining room. Typically this room ran across the center of the house from the bedroom zone to the exterior wall, terminating in a symmetrically disposed window, porch, or separate entry

vestibule. All rooms were just that, rooms, and not spaces that flowed into one another. This chamber-like quality was pronounced in the dining room. The repetitive arrangement of bedrooms was usually connected to the remainder of the house through a hallway.

The figural or decorative appearance of the house was frequently used to accentuate and visually qualify its strong overall formal qualities. These features were particularly apparent around the eaveline of the broad roof overhang, around the porch, and around wall openings. The craftsman-like quality of timber detailing was extended into the interior of the house through the use of architraves, dados, wall paneling, and built-in cupboards, features that are well illustrated in figure 44.

Sometimes a den or library adjacent to the living room was added. The physical extent of the living room across the front of the house also varied. By and large, however, the basic principles underlying the type were closely adhered to without much variation.

The Colonial Revival

The colonial revival house type consists of a simple, compact overall building volume, invariably two stories in height, with a square or rectangular floor plan. Typically the house was located at about the center to front third of a modest regular rectangular lot. In early examples the garage, if there was one, was located to the rear of the lot away from the house. Later the garage was often attached directly on to the house or through a connecting structure (Pickering 1951). Examples of this house type dated at least from 1920

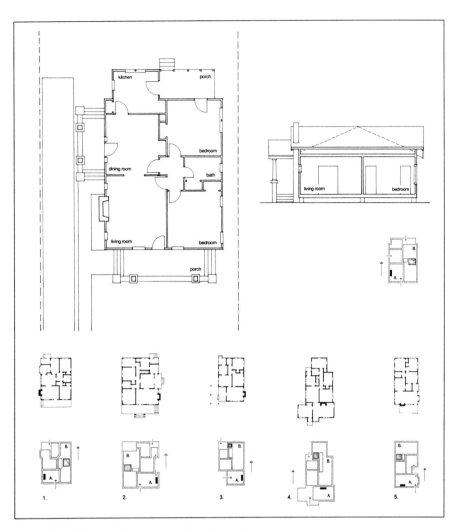

Figure 43   Plan, section, and transformations of the bungalow

Figure 44   A typical California bungalow

until the late 1940s, with additional examples found in each subsequent decade (Gowans 1986). Houses of this type ranged from about 1,200 to around 2,000 square feet in floor area, with an average size of about 1,300 square feet. Later models, however, were often considerably more opulent (2,500 square feet plus) and consistent with upward trends in the amount of floor area being provided (Rowe and Desmond 1986).

The layout of the house was usually divided into two distinct zones of use (figure 45). The first floor was given over to the formal and public functions of living room, dining room, and sometimes library or den. Spaces for service functions and family gathering, such as the kitchen, were also located on this level. By contrast, the upper-story zone contained bedrooms and related bathrooms, forming a private realm of the house, physically well removed from family gatherings and entertainment.

The plan of the lower floor was roughly quartered, with a stairway and incidental storage usually dividing the living room on one side of the house from the dining room–kitchen complex on the other. Typically the front entry of the house was centrally located, and the disposition of rooms around the entrance often made for a biaxial symmetrical composition. Consequently, in certain parts of the country, this house was referred to as a central entry colonial (McAlester and McAlester 1986). The living room and the dining room were distinct rooms rather than spaces, relatively formal in the placement of fireplaces, windows, doors, and furnishings. A summer porch frequently provided a less formal annex to the living room. The kitchen was always located to the

rear of the house with its own back entry and close access to separate laundry, basement, and pantry facilities, as well as to the garage at the rear of the site.

Consistent variations of the type featured a relocation or expansion of certain elements but within the strict order of the basic plan shown in figure 45. For instance, in cold climates, the fireplace was located near the center of the floor plan, whereas in moderate or warm climates, the fireplace, if present at all, was located on an exterior wall. Sometimes the formal entry sequence was elaborated through an external entry porch and an internal vestibule. Although the relationship of these elements to areas of formal entertainment was invariant, the central placement of the entry on the front facade of the house sometimes changed to the side. In such arrangements the rough symmetry of the two main rooms was maintained. Occasionally the dining room was placed to the rear of the house, sometimes with a porch attached, as well as some extensive use of climatically responsive devices such as verandas.

The second-floor bedroom suite also roughly conformed to the quartered floor plan layout. Typically between two and three bedrooms of roughly equal size were arranged around a stairway at the center of the home, filling at least three of the four corners of the square plan. The number of bathrooms varied from one in early years and in modest homes, located at the head of the stairway, to one bathroom per bedroom in later years, located en suite with each bedroom. Sometimes the quality of repetitive accommodations was broken by providing more floor area in the master bedroom and by adding the first additional bathroom to that part of the house.

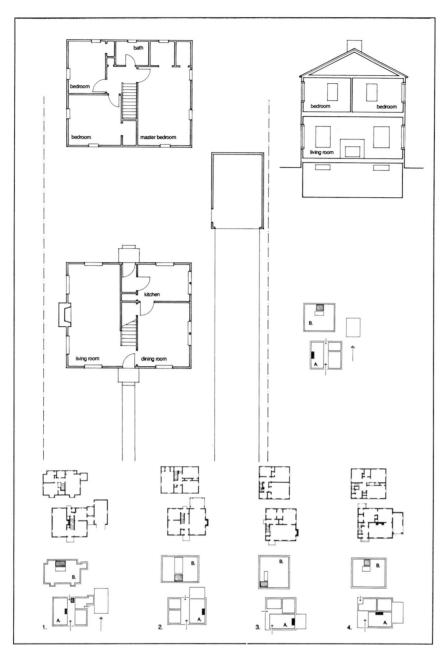

Figure 45   Plan, section, and transformations of the colonial revival

Figure 46   A typical prewar colonial revival home in New England, with a central entry

As its name suggests, the figural appearance, or styling, of the house type usually followed the compositional principles and motifs found in traditional period-style domestic architecture (figure 46). For example, homes were made to look colonial, Georgian, or federal. Far less frequently more exotic motifs, such as Spanish, Tudor, or Old English were to be found. Models of essentially the same house were typically advertised, through pattern books and the like, with a variety of facade treatments that attempted to give the product broad appeal (Jones 1929, Pickering 1951, Gowans 1986). In fact, one of the prominent features of this type is the comparative flexibility with which exterior appearances can be varied without changing the layout.

The Ranch

The modern ranch house type is clearly based, in mythos anyway, on its fabled predecessor of the nineteenth century. In fact, examples of the modern genre are strikingly similar to modest western ranch houses of the 1880s (Cassens 1953, 1955). Other examples also owe a considerable debt to F. L. Wright's prairie houses, in themselves something of a reinterpretation of the plains ranch tradition (Smith 1966, Brooks 1975). Wright's later usonian houses of the 1930s, expressing an ideal semi-agrarian way of life, also defined and developed themes that were often subsequently adopted in vernacular ranch house types (Sergeant 1984, Clarke 1986). Among these were the serial arrangement of rooms, the simple, strongly horizontal profile of the roofline, and the arrangement of the house toward the front of the lot, partially enclosing a larger private yard and patio at the back

(Rowe and Desmond 1986). Other influences are more diffuse, such as the use of natural materials, details like planter boxes, and horizontal arrangements of windows (Cavitt 1947). Wright also designed some twentieth-century equivalents of original ranch houses, such as the Raymond Griffiths house (1938), or ranch, in California, as well as his own Taliesen West on a much grander scale (Wright 1938).

Within the overall scope of the ranch house type, an evolutionary pattern of development is evident. Primarily both the size and complexity of the floor plan layouts increase. In fact, the house type evolves through three rather distinct phases from modest basic ranch type, on its way to the sprawling, highly articulated ranch rambler (Cavitt 1947, Clarke 1986, Rowe and Desmond 1986).

The basic ranch (figure 47) is a simple rectangular building mass, usually with a garage attached at one end, longitudinally located across its site. The floor area ranges between 1,000 and 3,000 square feet, with an average around 1,500 to 2,000 square feet. Including later split-level and bilevel variants, examples of the type were built between the late 1930s and the 1970s.

These houses are clearly composed of three functional zones, with varying degrees of expressive importance: a bedroom zone, which is arranged as repetitive rooms around a private hallway; a family living and entertaining zone, typically incorporating an open dining room or a dining alcove off to one side, and a kitchen area, often with a breakfast nook; and a garage with an adjoining recreation or hobby area. Typically the living zone is located in the center portion of the house, with a very open orientation toward the backyard, usually through glass windows, doors, and a patio. With the exception of the bedroom suite, which is still rather conventional in its arrangement and roomlike qualities, the interior space within the remainder of the house is relatively free flowing and uninterrupted. Wall partitions and similar devices are used to modulate the space and to create zones for special activities.

The exterior presentation of the house is primarily horizontal. A single-story appearance is usually maintained, parallel with the street, capped by a strong horizontal gable or hipped roof with wide overhangs (figure 48). Fenestration and other wall openings express this feeling of horizontally through arrangement and dimensions. The relationship of the house to its site is direct, and it frequently appears to grow out of the landscape. The addition of outdoor patios, pergolas, and screening devices adds to this sense of merger. Decoration and figural expression was typically kept to a minimum, appearing around and within windows and doors. The horizontal plane or visual datum of the house was gently articulated by serial rearrangement of major functional zones. Frequently the garage was pulled forward slightly beyond the remainder of the house, with a corresponding slight break in the roof line (May 1958).

Variations of the type typically occurred in the manner by which functional spaces were arranged on the interior, although the three-zone configuration was generally preserved. The most radical variations occurred later, during the 1950s and 1960s, with the introduction of split-level plans and units with bilevel entries. In all cases, the two and sometimes three levels of the house were used to distribute the three basic zones (Harrison 1973, Walker 1981). For instance, split levels often located the bedroom suite over the garage and family room, with a half-level change in grade downward and upward, respectively, to the main living zone. Sometimes the main living zone was located toward the rear of the house, with the bedroom suite in a forward position. The bilevel entry occurred on an intermediate landing at the front of the house, which was then usually arranged like a two-story house except that the formal living zone was on the same floor as the bedroom suite, with the family room(s) and garage below. In all cases, the overall massing of the house was compact and rectangular with a relatively horizontal appearance across the site.

With the house plan running parallel to the street, lot widths required to accommodate the ranch were usually considerably larger than for either the bungalow or the colonial revival. Dimensions in excess of 70 feet were often required. However, parallel development of streets with steep topography could be accommodated with reasonable ease by taking advantage of split-level arrangements and the relatively shallow depth required by the housing type.

The middle ranch was an evolutionary outgrowth of the basic ranch, with the earliest example dating from the mid-1950s. The floor area of this type was usually more generous than the basic ranch, ranging from about 1,600 to 3,000 square feet (Rowe and Desmond 1986), with building lots relatively wide across the front and units arranged parallel to the street. The floor plan layout of the middle ranch maintained the same three-zone distinction and basic relationships of the earlier type but with several im-

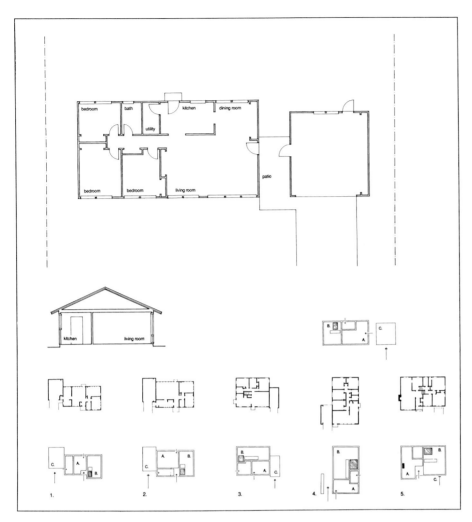

*Figure 47   Plan, section, and transformations of the
basic ranch*

*Figure 48   The horizontal lines of a typical single-story
suburban ranch*

portant elaborations. Typically the bedroom suite was larger, usually including three or more bedrooms and several bathrooms. The garage and hobby-recreation area was often expanded and brought into a closer arrangement with other parts of the house. Consequently the overall massing and formal composition of the house were much more highly articulated than the simple rectangular shape of the basic ranch. The three functional zones of the house were strongly expressed and their compositional arrangement used to heighten both the sense of entrance at the front and opportunities for outdoor areas such as patios at the back and side. As a corollary, distinctions between the front and back of the house, so prominent in earlier single-family houses, were less evident. In some variations both the bedroom suite and the garage were disengaged from the other living quarters, although the basic relationships among rooms and a coherent horizontal appearance of the house were maintained. More often than not, the garage occupied a prominent position to the front of the site.

Other variations took the form of highly articulated compositions (figure 49). Usually L-shaped plans and U-shaped plans used the overall massing and layout of the house as a bold gesture that embraced large outdoor areas as an integral part of the dwelling. Traditional distinctions between the sense of being indoors or outdoors were blurred in favor of a spatial continuum that extended from the landscape of the site by patios, broad roof overhangs, and full-length glass doors to the interior of the house. The family living area was frequently subdivided to provide an extensive variety of specific spatial realms, with wall partitions typically used to modulate rather than completely define the living space.

Like its predecessor the basic ranch, exterior figural expression in the middle ranch was subordinated to the overall formal composition of the houses. In fact, functional distinctions that lay behind the facade were often disguised through the consistent use of windows, shutters, window boxes, and other decorative motifs (Rogers 1962, Moore et al. 1983). Garages frequently received the same kind of exterior treatment as bedrooms. Again, considerable emphasis was placed on conforming the horizontal silhouette of the house to the landscape and vice versa. If anything, this feature was more pronounced than in the basic ranch. The higher levels of articulation in formal composition provided greater opportunity for engagement of the surrounding landscape.

The final, and in many ways logical, evolutionary expression of the ranch house type was what we might call the ranch rambler. As the name suggests, the simple formal unity of the basic ranch disappeared and became replaced by a highly articulated serial arrangement of building volumes spread out across the site. Almost all examples appeared in the 1950s and 1960s, and all were relatively large houses, built for families with above-average incomes. The typical floor area was around 2,500 to 2,700 square feet, although several examples were much larger, including separate guest or even maid quarters (Rowe and Desmond 1986).

Invariably distinct functional areas of the house were articulated separately, although the overall silhouette or profile of the house maintained the strong horizontal lines and planes characteristic of the ranch house type. Often the master bedroom suite was located apart from the other bedrooms, on the far side of the main living area. Furthermore, the program of specific accommodations often normally enlarged to include special family areas and other recreational venues.

While maintaining basic room-to-room relationships, the formal flexibility of the ranch type was fully exploited. Overall plan layouts show considerable variation, including L-shaped, U-shaped, and even courtyard configurations. Again, the degree to which outdoor areas were engaged within the house, and vice versa, was very high, with an almost complete lack of a distinct visual datum. In some extreme examples, each formal-functional component of the house took on its own shape under the overall rubric of strong horizontal roof planes, garden walls, pergolas, and other landscape elements. It is perhaps here in this type that the influence of the authentic western ranch house is expressed most dramatically (May 1946, 1958).

Figured Compact Plan

The figured compact plan type, a relatively recent development, combines the sophisticated planning of later ranches with the figural expression of earlier co-

Figure 49   Articulated variations of the ranch

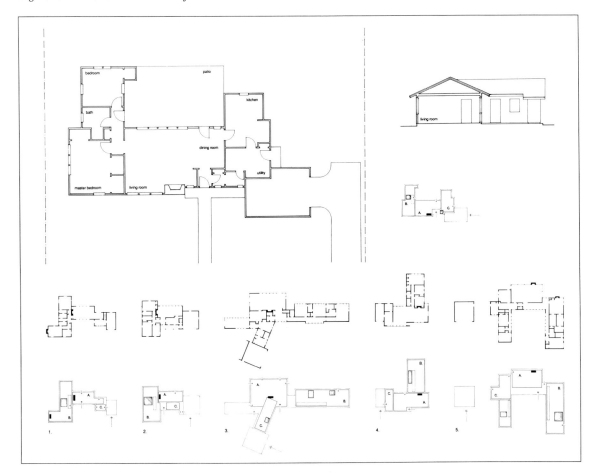

lonial revivals. Most examples of this type were built during the 1970s and early 1980s, although the type emerged during the later 1960s. In many ways, the figured compact plan expresses a merger of the two dominant earlier house types—the ranch and the colonial revival. In fact, beyond about 1975 it is difficult to find consistent examples of these earlier types (Rowe and Desmond 1986, Langdon 1987).

The floor plan layout of the figured compact plan is usually generous in at least the illusion of space (figure 50). Often one-and-a-half and two-story volumes are incorporated in the main living area and even in the master bedroom to convey a greater sense of spaciousness. This aspect seems to be borrowed, at least in part, from custom-built modernist houses. By contrast, the planar arrangement of rooms follows the three-zone configuration of the ranch, sometimes making use of the house's section to achieve visually interesting and efficient spatial distributions. More stately two-zone arrangements demonstrate perhaps a return to an earlier sense of Old World decorum.

Generally the overall form of the house is compact, and yet individual areas are often highly articulated in concert with a specific figural or decorative theme. For instance, neocolonial houses fit the classic profile of the original archetype, although entry vestibules, porches, and verandas are sometimes accentuated. The modernist plans and double-height room sections are also combined with period-style motifs from, for example, the Victorian era, where bay windows and porches were highly articulated. In short, a process of matching period-style decoration with appropriate small-scale formal gestures is followed but always within an overall design of considerable spatial coherence and efficiency. Unlike the earlier colonial revival house, where almost exactly the same plan in all particulars was clad in different stylistic motifs, the modern figured compact plan type is a little more rigorous, demonstrated by the example shown in figure 51. Figuration of the house form does have some influence on its articulation and vice versa.

Trade magazine descriptions of specific examples of this housing type stress tradition and authenticity (*House and Home,* 1967–1977, *Housing* 1978–1982, *Builder* 1983–1986.) Clearly an attempt is being made to interest buyers in these two characteristics and all the closely associated connotations of heritage, status, and respectability. Similarly, consumer surveys indicate strong preference for authentic and traditional building materials such as hardwood floors, windows with timber mullions, ceramic tiles, and the use of masonry (*Builder* 1983–1986).

Zero-Lot-Line Houses

As the label implies, each zero-lot-line housing unit is built on a narrow lot, at or near the property line on at least one side. Some span the entire width of the lot, with outdoor space arranged in either a townhouse or courtyard configuration. Others meet the property line on only one side, leaving a long, narrow side yard or easement on the other.

Although conceptually related to single-family European modernist courtyard projects of the 1920s and 1930s, the zero-lot-line house type has been used widely in the United States only since the late 1960s (Richardson 1988). The primary appeal of the type to developers is the accommodation of higher dwelling

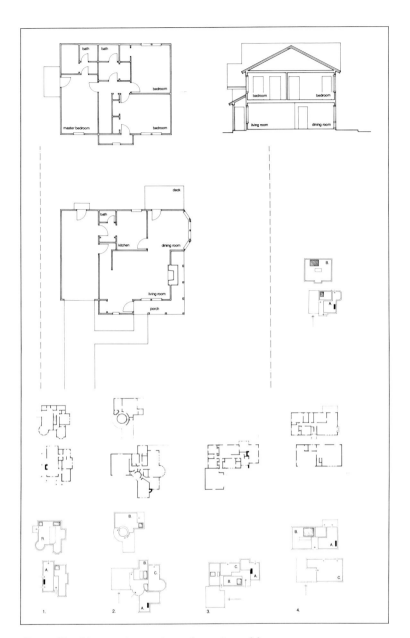

*Figure 50   Plan, section, and transformations of the
modern figured compact plan*

*Figure 51   Traditional exterior of a recent contemporary
house: Rosewalk Cottages, Seaside, Florida by Orr and
Taylor, 1983. Copyright Mick Hales, 1985*

densities without a complete loss of the all-important identity of a single-family unit. With the advent of more flexible municipal zoning practices in the late 1960s and early 1970s, such as planned unit developments, the way was clear for experimentation with higher-density single-family units. In many suburban, exurban, and tourist areas of the country, property values had risen to the point where it seemed provident to break the hegemony of single-family detached housing construction so long as a single-family character could be maintained. There was also increased interest, as the term *planned unit development* implies, in maintaining a relatively uniform, thematic public appearance. Clearly there were also market advantages to this strategy. A clustering of units expressing a coherent architectural theme made a more significant and inviting impression within the suburban landscape, offering, in addition to an individual unit, a sense of place and community (Langdon 1987).

Within the category of house type are several variations. In townhouses (or townhomes) the spatial organization and overall public appearance of units are based on nineteenth-century row houses found in older East Coast cities. Usually, however, the units are set back from the street, respecting municipal building lines for neighboring conventional single-family houses and providing for a small garden or enclosed front yard. Nevertheless, units are invariably constructed as close to the street as possible, allowing the rear portion of a typical 30 by 100 foot lot to be used as a private garden. The interior arrangement of rooms within the house adheres to a three-zone configuration, although the more public, formal enter-

taining spaces are often found on the second floor. Generally houses are from two to three storys in height. Figural expression can vary widely from eclectic traditional styling, such as William F. Stern's Wroxton Street houses in Houston, Texas, to the modern and abstract in the case of Arquitectonica's Milford Townhouses in the same city, shown in figure 52 (Arquitectonica 1984, Langdon 1987, p. 13). In both cases, considerable skill is used to balance expression of individuality with that of public uniformity.

The second type is the zero-lot-line arrangement where the units are not fully attached to one another, except perhaps by garden walls. The lots are usually a little wider, on the order of 45 to 50 feet, and sometimes shallower in depth (Richardson 1988). Units vary in spatial arrangement from one to two storys in height but usually expand horizontally to occupy

Figure 52   The abstract forms of Arquitectonica's Milford Townhouses, Houston, 1979

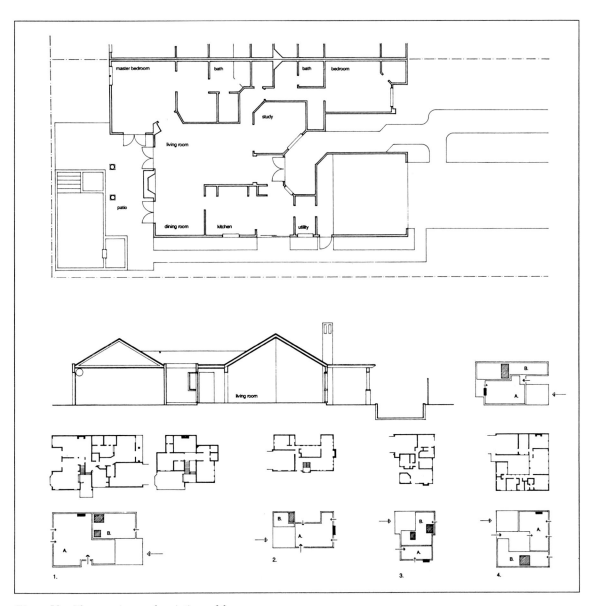

Figure 53   Plan, section, and variations of the
zero-lot-line house

large portions of the site, as shown in figure 53. Special problems with the type include accommodation of the automobile, especially in two-car garages; dealing with long, windowless side walls along a property line; and maintaining a clear sense of entry and spacious sense of individual identity. The last is often solved by arranging building volumes diagonally across the front of the site to give the impression of greater width. Alternatively the lots themselves are arranged at an angle to the street, accomplishing much the same visual effect (Langdon 1987, Richardson 1988).

A third subtype is the zero-lot-line courtyard house. Usually composed as a single-story unit, the house extends across most of the lot, with private garden courtyards contained within the overall plan. The spatial arrangement of rooms can be quite complex, with the courtyards and galleries between acting as ways of achieving functional mediation and focus. In these respects, units embrace many of the principles espoused by Chermayeff and Alexander in their relatively early work on ideal urban and suburban houses (Chermayeff and Alexander 1963). Public architectural expression of these units is usually anonymous, subordinated to the articulation of an exterior garden wall. On occasion a sense of individuality and stylistic expression is achieved by the use of an entry pavilion on a double-story portion of the house along its front.

The Contemporary House

The final house type remains the least favored in the popular marketplace and is clearly the most radical in design and layout (Rowe and Desmond 1987). The house is almost entirely represented by custom-built examples, often by notable architects. Ranging over the period from the late 1930s until the 1960s, most examples date from the 1950s, including many of the "Case Study Houses" in Los Angeles (McCoy 1977), examples from Quincy Jones, Nelson, and the Fords, as well as a variety of research homes (Ford and Ford 1940, Wright and Nelson 1943, Jones and Emmons 1957, Mason 1982). All were developed as prototypes for mass production. Other examples that did achieve some commercial success include Ned Eichler's contemporary houses built in the Palo Alto area of California in the early 1950s (Eichler 1982).

A hallmark of the type is a loose, well-organized floor plan, where specific functions are quite evident and sometimes arranged in an unusual manner (figure 54). For example, the use of separated individual pavilions for specific spaces, like bedroom-linked circulation areas, is quite common. Typically the program of uses is pulled apart so to speak, in its physical expression. Or, to put it another way, the appearance of the house is primarily about its use program, and other matters of identity are considered secondary (Ford and Ford 1940). The use of standardized planning modules for organizing the layout of the house, in both plan and section, is another common feature.

Overt expression of modern technology in the appearance of the house is a second hallmark of the type. Any figural expression on the facade, other than under principles of "form follows function," are banished (Wright and Nelson 1943). Post and beam construction is often used, together with bold, simple roof planes and large areas of glass infill. Decks, patios, and other accoutrements of outdoor living are

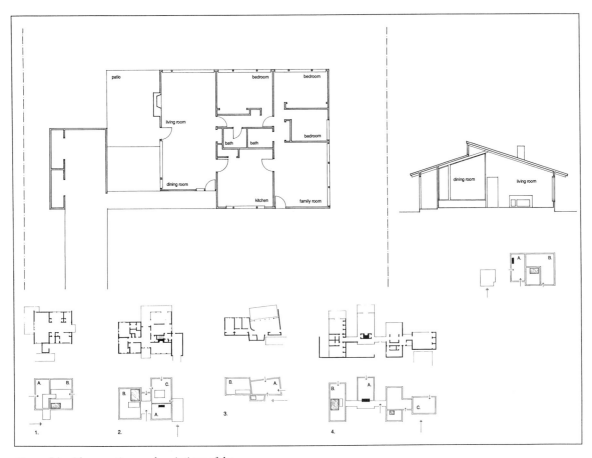

Figure 54   Plan, section, and variations of the contemporary house

Figure 55   An experiment in modern domestic architecture: Neutra House, Los Angeles, 1933. Rebuilt in 1964.

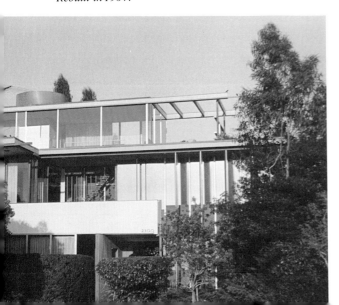

frequently employed (figure 55) (Mason 1982, Eichler 1982). In short, the visual appearance of the house is bound up in both its functional program of uses and the materials of its construction. The type conveys no sense of history, heritage, or continuity with the past. On the contrary, its expression is rooted in the here and now and the specific circumstances of its own manufacture.

Houses in Gardens

SPATIAL TRENDS AND VARIATIONS

Among the single-family housing types, a number of distinctive and related design trends can be discerned. They can be grouped into five domains of interest, each corresponding to a particular physical feature: accommodation of the automobile, the spatial arrangement of rooms and other spaces within the house, the site layout and landscaping around the units, the formal and figural appearance of the house, and the material and construction of the house (Rowe and Desmond 1986).

Accommodation of the Automobile

Certainly by the 1930s the use of private automobiles had expanded considerably to the point where the automobile suburb was established where the streetcar suburb left off (Wright 1981, Stern 1981, Clark 1986). At first the automobile was accommodated at the home site in a direct and pragmatic manner. In many cases the car was parked on the street next to the house or in a driveway by the side of it (figure 56). In others it was parked in a detached garage, usually located to the side and rear of the dwelling. A number of trade journals in the 1920s carried articles specifically dedicated to the matter of garage design (*House Designs* 1929). The dominant theme was one of disguise, whereby the garage would both hide the car from view and blend into the surrounding landscape like a traditional garden house or farm outbuilding. Sometimes the shape and appearance of the garage nearly matched that of the house in its roofline, material composition, and decorative treatment. This lat-

Figure 56   Early suburban accommodation of the automobile

ter response was strongly evident among period-style, larger versions of the colonial revival house type and less apparent among the bungalow house types of the same general period.

From the 1930s on, a gradual transition took place toward including and articulating the garage as a fundamental spatial and formal component of the house. First, the garage was placed near the house, connected to it through a covered breezeway (figure

57). The garage and the breezeway became additional building elements that were actively used in composing the overall appearance of the house. The garage was no longer disguised by its placement at a remote location of the site. Some architects, such as Royal Barry Wills, used this opportunity to give the house a larger and grander appearance from the street, a trend that was to continue (Moore and Oliver 1977).

During the late 1930s and throughout the post–World War II era, the garage was incorporated into the overall massing of the house. This was particularly pronounced in the ranch type and its variations, such as the split level shown in figure 57. Here the linear and serial arrangement of major components of accommodation across the site, such as bedrooms and living room areas, was continued with the garage. This compositional strategy allowed the horizontal lines of the ranch to be more fully exploited by extending the overall form of the house to include the garage. Furthermore, the horizontal appearance of the garage door and associated window openings, read against the background of the facade, could be aligned with horizontal fenestration in the remainder of the house to enhance the desired appearance of the low-lying horizontality, a conspicuous feature of the ranch type.

By the 1950s the garage was also used as a multipurpose space for recreational and other leisure-time purposes. Either these activities took place in part of the garage, or the garage formed a convenient annex to a recreation area. For obvious reasons of convenience, connection to the living–family room area of the house was usually made directly through the kitchen. The full integration or domestication of the garage, sometimes replete with window coverings and window boxes, was no different from devices used on other parts of the house.

By the 1970s in variations of the ranch, compact plan, and zero-lot-line types, the garage had become a prominent element in the overall formal composition of the house. It can be pulled forward on the site, or articulated in a similar manner, to vary the overall massing and to provide a heightened sense of entrance to the house, or it can form the base component of a two-story structure, typically with bedrooms above, to achieve the same kind of effect. Homeowners prefer single doors, presumably for the width of access that they provide, but also because they soften the intrusion of the car, now in a more prominent position on the site (*Housing* 1978–1982). Throughout, the domestication of the automobile as a design strategy was maintained. Another pragmatic reason for the forward location of the garage is no doubt the reduced cost of driveway and related site improvements, as well as the ability to accommodate houses with this configuration on smaller lots (Eichler 1982).

There has never been popular enthusiasm for the carport or, in later times, for the detached garage (*Housing* 1978–1982). If nothing else, the trends suggest that overt presentation of the automobile has been viewed with a certain awkwardness. First it was removed or disguised, then integrated, and finally fully assimilated into the design agenda for shaping the house.

From the twin vantage points of the intrinsic dependence of the suburbs and most single-family

Figure 57 Connected and integrated accommodation of the garage into suburban single-family homes

housing on the private automobile and a modern romance with the car itself, this trend may seem paradoxical. However, if one views the car either as a begrudged necessity in these circumstances or as a plaything with its own related though distinct identity, then the paradox is less strongly evident. There still remains, however, a certain confusion between the symbolic realms of house and garage, in spite of attempts at assimilation, an awkwardness that never fully disappeared. Symptoms of this confusion can be seen, for example, in the full fenestration and integration of the garage below the roofline so that it appears to be like other parts of the house, yet with the roofline invariably broken, deferring to its special function. It is as if the idyll of the house as home has never been fully reconciled with the automobile as machine and artifact of technical progress.

The Spatial Arrangement of Rooms

A clear trend in the spatial organization of rooms and other spaces within the house began to occur in the late 1930s and became a persistent feature by the mid-1950s. At this time the general zoning of spaces within the house changed from a two-part division of formal and informal areas to a three-part division along the lines of private bedroom suite, formal living area, and spaces for family living.

Invariably within both the colonial revival and bungalow house types of the 1920s and 1930s, a sharp distinction was drawn between the private bedroom areas of the house and the more familial or communal realm of the living room, dining room, and their service functions. This was a time during which the program of spaces to be accommodated within the

house was relatively minimal and straightforward. For example, there was undoubtedly multiple use made of the living and dining room for formal and informal family functions. However, the layout of these spaces, with some notable exceptions, was almost exclusively inclined toward formal entertainment. No special accommodation was made for informal family leisure time and recreation. Similarly the kitchen and other utility spaces were generous in size and straightforward in their arrangement. No doubt developments in household appliances for cooking and laundry, for example, began to obviate the need for the specialized accommodations of the Victorian era (Wright 1981, Clark 1986, Forty 1986). Multiple use was also made of the kitchen for family eating and recreation simultaneously with that for food preparation. Nevertheless, again like the living and dining areas, the kitchen's layout was inclined primarily toward one use—food preparation. The appearance of breakfast areas or dining nooks in or immediately adjacent to the kitchen did not occur with any regularity until later.

In most respects the two-zone arrangement of the house, with the relatively straightforward designation and layout of rooms, fitted social circumstances. Moreover, the layout of spaces in the house appears to have reconciled two otherwise exclusive requirements and social themes. First, although the more public aspects of family life-styles were certainly less formal and ritualized than those of the Victorian era, they played a significant role in maintaining a prevailing sense of decorum. Second, an important feature of the progressive movement in housing, of which these houses were a direct outgrowth, was an

Figure 58   Craftsmanlike detailing and functional simplicity of early interiors: the dining room of Greene and Greene's Gamble house, 1908

emphasis on a simpler way of life (Wright 1981, Clark 1986). Interiors were functional, as amply illustrated by Greene and Greene's Gamble house of 1908 (figure 58), and yet rich in craftsmanlike finishings.

Curiously, in the bungalow housing type one finds an inversion of the expected formality of the living room, or parlor, with that of the dining room. Here the dining room, located in the middle of the house, exemplifies the highest investment in the use of biaxial symmetry and other formal compositional devices for arranging rooms. By comparison, the interior arrangement of the living room, the traditional location for the use of such devices, was usually rather informal, with a direct orientation through a porch to the outside. Gone, in most cases, was the traditional entry vestibule and ritualized sequence of spatial events usually associated with the living room, especially in contemporaneous examples of the colonial revival house type.

Strange though this arrangement may seem at first, it can be accounted for under a principle of use and social value in which the shape and appearance of the house had to convey a sense of informality and simple living while still preserving some sense of traditional decorum. In the overall formal appearance of the bungalow, the balance was clearly struck in favor of informality and simple living, within which a more traditional sense of decorum could then be addressed. What easier way to handle the latter than appealing to the irreducible spatial ritual of dining? By contrast, the colonial revival house type was inclined in the other direction, favoring a traditional hierarchy of formal entertainment spaces centered on either the

living room alone or on the living room and dining room as a symmetrical ensemble. Within this house type a feeling of informality, though never really the sentiment of a simpler way of life, found its way into the spatial arrangement by way of dens and verandas leading to the outdoors at the side or rear of the house.

The three-zone division of the house is exemplified by the ranch house type that gained in popularity during the 1950s. Here the distinction between formal and informal family living and entertainment was given full expression. Rather than relying on the multiple use of spaces to accommodate both aspects, separate, more specialized accommodations were developed. Furthermore, the garage became annexed as part of the informal living zone of the house, together with outdoor patios and yards. By contrast the arrangement of bedroom en suite with a hallway and bathrooms, with some minor elaboration, remained unchanged from the earlier types.

The spatial relationship of the three zones was typically handled in a serial arrangement whereby the bedrooms were located next to the living areas and, in turn, to the family area–garage ensemble. The distinction between formal living and informal living was usually not sharply drawn. Rather, we can often see a graduation in areas of use, as shown in figures 47 and 49, from formal parlor, through dining area, to breakfast room and family room, to open recreational and hobby areas near the backyard. More often then not, the spatial definition and articulation of these functional areas shifts in a corresponding manner from the more fully defined roomlike quality of the parlor to the more open and locally defined family areas. Within this kind of hierarchical arrangement, the formal living areas are usually located to the front of the house and the informal areas to the rear. As might be expected, the perceived relationship between interior and exterior becomes less pronounced and ambiguous toward the rear (figure 59).

Once again the general three-zone arrangement of spaces within the house coincided with social circumstances. The greater emphasis on family entertainment and recreation, especially for children, fulfilled the needs of the emerging baby boom in the

Figure 59 Patios and other outdoor living areas formed highly accessible extensions to the modern house

1950s. This was also a period of rising affluence for many, in which a structured yet rather casual sense to the mode and manner of everyday life was encouraged (Masotti and Hadden 1973, 1974). In spite of several national economic setbacks and a rising sense of social unrest, there was a feeling of optimism and opportunity. This appears to have further dispensed with the need for highly formal behavior (Blum et al. 1963). Suburban development, with its social and economic tendency to form communities of similarly situated people, effectively did away with the need for marked distinctions between public and private forms of conduct. Nevertheless, a certain paternalism also pervaded daily family life.

Both social influences are evident in the evolving shape and appearance of the ranch house type. The basic plan of this house maintained a traditional hierarchy of rooms and living spaces, organized from the more public realm at the front of the house toward the private and informal realm at the rear. The colonial revival house type persisted in many parts of the country, often with the addition of family-oriented programmatic spaces to the rear and side of the formal living zone. By contrast, some other versions of the ranch displayed far less of a distinction between the public front and private rear.

By the 1960s, strict zonal distinctions among rooms in many houses had almost disappeared. The single exception was the bedroom suite, which maintained a regular repetitive arrangement of roughly equal-sized rooms around a hallway. The number of bathrooms increased, at times reaching a one-to-one ratio with the number of bedrooms. The master bedroom invariably was a little larger and had a private bathroom attached. Nevertheless, at least into the 1970s, a more or less egalitarian arrangement of bedrooms in terms of relative size, amenity, and orientation persisted.

Other more compact versions of the ranch plan—the bilevel, split-level and double-story arrangements—reemerged and became prominent in the 1970s. Fundamentally the three-zone configuration was preserved and organized around the vertical section of the house. Typically, different levels corresponded to the separate zones of the house. When two zones shared the same level, often the case with the bedroom suite and formal living-dining areas, they were not merged and were linked by a hallway. The impetus behind these compact layouts seems to have been primarily economic. Rising costs of home construction, site improvements, and consumer concern for operating and maintenance functions, especially energy efficiency, logically guided house design in the direction of minimal building envelopes and a compact massing of form.

The expansion, degree of elaboration, and specialization of the program of rooms and other spaces within the home reflected a related long-term trend: more space and more spaces with different and overlapping functions. Between the 1920s and 1930s houses typically had a basic complement of rooms that accommodated various household functions; where necessary, rooms took on multiple purposes. During the late 1940s and 1950s this basic complement of spaces was expanded to incorporate other specialized outdoor living areas, interior breakfast alcoves, storage facilities for food and other household items, family rooms, TV rooms, hobby areas, recre-

ation spaces, and others. Forerunners are to be found in houses of Frank Lloyd Wright, such as the Wiley house (1934) (figure 60). Some versions specialized spaces according to the life cycle of family members (McCoy 1977). In most respects this general trend persists today, although contemporary plans often display higher levels of sophistication and efficiency in accommodating the expanded program.

Rising affluence, and with it the rising expectations of homeowners, undoubtedly contributed to this trend. Characteristics of household formation, particularly during the years of the baby boom, also account for certain aspects of the programmatic proliferation, as did changes in the retailing of household goods and services and an increase in and more diversified use of appliances (Cowan 1982). The question still remains, however, as to whether these trends required expansion of the program of room accommodations and specializations of spaces within the home. Clearly with emphasis on the home as the site for a variety of leisure-time activities for family

Figure 60   Specialization of functions within the open plan: eating area in the Wiley House, by Frank Lloyd Wright, 1934

members, the dictates of privacy and the need for additional facilities support the trend. Nevertheless, other cultural influences were also at work.

Although the modern architectural avant-garde was never singularly important to popular American single-family housing, it did exert an influence on the use program and some of the spatial sensibilities by which houses were produced. As early as the late 1930s numerous home magazines carried articles extolling the virtues of modernist houses and the design doctrine of "form follows function" (*Architectural Forum* 1936, Wright and Nelson 1943). By the 1940s at least two strains of thought could be discerned in this direction. First, an argument was made that houses should not be regarded as simply being made up of rooms with separate functions but as an ensemble of more finely desegregated spaces, each ergonometrically designed to suit its function. For example, the leisure-time activity of reading the evening newspaper was to be accommodated with the proper seating arrangement, lighting, and acoustical privacy. Second, a related though less extreme view was adopted whereby specific functions in a house were first to be identified and analyzed as a system of events and then the space of the house designed accordingly. The materials for constructing and furnishing the house were to be used in a manner most appropriate to their technical characteristics.

During the 1950s, and possibly earlier, this functionalist architectural doctrine was beginning to have some effect. The spatial configuration of living areas, placement of room dividers, organization of furnished areas, and so forth exhibited more of an atmosphere of flowing interrelated spaces than ever before. Greater design attention was clearly being focused on specific functions within rooms. However, rather than mass housing being directly influenced by modernism in some direct imitative fashion, it seems more likely that demands for an expanded program and more specialized spaces found reinforcement and sympathetic expression under a functionalist architectural paradigm.

A further widespread devolution of the early standard program of rooms in the house was apparent during the 1970s, now centered on the master bedroom. Until recently the bedroom suite had remained unchanged in both layout and accoutrements. Now considerable architectural emphasis was placed on increasing the amenity of at least the master bedroom suite through the use of, for example, increased ceiling heights, special fenestration, private outdoor patios and decks, separate exercise areas, and opulent bath and dressing rooms (Langdon 1987, Vogel 1987). On most contemporary plans, the size of the master bedroom, relative to other bedrooms in the house, has also increased. And recent preference surveys indicate high levels of interest in this part of the house (*Housing* 1978–1982, *Builder* 1983–1986).

The changing roles of family members are reflected in this and other trends. Smaller families, a significant number of empty-nesters, and a complete absence of children among many younger couples and singles logically would seem to promote an emphasis on the private realm of a house. Elaboration of the master bedroom suite as an integral part of leisure-time activity also follows a pattern similar to other domains of the house in earlier times. In short, as soon as the ritualized use of the house is relaxed and pressures for multiple use are developed, the program and spatial design expand accordingly. Higher participation of women in the work force and labor-saving home appliances may also mean some de-emphasis in other programmatic aspects of the home associated with housekeeping (Cowan 1982, Vogel 1987). It is certainly clear from a number of surveys conducted in different eras that, if anything, the housekeeping and child-rearing functions increased during the pre– and post–World War II eras as much as a consequence of the demands of the modern house as anything else (Cowan 1982, Hayden 1982, 1984).

In brief summary, a strong sociological rationale can be advanced to explain the gradual expansion and elaboration of the basic program of accommodations within the single-family house of all types. Trends in this direction closely follow patterns of household formation between 1920 and the present. They also built on each preceding generation of developments in house design and were guided by functional trends in modern architecture, especially those involving use of the open free plan.

Landscaping and Site Layout

Situation of the house, in both the immediate landscape of the lot and in the context of neighboring houses, shows some subtle though distinct differences among housing types, and consequently from one era to the next. More often than not these differences appear to reflect changing cultural attitudes toward natural landscapes in general and domestic landscapes in particular.

There were also changes in the housing lot configurations themselves, although in almost all cases the layout strongly reflected prevailing programmatic conditions. In addition, rather uniform lot sizes and geometries were commonly adopted throughout the country as minimum acceptable standards. Invariably these sizes and geometries were defined by practical considerations like zoning setbacks, municipal easements, and sufficient space for house, garage, and driveways.

The siting of both the colonial revival house type and the bungalow of the 1920s and 1930s was straightforward. Typically the house was located in what might be called a standard tract configuration, toward the center and front third of a rectangular lot of approximately 50 to 55 feet by 100 to 120 feet on adjacent sides, arranged perpendicular to the street. It was an economically efficient arrangement, where relatively narrow, deep lots minimized infrastructure investments. It also essentially divided the site into a front yard and backyard, with smaller side yards. A hierarchy of public to private spaces was thus created from front to back, with the internal configuration of rooms in the house directly reflecting this arrangement. For example, the living room was typically located at the front and bedrooms either to the rear or on the second floor.

Some exceptions to this spatial gradation are to be found in the bungalow, where the dining room, located to the center and one side of the house, often had a prominent porch. The visual effect of this intrusion into the exterior side space, illustrated by the house in figure 44, was to create a more expansive frontal presentation of the house to the street. In most subdivisions the bungalow was rather narrow in frontage and typically located on a narrow lot. This compositional arrangement also allowed the dining room, one of the formal spaces of the house, to be brought into more prominent alignment with other formal spaces and therefore to approximate more closely in appearance the typical side-by-side arrangement of the colonial revival house type built during the same era. A similar tactic was also employed much later with the diagonal composition of zero-lot-line houses across their sites.

By comparison to later housing types, the bungalow and the colonial revival were relatively removed from their landscape setting. Typically the ground floor was raised above grade, and access to the outdoors was mediated through porches or verandas (figure 61). The gardens usually expressed distinctions between front and back and the corresponding formal and informal presentation or use of the house. The sentiments about the natural landscape expressed by this arrangement seem to be ones of selective engagement and "being next to," an attitude that is perhaps not surprising given the times. Toward the end of the last century, the awe and curiosity with which American culture had usually regarded natural landscapes began to change (Nash 1980), and by the early 1900s, there was a more benign sense of adventure and romance. Nature clubs were established in various parts of the country, the Boy and Girl Scouts were formed, and the outdoors was seen as a healthy, invigorating place to be (Clark 1986). This attitude permeated the domestic realm, particularly in the new suburban and exurban environments. Exposure to the natural elements of the outdoors, even if only from the comfortable vantage point of the front veranda or screened porch, replaced the more claustro-

phobic surroundings of the Victorian parlor as being both more healthful and mentally stimulating. The stage had not yet been reached for complete involvement in the outdoors, however. The experience was clearly enjoyed as part of day-to-day life but selectively and largely from the surroundings of the house looking out.

With the ranch house type of the 1950s, the relationship of the house to the outdoors shifted more dramatically. Here the house extended out into the landscape, which was embraced and incorporated both literally, at times, and metaphorically within the dwelling. In short a continuum was established, moving from the garden landscape through the patio, glass external wall, and into the rooms of the house (figure 59). Rather than being a gradient from public to private realms, this spatial arrangement was con-

Figure 61   Selective engagement: a colonial revival house and summer porch in a naturalistic garden setting

trived to bring the out-of-doors indoors, and vice versa.

A shift can also be perceived in the metaphor for the domestic landscape from a kind of naturalism to something more closely akin to rural life and even agriculture. The garden was a place to be in, to be worked and shaped and to be used for recreation. Landscape designs featured large expanses of lawn, shrubbery, and sweeping horizontal curves. As a consequence, sharp distinctions between formal front yard and informal backyard became subsumed in one continuous flow of garden elements. Again the role of family structure was consequential. An abundance of recreational venues and outdoor family areas was demanded in the baby boom era, particularly when the house continued to be a primary site for family activity (Masotti and Hadden 1974, Clark 1986).

Lot configurations changed to support this program. First, they changed proportion, becoming much wider across the front to allow full presentation of the horizontal lines of the house in its landscape setting (figure 62). Second, when possible, lot subdivisions tended to be more irregular and curvilinear, accentuating the flowing horizontal lines of the dwelling environment. Site irregularities could be easily accommodated in the ranch house type through articulation of the floor plan and through the use of patios, pergolas, and other similar landscape features. Third, in a manner similar to Frank Lloyd Wright's much earlier Usonian and garden wall houses (Sergeant 1984), placement of the house across the front of the lot and often down one side effectively created a large single private garden for extensive family use.

During the 1970s another shift in attitude toward the domestic landscape can be perceived—away from direct recreational use and toward the garden as an object of contemplation. In short, a transition had occurred in the role of the domestic landscape from matters of hygiene to physical occupation and finally to engagement of the mind. It also matched the scale of smaller lots due to higher-priced land.

In many examples of the later compact and zero-lot-line house types, landscape themes extended into the house, and vice versa. Unlike earlier ranch plans, however, the conjunction between house and garden appeared to be oriented more toward visual contrivance than active recreation, a condition well illustrated in figure 63 by the Rosewalk complex (1983) in Seaside, Florida. Landscape designs became more artificial, varietal, visually interesting, and even exotic. From the vantage point of paths, gazebo, courtyards, balconies, and decks, occupants were invited to partake in these landscape qualities. Outdoor recreation activities were now usually confined to specific locations within the garden rather than being spread out and largely undefined, as in the late 1950s.

Lot sizes were often reduced in these later house types, usually under pressure from rising land and development cost. In 1949 a finished lot accounted for around 11 percent of total costs, increasing steadily to about 24 percent by 1982 (Sumichrast and Enzel 1974, Merrill Lynch Fenner and Smith 1982, and *Banker and Tradesman* 1986). Novel site configurations, like interlocking z-plans and zippered layouts, allowed the potential for gardens to be maintained in spite of cramped quarters (Richardson 1988). Courtyards and walled-in gardens even became like addi-

Figure 62   Cultivation and recreation: a contemporary suburban house in its expansive yard

tional rooms, a further rearrangement of "house" and "garden."

In summary, a subtle though definite trend can be perceived in landscape qualities and the relationship of the house to the garden—a trend that reflects changing cultural attitudes toward the siting and landscaping of the house, in concert with changing site development economies. Throughout, the geometry and size of lots depend upon the housing units, not vice versa. As much as anything else, they are extrapolations, within the framework of zoning codes, of functional exterior requirements stemming from the house types themselves.

Formal and Figural Appearance

The distinction between formal and figural appearance of house types is strongly reflected in many examples of modern suburban housing. The formal character of a house refers to its plan, volumetric or-

Figure 63   Fences, pergolas, formality, and contemplation: Rosewalk, Seaside, Florida, by Orr and Taylor, 1983. Copyright Mick Hales, 1985.

ganization, and general compositional massing. In other words, when stripped of ornamentation, specific cladding materials, and other stylistic devices, the form of the house remains. The figural dimension refers less to spatial organization and more to the particular appearance of elements, ornamentation, and decoration. In principle, both dimensions are interrelated and together constitute the concept of style (Norberg-Schulz 1965, Colquhoun 1978). This distinction is particularly important when dealing with examples in which the form of the house corresponds to one typological category and the figuration to another. For instance, without this distinction, a colonial ranch, quite common in various parts of the country, would appear as a contradiction in architectural terms. In fact, most examples other than those built during the formative era of a particular house type exhibit this tendency. It suggests a separation in preference between matters of accommodating spatial layout, room arrangements, and so forth and matters of symbolic presentation and identity. If any specific characteristic exemplifies the appearance of the single-family American home, it is this distinction and the facile use of figural devices independent of their authentic formal roots.

Two broad parallel themes can be discerned behind the formal and figural expression of single-family housing: sensibilities associated with the new, the progressive, or the modern and sensibilities associated with the old, the stable, or the traditional. Preoccupations with one or the other appear to occur simultaneously, in cycles, or as dominant themes in particular geographic locations. For instance, the overwhelming preference of homeowners in Wash-

ington, D.C., is for traditional colonial or similar period-style housing (*Housing* 1978–1982, *Builder* 1983–1986). And housing in New England often reflects the area's early colonial heritage. By contrast, but just as understandably, suburbs in the Midwest and West are full of various ranch types.

Expression of the new, progressive, and modern was influenced by two quite dissimilar metaphors. The first, and by far the more compelling to a majority of families, centers on the aura of the American West, the frontier, and the good life and closely associated feelings of informality, optimism, social progress, and opportunities for personal advancement. The second centers on technology as the symbolic realm for expressing similar aspirations of progress, advancements in the quality of life, and modernity.

The bungalow and ranch clearly express sensibilities of the frontier and the West (figure 64). During the formative years of both types, allusions to these quintessential American symbols of progress were somewhat more than illusions. The so-called California bungalow closely coincided with in-

Figure 64   The real thing: a western ranch in modern times

creased settlement in the western United States through the rapid suburban expansion of cities like Los Angeles (Clark 1986). Similarly, later suburban expansions in other parts of the West and Midwest drew heavily on the authentic ranch house archetype because of its appropriateness to the setting, its symbolic sense of progress, and its accommodation to relaxed routines of daily life.

In appearance, the bungalow and the ranch subordinate figural expression in favor of a distinctive formal outline and composition. In spite of applied decorative motifs, the strict single-story planning, strong roofline, and porches of the bungalow remain its most distinctive features. The strong horizontal lines of ranches, their integration with the surrounding landscape, and the relative absence of opportunities for decoration are prominent features. The ranch rambler, for example, relies almost entirely on formal devices for its appearance. Conversely, it has a spatial organization that is inherently very difficult to refigure as anything else but a ranch rambler. Figuration in both classes of house type is generally confined to doorways, fenestration, and decorative elements around the main entry and the roof. Nevertheless, these motifs form a weak counterpoint to the formal elements of appearance such as roofline, massing, and situation within the landscape.

Expression of the new through the symbolic dimensions of technology has been a largely unfulfilled and unsuccessful enterprise in spite of fine architectural examples, such as the Eames house (1949) (figure 65). Only relatively few merchant builders have successfully marketed modern houses and most of those to a rather limited cross-section of the mass

Figure 65   A modern aesthetic of standardization: mass production and new materials, Eames house, by Charles Eames, 1949

market (Eichler 1982, Mason 1982). The failure of this modern technological aesthetic can be explained in several ways. First, there were pragmatic difficulties in producing dwellings of this kind relative to others. Material and labor requirements for this mode of construction were comparatively expensive. In fact, Eichler Homes, one of the most successful modern home builders, had to suspend several early product lines because of rising labor and material costs (Eichler 1982). As a corollary, the amount of exposed structure work and complicated joint detailing demanded by this aesthetic orthodoxy required high levels of workmanship and trade specialization (*House and Home* 1954). Second, many contemporary house types had unconventional plans, and although many of these space-planning ideas later became influential in conventional home building, others did not. The fragmentation of the bedroom zone, for example, a hallmark of the modern technological home, was strongly rejected by the market. The third, and probably most pervasive, reason for the failure of this style of housing was a cultural lack of enthusiasm for its immediate sensibilities and certain of its connotations. For many the appearance was not cozy, warm, inviting, and familial. There were also strong associations with mass production, standardization, provision of low-income housing, and a "brave new world." The related "dream of the factory made house" languished for similar reasons (Herbert 1984).

The metaphorical realm for expression of the traditional clearly resides in the colonial and early American heritage largely found in the East (figure 66). Perhaps just as the West has represented the pioneering spirit of optimism and opportunity, the East has exercised the minds of Americans in the direction of tradition, social respectability, and continuity with the culture of Europe. The only exception was Spanish colonial in the West and Southwest, although here also the tie was in the direction of Europe (Banham 1971).

By contrast with expressions of the new or modern, the formal appearance of traditional housing types is generally compact and uncomplicated. The various colonial revival configurations are formally simple. There is a straightforward boxlike volume, with simple lines, placed on the site. Later modern compact versions, though often more complicated in internal organization, appear as simpler overall forms. Against such a plain and nondescript visual datum, it is easier to give full expression to the figural appearance of the house, a circumstance amply demonstrated by the wide variety of styles in which a single basic plan could be clad (Architects' Small House Service Bureau 1929, Gilles 1946).

The choice of figural themes and motifs not only reflects period styles but period styles authentic to the United States and its heroic periods and historical time line as a nation. During the 1920s and 1930s there was something of a revived national interest in America's vernacular and colonial past, exemplified perhaps by events like the Williamsburg restoration of 1927–1935. Consequently various kinds of domestic colonial architecture were used as models, as well as Federal style, Regency, and, more recently, the figured compact plan type, a return to the Victorian (Langdon 1984). The only significant non-American styles of any significance were the Tudor and the English cottage, both traditional picturesque themes that seem to have lent themselves well to certain woodsy kinds of suburban development. As early as the 1920s, however, popular journals carried warnings against the "whimsical" nature of these themes and how they could quickly be seen as out of place and anachronistic (Gilles 1946).

Since World War I, both broad vernacular cultural themes—the West and the new and the East and the traditional—have simultaneously exerted influence on the appearance of single-family housing. At certain periods and in certain places one theme may have predominated but never at the exclusion of the other (Clark 1986, Rowe and Desmond 1986).

In the 1920s and early 1930s the bungalow and the colonial revival house types were popular, with the bungalow more prevalent in developing areas. In some cities and towns where both kinds of house were being constructed, one study found that higher-income professionals tended to acquire houses with a traditional appearance expressing values of stability, status quo, and social position, whereas the bungalow appealed to younger couples with a certain sense of adventure, upward social mobility, and lower income (Clark 1986). At the time, the bungalow was probably slightly less expensive, although the data are not clear (*Construction Review* 1955–1986).

After World War II, and especially during the 1950s, the ranch was an especially popular suburban home type. It was relatively inexpensive to build, and the underlying aesthetic theme dovetailed with a rise in informality, a sense of optimism, and the promise of a new era. But numerous traditional house types were also constructed. Probably the most notable was the so-called Cape Cod, an inexpensive one-and-a-half- to two-story unit that usually came equipped to

Figure 66   An early colonial dwelling: Fowle-Reed-Wynn-Belcher house, Arlington, Massachusetts, 1706

Figure 67   Old form and contemporary use a suburban Cape Cod in New England

allow for later expansion and accommodation of larger families (figure 67).

In spite of significant climatic, demographic, and historical differences among the geographic regions of the United States, the predominant trend has been toward providing similar kinds of housing stock regardless of region (Mason 1982, Eichler 1982). The concept of a "house for all America" was not only widely advertised at various times since 1920 but also supplied. When two or more housing types were simultaneously popular, particular regions sometimes received more of one type than the others. For instance, bungalows were developed extensively in California, but not in Washington, D.C. Nevertheless, such regional concentrations may have been a reflection of shared senses of purpose and social goals. In other words, the bungalow perhaps befitted the image that younger Californian couples had of themselves better than a traditional colonial cottage, though their social and economic circumstances may have been much the same as counterparts in Washington, D.C., with quite different tastes.

The dominance of the concept of a "house for all America" is perhaps surprising for other reasons. Today there are few, if any, firms of home builders that construct housing units in many different locales and regions of the United States (Eichler 1982), and there were even fewer in the past (Mason 1982). On the contrary, most firms construct a modest number of units each year and tend to operate in and around one or maybe two metropolitan areas. Nevertheless, their product lines are strikingly similar in appearance.

The geographic mobility of home buyers may influence this similarity in appearance. Broad segments of new home markets come from outside a city or region. Consequently houses are developed to appeal to that "other market," and nationwide rather than regional trends in shape and appearance occur. Clearly this kind of trend might be offset in a region that is strongly identified with a particular style of housing stock. However, it is also perhaps surprising, for example, how many ranches have been built in New England in the past fifteen years (*Housing* 1978–1982).

The home-building industry itself has been actively projecting a national image in spite of the lack of truly national firms. The National Association of Home Builders has risen in prominence to a position of significant leadership from relatively obscure beginnings and from competition with rival organizations (Mason 1982). Furthermore, in efforts to capture wider attention, popular media, journals, pattern books, and so on have concentrated from their early beginnings on national rather than regional tastemaking (Forty 1986).

Casual observation of housing stock in almost any American town or metropolitan area usually reveals an extensive array of house types. Regions are not homogeneous in this regard. Rather, the suburban landscape is strewn with houses that gained national as well as local appeal during different eras. Consequently the aphorism "what time is this place?" (Lynch 1972) is more illustrative of the process of changing appearance than notions of enduring local traditions and building practices. In short, the predominance of particular housing types is largely a reflection of the times during which development took place, not the locale.

The shape and appearance of the American single-family home can also exhibit variety and uniformity for other reasons. While we may be often struck by the inventive vitality of individual efforts to personalize the home and to use it to project a sense of personal identity, the suburbs are frequently criticized as being monotonous, experiential deserts (Keats 1957). For good sociocultural reasons, both characterizations hold a certain amount of validity. An important facet of the equation that linked the prospects of national identity with the family and the home was broad provision of the rights and opportunities for individual homeownership. With both this right and these opportunities went the capacity for self-expression. The variety of ways in which single-family houses present themselves across the country is ample testament to this phenomenon. Home builders responded with basic plans that could be customized to suit a purchaser's circumstances by refiguring the architectural character of facades, details of room layouts, and so forth. In fact, the real flexibility of the American single-family house seems to reside in this capacity for a change of clothes, so to speak, rather than in functional rearrangement.

This expression of variety can also be accounted for by other explanations. For instance, the develop-ment in a product of numerous distinct yet finely disaggregated differences among specific versions increases its market appeal (Forty 1986). A broad range of options allows most people's tastes to be accommodated, and the fine dissimilarity of products within that broad range increases the probability that at least one product will be just right, or close enough to sell.

Several other related influences, however, work in the direction of uniformity. First, for most homeowners, the house is their largest single financial asset, and future realization of the full potential of that asset depends upon its resale. Wide divergences in appearance from perceived cultural norms would adversely affect this potential, leading to a certain uniformity in the appearance of houses. Second, homeownership, and with it a higher position on the social ladder of life, was and probably remains a fundamental part of the American dream. The projection of social position is strongly reflected in the appearance and related characteristics of house, neighborhood, and community. To interfere with these important mechanisms for sustaining a personal as well as a community identity would not only gain the wrath of neighbors but eventually also confound the whole economic and cultural enterprise of American home building.

A considerable amount of evidence also suggests that choices about a home's appearance conform to realities and perceptions about socioeconomic status (Rowe 1972). Lower-income groups tend to want what upper-income groups appear to have. Consequently an interest in period-style traditional forms of single-family housing by upwardly mobile younger families, for instance, often reflects their perception about what is considered most socially acceptable. A number of preference surveys clearly show this kind of trend (*House and Home* 1967–1977, *Housing* 1978–1982, *Builder* 1983–1986). Predictably, perhaps, the same surveys indicate a complete lack of clear stylistic preferences among homeowners in upper-income groups because of their personal position at the apogee of tastemaking. These trends, however, may indicate a process less of lower-income groups actually emulating preferences of upper-income groups than acquiring formal and figural qualities for their homes that they believe stand for success and stability. This explanation also has the advantage of admitting formal and figural variation at different times and in different eras rather than all upwardly mobile preferences directed toward an invariant range of choices. In short, what is important is not what one group actually perceives the other as doing but the qualities they see as epitomizing their own sense of social position.

Yet another kind of trend can often be perceived. During socioeconomically less stable times with some uncertainty about prospects for the future, there seems to be a rise in the socially structured figuration of the house. For example, recently, particularly in the 1970s amid economic recession and related tensions, the figural appearance of many new houses was both prominent and mannerist. Now the output of technically sophisticated homes with a nostalgic Victorian appearance is not exactly commonplace but not unusual (Langdon 1984). By contrast, the ranches of the late 1940s and 1950s, a period of relative national optimism in spite of setbacks, are largely devoid of broad figural variety and overt expression. Perhaps when individual positions on the so-called social ladder of life are uncertain or threatened, higher levels of expression motivated toward social status can be expected. Consequently the preferred appearance of homes is likely to be both more figural and traditional in orientation. For some segments of today's young professional middle class, this form of figuration also seems to satisfy urges in the direction of both individuality and traditional authenticity in their possessions (*Builder* 1983–1986, Langon 1987, Vogel 1987).

Materials and Building Practices

Among manufacturing processes, home building is generally a decentralized, relatively fragmented, low-technology industry. Few firms have sufficient volume of production and geographic spread of operations to be regarded as truly national (Mason 1982). The size of most firms is modest, on the order of 100 to 500 housing starts per year, with roughly 50 percent of all starts distributed among 25 percent of the firms (Urban Land Institute 1987). Few aspects of building construction are standardized and certainly none to the extent of highly integrated industries like aerospace and automobile manufacture. Finally, construction technologies place a heavy reliance on traditional, pre–twentieth century balloon and platform frame building systems. Most modern single-family detached houses consist of a load-bearing slab, poured in place on the site, over which is erected the frame of a stud-wall, over which span roof rafters and purlins or simple wooden trusses. The inside walls are usually lined by plasterboard with insulation as required. Exterior cladding involves a variety of materials from masonry to aluminum siding, although the most usual materials are timber of fibrous materials. The roof is usually built up on a plywood deck, or similar foundation, by layers of bituminous sheeting, conformed to look somewhat like traditional tiles. Mechanical systems and utilities are relatively unsophisticated by commercial building standards and service the house in a straightforward manner. This traditional building technology has consistently proved to be cost-effective and admirably flexible (Eichler 1982).

Improvements in home-building technology have been both episodic and evolutionary. Moreover, only during periods of intensive development has technology been at all visible in houses' appearance, and even then many improvements passed unnoticed. Extensive use of prefabricated roof trusses in the 1940s and 1950s may have led to a simplification of roof forms but ones whose appearance was hardly significant. The design of more environmentally efficient homes after the energy crisis of the early 1970s, produced compact shapes and volumes that were a little more noticeable. Generally, though, in matters of appearance, building technology has been clearly subordinated to other influences.

During the early years of the Federal Housing Administration, the formulation and promulgation of minimum housing standards were influential in shaping the layout, ceiling heights, and other spatial parameters of the single-family house (Weiss 1987). However, not until the late 1930s did selected stickbuilding procedures become mechanized and aggregated into larger preconstructed components (Mason 1938). At much the same time, the precutting of ma-

terials into standardized lengths was also undertaken. During the war years experimentation with industrialized building processes led to the streamlining of "production lines" (figure 68) with the use of new management techniques (Mason 1982). A number of building contractors and developers who were involved in the war effort to mass produce worker housing applied their knowledge during the postwar boom. Levitt and Sharp, among others, eliminated the traditional basement, built unprecedented volumes of simple, economical houses on extensive tracts of land, and in so doing exerted high levels of coordination over the construction process (Mason 1982). Other merchant builders, like Eichler and Ryan, operated smaller and more dispersed operations but employed sophisticated management procedures and highly specialized labor to produce at similar rates of around 5,000 units per annum (Eichler

Figure 68   An assembly line in reverse: tract housing development in California, 1955. Copyright William Garnett, 1955.

1982). In fact, the late 1940s and first half of the 1950s saw considerable innovation and improved efficiency in the coordination of labor and materials. Typically small labor crews moved from site to site specializing in a relatively small number of building operations. Trades were highly coordinated, and a daily schedule of required tasks was preissued and adhered to, often in spite of weather and supply problems (Eichler 1982). Lower levels of uncertainty about the overall schedule of building operations also appreciably improved the timely supply of materials to sites and minimized the need for extensive nearby staging areas. The use of precut materials, prefabricated components, and power tools (figure 69) continued with particular improvements in services, such as installation of complete plumbing trees, wet-wall units, and coordination of mechanical risers (Mason 1968).

The period from the mid-1950s on was one of evolution and continual refinement of existing practices and technologies. Scarce or increasingly expensive materials were replaced by close substitutes. For instance, timber bearer, joist, and board systems for flooring were replaced by plank and beam ensembles and then by beam or truss and plywood structures. Objectives for building cost and building performance continued to be instrumental in shaping the change. Developments in parallel industries, such as the application of information processing and analysis techniques to management and scheduling, were incorporated where appropriate into building practice. Responses were made to consumer demands for better quality at affordable prices. Generally these demands also came as episodes, typically prompted

by factors outside the housing industry. For example, the energy crisis of the early 1970s, together with the environmental movement, increased demands for use of renewable sources of fuel and improved insulation. Initially these responses required or encouraged rather dramatic changes in the appearance of many houses (Davis and Schubert 1976). Lately, however, comparable and even superior levels of performance can be achieved without such impositions on the form of the house. Experiments and promising modifications continue to develop, for example, through research projects, such as those sponsored by the National Association of Home Builders (Mason 1982).

Each decade in the development and improvement of traditional building techniques was greeted with prophecies of revolutionary change occasioned by new materials and construction techniques (Eichler 1982). A number of experiments and pilot pro-

Figure 69   Traditional frame construction using precut materials, prefabricated components, and power tools

grams were initiated during these moments of enthu-siasm (Mason 1982, Herbert 1984). Plastic houses were investigated, and some prototypes were built (Dietz and Cutler 1972), as were steel structures or-ganized around standardized spatial modules and us-ing panelized infill systems (Mason 1982). In the late 1960s and early 1970s, the U.S. Department of Housing and Urban Development launched Opera-tion Breakthrough, the largest and best publicized ef-fort to date in the realm of industrialized building. Al-though these enterprises undoubtedly had some influence, they did not radically change building practice or interrupt the spasmodic and incremental development of improvements (Schodek 1975) be-cause improvements in traditional building methods proved to be appropriately flexible and cost-effec-tive. In spite of beliefs to the contrary, there was no compelling reason to do otherwise (Eichler 1982). Later, rather dramatic changes in the home-building industry certainly did occur, including some applica-tion of industrialized building procedures (figure 70). These changes, however, appear to have more to do with solving chronic problems of undercapitalization and other scalar problems of business than with tech-nological revolution or any marked difference in atti-tude on the part of suppliers to houses' shape and ap-pearance (Mason 1982, Eichler 1982).

Technical changes occurred in the construction of the single-family house in order for it to appear to stay the same. Technical advancements were made within the industry to maintain affordable prices and to meet rising consumer expectations with regard to performance; however, considerable care was taken to suppress and disguise these changes so that they would not intrude on matters of appearance. This is not to assert an entire absence of any kind of techno-logical determinism in shaping the form of the house but rather to suggest its avoidance purely on technical grounds. Above all, there is the need for a convincing symbolic conception of the house. For example, sig-nificant improvements in energy consumption often necessitated more compact overall shapes. Neverthe-less, it seems unlikely that this change would have been so readily accepted unless it could also be made to conform to appropriate cultural norms of formal and figural appearance. Similarly, both the ranch house and the neocolonial Cape Cod seem to have conveyed a positive social image for the otherwise small size and spartan circumstance of postwar af-fordable housing.

A persistent feature in the physical composition of houses, particularly in recent years, is the ex-pressed preference, all other things being equal, for "natural" materials (*House and Home* 1967–1977, *Housing* 1978–1982, *Builder* 1983–1986). Here the concept of an ideal, traditional form of material seems to be at work. It is not simply a matter of au-thenticity. After all, "gold flake" sheets of "fiber board" are authentic and express the full potential of their inherent composition and manufacture no less than do ceramic tiles. Nevertheless, surveys show that most consumers prefer the tiles as counter tops when the price is right. In short, preference is strongly oriented in the direction of both authenticity and traditional forms of material and manufactured finish.

This has not always been the case, or to put it an-other way, there have been times when adherence to these qualities in materials and finishes has not been so marked. During the 1950s, a period of relatively enthusiastic reception of new technology and its products, plastics and exposed metal finishes were widely accepted as materials without disguise (Forty 1986, Sparke 1987). However, in parallel with socially structured figuration of houses' facades, during other times preferences swing back in the direction of the authentic and traditional.

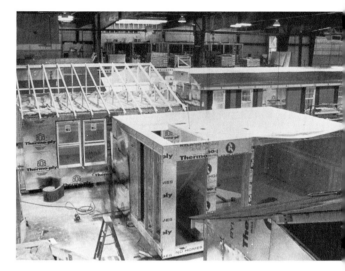

Figure 70   Complete housing modules produced in a factory environment, Ryland Homes, 1983

FORM, FIGURE, AND FUTURE FUNCTION

During the modern period, production of the single-family home, enthusiastically received by the American public, accounted for the overwhelming majority of housing starts. Government-supported loan programs greatly widened the opportunity for home-ownership, and a supply of houses was sustained at widely affordable prices. A decentralized home-building industry, using traditional, low-technological means of construction, proved to be highly robust and responsive to both demographic trends and family economic aspiration. In short, a broad niche was carved out in the overall housing market defined by widespread socioeconomic parameters of supply and demand. Within this niche, however, on matters of shape and appearance, the economic and technological dictates of production seem to have assumed a subordinate role to sociocultural influences from other directions.

At this juncture, the question remains as to whether the cultural themes and ideas that have so strongly influenced the shape and appearance of the

single-family house will persist. In one way we appear to have come full circle. The newest type, the zero-lot-line configuration, is attempting to provide affordable single-family housing in the same manner as the bungalows and modest colonial revivals of the 1920s. However, a similar observation could also be made about another revival form, the Cape Cod cottage of the early 1950s. But, the past aside, will we see radical changes in the shape of the single-family house? Or, to put it another way, will there come a time when the hegemony of the cultural dimensions controlling the house's appearance will relax sufficiently to allow freer rein for experimentation with new types? To both these questions the answer seems to be equivocal.

Should the broad socioeconomic parameters that define the identity of the modern single-family house alter appreciably, then radical change might be expected. In some regard this is already happening.

Demographic trends in household formation among the generation of post–World War I home buyers exhibit strong differences from those of the baby boom generation. Now the distribution of families has spread out among many different household types (Masnick and Bane 1980). The nuclear family is no longer so prevalent, and, therefore, one of the terms in the original equation of nation, family, and home, which empowered the single-family house with its special status, has begun to crumble. Furthermore, the single-family house is fast moving out of the economic reach of broadening segments of society.

Whether these turns of events will materially affect future single-family housing is debatable. Sustained levels of housing starts through second homes, the process known as trading up, and consumer preference will undoubtedly continue to perpetuate the typology. Unless consumer preferences in domestic real estate change radically, the apparent dichotomy between the single-family house and changing family needs will matter little. People, regardless of demographic or other sociological circumstances, will continue to buy in, so to speak, for the economic returns to be made. However, it is also likely that the related slide in the general perception of the single-family house from dream home to commodity will shake it loose from its cultural underpinnings. Eventually this disengagement, together with substantial alterations in the socioeconomic circumstances defining the house type, may cause a fall in continued production. Until then it seems most likely to remain a prominent artifact in the American middle landscape.

4   *Retail Realms*

In the American suburban landscape, the automobile-oriented shopping center is a prolific companion to the single-family home. From roadside franchises and strip commercial developments to regional shopping malls, this phenomenon has become an icon of contemporary metropolitan life. Indeed, the rise in the sheer number and importance of suburban shopping centers has been staggering. Between 1950 and 1960 the number increased from about 100 to around 3,000, and by 1975 it was 18,500, accounting for 25 percent of all retail sales. In the following ten years the number of centers increased to around 25,000, with over a 50 percent share of total retail sales (Sternlieb and Hughes 1981, McKeever, and Griffin 1977, *Shopping Center World* 1985). These statistics underline the wholesale geographic transformation of American life that has taken place during this century.

In addition to retail activities, suburban shopping centers, for better or worse, have assumed the social roles of public gathering places and community centers. They have also become prominent leisure-time venues and sites for recreational activities. According to some, perhaps the most popular tourist activity today is to "go look at the shops" (Beddington 1981, p. 2).

Undoubtedly, lamentable tendencies toward material consumption as a dominant form of recreation have been accommodated by the emergence of malls and other suburban shopping facilities. In themselves, however, these facilities cannot be so easily branded as causes for this assumed decline in civic life. At the very least they are simply cultural artifacts and, at most, the new centers of metropolitan life.

TYPES OF RETAIL CENTERS

The nineteenth century saw a dramatic rise in retail shopping, or the distributive trades. Burgeoning urban population growth brought with it a mass demand for goods and services. Improvements in transportation greatly increased mobility and the availability of consumer goods. Industrialization broadened manufacturing, introduced mass production, and made available a wide variety of affordable goods to the general public. Over time, technical developments in packaging and preservation greatly added to the security and longevity of consumer items well beyond the stage of production or manufacture (Beddington 1981).

Amid this proliferation of activity, rudimentary business relationships between producers and consumers became much more complex, requiring the services of so-called middlemen. Thus the present general functions of manufacturer or producer, wholesaler, and retailer were developed. In this arrangement, the role of the wholesaler is to ameliorate the stockholding and cash-flow problems of the retailer, especially under emerging conditions of accelerated production to meet increased demand. The distribution function of the wholesaler also allows retailers greater direct access to consumers. Consequently the location of stores occurred not only in special districts but at all scales of community life (Beddington 1981).

During this century the location, layout, and general form of the retail realm has evolved considerably. This is particularly apparent in suburban metropolitan developments, where a new set of building types has emerged. A common classification of these types is based on definitions of trading area, primary function, and tenant mix (Baker and Funaro 1951, McKeever and Griffin 1977, 1985). The resulting categories of neighborhood, community, and regional facilities are sometimes broadened to accommodate different conditions of accessibility, with the addition of categories like convenience center and strip commercial development. Others have adopted a longitudinal viewpoint, enumerating different types of retail establishments as they have emerged in the metropolitan landscape (Liebs 1985).

In the typology presented here, the spatial organization of the retail facility is the dominant characteristic, resulting in four types: the strip commercial center, the roadside franchise, the shopping village, and pedestrian malls. Each category is more or less descriptive of its place within an overall geographical hierarchy of commercial facilities, but the typology avoids awkward designations when types, such as strip commercial centers, act simultaneously as providers of neighborhood, community, and regional services. A rough chronology of development runs through the sequence, from strip commercial development to the emergence of pedestrian malls, although this chronology is by no means firmly established.

Strip Commercial Centers

As the early suburbs developed, beyond easy reach of traditional downtown centers, commercial strips began appearing along trolley lines and more highly traveled roadsides. The objective of these retail establishments was simple: to turn a high profit by attracting as many customers from passers-by as possible. Soon stores became concentrated along streets, vying with each other for the most accessible and convenient locations. The vernacular expression "ten-foot store" was coined, referring to the narrow frontage produced by such high concentrations of stores within easy walking distance of transit stops (Liebs 1985, p. 12). By 1900 storefronts lined major streets leading out of town in many American cities, a practice that persisted into the first decades of this century (Warner 1962).

The earliest version of the strip commercial center was the so-called taxpayer block consisting of "a row of stores united under a single roof, housing a wide variety of neighborhood business, built along streetcar lines and major routes" (Liebs 1985, p. 12). Sometimes these commercial buildings were single-storied and at other times consisted of two stories with loft, office space, or residences above the ground floor; both versions are illustrated in figure

71. Apart from the overall linear form, the most prominent architectural feature was a strong tripartite building facade along the street. Typically glazed shop fronts were surmounted by a flat wall with domestic scale windows, capped by a large ornamental cornice or frieze that protruded above the lower extremity of the roofline. The applied decoration generally conformed to prevailing aesthetic tastes and usually stressed compositional symmetry around the center of the building or around prominent corner details. In most respects this building type emerged around the mid-nineteenth century and continued to be built well into the twentieth century. One of its great functional advantages over earlier stores, with a more singular house- or barnlike quality, was the flexible provision of adequate store space for a variety of firms under a unified and impressive facade. However, because of competition for the attention of passers-by, signs and billboards often began to obscure the buildings. Contrary to popular opinion, American commercial areas were already heavily cloaked in signs well before the arrival of the automobile (Liebs 1985).

The term *taxpayer block* or *taxpayer strip* stems from the temporary manner in which these commer-

Figure 71   Taxpayer blocks along Massachusetts Avenue in the Boston metropolitan area

cial buildings were regarded. In the mind's eye of their developers, they were nothing more than an interim use until the land under them became sufficiently valuable to build more permanent commercial facilities in the concentrated manner of established downtown centers. More specifically, they produced enough revenue to pay the ad valorem taxes and to hold the land for future redevelopment. Ironically, in many locales the concentrated development envisaged by the early developers did not arrive to take over the suburbs (Liebs 1985). Instead they continued to expand at relatively low densities, and the interim use became far more permanent. Even today, mile upon mile of former taxpayer strips line the inner suburban streets of many metropolitan areas.

The interdependence between transportation improvements and the early development of strip commercial centers is well illustrated by Shaker Square within the planned community of Shaker Heights, now in Cleveland, Ohio (figure 72). In 1911 the developers O. and M. van Sweringen purchased a tract of suburban farmland in the township of Shaker Heights and then proceeded to develop a well-appointed planned community, which opened around 1916. It developed only slowly because of a lack of adequate transportation. This problem of accessibility was resolved later in the 1920s through the private sponsorship of a transit line linking Shaker Heights with downtown Cleveland. By 1929 the community was large enough to warrant opening the Shaker Square Shopping Center to serve local needs (Stern 1981, p. 46).

Shaker Square, designed by Small and Rowley, represented a departure from the typical strip commercial block of the time. Instead of a linear arrangement of buildings flanking the boulevard, with transit in its median, twelve commercial buildings were carefully arranged to make a formal square and symbolic community center (figure 73). The experiment was very successful, attracting development of several period-style apartment buildings immediately adjoining the square (Cleveland Chapter AIA 1958, p. 34). Subsequent development has continued well into the automobile era, although much of the clarity of the original urban concept was dissipated in order to provide parking. The division of the center by a wide and well-traveled boulevard also proved to be less than successful from a business viewpoint (Baker and Funaro 1951, p. 185).

The architecture of Shaker Square is in keeping with the tone of the surrounding community, which at the time of its construction was generally regarded as a high-class residential neighborhood (Stern 1981, p. 46). The stores have neo-Georgian facades of one and two stories, and there is a picturesque quality to the scene reminiscent of some of the qualities of the

high street of traditional English towns. No doubt this was an appropriate image for marketing to the community, although the appearance of individual stores, and their associated histories, was in fact a contrivance. The development was more or less constructed at once.

During the post–World War II suburban boom, strip commercial centers flourished as major roadways took the place of earlier transit lines. In rapidly developing communities, these strip centers began to incorporate civic functions and became local town centers. The basic form remained the same, however: a linear arrangement of stores distributed along a street, one store deep and with parking in either the front or the rear, or in both locations. If anything, the architecture of these centers was reasonably coherent in its expression of a singular image. Unlike Shaker Square, there was no attempt to appear to be the result of a lengthy development process. Moreover, intersections between two major roads became prime locations for these centers, and it was not unusual to find them built in advance of oncoming suburban development (Baker and Funaro 1951, McKeever and Griffin 1977).

The commercial and town center of Port Edwards, a small industrial town in Wisconsin built in the late 1940s, epitomizes many of these attributes. The center, designed by Donn Haugen, unifies a linear arrangement of stores and other facilities behind the carefully composed moderne facade along a main street (figure 74). In plan the complex bows slightly to accommodate convenient parking off the street and to provide an axial orientation with a perpendicular cross street (see figure 73). This compositional for-

Figure 72   Shaker Square, developed by Small and Rowley in 1929, as it appeared in the 1950s

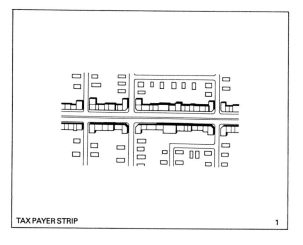

TAX PAYER STRIP   1

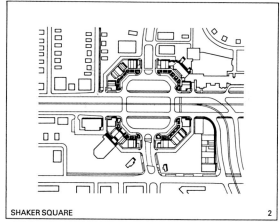

SHAKER SQUARE   2

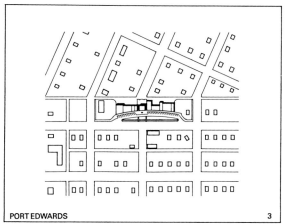

PORT EDWARDS   3

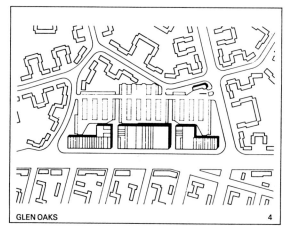

GLEN OAKS   4

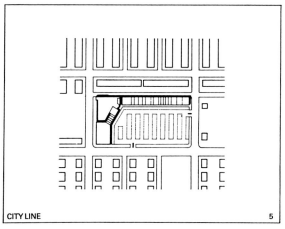

CITY LINE   5

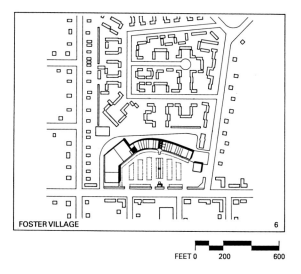

FOSTER VILLAGE   6

*Figure 73   Evolution of the strip commercial center from
the taxpayer strip to postwar convenience centers*

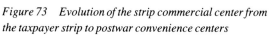

FEET 0   200   600

Retail Realms

Figure 74   The modern facade and parking lot of the Port Edwards Shopping and Civic Center

mality is reinforced by the placement of a war memorial on the same axis with the town hall, located immediately behind in the strip complex. The development is surrounded by single-family dwellings (Baker and Funaro 1951, p. 113).

Another strip center with a similar program of uses was built in Glen Oaks, New York, in 1948–1949 to provide immediate local facilities for a fast-growing suburban area on Long Island. Integration within the surrounding context was carefully considered by locating the center along the Union Turnpike yet within walking distance of a large garden apartment complex housing some 3,000 people. Parking was located at grade in the rear of the center, as illustrated in figure 73, thus forming a 1000-foot line of two-fronted stores along a city block. At over 115,000 square feet in area, the facility was large in comparison to some predecessors although fairly typical of the scale of emerging all-purpose, one-stop suburban shopping facilities. Like Port Edwards, there was a significant presence of public facilities, including a library, a post office, and administrative offices (Baker and Funaro 1951, pp. 264–65). Also like Port Edwards the massing of the building complex was symmetrical, although application of compositional principles went beyond the facade and into

the overall formal organization of the complex. The two-story portion of the building was located centrally, with two pedestrian arcades on either side moving out into the parking lot in the form of raised walkways under rows of trees. The public facilities were located prominently on the parking lot side, with a small plaza in front of the complex. Formal articulation of the building was achieved by varying the building width from 75 feet at the ends to 150 feet at the center, thus diminishing its overall scale.

From the turn of the century until the early 1950s an evolution took place in the relationship of buildings to parking lots within the strip commercial center. For the taxpayer strips, parking was located in front of the row of stores on the street. By the late 1920s and the 1930s with Shaker Square and other contemporary developments, the buildings of commercial centers were set back from the street, allowing a zone of car parking in the front. This was to be followed by off-street parking and the removal of commercial buildings some distance back from the street, or, as was the case in Glen Oaks, off-street parking was provided behind the building complex. The former configuration first started appearing in the late 1930s, with developments like Leland Champlin's Dey Wilcox Center (1938) in Pennsylvania (Jackson 1985). Here an L or a U shape was adopted for the overall plan of the complex in order to shorten walking distances from car to store and to maximize the linear exposure of the storefronts to the frontage of the building complex. Usually ratios on the order of 3:1 were employed for the amount of space to be left in front of a complex for car parking (Baker and Funaro 1951).

Figure 75   Integration of the Foster Village Center into an adjacent residential development

A clear example of this last phase of the evolutionary process can be found at the City Line Center in Philadelphia, (1948–1952) by Harry Fried. Developed in two phases across an extensive frontage, the complex began in the overall form of an L shape, as shown in figure 73, with two wings of stores pivoted around a cinema complex in the corner. A later phase of development was to have incorporated a department store at the far end of the complex, thus converting the L shape into a U shaped configuration. This type of commercial center was repeated often in different suburban locations throughout the country, complete with a familiar streamlined moderne styling, no doubt signaling to the world a progressive, optimistic, and up-to-date image. The City Line commercial complex incorporated public facilities, like a post office, and it was located adjacent to and in conjunction with an extensive garden apartment residential complex (Baker and Funaro 1951). Other versions of the L-shaped strip commercial complex were also developed in the form of slanted L's, like Kelly and Gruzen's early (1951) center in Hackensack, New Jersey, whereby visibility to one direction of oncoming traffic was enhanced (Jackson 1985).

The thematic development and cumulative evolution of the strip center is well illustrated by the Foster Village center (1947) in Bergenfield, New Jersey, by Alan Wood Fraser (figure 75). The shopping center was integrated into the surrounding residential area of garden apartments housing some 646 families through the extension of an arcade into an open space that effectively formed a residential square. In this regard it was like Shaker Square. Strong compositional principles were employed in the overall L-shaped configuration of the center's plan. The axial arrangement, which extends back into the residential area, was brought forward through the parking lot, giving structure to the lot and a strong sense of a center to the whole complex. In order to avoid dead space, a persistent problem in the corner of all L-shaped configurations, the plan was curved, presenting a continuous surface of store fronts to the main street. Off-street parking was generous and sufficiently well structured to provide convenient access and a minimum of visual blight. The complex incorporated civic functions, including a bus stop, and also encouraged walk-in trade through pedestrian connections to surrounding residential areas. The clean line of the front facade masked irregularities in the floor plan toward the rear, as well as symbolically acknowledging the presence of a major use, in this case a one-stop supermarket. Finally, the moderne styling and figural program of the architecture coincided to project to customers a feeling of progressive, up-to-date, and efficient retail service.

In the intervening years, numerous strip commercial centers were developed according to the fully evolved type that first appeared during the late 1940s and early 1950s. Many began as local community shopping and civic centers, conveniently serving both pedestrian and automobile access. Alas, however, with continued mobility and wider-ranging shopping patterns, the local character of many of these centers has diminished. Strip commercial centers have become oriented almost exclusively to the roadway and passing traffic. Public facilities are less common, and often the architecture has an ill-considered and temporary quality that reflects rising land costs, intensive competition for shares of the retail market, and interim use.

Roadside Franchises

Along the nation's major suburban thoroughfares, a parallel and nearby development to strip commercial centers was the roadside franchise. Facilities within this general building type had a number of different functions, including convenience stores, filling stations, motels and, perhaps above all, fast-food restaurants. Almost without exception they incorporated aggressive advertising with a distinctive building image, aspects well illustrated in figure 76.

Several broad observations can be made about the class as a whole. First there are obvious physical characteristics. The facilities are small, designed for customers to pause, purchase, and leave without lingering. They are usually set back from the road, amid a broad apron of car parking, often on three sides. The buildings either possess a mimetic form consistent with their advertising program or are closely associated with a prominent road sign. Whether they are so-called ducks, referring to buildings shaped as signs, or decorated sheds, both buildings and advertising are tightly and expressively intertwined (Venturi and Scott Brown 1968, 1971).

Second, the need to project consistency and predictability in the product and services being marketed has led to a high degree of standardization in design. The underlying logic of this trend is well illustrated by the following excerpt from a brochure of the White Castle hamburger chain, which grew from five outlets in 1921 to 115 only ten years later: "Remember that you are one of several thousands, you are sitting on the same kind of stool, . . . the hamburger you eat is prepared in the same kind of way" (Langdon 1986, p. 30). Standardization is clearly linked to the consistent quality of the product and therefore to consumer satisfaction. Another closely related quality of standardization is the predictability of the range of services offered and concomitant levels of consumer

Figure 76   Flags, arches, and familiar form: a McDonald's fast-food restaurant

assurance in their expectations. Finally, standardization seems to help rationalize choice and to form habitual behavior. By offering a strong image aligned with a particular product, prior satisfaction is immediately recalled, thus helping to prompt further consumption.

An unfortunate consequence of standardization coupled with a highly distinctive image is the difficulty of meeting the dictates of existing physical contexts. A particular franchise is the same no matter where it is located. Recently, however, some local planning boards have insisted on specific design variations in conformance with the physical character of surrounding neighborhoods (Langdon 1986, pp. 169f.).

The third general characteristic of roadside franchises is an overwhelming emphasis on economy and efficiency in service and product delivery. Popular insistence on this characteristic seems to take precedence over all other design elaborations. Unfortunately, it also contributes to the propensity for visual blandness and a predictable sameness in the suburban landscape (Langdon 1986, p. 197).

Economy and efficiency are exhibited in a number of ways in the design and physical layout of franchise facilities. Throughout, standardization is a strong contributing factor. Richard and Maurice "Mac" McDonald pioneered the self-service fast-food roadside restaurant by standardizing their operations. In 1940, restaurants paid out 27 percent of their receipts in wages, rising to 35 to 40 percent by 1947. A year later, in order to counteract these costly inroads into profits, the McDonald brothers introduced into their drive-in restaurant a rigidly standard-

ized menu and dismissed most of the help. By 1952 the idea, in spite of a shaky start, became formally established, and they began to franchise their chain of restaurants (Kroc 1977, Langdon 1986, pp. 81f.).

A second way in which economy and efficiency were exhibited was through the material composition of buildings and their surface finishings. With regard to the Dairy Queen chain, Langdon made the folowing observation: "The straightforward construction . . . [was] characteristic of ordinary people, functional and unselfconscious, dictated by the need for economy rather than by sophisticated aspirations" (Langdon 1986, p. 68). Nevertheless, striving for economy and efficiency sometimes also leads to a lack of authenticity in design and outright kitsch. For instance, within a prevailing mood of comfort and coziness it is not unusual to find wood-grained plastic finishes in lieu of the real thing where the latter might unduly complicate the functions of cleaning and maintenance (Langdon 1986, pp. 193f.).

Finally, there seems to be common agreement that the shape and appearance of franchise facilities, in spite of the need for standardization, change to reflect prevailing cultural attitudes (Liebs 1985, Langdon 1986). Moreover, in a manner rather similar to houses, symbols of traditional values and status are preferred during times of uncertainty, whereas technological symbols of progress dominated during the confident postwar period. For instance, of all the images used in roadside commercial buildings during the turbulent 1920s and early 1930s, those that evoked hearth and home were most prevalent, signaling, as some commentators put it, "a return to normalcy" (Liebs 1985, p. 44, Gowans 1964). By contrast, the era of contemporary modern and moderne styling, which began in the 1930s, continued into the 1960s. Here the visual celebration of frictionless machines coincided in the marketplace with ideas of forthrightness, efficiency, progress, and modernity (Meikle 1979, Hillier 1975, 1983). As Hillier put it, "It suggested a people who were not content to remain static in the doldrums, but were determined to ride forward . . . into a shining future" (Hillier 1983, p. 107). In the end, however, an interesting paradox was presented by modern architecture in the service of commerce: "How could a building be modern, express its function, and yet still sell a product along the highway, without resorting to applied imagery" (Liebs 1985, p. 61). The response, illustrated in figure 77, was to exaggerate various aspects of its form, such as the structure of rooflines. This formal manipulation could be sustained for only so long before exhausting its novelty or reaching bizarre extremes.

Following the 1960s, a certain amount of contextualism and environmental responsibility overtook franchise facilities. Chastened by the thrust of attacks like Blake's in his *God's Own Junkyard* (1964) and by a general disenchantment with the technically oriented world of tomorrow, franchises assumed a rustic appearance (Hess 1983) or what Langdon has referred to as the "browning of America" (Langdon 1986, p. 133). Chains like Dennys and Burger King built in earthen-colored bricks and shingled mansard roofs and covered their sites with relatively liberal amounts of landscape materials. Predictably, in the late 1970s, this tendency turned toward a broad spectrum of historical references, as shown in figure 78, presumably coinciding in the

Figure 77   Bold rooflines and simple forms: Howard Johnson's on Route 2, Massachusetts, 1989

Figure 78   Wayside dining with traditional architectural references: Pillar House on Route 128, Massachusetts, 1989

mind's eye of the consumer with ideas of status, selectivity, unusual merchandise, and a hankering for tradition (Liebs 1985, Langdon 1986). In short, the styling of the highly functional and technically sophisticated franchise followed cultural norms. To do otherwise would have meant being at odds with the consumers.

Shopping Villages

Ever since the development in 1908 of J. C. Nichols's influential Country Club District on the outskirts of Kansas City, Missouri, shopping villages have been an integral part of the American suburban landscape, especially in the Midwest, the Southwest, and the West. By the late 1920s Nichols began constructing

Country Club Plaza, the main shopping center for his ambitious overall 5,000-acre development (Funaro and Baker 1949, Nichols Company 1983). Based on creating a small town atmosphere for shopping and professional commerce yet incorporating the convenience required in a modern automobile era, the complex was composed of an aggregation of relatively small blocks, with stores facing the street and with car parking interspersed within the overall block layout (Kansas City Chapter of the AIA 1979, Nichols Company 1983). The result was a deliberately picturesque commercial environment, strongly reminiscent of a traditional southern European town center, and the first modern suburban shopping center offering a full variety of goods and services (Baker and Funaro 1951).

Many of the hallmarks of the modern shopping village, first established in the Country Club Plaza, were maintained and elaborated upon in subsequent developments. Of primary importance was the overall form and layout of a shopping complex and the image it projected. Until the type became more firmly established, almost all early examples referred back to a traditional model of development, one that stressed small-town, villagelike values of cheerful familiarity, personal service, convenience, and quality. Individuality in the architecture and the appearance of specific stores took precedence over mass consumption, though centers included supermarkets and many other modern shopping conveniences.

A fine example of this mimetic orientation is evident in the Highland Park Village of 1931 (figure 79), now a suburban area of Dallas, Texas. Developed by Hugh Prather and strongly influenced by

J. C. Nichols, the layout of the center was based on the central plaza of a traditional Texas county seat (Baker and Funaro 1951). The Spanish architectural style of the overall complex was far from coincidental and was used, at Prather's insistence, in an attempt to recreate the appearance of a villagelike atmosphere with a certain well-worn historical license.

In spite of its historical styling, Highland Park Village was, in its day, very modern. Approximately 100,000 square feet of public and private uses were aggregated together, offering a full range of retail functions, a restaurant, a theater, and professional offices. Great care was taken to provide a highly functional layout and service infrastructure, well disguised from the surrounding neighborhood by walls incorporated into the complex's architecture (figure 80). Above all, convenient automobile access was emphasized within the precinct of the center itself, away from surrounding streets.

Another example within the modern suburban context that harnessed a traditional image of day-to-day shopping was the chain of Farmers Markets that became popular in the West shortly after World War II; they were "the modern equivalent of the old-time market square with parking added" (Baker and Funaro 1951, p. 94). Small and pedestrian in scale, they placed an emphasis on individuality and produce with a direct-from-the-country freshness. Cars were kept entirely to perimeter parking lots, and the markets themselves consisted primarily of closely packed stalls rented by tenant-producers.

The original Farmers Market was begun by Roger Dahlhjelm in Beverly Hills during the depression years. The idea quickly caught on, and the Farm-

Figure 79 A shopping village in a suburban context: Highland Park Village, Dallas, 1931

ers Market Co. became a chain, building markets in Fresno and Los Angeles proper, among other places (figure 81). All tended to be located toward the outskirts of town where land was inexpensive and the location accessible to both customers and tenant-producers. Generally a perimeter band of permanent buildings subdivided into stores was provided, the area inside of which was filled with market stalls (figures 80 and 81). In certain respects, the totally pedestrian environment was the forerunner of pedestrian malls (Baker and Funaro 1951).

Generally the disaggregated layout of shopping villages, in the form of buildings, blocks, and streets, came in two versions: those that emulated traditional urban commercial areas that might have been found near the center of a town and the plazas and bazaars like Highland Village and the Farmers Market where shops and customers gathered together in a predominantly pedestrian precinct within a suburban superblock structure.

Cameron Village (1948) in Raleigh, North Carolina, was of the first kind. Developed by Wilke York

and designed by Seward H. Mott of Garden City and town planning fame, Cameron Village consisted of a number of solidly built blocks of stores (see figure 80) separated from each other by public streets and wide belts of perimeter parking. Located toward the center of a rapidly growing planned community development, Cameron Village offered a full range of commercial goods and services. The layout of buildings, car parking, and streets was clear and straightforward (Baker and Funaro 1951). Several other suburban shopping centers, such as the Rice Village in Houston, Texas, of the 1930s and 1940s incorporated the same basic approach. In almost all cases the shopping precinct was located adjacent to a major metropolitan thoroughfare.

The second type of shopping village included the Town and Country chain of medium-sized shopping centers that became popular, particularly in the West and Southwest (see figure 80). Regarded by some as the "sophisticated step sisters of farmers markets," these complexes consisted of blocks of shopping threaded through by picturesque pedestrian alleyways, surrounded by curb and lot parking (Baker and Funaro 1950, p. 100). Throughout, emphasis was placed upon rustic charm and informality. A number of different complexes like this were built during the late 1940s in California, including those in Sacramento and Palm Springs by Strizek and Quincy Jones, respectively. Other centers were built in other parts of the country well into the late 1960s and early 1970s.

The orientation of the shopping villages to the street varied. Highland Park Village was the first major shopping center to turn away from a major street,

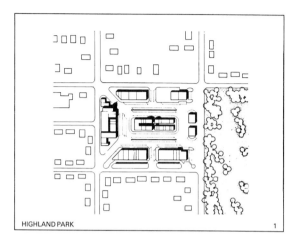

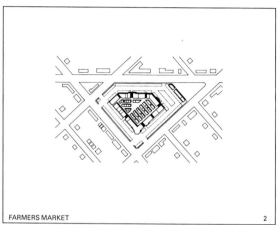

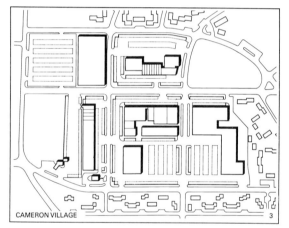

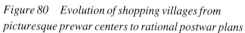

Figure 80   Evolution of shopping villages from picturesque prewar centers to rational postwar plans

FEET 0   200   600

creating its own pedestrian and vehicular area (figure 82). Unlike the strip commercial centers that were built parallel to the street, the Highland Park complex was organized perpendicular to Preston Road, the adjacent thoroughfare. Its spatial organization was highly symmetrical and centered in on itself, not toward some external referent. The area across the major street frontage was a golf course, adding to the complex's prominence. Like the early strip commercial centers, however, Highland Park Village was

also well integrated into the surrounding community of single-family homes. A school lay immediately to the north, reinforcing an overall institutional presence (figure 79). Moreover, the scale of the development was well gauged to its surroundings, and the complex was centrally located for convenient access.

The Farmers Market and the Town and Country shopping complexes were internally oriented away from surrounding streets. In the case of the Town and Country Shopping Villages, however, a certain ambivalence was also noticeable, with many stores fronting on curbside parking and thence the street (figure 80).

All stores in Cameron Park and the Rice Village, on the other hand, were clearly oriented toward the street in the traditional manner of small towns and earlier urban developments (see figure 80). Curbside parking running perpendicular to the street frontage was provided for convenience. At the Rice Village this was augmented by rooftop parking above stores. Unsightly service areas were kept from view by aligning blocks lengthwise, with a service alley down the middle between stores facing onto two separate streets. Other earlier shopping centers, like Houston's River Oaks Shopping Center by Prather (1937), had similar arrangements, although here small parking lots similar to those in strip commercial centers were provided.

The shopping village declined as a prominent building type as commercial attention became focused on large, centralized retail malls. Nevertheless, a few were still constructed, usually with a nostalgic, historicist theme that sought to embody traditional values of individuality and personal service. Some, such as Westbury Square in southwest Houston developed by Ira Berne during the late 1960s, went to extremes in which the complex was more like a stage set than a shopping center. More recently small resort towns, such as Florida's Seaside (1981) by Duany and Plater-Zyberk, have commercial centers under development that are designed based on the traditional vernacular of small towns (Langdon 1988, Ellis 1988). Many of the shopping villages of the 1930s and 1940s are undergoing a re-

Figure 81   A commercial Bazaar from the depression years: Farmers Market, Los Angeles, by Deleena and Barber

naissance, much to the appreciation of surrounding upper middle-class residents. This is certainly the case at Highland Park Village.

Pedestrian Malls

Regional pedestrian shopping malls emerged during the early 1950s, first as complexes of retail stores surrounding an open pedestrian concourse and then as fully enclosed air-conditioned precincts. Later some became multiuse complexes of considerable complexity and scale. All aspired to markets beyond their local communities, serving regional needs of a similar kind to traditional downtown shopping districts. Regional shopping malls were usually located on the urban periphery of metropolitan areas with good highway access. Generally the centers were created in advance of suburban development, anticipating the outward expansion of residential areas adjacent to the expanding freeway system and interstate roadway network linking major cities. Particularly favorable sites were found next to highway interchanges and major grade-level arterial roads.

Open pedestrian malls were of three types, all constructed more or less contemporaneously and all consisting of a building complex surrounded by a large continuous expanse of grade-level car parking: an irregular arrangement of stores and other commercial facilities around an open, well-landscaped pedestrian spine, linking one part of a neighboring community to another; a centralized overall organization around a single, large department store; and the highly influential dumbbell plan, commonly attributed to the architect Victor Gruen, where a pedestrian concourse ran between two large department stores, flanked on both sides by storefronts of smaller retail outlets (Gruen and Smith 1952) (figure 83). The term *magnet store* is often used to describe larger department stores, referring to their relative attractiveness within the regional market area and to their function within the mall itself. In principle the magnet store, or stores, because of its familiar name and line of products, attracts shoppers to the building complex. Once there, consumers are attracted into impulse buying by the convenient and pleasant arrangement of smaller stores (Funaro and Baker 1949, Gruen and Smith 1952, *Architectural Forum* 1953, p. 125). Similarly, pedestrian movement is encouraged between department stores, in the two-store configuration, toward the same end.

A good example of the first type, the irregular pedestrian spine, was the Park Forest shopping center of the early 1950s, located in the planned community of Park Forest, some 25 miles south of central Chi-

Figure 82   The appearance of a traditional shopping street adjacent to off-street parking, Highland Park Village, Dallas, 1931

Figure 83   Open automobile-oriented pedestrian malls

cago. The community itself was based on the Greenbelt towns of the Federal Resettlement Administration, built during the depression years. It was also the subject of Whyte's *Organization Man* (1956).

The shopping center was the community focus, centrally located between a large public park and nearby residential neighborhoods (Baker and Funaro 1951, Gillette 1985). The layout of the shopping center, though rational and roughly symmetrical in overall organization, was deliberately made irregular to offer a variety of spatial experiences along the interior mall and to provide inviting access from the adjacent parking lots on the outside (Baker and Funaro 1951). The theme of this open interior plaza was clearly rooted in the idea of a community green, harkening back to the main civic space of early American towns. The irregular layout also allowed different functions, with their own distinctive forms like movie theaters, some expressive latitude. This variation in scale and expressiveness reinforced the central idea of a town center "growing up" around a common green space. The analogy goes still further. Unlike many other pedestrian shopping complexes, the central mall was an extension of a major neighborhood

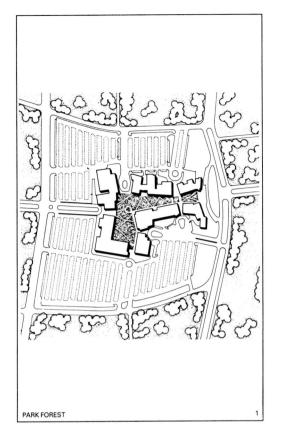

PARK FOREST   1

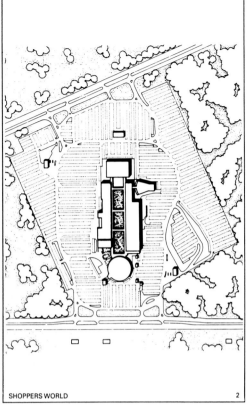

SHOPPERS WORLD   2

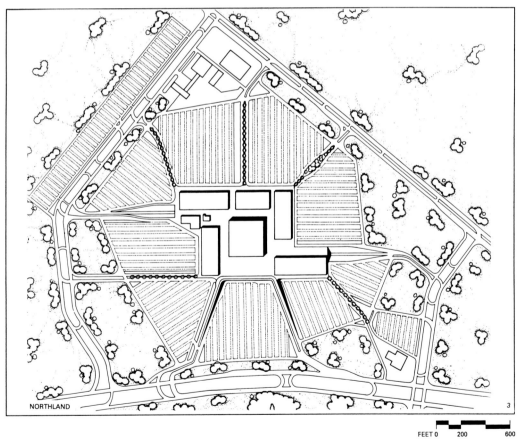

NORTHLAND   3

FEET 0   200   600

street, terminating in a formal compositional arrangement on the north side at the intersection with the major route out of the community toward Chicago. In keeping with other shopping centers of roughly the same era, public functions, including a clinic, a post office, and administrative offices, were prominently incorporated into the building complex.

The second type, incorporating a single large anchor or magnet store, is well illustrated by the Northland Regional Shopping Center, built in Detroit between 1952 and 1954 by Victor Gruen Associates, Inc. Often referred to as the first modern pedestrian shopping center, although Shoppers World in Framingham, Massachusetts, seems to have opened earlier, the main idea behind Northland was a modern version of the preindustrial town market (*Architectural Forum* 1954, p. 102). Shops were arranged in a compact overall form around ten open courts and terraces, many leading out into the parking lot beyond. The overall length of storefront, obtained in this manner, was well over 1 mile.

Northland was unprecedentedly large. The total site area was 163 acres; 15 acres were in buildings, 68 acres in parking, and the remainder in roads and peripheral areas. The building complex provided for 1,045,000 square feet of rentable space, with expansion capability for another 1.5 million square feet. Parking was provided initially for 7,400 cars, to be increased later to 12,000. The trading area north of downtown Detroit and due west of Grosse Pointe had a population of over half a million people within a convenient 20-minute drive, and the mall was located adjacent to several major thoroughfares. In keeping with the scale of the enterprise, the J. L. Hudson de-

partment store chain, the clients for the project, built the largest branch department store to date as the centerpiece of the overall complex (*Architectural Forum* 1954).

Unlike Park Forest and other malls with irregular plans, the architecture of Northland was regular, unified, and modern. Stores were grouped in rectangular blocks, with common bay widths of 110 to 120 feet. Tall colonnades were provided from standardized storefronts onto open courts in the middle of the complex. Several of these courts contained abstract water features, such as the Fountain Court and the Great Lakes Court, and all had large pieces of modern sculpture by contemporary artists such as Arthur Kraft, Malcom Moran, and Libby Saarinen. The landscape architecture of these exterior spaces, designed by Edward Eichstedt, was restrained and modern, in keeping with the surrounding architecture. No architectural reference was made to the rural common or common green of early American towns. On the contrary the architecture was a reaction against this metaphor in the direction of a higher level of urbanity (*Architectural Forum* 1954).

Another prominent feature of the overall organization and planning of Northland was the traffic circulation and attempts to integrate parking with the central building complex. An elaborate basement zone serviced the entire complex, and truck ramps were located so as to minimize contact with automobile traffic. Husdon's department store was directly accessible at the second level by a separate ramp road, in the manner of an airport, which also served as a bus stop for the 10 percent of customers who came by public transit. Finally, the vast expanse of grade-level car parking was given a significant amount of structure by heavily landscaped and raised pedestrian zones that extended out into the lots from the central mall area (*Architectural Forum* 1954).

The third type of open pedestrian shopping mall is epitomized by an early example: Shoppers World in Framingham, Massachusetts, which opened in 1951 (figures 83 and 84). Located 19 miles west of Boston on the Worcester Turnpike, Shoppers World was organized with an anchor department store at either end of a linear mall, 665 feet long. The distinctive dome of the Jordan Marsh department store was visible from the turnpike; the profile of the second-phase department store was to be visible from Route 30, on the other side of the complex. At 500,000 square feet, the total rentable area was roughly half that of Northland and a relatively compact overall shape was provided through a two-level mall, referred to by the architects, Ketchum, Gina and Sharp, as a "double-decked mainstreet" (*Architectural Forum* 1951, p. 182). The resulting depression of the lower level of this central mall area allowed covered entry and egress to remote areas of the surrounding parking lot through underground pedestrian tunnels. The complex was roughly the equivalent of eight to ten city blocks of commercial retail development.

The image expressed by the architecture of Shoppers World incorporated both the earlier metaphors of traditional common and contemporary modernity. Referred to at the time as "one-stop shopping machinery," the external appearance of the mall was almost that of a spacecraft that had landed in a clearing within the woods (*Architecture Forum* 1951,

Figure 84   A dumbbell plan surrounding a reinterpreted village green: opening day at Shoppers World, Framingham, Massachusetts, by Ketchum, Gina and Sharp, 1951

p. 181). The technological imagery brought with it parallel ideas of progress and being up to the moemnt. By contrast, the central mall was referred to as a community common or community green, clearly an attempt to recreate, in modern guise, the town green of yore. Even in early renderings of the scheme, the central mall was landscaped with shrubs, trees, and meandering paths (Baker and Funaro 1951, *Architectural Forum* 1951, p. 181). Far from being discordant, both metaphors worked together to proclaim modernity and Old World familiarity simultaneously.

A number of other open pedestrian shopping malls were planned and constructed in the early post–

World War II period, beginning perhaps with North-gate, Seattle, in 1948 (Clausen 1948). Most were linear in overall configuration, invariably incorporating one or more large department stores. Many clearly recognized the problem of accommodating large numbers of automobiles and the need to construct an overall landscape of which the building complex was a part. Some went to extremes; the Skidmore Owings and Merrill proposal for the Marshall Fields Shopping Center in Chicago called for depressed parking courts with ramp access up to the store-level pedestrian concourse (*Architectural Forum* 1951, p. 195).

The closed pedestrian shopping mall followed closely after the initial open mall projects, more or less as an evolutionary development (Gruen and Smith 1960). In fact, many early open pedestrian malls, such as Northland, are now fully enclosed. By the 1960s this closed form was the rule rather than the exception.

The first fully enclosed pedestrian shopping mall was considered a distinct building type (Gruen and Smith 1960, McKeever and Griffin 1977). Designed by Victor Gruen in 1953, Southdale was finally opened in 1955 on an 84-acre site owned by the Dayton Company, south of downtown Minneapolis. At 560,000 square feet of rentable retail space, Southdale was sizable but not enormous. The site, like many others at the time, was placed in advance of community development. In fact, the Dayton Company purchased 378 acres more as a buffer to ensure blightproof development adjacent to the mall, in a deliberate attempt to stave off the same sort of deterioration of neighborhoods that had occurred around commercial downtown areas (*Architectural Forum*

1953, p. 127). By providing an enclosed, fully air-conditioned environment, the 123 good outdoor shopping days per year in Minneapolis were extended indefinitely.

The mall had a compact overall shape that was almost square in plan (figure 85). Shops were distributed in clusters among four levels, all opening onto a large indoor plaza skylit from above so as to provide a "high outdoorsy space" (*Architectural Forum* 1953, p. 124). Gruen's model was of a market square with side streets providing lateral access to stores away from the main space. In addition to providing year-round comfort to shoppers, the enclosure of the mall resulted in significant internal cost savings on store-front building materials, now buffered from the harsh winter climate (*Architectural Forum* 1953).

Care was taken to integrate the central building complex into the surrounding automobile environment (figure 86). A peripheral belt road was provided just inside the site to improve internal vehicular circulation, and, more important, each major parking lot, roughly in the quadrants of the site, was arranged in a split-level fashion with regard to adjacent lots. This was justified both to improve the site drainage and to avoid the necessary separation of levels inside the multilevel building that comes from a single ground plane. The result was a formal and functional merger of building with the rest of the site landscape, one that provided considerable clarity and amenity for pedestrian and vehicular movement. Again in keeping with by now common practice, a basement-level full-service zone was provided with ample truck access.

Other centralized plans were also proposed for

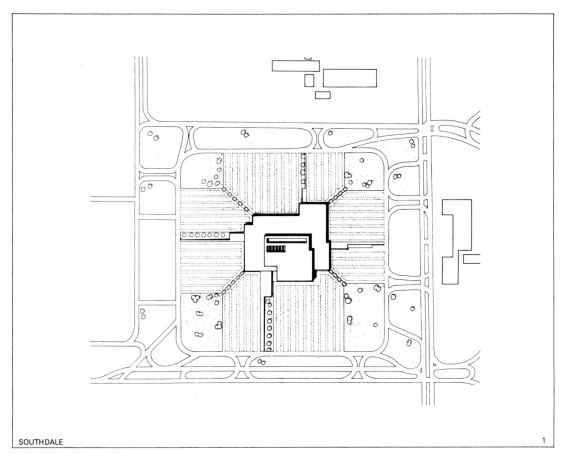

SOUTHDALE

1

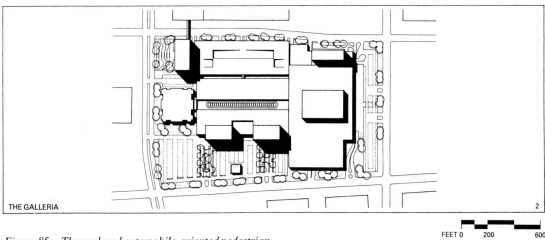

THE GALLERIA

2

FEET 0   200   600

Figure 85   The enclosed automobile-oriented pedestrian
mall and the mixed-use center

Figure 86   Integration of the mall into a larger landscape: Southdale, Minneapolis, by Victor Gruen, 1953–1955

other developments. Ketchum, Gina and Sharp's scheme for Parker Square in Wichita, Kansas, proposed a compact building complex all essentially under a glass roof. The majority of enclosed malls, however, followed a variant of Gruen's original dumbbell plan, in which the central mall between the anchor or magnet stores was enclosed and usually glazed. Storestown, in the San Francisco area, by Welton Becket of 1953–1956, is an early example.

In the late 1960s, the enclosed pedestrian mall evolved in the form of mixed-use developments and so-called supermalls. One of the first and certainly one of the most illustrative of this type was the Galleria complex, in Houston, Texas, opened in 1971 by the Gerald D. Hines Interests. When construction began in the late 1960s adjacent to a major arterial and a freeway loop road, the surrounding sites were scarcely more than pastureland. Now the City Post Oak, as it is known locally, is second only to Houston's central business district in commercial concentration.

The first phase of the Galleria, designed by Hellmuth, Obata and Kassabaum in association with Neuhaus and Taylor, incorporated 788,000 square feet of retail space, almost 1 million square feet of of-

fice space, a 400-room hotel and a large recreational facility (figure 87). The total area was over 2 million square feet of facilities located on 32.9 acres of land in a single rectangular city block. Parking for over 7,000 cars was provided, mostly in multilevel structured garages. The anchor store was Neiman-Marcus, a high-quality and expensive department store. The high-rise hotel and office building were located between the street frontage of the complex and the mall proper (King and Cannady 1973, Zeidler 1983). The Galleria, as its name suggests, was both inspired by and refers to the nineteenth-century Milanese

Figure 87   Suburban mall becomes regional mixed-use center: The Galleria in Houston, by Hellmuth, Obata and Kassabaum, 1968–1982

grand arcade of the same name (Beddington 1981). A second phase subsequently added to the original complex increased the total area to well over 3 million square feet and distributed the commercial uses almost equally among retail, office, and hotel-recreation uses. Another hotel was added, along with more office space in a small atrium tower, several other department stores, and additional parking.

The complex is distributed over a large single, rectangular block with its long side facing Westheimer, the major street. The general layout of the plan is composed within the geometry of the block in the form of a classic dumbbell plan anchored at both ends, with three levels of small shops in between. Large, enclosed public areas are devoted to recreation, in the form of an ice rink (figure 88) or to well-appointed plazas. The whole development constitutes a comprehensive environment that can be used for both business and family activities. In fact, the Galleria has become a tourist attraction in its own right, with families from out of town spending an entire short vacation there in shopping and recreation.

The architectural character of the complex is a well-harmonized assemblage of individual building components, each with its own identity. This approach clearly helps define various parts of the complex from the street and promotes an urban appearance of building facades, forecourts, and sidewalks. Inside, the sense of urbanity is not entirely relaxed; the pedestrian concourse itself is structured as an urban street. Those nonretail spaces that share both realms have two public faces—one on the exterior amid an urban-suburban landscape and one in the inside between mall and "street."

Figure 88   Enclosed public recreation and commerce: The Galleria, Phase I, Houston, 1969

A number of similar urban-suburban projects have been constructed, including the Dallas Galleria by the same developer. Opened in 1982, this complex follows much the same formula. It is a multilevel regional mall with about 1.5 million square feet of retail space, a hotel, offices, and structured car parking, prominently located on 45 acres of land beside a freeway in north Dallas (Rathbun 1986).

The world's largest mall is probably the most bizarre in its extreme merger of shopping and recreation. In the West Edmonton Mall (1981–1985) in Alberta, Canada, material consumption becomes recreation. Built in three phases by the Ghermezian brothers of the Triple 5 Corporation and designed by Marice Sunderland, this behemoth contains well over 4 million square feet of retail space in the form of 11 major department stores and nearly 1,000 other smaller outlets. Perhaps the most fantastic feature of this supermall is the approximately 500,000-square-foot waterpark, partially depicted in figure 89, and the additional amusement and recreation areas of the same order of magnitude. Included within either the leisure or retail portions of the complex are a roller coaster, a wave pool, submarines and other boats such as a replica of the *Santa Maria,* a golf course, an aviary, and a facsimile of Bourbon Street in New Orleans. Fantasy settings even invade the hotel, which features 120 rooms with theme room decor. To date the total area of the complex is 5.2 million square feet (Hemingway 1986, and Knobel 1986).

The overall form of the West Edmonton Mall is compact and distributed within an overall rectangular plan. A central pedestrian spine runs down the middle of the complex, intersecting major theme parks and shopping environments along the way. Smaller cross-axial concourses lead into other shopping precincts, including the many department stores. Unlike either Shoppers World or the Galleria, the exterior architecture of the mall is almost inconsequential and totally subordinated to interior contrivances of mock plazas, streets, and parks. The spatial integration of leisure and shopping is almost total throughout, although the first phases of the project were less successful in this regard (Hemingway 1986, Knobel 1986).

During nearly forty years of evolution, the design of pedestrian shopping malls has continually blurred distinctions among shopping, leisure, and recreation, although the primary recognizable function has always been the retail distribution of goods and services. With the West Edmonton Mall this appears to have changed. Here a commercial leisure phenomenon has been produced that purports to be as

Figure 89   Recreation as consumption in fantasy world: West Edmonton Mall, by the Ghermezian Brothers, 1981–1985

much a resort and tourist attraction as a place to buy goods. Parallel developments in packaged commercial recreation have also begun to appear in the form of Fame and Fat Cities, or similar mall-like recreation facilities, in the South and Southwest of the United States. It is not surprising to find that a principal source of revenues in the West Edmonton Mall is not the rental of retail space but receipts from leisure activities. In fact, the average visitor spends more on various rides than in the stores (Knobel 1986).

What started out in shopping malls as civic leisure-time references have now been transformed to the fairground of ferris wheels and palaces of mirrors. In its crass materialism and antiurban stance, this trend may be seen by many as degenerative. Nevertheless, we should also remember that the fairground, carnival, and state fair also formed an important part of civic life.

SPATIAL, FORMAL, AND FUNCTIONAL TRENDS

Among the shopping centers of various types, several spatial trends and consistent variations in building function and form can be discerned: location, scale and diversity, community function, and identity. Primarily they are responses to changing operational conditions within the retail trade.

Location

The location of retail activities in a metropolitan region has varied largely with transportation technology and related concepts of shopping habits and trading areas. As residential developments grew, retail goods and services continued to be demanded convenient to homes, although convenience varied according to the good or service in question. For instance, stores carrying items households consumed daily tended to be more numerous and located closer at hand than those selling specialty goods. Thus, general categories of outlet—neighborhood, community, or regional stores—were formulated based primarily on trading area, location in the community, and retail function and tenant mix (McKeever and Griffin 1977). Often, however, in spite of this seemingly reactive stance, shopping centers were located in advance of full-scale residential development.

This phenomenon was particularly evident during periods of rapid suburban expansion, when growth appeared to be more or less predictable (Converse 1946, Holden 1960).

From early beginnings as taxpayer blocks, strip commercial shopping centers have had a primarily local community orientation. While the ribbonlike appearance along major roads and transit routes suggests more than local patronage by numerous passersby, most stores served nearby residents. Location next to transit stops provided convenient access on the way to and from home, as did corner locations along major roadways before entry into a residential subdivision. Many strip commercial centers, especially during the post–World War II period, had explicit pedestrian links into neighboring residential areas, and the inclusion of public facilities reinforced their role as local community centers.

Although similar in their location along major roadways or at important intersections, shopping villages usually had a more than local orientation. They were roughly equivalent to small town centers and typically became the focus of community life in the larger subdivisions and planned communities of which they were a part. The size and variety of stores was often intended to meet most of the shopping needs previously satisfied by downtown commercial locations. Unlike the strip commercial centers, which provided only convenience and regular shopping services, as well as some local entertainment, shopping villages usually had a broader focus. The exceptions were the Farmers Markets, although here there was subregional appeal involving more than routine daily shopping trips.

With the development of regional shopping malls, the hierarchical pattern of shopping behavior was turned away from central and downtown commercial areas in favor of outer suburban locations for almost everything. Malls were usually dispersed near the perimeter of metropolitan areas where they could be well served by high-speed, high-capacity thoroughfares. In many cities they were constructed in advance of expanding suburban residential development, where access was good and land relatively inexpensive (Baker and Funaro 1951, Holden 1960, Beddington 1981) (figure 90). For most suburban areas, the location of regional shopping malls effectively reversed the direction of shopping trips away from the city toward the countryside and into an environment more suited to the exclusive use of automobiles. Recently this pattern has shifted again as malls compete with one another and become more specialized in function. The net effect in travel behavior is more highly dispersed patterns of shopping trips, involving numerous locations within a region. Aggregations of strip commercial centers and shopping malls have created centers to subregional urban realms that have effectively replaced traditional downtown commercial locations (Muller 1981).

With this rearrangement of metropolitan shopping patterns, the locational response of shopping centers to their sites has been reasonably consistent. The early taxpayer strips served to hold land for future use in more intensive forms of development. Gradually, as automobile use intensified and roadway networks proliferated, location of retail commercial centers became less contingent on but no less responsive to the abstract gradients of transportation accessibility that favored some locations more than others. Similarly regional malls required good access in competitive proximity to a large number of residents.

By the same token, the presence of shopping centers in convenient locations spurred on residential and other forms of development. Throughout, good access to a wide range of commercial facilities was a distinct asset—so much so that in most cases the density and often the quality of housing intensified around these suburban commercial centers. Just as gracious apartment blocks were located next to Shaker Square in the 1920s, high-priced condominiums are located close to the Galleria complex.

The location of retail commercial facilities in relationship to car parking and street access has also shown a consistent trend toward more structure. The first strip commercial centers provided for car park-

Figure 90 Shopping centers in advance of metropolitan development: Bellevue Center outside Seattle, 1946

ing on the street. Sometimes parking lots were to be found behind taxpayer strips, although this was often a later adjustment to more intensive automobile use and therefore demand for parking. Formalized off-street parking was to follow, either beside or within a shopping complex (figure 91). Highland Park Village (1931) was one of the first major centers to provide off-street parking for its patrons. Commercial development along the now-renowned Rodeo Drive in suburban Los Angeles featured buildings along the street, in the typical urban fashion, but with elaborate automobile entries to parking lots in the rear. In contrast, by the 1950s, strip commercial developments were almost always set back from the street with parking in the front, an arrangement that roadside franchises tended to use. Intensive mixed-use mall developments that followed in the 1970s and 1980s invariably provided structured parking with direct access into the shopping mall. Even some relatively early malls, like Sharpstown, were retrofitted with structured multilevel parking garages, not to accommodate excess parking but to provide more convenient covered access into shopping areas. Throughout the development of suburban shopping centers, a continuous striving for higher levels of convenient access has been a major determinant of both site location and building form.

Size and Diversity

Changes in the size and composition of retail outlets have been largely episodic, conforming to changes in operating and management conditions that reflected both the costs and opportunities of doing business. For instance, the trend away from full-service stores toward self-service was motivated, as much as anything else, by a need to cope with rising labor costs. Similarly, diversification of goods and services within a single outlet was an attempt to maintain economic stability amid a spread of profit margins. Low-profit margins on food produce could be balanced against higher margins on household goods. Throughout, the sizes of operations have generally risen in response to economies that seem to have accrued to increases in scale. Retail facilities have increased in physical size and in the mixture of uses.

Not all trends have moved in a single direction toward increased magnitudes. Contemporary specialty stores and specialized retail complexes are often smaller in size than their counterparts in mass markets and increasingly offer a fuller range of service (McKeever and Griffin 1985). So-called fashion malls and high-end limited department stores are cases in point. Recent rises in the diversity of uses housed within a single building complex can be seen as a contemporary phenomenon—or as a return to earlier models of a traditional central commercial district that incorporated a wide range of uses.

Before World War I, retail commercial activities in a city or town were an agglomeration of small, specialized outlets, with some department stores in central areas. Ownership was invariably independent and in the hands of individual shopkeepers. Full service was universal. A shopper presented a list of goods to be purchased, or asked to inspect a particular item, and was served individually by a shopkeeper or clerk. Personal relationships were often fostered by this mode of operation between vendors and their buying public (Beddington 1981, Liebs 1985).

Figure 91   Off-street parking along commercial strips: an early prewar example and a contemporary example

Shops were often small and usually housed below the living quarters of the shopkeepers in a "main street" row of retail establishments (Liebs 1985, p. 39). At the other end of the scale, that turn-of-the-century retailing invention the department store was invariably located downtown on a busy intersection, sometimes referred to as a "100 percent corner." In keeping with this description, department stores were multistory buildings filling out the available building volume of a site. Display and service areas for spe-

cific kinds of goods, or departments, were arranged across each floor of the building, which effectively became like a shopping district under one roof.

During World War I prevailing forms of merchandising began to change. In 1916, Clarence Saunders converted a grocery store in Memphis, Tennessee, into the first self-service store. By the end of the war his Piggly Wiggly stores were in operation in many cities across the nation (Liebs 1985). Furthermore, these stores began to combine goods from several separate stores. Typically self-service combinations, as they were called, incorporated groceries, produce, and meat sections under one roof (Dipman 1935). The advantages of the self-service mode of operation were twofold. First, since customers selected and handled the goods themselves, less labor was required to run the store effectively. This, in turn, resulted in labor cost savings, as well as reduced labor demand at a time of wartime shortages. Second, the presentation of goods for self-service merchandising (figure 92) encouraged customers to peruse shelves filled with goods, adding significantly to the tendency toward impulse buying. By the early 1920s most of the industry had converted to a self-service mode of operation (Dipman 1935, Baker and Funaro 1951, McKeever and Griffin 1985, Liebs 1985).

The emergence of both corporate and voluntary chain stores in the 1920s added to increased levels of merchandising and improved economies of operation. Wholesale inventories and distribution could be rationalized because of standardization within a chain, resulting in potential cost savings. Like the roadside franchises, standardization helped to improve relations with potential customers, who knew what to expect about the range and level of service.

Naturally enough the physical layout and architecture of retail stores changed in order to accommodate the self-service mode of operation. Larger and wider expanses of floor space were required in order to display the goods effectively and to accommodate more than one kind of merchandise. The separation of inventory from goods accessible to consumers necessitated a division of the facility, although this diminished as the practice of holding the inventory on the open shelves increased. Standardization within chain store outlets fixed not only the internal layout of facilities and signage but the building envelope and architectural form as well. A Kroger or Piggly Wiggly store in one place looked like one in any other place. Gradually whole streets, dominated by chain stores, began to look alike, regardless of other regional differences or potential local variations.

The next major change occurred with the depression years and resulted in a further increase in store size and diversity of goods. In 1930, Michael Cullen suggested to the management of the Kroger chain of stores that a huge self-service market could be advantageously established by offering large quantities of goods at low unit prices. Thus the modern high-volume, cash-and-carry so-called supermarket came into existence (Zimmerman 1955, Liebs 1985). Subsequently the basic idea was extended to provide one-stop shopping whereby a broad range of goods was housed under one roof. In fact, to be most effective the diversity of goods was to allow for comparative shopping among competing products. This diversification also had other advantages. Low profit margins on goods like food could be offset by much higher margins on goods like household appliances and furniture (Baker and Funaro 1951).

By the 1940s approximately one of every three retail stores built was a supermarket, and other related trends were significantly affecting the geography of the retail industry. For example, the large supermarket chains eliminated smaller retail units and increased store sizes appreciably (Zimmerman 1955). In 1930 the maximum size of supermarkets was on the order of 10,000 square feet. By 1950 this was the minimum size for effective operation. Total sales volume for a prominent firm like the A&P Stores (The Great Atlantic and Pacific Tea Company) more than doubled between 1927 and 1951 with a quarter the number of stores (Baker and Funaro 1951, pp. 5f.). Thus the number of retail outlets decreased in relative terms, and each became larger in size. Technical innovations in areas like refrigeration also helped make each store more self-contained (figure 93).

During the 1950s and 1960s the scale of retail operations continued to increase. In fact, with the de-

Figure 92   Perusal and self-service: an early Piggly Wiggly store, Ohio, 1926

velopment of the pedestrian mall in the early 1950s, there was a substantial jump in the size of a single retail facility from around 150,000 square feet to about 500,000 square feet. Moreover, different shopping activities became more integrated, and the combination of large department stores, supermarkets, and smaller variety and specialty stores broadened the base of market appeal at a given locale. Not only did economies of scale change; so did opportunity costs. Fundamentally retail malls were designed to provide convenient and comfortable shopping conditions for all retail needs.

In the 1960s shopping centers proliferated rapidly. From approximately 3,000 outlets in 1950 the number rose to 13,000 in 1970—the most dramatic historical increase to date (Sternlieb and Hughes 1981, McKeever and Griffin 1985, Shopping Center World 1985). With this rapid rise in the number of outlets came higher levels of standardization in product lines and a corresponding segmentation of the mass consumer market. Typically markets, and therefore shopping center stores, became stratified economically between so-called high-end and low-end goods and services. With some exceptions like the chain of Best Stores, where each store was architecturally different, higher levels of standardization also brought architectural uniformity (figure 94), especially the case given the continuing suburban model of freestanding building complexes on a large, accessible site.

Since about 1970 two related though dissimilar trends have emerged. First, regional shopping centers have generally continued to increase in size and diversity in most parts of the country, often gaining the stature of so-called supermalls. Second, there has been an emergence of specialization within regional markets and closer targeting of consumers assumed to be between existing major markets (McKeever, Ross, and Griffin 1985). The result of the first trend is multilevel facilities in mixed-use developments, like the Galleria complexes, where the retail mall is no longer a freestanding building on the site. The overall size of development has jumped to on the order of 2 million to 3 million square feet. The result of the second trend is a decrease in the size of shopping centers and the emergence of mall-like complexes around freestanding stores like home improvement centers (McKeever, Ross, and Griffin 1985). Certainly in the case of specialty festival and fashion centers, the spatial experience and iconography of the building complex often takes on a special theme. By contrast the architecture of most discount centers is usually much more prosaic. Among other factors, the net effect of

Figure 93   Frozen food, modern convenience, and supermarkets: an Empire Mart, Troy, New York, 1947

Figure 94   Standardization with architectural
distinction: The indeterminate facade of the Best Store,
Houston, by SITE, 1974

these two trends has been a relatively stable growth in the number of shopping centers built within the United States. Between 1980 and 1985 some 3,000 to 4,000 were constructed, somewhat fewer than in the preceding decade (Shopping Center World 1985). In addition to an increasing tendency toward mixed-use development, in which leisure and recreation facilities seem likely to play a significant role, this twofold trend probably will continue.

Community Function

Within the suburban context, shopping centers have fulfilled the roles of both selling merchandise and, paradoxically perhaps, attempting to improve social and civic life. According to one thesis, shopping centers are not only a fundamental part of community life but vehicles of social reform as well. Distressed by

metropolitan sprawl, businessmen and planners saw the planned development of shopping centers as a way to instill and maintain civic pride (Gillette 1985). Early reformers of the 1920s and 1930s, such as Clarence Stein and Arthur Perry, clearly equated the roles of shopping centers with schools and playgrounds in any attempt to create a sense of suburban community (Stein and Bauer 1934, Gillette 1985). Similarly, during the early days of the large-scale pedestrian shopping malls, many designers, such as Victor Gruen, explicitly regarded retail activities as part of social life and incorporated as many nonretail functions into their malls as possible. In fact, as we observed at Northland and Southdale, Gruen saw the shopping mall as a surrogate for the conventional town center or downtown area of a city. As he put it, in the appropriate design of shopping centers, "we

Figure 95   Community life in the suburban mall: public art and display at Southdale, Minneapolis, 1955

can restore the lost sense of commitment and belonging; we can counteract the phenomenon of alienation, isolation and loneliness and achieve a sense of identification and participation" (Gruen 1973, p. 11). It was no idle boast. The Southdale Center outside Minneapolis, for instance, annually hosted the Minneapolis Symphony, among other events, and deliberately incorporated public art (figure 95). In his detailed discussion of the role of shopping centers in providing structure to metropolitan development, Muller (1981) enumerates many other regular occasions when the civic life of a community has literally converged on the plaza areas of suburban malls. The central metaphors at work in shaping the architecture of pedestrian malls, like the town green, all had a strong civic orientation. Almost all the early examples of shopping centers and many of the later ones incorpo-

rated public uses into the program of functions. They were the community centers for many towns and metropolitan districts.

In spite of the efforts of planners, social reformers, and civic-minded businessmen, however, the public role of shopping centers has usually remained ambiguous. Property rights are private, not public, although the de facto public nature of malls has given rise to a recent judicial propensity to regard them as essentially public places, at least with regard to First Amendment rights (Muller 1981). Nevertheless, most mall developments remain sealed off from the rest of a community, as well as appearing selective and controlled in the activities encouraged to take place there. Moreover, the monumental architectural rhetoric of many malls often seems out of place with their immediate retail role and more consistent with grandiose civic functions.

Several trends can be discerned in the community orientation of suburban shopping centers. At the outset, there was a strong degree of spatial integration within the local community and incorporation of public uses like post offices, administrative offices, and libraries. Strip commercial centers like Shaker Village provided a public focus for surrounding apartment dwelling. The center at Port Edwards, Wisconsin, was symbolically and functionally the community center. Similarly, Foster Village in Bergenfeld, New Jersey, was closely linked with adjacent residential areas through an arcade and a community park. Although they were all freestanding buildings on sites designated for nonresidential uses, strong pedestrian connections were maintained with surrounding neighborhoods. Moreover, use of these connections was actively encouraged by the location of higher-density residential developments, such as apartment complexes, immediately adjacent to the centers themselves.

Shopping villages also enjoyed strong ties with surrounding residential areas. Here the practice of continuing the pattern of public streets into the shopping centers to form sites for commercial development almost guaranteed a strong spatial connection. The scale of building was also usually harmonized with adjacent residential areas. Finally, piecemeal development of commercial lots and blocks added to the prevailing sense of a traditional town center with its lack of strict uniformity and its possession of a history.

With the development of large-scale pedestrian malls in the 1950s, shopping centers acquired a separate presence and autonomy, particularly from surrounding circumstances. The sheer size of these facilities and the practice of surrounding them by parking lots immediately set them apart from any adjacent buildings, in spite of some reasonably successful efforts to integrate pedestrian landscapes (figure 96). They were no longer local or community centers in the manner of earlier strip commercial developments. Social and economic ties to the public at large were regional in scope and therefore a difficult source of meaningful physical manifestation. One potential source of such expression was the road and freeway system upon which the regional shopping centers were so dependent. But the scale and presence of this infrastructure in the metropolitan landscape was usually so vast and abstract that a sense of community propriety could not be easily established. The irony

Figure 96   Pedestrian landscapes in automobile environments: Northland Shopping Center, Detroit, 1952–1954

was that the early malls had all the hallmarks of public places, but the important community link fell victim to the ubiquitous and therefore specifically aspatial realm of automobile movement. To transform Gertrude Stein's famous comment, "There may have been some there there, but there was no there in getting there."

Recently, as suburban commercial developments have continued to consolidate and assume the role of metropolitan subcenters, their public function is becoming more manifest (Fisher 1988). Many are no longer freestanding and spatially isolated. Instead mixed-use developments on the same site, as well as developments of comparable scale nearby, provide the means for higher levels of spatial integration. Nevertheless, the identity of a public realm still remains relatively suppressed as space rather than a sense of place continue to exist between individual subdevelopments.

Another trend running through the longitudinal development of suburban shopping centers is a changing role in the expectations of customers. Initially service and convenience were predominant requirements. Customers patronized shops because they were readily accessible and convenient to use. Comfort and consistency were added with enclosed, air-conditioned facilities. Soon the malls increasingly assumed the function of leisure-time and causal recreational venues. Formal commitments were made to this role by incorporating explicit recreational uses into the facilities program. In some cases, like the Galleria complexes, this use, in the unlikely guise of a skating rink, became a central feature of the mall complex. Contemporary developments have pushed this role still further in the direction of play and now fantasy. Supermalls and festival malls are no longer places just to go to shop; they are other worlds in which to be delighted and be entertained.

Identity

The common agreement that has already been noted with regard to the appearance of roadside franchises (Liebs 1985, Langdon 1986) extends to suburban shopping facilities in general. First was a trend toward a domestic homelike or villagelike appearance during the 1920s, parallel to developments in single-family housing, where small cottages and bungalows coincided with market economics, a conservative attitude toward traditional family values, and a return to normalcy (Gowans 1964, Cohn 1979).

From the 1930s until about the mid-1960s, there was a reaction, from the direction of the architectural avant-garde, against traditionalism and historic revivals (Hiller 1975). Designers and influential sylists promulgated a moderne visual language, bound closely to idealized images of technology (Miekle 1979, Corn 1984, Liebs 1985). Increases in building size and a strong automobile orientation also made it difficult to follow traditional architectural models. The art deco and moderne shopping centers that followed appeared efficient, contemporary, and progressive. This uncluttered, streamlined styling that was eschewed in the domestic environment was found not only acceptable but desirable in the world of commerce. A rough equivalence was also struck between the appearance of artifacts of mass production, such as appliances, and the automobiles that provided access to stores. Appropriately perhaps, both the mechanical consumer products, and the realm to which they were most closely attached seemed to be alike. This design idiom readily allowed the almost instantaneous development of shopping centers to forthrightly appear as single, new and unified projects.

As disillusionment with the promise of technology became evident, a conservationist attitude developed. In order to show a sense of environmental and contextual responsibility to the consumer public, modern styling was replaced by rusticity (Liebs 1985, Langdon 1986). This shift took two forms, roughly in sequence: first, compliance with forms appropriate to the environmental movement of the late

Figure 97   Modern styling and the automobile realm: Stan's Drive-In Restaurant, California, 1950s

1960s and 1970s, and second, an interest in broader issues of contextualism and a certain reverence for continuity with the past. Apart from a real societal concern for conservation, this turn also coincided with the unprecedentedly affluent baby boomers' penchant for acquiring symbols of status, which allowed them to differentiate themselves from others and yet maintain the hegemony of a postmodern blend of old and new (Liebs 1985).

Throughout this account, the underlying cultural model has been that building form follows social dictates. In order to appeal to the consumer public, retailers must conform to that public's sense of a responsible retail commercial sector and mass consumption. There is considerable merit to this type of interpretation; it explains much about the shape and appearance of suburban retail realms. But it largely ignores reciprocity between form and social response, especially the processes by which that might take place. It also largely ignores how a particular aesthetic doctrine happens to coincide with a set of social beliefs. Finally, important intrinsic processes of design, formal adaption, and transformation that occur in parallel with but independent of social responses also go unnoticed.

In the light of the earlier model, it must be asked how those in society, apparently satisfied with the shape and appearance of retail commercial facilities, change their collective minds. What transpires within the realm of these facilities to cause dissatisfaction? One explanation may be developments in the facilities themselves. At its outset each building type was carefully considered, well designed, usually well integrated into its surroundings, and displaying completeness and unity to the characteristics of the building type. Once a building type was firmly established, some of its salient features could be changed without great loss of recognition or symbolic value; in other words, a building that approximated a building type sufficiently was assumed to be a member of that class. But as the salient features of that type were consistently degraded (for example, by increased competition and pressure to reduce costs), the entire class of development could be called into question. At that point the reduced quality was rectified or a different approach was adopted.

The strip commercial development that has become an unfortunate part of most American metropolitan areas well illustrates this process. The early strip commercial centers were well designed and positive in their social contributions. But as they began to develop endlessly and independently from adjacent residential neighborhoods, they lost important features, and the design frame of reference was sorely reduced. As greater competition in these strips lowered marginal returns on investment, the resources for good, socially responsible design plummeted. Today there are numerous undistinguished boxlike buildings in bleak roadside landscapes, well beyond the point at which society began to see commercial strip development in general as being a contemporary problem and blight on the landscape (figure 98). In come cases, criticism and opportunity have conspired to rectify the situation. Rising land costs and the appearance of so-called minimarkets in the increasing segmentation of consumers' shopping behavior have created conditions whereby redevelopment is taking place, to positive effect, in these bleak landscapes.

Additions and links being made to blank freestanding buildings will unify the commercial strip and allow it to regain some of its earlier positive features (Fisher 1988). Similarly the vast featureless expanses of parking lots, never part of the original building type, are being upgraded and given structure. Clearly there exist sociocultural processes by which there can be considerable reciprocity between the physical form of a development and its social response. These processes stand well beyond matters of taste or the prevailing spirit of the times.

The matter of how a particular aesthetic doctrine happens to coincide with a set of social beliefs about the retail commercial environment is complex. Adoption of a moderne idiom of architecture in many suburban retail facilities was bound to a fascination with a machine aesthetic and its successful symbolization of the contemporary and efficient qualities that we might seek in our products (Meikle 1979, Corn 1984, Liebs 1985, Forty 1986). And there was a deeper or more pervasive conjunction of ideas at work. The moderne designers' interest in machines arose because of the clarity these objects brought to the doctrine that form should follow function (Conrads 1964). This is an attitude that actively eschewed unnecessary artifice, preferring instead a straightforward reckoning with circumstances and a certain relish for technological possibilities. This was also a general societal outlook in a time of rapid change and eventual prosperity.

Curiously, society's heightened environmental concerns did not find adequate aesthetic expression in the retail realm. The number of shopping centers did not diminish in spite of threats from the energy crisis and the Clean Air Act (McKeever, Ross and Griffin 1985), nor did their building form change fundamentally, even when the figuration displayed a certain rusticity. The contextual conservationist impulse led back to stylistic revivals and so-called old buildings but without any real focus. Almost any style would do so long as it appeared to be from the past. Ironically during the course of this revivalism moderne architecture has reappeared and been embraced by many preservation-minded purists. Perhaps they are correct that modernity in its manifold forms is the authentic mode of expression for suburban shopping centers.

The formal adaptation and transformation that occurs by a logic largely intrinsic to building types themselves can be illustrated in a number of ways. For example, strip commercial centers with offstreet parking incorporated within the same precinct can be viewed reasonably as an adaption of the off-street parking schemes found in earlier shopping village types, like Highland Park in Dallas. Similarly, both Nichols's Country Club Plaza (1922) and the Shaker Village, built a few years later, harken back to earlier models of commercial development around town squares. In a slightly different vein, the intrinsic difficulty of providing a unified and highly integrated design, a common feature of most shopping centers, becomes greater as the mixture and magnitude of uses expand. Consequently, in cases like the Galleria complexes, a different doctrine was adopted—one that emphasizes the separate articulation of recognizable buildings within a complex (figure 99). But here again a preexisting model for the development was followed: the idea of a traditional urban block with a

Figure 98   Roadside landscapes of cluttered signs and bland boxlike buildings: Route 9, Massachusetts

central shopping arcade, more specifically, the Galeria of Victor Emmanuel in Milan.

From this typological vantage point, another kind of explanation might be offered for the formal developments in the shape, appearance, and identity of suburban retail realms. Instead of changes according to prevailing socioeconomic circumstances, the assumption might be made that, throughout the past seventy years, there has been the constant presence of a single metaphor guiding development: the traditional European and early American market street, plaza, or village green. Certainly it is a recurrent theme found in all shopping center types. It seems to be reified during the initial stages of each major typological development. In both physical form and surrounding rhetoric, early strip commercial shopping centers were designed as local town centers with public functions and a symbolic presence. Shopping villages, almost by definition, were based on the metaphor of the market town. Pedestrian malls of all kinds have expressly made reference to traditional market places or the village green. Even mixed-use supermalls incorporate an interior streetscape that is overtly urban and traditional. In an extreme case, the

West Edmonton Mall contains a replica of Bourbon Street in the old quarter of New Orleans. In summary, most of the development that has taken place accommodates a greater diversity and scale of activity to this simple root metaphor.

Each of these interpretations conveys some truth about the identity of the suburban retail realm. Certainly many of the varied surface features are explained well by the socially deterministic model. Indeed, at different times, much the same type of facility has appeared to don a different guise. Nevertheless, much of the early enthusiasm for various forms of retail development has certainly worn off for reasons that are much more than only circumstantial. Poor design and shoddy development have contributed to public disfavor. In the absence of a useful and strong underlying aesthetic doctrine, public sentiment notwithstanding, design invariably lacks focus and falls into eclecticism and kitsch. Finally, there is something to be said for the sustaining power of the traditional metaphor of the market town. It has sustained retail trade, in a variety of socioeconomic and cultural circumstances, for several centuries.

FUTURE VARIATIONS

What the future holds for the development of the suburban metropolitan retail realm is hard to say with any precision, although certain trends and emerging themes seem likely to persist. First, we are likely to see consistently higher and more intensive levels of mixed use within a single building complex, regardless of size. The mixed-use supermall has reached

city proportions, and diversified development of minimalls is taking place within the precincts of relatively modest commercial strips. Subregional centers seem certain to grow, intensify, and mature. The first generation of development, geared primarily toward the straightforward role of a suburban shopping center, is being replaced by a higher density of building with a strong mixed-use character (Fisher 1988). Furthermore, the interdependence among separate uses and projects seems likely to be much higher than in the past, producing truly urban metropolitan subcenters. With this higher level of functional and proximal interdependence, the future of a public domain seems brighter within these commercial realms because of the necessity for higher levels of cooperation among private entrepreneurs and a greater dependence on public services like transportation and environmental management.

Second, the twofold trend in the size and diversity of development appears likely to continue. Increasing levels of consumer market segmentation will bring greater specialization in the type and style of merchandising and hence facilities. Economies of scale, especially in rapidly growing metropolitan subcenters, also seem likely to persist, maintaining large sizes of development. The merger of the two sides of this trend could make for a richer commercial environment by bringing a higher degree of thematic variety. Once again, mixed-use developments will predominate.

Third, retail trade may well take on a subordinate role to other leisure-time activities and workaday functions. The mix of uses in complexes like the Galleria is already divided roughly equally across office,

*Figure 99   Separate articulation of recognizable
buildings within a singular complex: the Galleria,
Houston, 1969–1982*

leisure-recreation, and retail functions. If the fantasy
world of the West Edmonton Mall is a harbinger, then
retail trade will revolve around an array of special
recreational environments. Shopping and contrived
leisure-time activity will become intertwined, probably with a emphasis on the latter.

Finally, the physical shape and appearance of the
metropolitan suburban commercial landscape will
probably lose much of the desolate and formless
quality of its extensive parking lots and isolated
buildings. Rising land costs, higher intensities of development, and a greater diversity of uses will require
higher densities and much more integrated forms of
development. The land-banking function of grade-
level parking lots will become exhausted in most locales. Similarly, the distinctive image and identity of
individual premises may persist but in conjunction
with a more pronounced public infrastructure required to handle the higher densities of development
and demand for higher levels of amenity. In short, the
suburban retail realm may well move closer to becoming like the cosmopolitan marketplaces of old.

5   Corporate Estates

As homes and shopping centers dispersed into suburban locations, so did commercial offices and corporate headquarters. Relocation was based on the belief that corporate administration would become more efficient away from the distractions of the central city and offer the convenience of a shorter commute (Herrera 1967).

In the New York region the mass exodus of corporate offices into the suburbs was relatively slow. General Foods led the way in 1954, moving 30 miles north of its midtown Manhattan address to suburban White Plains. Over the next ten years only ten other big firms followed. Some companies viewed suburban sites as too isolated. Royal McBee, now part of Litton Industries, for instance, found that clients, business associates, and support services disliked their new location near Rye, New York, though it was only about 35 miles from downtown Manhattan (Herrera 1967). Nevertheless, by 1965 the mass exodus was well under way. IBM, American Can, Pepsi Co., Avco, and other large corporations moved out north of the city. Eventually some fifty firms would abandon their inner-city locations.

These corporations decided on relocation because of the ready availability of comparatively inexpensive space for expansion, the positive effect of a more tranquil site on employees, a shortened commute for many, especially white-collar workers, and the rising cost of good office space in Manhattan. American Cyanamid, for instance, estimated an annual savings on the order of 8 percent by owning its own building in suburban New Jersey compared to the costs of renting in Manhattan (Herrera 1967). Between 1972 and 1985, it was estimated that about 16 million square feet of prime office space was built in the New York suburbs alone (Muller 1978).

Corporate offices in other major cities relocated as well. In Boston the new highway system, and especially Route 128, had an immediate impact on relocation. Today over forty-seven high-technology firms are located on Boston's periphery, with employment in excess of 1 million people (Visitor's Guide 1987, *Boston Globe* 1989). The suburbs of nine of the fifteen largest metropolitan areas within the United States were the principal source of office employment by 1970, their share rising to around 67 percent by 1980. In San Francisco alone, 75 percent did not work in the core city, and 78 percent of New York suburban residents also worked in the suburbs (Jackson 1985). Although there were numerous interregional relocations of corporate offices, especially to the sunbelt during the 1970s, most relocations were from city to suburb within the same metropolitan region (Muller 1978).

TYPES OF CORPORATE OFFICE

With the rapid growth in demand for office services during the nineteenth century, both the needs and requirements for commercial office space became strongly defined and visible in American urban centers. First, banks and comparatively new financial institutions, like insurance companies, constructed buildings to house clerical, bookkeeping, and supervisory functions. In keeping with the spirit of free enterprise, these buildings often presented an edifice that reflected the occupants' business successes (Gibbs 1984).

According to time-honored tradition, professional offices were typically located together in order to provide for easy consultation and to attain higher overall visibility. Consequently certain areas of town might be known for the presence of lawyers, stockbrokers, or doctors. As times changed, however, a strong need developed quickly for special employees in manufacturing industries to cope with the increasing magnitude and complexity of managerial tasks. Primarily this need arose because of increased functional specialization within firms and the concomitant requirements for supervision and management.

With the ensuing rise of the white-collar worker, the need for a great many offices occurred in conjunction with most economic activities. Later improvements in reliable communications gradually made these functions increasingly independent (Hohl 1968). It was no longer necessary for office functions to be located next to industrial production or for headquarter offices to be adjacent to support services, or so-called back offices.

In the dispersal of office functions that often accompanied increases in corporate size, the headquarter's function, not unexpectedly, received special attention. It was the shift of these corporate activities into suburban locations that set the design standards for similar functions, such as office parks and other speculative commercial developments. Even when they were not directly emulated, they still remained highly influential.

I employ a typology of six categories of suburban corporate offices, each reflecting a particular type of development: factory offices, functional layouts, campus plans, systems complexes, court buildings, and hierarchical configurations (figure 100).

Factory Offices

From the 1930s on administration and executive office buildings, designed in conjunction with industrial plants, were relatively common features in the suburban landscape. Certainly on a massive scale, Ford's River Rouge plant and associated offices (1927) was one of the first. The Johnson Wax com-

Figure 100   A typology of corporate offices: (1) Noxell offices at Cockeysville, Maryland, by Gordon Bunshaft of Skidmore, Owings and Merrill, 1971. (2) Youngstown Steel and Tube Company in Ohio, by Gilbert P. Schafer, 1957. (3) General Motors Technical Center near Detroit, by Eero Saarinen in Association with Smith, Hinchman and Gryll, 1947–1955. (4) American Can Company, Greenwich, Connecticut, by Gordon Bunshaft of Skidmore, Owings and Merrill 1970. (5) E. R. Squibb and Sons, Inc. World Headquarters, Lawrenceville, New Jersey, by Hellmuth, Obata and Kassabaum, 1969–1972. (6) IBM World Trade Americas–Far East Corporation Headquarters, by Edward Larabee Barnes Associates, 1975.

FACTORY OFFICES   1

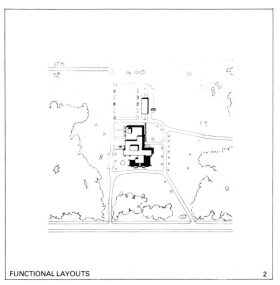

FUNCTIONAL LAYOUTS   2

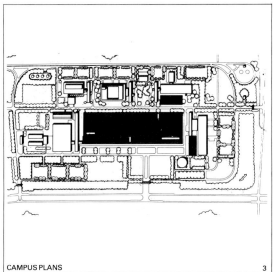

CAMPUS PLANS   3

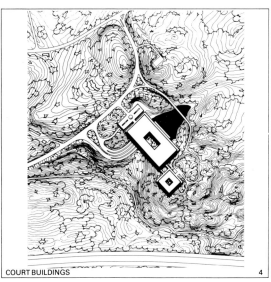

COURT BUILDINGS   4

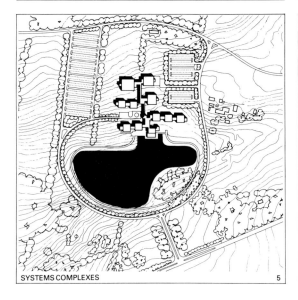

SYSTEMS COMPLEXES   5

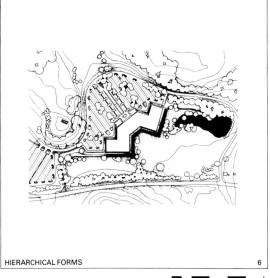

HIERARCHICAL FORMS   6

FEET   0   200   1000

plex, by Frank Lloyd Wright, was constructed not long after, between 1934 and 1937 (Scully 1988). With changes in industrial processes because of automation, suburban industrial sites became particularly attractive as requirements for large floor areas and low land costs made decentralization inevitable.

Factory offices were designed either as an integral part of an industrial plant or as separate nearby buildings. Many of the design considerations that were to shape other suburb office types quickly began to emerge: convenience of access, including a prominent and gracious entrance; comfortable, restful, and interesting surroundings for visitors; common areas for employees; a carefully considered environmental quality of work areas; and placement of office buildings away from the street in parklike settings (*Architectural Record* 1951).

Two different attitudes seem to have pervaded the design of factory offices. The first, especially during the late 1930s, was a concern for completeness in a design, as well as a certain monumentality. The plant and offices for the chemical company G. D. Seale of Skokie, Illinois, completed in the early 1940s by Herbert G. Banse, were rendered in a streamlined moderne styling typical of the period (figure 101). The semicircular tower, containing lobby and conference space for all the office floors, protruded unabashedly at the front of the building, marking the entry and providing an unusual sense of grandeur. By contrast, the bold horizontal lines of walls, fenestration, and sun screens appeared to stretch the building tautly across its site. The overall composition was at once abstract and monumental yet complete. A simple parklike setting with broad

grassy areas and a single hedgerow paralleling the horizontal lines of the offices provided a strong complement to the building complex (Goble 1957, p. 187).

The other attitude reflected an opposite opinion. According to some authorities at the time, a designer should "lead his client away from institutional monumentality, in favor of flexibility, expendability, perhaps even demountability." Furthermore, plant and office should not be thought of "as the ancestral home of a corporation" but as "a design for fast-changing times" (Whitney 1957, p. 187). According to this view, a fundamental aspect of the building complex was the external wall, which could be economically expanded or revised as the production facility changed. Furthermore, the office building was an integral part of this wall. In short, offices were expected to expand in much the same orderly and rational manner as the production processes themselves.

The plant and offices developed in the mid-1950s for Parker Pen in Jamesville, Wisconsin, by John J. Flad and Associates was a fine example of this second approach (see figure 115). The long horizontal lines of the double-story office building almost appeared to cantilever over the plant on both sides (Goble 1957). These double-story configurations where prominent upper floors appeared to float over lower floors, suggesting a sense of both extension and spaciousness, were common. In some other complexes the principle was exploited further by raising the upper floors on columns (Hunt 1961). Throughout, most offices conformed to a strictly linear arrangement of about 30 to 50 feet in width, depending on the corridor loading (Goble 1957).

Figure 101   Monumentality and moderne styling in the factory office: G. D. Searle, Skokie, Illinois, by Herbert G. Banse, 1943

A contemporary version of the factory office from the early 1970s shows an evolution of the type toward the court building. At the Noxell Offices at Cockeysville, Maryland, by Gordon Bunshaft of Skidmore, Owings and Merrill (figure 100), the office building is separated from the plant and placed toward the rear of the site where the trees are denser and the site offers more amenity. The single-story building on the approach from the entrance appears to hug the site, registering almost as a bold single line. An inner courtyard allows natural light to enter directly into the complex, especially into the lower basement level (Schmertz 1975).

Functional Layouts

One logical outgrowth of the factory office was a straightforward functional layout of freestanding office space within a suburban setting. As the name suggests, offices were informal yet efficient arrangements of specific functions expressed architecturally as building volumes, usually within a comparatively neutral landscape. Often the overall impression was

of a building complex that had expanded over time to meet new spatial requirements. In fact, this may well have been the case. The generative idea of the type fundamentally resided in the building's plan and an efficient functional layout of spaces within that plan. Examples of the type did not appear to conform to any other organizational concepts.

A clear example of this type was the headquarters building for the Youngstown Steel and Tube Company in Ohio of 1957, designed by Gilbert P. Schafer (*Progressive Architecture* 1959). Situated on a 52-acre flat and rather featureless site in what was a rapidly growing suburban area, the building was, in the words of its architect, "to be particularly attractive and comfortable for the employees to offset any reluctance [on their part] to leave for the new site seven miles south of the city" (*Progressive Architecture* 1959, p. 79). In plan the building complex was arranged at the center of the site (figures 100 and 102), with a three-story, horizontal band of offices forming a dividing line between a library, lobby, and concourse pavilion, at the entry, and the horizontal expanse of other office and service space behind. A light court provided natural light to an inside annular configuration of offices. Parking was located directly at the rear of the complex, some of it under cover, and vehicular access was provided by a simple system of loop roads. The most prominent feature at the front of the site, apart from the 600-foot expanse of lawn between the building complex and the road, was a ramped entrance drive and a series of platforms that formed a bridge to the visitor's lobby (*Progressive Architecture* 1959). Everything was simply placed where it should be, and there was very little contrivance, except, perhaps, for the comparatively elaborate main entry. Generally the building complex exuded an air of informality and modernity.

Although as directly functional in their spatial organization, several other examples of this type were far more controlled and formal in their architectural presentation. The home office for General Mills of the late 1950s, for instance, by Skidmore, Owings and Merrill with Edmund Phelps as the landscape architect, consisted of a compact, highly functional layout of two buildings linked by a short, double-level, glazed skyway. One building housed the cafeteria and the executive offices and the other the main office. The architecture was precise and uniform, expressing in an elegant pattern the structural frame and curtain-wall mullions. There were no references anywhere to the specific activities that lay behind this fenestration (Hunt 1961).

Another example that was as disciplined and predetermined in its overall form was the proposal for the Liberty Life Insurance Building in Greenville, South Carolina, by Carson and Lundin, dating from the 1950s. The overall cruciform plan was inflected, where necessary, from its strict geometry. Furthermore the practice of expressing certain peculiar functional forms occured in several places, most noticeably at the rear of the project, where a terrace ramped down into the garden around a cafeteria.

In all these formal examples of functional office layouts, a design preoccupation with the office planning module was evident. Common during the postwar era, these modules were the loci around which all lighting, structure, and wall partitions were planned. In theory and sometimes in practice, they were to provide both flexibility and easy variation in spatial accommodations (Manasseh and Cunliffe 1962). The effect on the shape of office buildings was to regularize their appearance. In effect, functional layouts that might have emerged from a direct although rather ad hoc reckoning with office functions now became subordinated to abstract rationalizing frameworks. And an exuberant and occasionally unruly architecture of circumstance and expediency gave way to a more disciplined, coolly rational approach. In addition, the earlier neutral field of site conditions, well matched to the informal layouts, became replaced by much more deliberate landscape designs that sought to complement the office buildings.

Campus Plans

The other logical outgrowth of the factory office complex was a separation of office functions and their placement into a campus like setting. Expansion and adaption over time could be handled by building new

Figure 102   Functional layout of a freestanding suburban office complex: Youngstown Steel and Tube Company, Ohio, Gilbert P. Schafer, 1957

facilities and linking them to existing structures. A master plan that incorporated access routes, building sites, and landscape design gave overall coherence to the complex. The welfare of workers could also be enhanced through the relaxed atmosphere of a bucolic environment reminiscent of many universities throughout the United States.

Certainly one of the most extensive and prominent early office complexes with a campus layout was the General Motors Technical Center near Detroit, Michigan (figures 100 and 103). Designed by Eero Saarinen in association with Smith, Hinchman and Grylls, the complex was built on flat farmland between 1949 and 1955. The site was immense, 3,000 feet in length. Both the internal streets and the layout of specific buildings conformed to a simple rectilinear plan, with a large rectangular artificial lake at the center, measuring some 1,780 feet in length. Moving clockwise around the lake from the west, the complex encompassed the Research Section with its offices, the Service Section and power-generating facilities, the Process Development Section, a freestanding restaurant, the Engineering Section and engine-testing center, finally ending on the other side of the lake with the Styling Section and an auditorium under a dome (Manasseh and Cunliffe 1962, and Joedicke 1962). The site works were carefully organized by Thomas Church, the landscape architect, in a manner that reinforced the rectilinear layout of the complex and the precise, rectangular forms of its architecture. The extensive rows of trees, together with the well-defined rectangular parking lots and grassy open spaces, formed an almost exact complement to the architecture in both scale and defined volume. The overriding geometry of the entire complex was unequivocally modern, suggesting patterns from a Mondrian canvas.

In an early scheme for the Technical Center designed before his death in 1948, Eero Saarinen placed a pristine glass and steel administration center in the lake itself. There was also an even greater merger between buildings and vegetative elements of the landscape in this plan (Holleman and Gallagher 1978). As built, all buildings architecturally conformed to a machine-finished aesthetic of low rectangular objects with standardized steel frames, glass or vitreous-enamel curtain walls, and infill panels of richly colored glazed bricks. Of the massive yet finely wrought complex, one commentator observed, "The scale of the whole complex is designed for the car traveller . . . the technical center site module is a speedometer!" (Manasseh and Cunliffe 1962, p. 131).

A recent office, complex with a campus layout that has certain strong similarities to as well as significant differences from, the General Motors Technical Center is Kevin Roche's Conoco Inc. headquarters, located beside a suburban freeway 17 miles west of downtown Houston. Built between 1979 and 1984, Conoco is a massive complex at 1.2 million square feet of office space for some 2,500 to 3,000 employees (Knight 1986). Like the General Motors Center, the underlying spatial organization of the Conoco Headquarters is a rectilinear grid. There are lines of general symmetry, only this time they are axial and revolve around a bridgelike central spine that links parking lots together from the outer extremities of the site instead of around a monumental artificial lake (figure 104). There is a lake at Conoco, although its

156

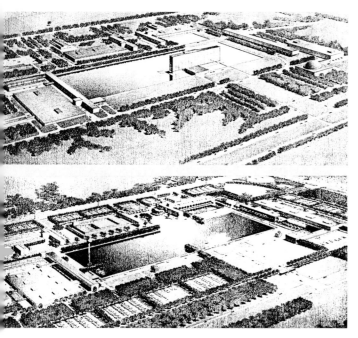

Figure 103   Two proposals for the General Motors Technical Center near Detroit, Michigan, 1947–1955: at the top, an original layout by Eero Saarinen: below, the complex as developed in association with Smith, Hinchman and Grylls. Copyright Wayne State University Press.

form is irregular and naturalistic, offering a counterpoint to the long rectilinear forms of the buildings. The overall grid pattern of the building complex "dematerializes," to use Roche's terms, evolving into a collection of sixteen separate but linked office buildings (Knight 1986, p. 57). Canopies are provided for the 2,000-vehicle parking lots, and an extensive system of arcades and trellises provides a climatically appropriate and pleasant system of walkways along the perimeter and between the buildings. One of the central ideas for the complex was, in Roche's words," a campus that will have the same felicitous effect on the occupants as if they were working in a

well-planned university campus" (Dal Co 1985, p. 58). This collegiate institutional theme was used, more traditionally, by Kallmann, McKinnell and Wood, in collaboration with Morgan Wheelock as landscape architects, in their design of the Becton Dickinson Headquarters in New Jersey of 1987–88 (Davey 1988).

A different model of the corporate campus appears in the Arco Research and Development Center at Newton Square, Pennsylvania, about 20 miles west of Philadelphia (Brenner 1982). Designed and built between 1978 and 1981, the landscape architecture of Hanna/Olin and the architecture of Davis Brody and Llewelyn-Davies evokes the metaphor of an English country estate (see figure 113). Indeed the arrangement of buildings within the meadowed and sylvan setting closely parallels the model of the country estate, although with a certain functional reversal. The expansive meadow that occupies a substantial portion of the 312-acre site is ringed by a road and small buildings formerly belonging to a boarding school and now in various forms of reuse. The primary research and engineering facility is located nearby, along one side of the site, where, to continue the analogy, large barns and other farm buildings might have been situated. Both the buildings and the landscape thus form layers that provide a backdrop to the prominent meadow. An orchard at the front entry to the complex continues a strong pastoral image (Olin 1988). Skillful use of hedgerows mediates between the research facility and the broader natural setting beyond. The resulting arrangement of buildings and landscape serves simultaneously to restrain any overwhelming impact from the architecture of such a large facility and to convey a dignified sense of corporate identity. A certain cultural continuity has thus been established between today's corporate estates and those of the landed aristocracy of the eighteenth century (Olin 1988).

These three examples show the evolution of the corporate campus from functional yet abstract modern compositional principles to a narrative form that draws on traditional historical models. The symbolic enterprise of providing a strong corporate image has not changed, however, although it is certainly more self-conscious in this type than in either of the earlier types. Nor has the corporate desire to provide a congenial workplace. A need has simply been reached to move beyond the corporations themselves in search of a broader legitimizing framework for their identity. The 1950s was a time of considerable public confidence in business, especially the technical progress it offered. A straightforward modern portrayal of the corporate world could thus be presented. Today

Figure 104   Systematic layout and symmetry in the campus of a corporate headquarters: Conoco Inc. Headquarters, Houston, by Kevin Roche John Dinkeloo and Associates, 1979–1984

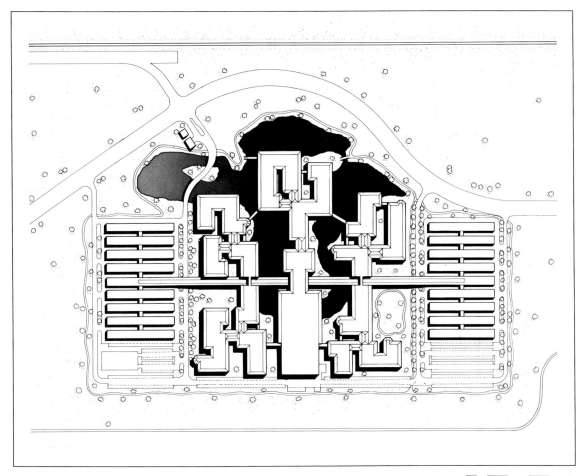

FEET 0   100   500

that progress is often severely questioned, requiring qualification and placement within a broader cultural matrix.

Recently another type of campus plan has emerged for the corporate estate; this time the reference is less institutional and more in the direction of a traditional small town center (Iovine 1987). An example is Princeton Forrestal Village by the Toombs Development Company, where two and three-story mixed-use buildings are grouped around a walking street environment, with parking on the periphery. Another example with a similar orientation is the Carnegie Center project, also in Princeton, New Jersey, by Hugh Stubbins Associates and Hanna/Olin, Ltd. With a first phase completed in 1985, the center's master plan calls for a 250-acre office park with about 2.4 million square feet of rentable space. The main organizing feature of the plan is a central greenway in the form of a suburban version of an urban park (Olin 1988). Another recent mixed-use example, this one with a regional theme, is the sprawling Solana Westlake–Southlake complex (1984–1989) near Fort Worth, Texas, by Mitchell Guirgola, Ricardo Legorreta, and the landscape architects Peter Walker and Martha Schwartz (Barna 1989).

Court Buildings

During the early 1950s, centralized symmetrical arrangements of office space around open courtyards began to emerge in what was to become a commonly used spatial organization for the suburban offices building. Formally more self-conscious than the straightforward functional office layout, the court building provided a compact yet simple architectural solution for large areas of clerical and managerial workspace. Courtyards were introduced, interrupting large office floor plates in order to admit natural light into the building and to offer outside views. Such arrangements generally provided flexibility for rearranging offices, clarity in overall office layout, and an economy derived from repetitive use of planning modules (Hunt 1961, Joedicke 1962, Hohl 1968). The relationships of building to site varied from a relatively stark contrast between pristine, machinelike objects in bucolic naturalistic settings to objects in a cultivated landscape. In all cases the buildings usually had a strong figural presence. Invariably two different outdoor realms were created: one inside within the courtyards and the other outside in the garden- or parklike setting. Rarely were the landscape qualities of each the same.

A fine early example of the court building type, built between 1954 and 1957, is the Connecticut General Life Insurance Company in Bloomfield, Connecticut, by Skidmore, Owings and Merrill, with landscape architecture by Isamu Noguchi. The client's desire for large, undivided office halls with smaller rooms for senior executives (Joedicke 1962) led the architects to a general organization of three buildings: a small executive office building, a large clerical block, and a separate cafeteria pavilion, all interconnected in a roughly diagonal composition, with parking split into two separate lots on each flank of the large clerical block (figure 105). According to the architects, the complex was to have an "air of security and permanence" and provide "an attractive enough environment to draw staff to its out-of-town location" (Manasseh and Cunliffe 1982, p. 182).

The clerical block took the form of a low three-story building, hugging the site, with external dimensions of 470 feet by 330 feet. Four enclosed yet open-air courtyards were placed symmetrically within the rectangular office plan in order to provide views and natural light. Each court was exquisitely landscaped by Isamu Noguchi with a simple palette of materials and in an abstract modern formal design. A similar approach was taken to the plinth separating the lake side of the building from the cafeteria (Joedicke 1962). Beyond the building complex, the overall setting had an informal pastoral quality of grasslands and trees. A large artificial lake created on the expansive south side of the site offered a splendid middle-ground focus to views from the offices and cafeteria. Noguchi's sculpture *Family Group* was placed in the lake (Manasseh and Cunliffe 1962).

A basic example of the court building is the Reynolds Metal Company regional sales headquarters in Neutland, just outside of Detroit. Completed in 1959, the symmetrical, rectangular three-story building was designed by Minoru Yamasaki and Associates (Hunt 1961, Manasseh and Cunliffe 1962). The top two floors of the building were partially raised on steel columns, forming a perimeter colonnade at the ground floor level. The upper floors were also covered with a light metal screen, sufficiently transparent to reveal the structural bays and fenestration behind. The 4½-acre site, near the Northland Shopping Center, was formally landscaped in the front of the building with clipped hedges and geometric arrangements of trees. Elsewhere Eichstedt's landscape design incorporated an informal planting of trees on a carpet of grass (Manasseh and Cunliffe 1962).

Figure 105   An early example of the court building type in a rural setting: Connecticut General Life Insurance Company, Bloomfield, Connecticut, by Skidmore, Owings and Merrill, 1954–1957

A larger and starker version of the court building, by Skidmore, Owings and Merrill, is to be found in the offices for 2,200 employees of the American Can Company in Greenwich, Connecticut (see figure 100), completed in 1970. The site for the building consisted of 175 acres of rocky, heavily wooded land that originally formed the grounds of a large house, now retained as guest quarters (*Architectural Review* 1971). Gordon Bunshaft's design took advantage of the site conditions by locating the building across the steeply sloping land and using the lower floors, within a ravine, for car parking (Krinsky 1988). The office building sits on top of this plinth of parking and service, rising to a height of three storys, all organized around a single well-landscaped courtyard (see figure 100). Like Connecticut General Life and General Mills, a smaller executive office suite was provided in a nearby separate building, preserving the presence of the corporate hierarchy. A repetitive and highly expressive concrete structure dominated the building's architecture and was placed in stark contrast with the immediacy of the sylvan surroundings. An artificial lake was also provided, dammed up at one end of the ravine and traversed by an internal loop road leading from the executive building to the main entrance (*Architectural Record* 1971, Krinsky 1988).

The 1978 Texaco headquarters building by Skidmore, Owings and Merrill takes the idea of the singular court building and expands its size and scale to monumental proportions (figure 109). Located on a secluded 107-acre site on the suburban fringes of New York City, this three-story, 1.2-million square foot complex, with a prominent, sweeping roadway, is in scale with the adjacent expressways (Bush-Brown 1983). The central location of a single building conserved the wooded landscape of the site, and the roof of the underground parking at the front of the building was landscaped as a grassy forecourt, complete with circular entrance driveway. Apart from the enormous scale of the building, one cannot help recalling the image of a large house with its front lawn. The open-air interior courtyards were terraced to provide enjoyable outdoor spaces for employees. Provision was also made around the site for a variety of other amenities, such as a pool and nature trails. Both enclosed and open office plans were provided.

A final variation of the court building type is the office complex organized around an enclosed atrium. Popular in many parts of the country with climates that are either too hot or too cold, the compact midrise suburban atrium office building has become com-

monplace—and much of the architecture mundane, designed as if by rote. One outstanding exception is Koetter, Kim and Associates' Codex Corporation headquarters in Canton, Massachusetts, constructed between 1983 and 1987 (see figure 111). The result of a limited architectural competition on a difficult site beside Boston's Route 128, Koetter and Kim's design formed a sophisticated commentary on urban offices and rural dwellings. First and foremost, the complex was conceptualized as a country villa in the manner of the great Roman and Renaissance examples, where numerous civil, domestic, and agricultural functions were regularly incorporated within a single ensemble of buildings (Anderson 1987, Koetter 1987). Literally engaging a horse training course and stables for pacers, the corporate headquarters easily takes on this role (illustrated in figure 111). Functions within the overall plan are allowed to be expressive, breaking down the appearance of the overall mass of a relatively large building, again coinciding well with the model of the country villa. By avoiding either an arcadian or high-tech image, the architecture for Codex is reminiscent of the New England mill, another obvious architectural antecedent for the project. The exterior cladding is a regional red brick with individually framed windows and gray slate roofs (Anderson 1987, Johnson 1988).

On the urbane side of the design commentary, the three floors of offices are organized primarily around a network of urban streets that rise up the full height of the building and are skylit from above. A central feature of the complex is a large winter garden rendered as a town park (figure 106). Located at the building's entrance, the enclosed garden rises above the surrounding offices and also acts as an integral part of the building's environmental control system. With numerous roof terraces and indoor, as well as outdoor, gardens, Hanna/Olin's landscape architecture provides inventive variety and yet reinforces the overall architectural themes of the building complex. Particularly noteworthy are the sunken, bermed, and heavily landscaped parking garages that succeed in avoiding the usual visual intrusion, as well as shielding the remainder of the project from the adjacent expressway.

Systems Complexes

Systems complexes date from the mid- to late 1960s and coincide with a strong international architectural interest in processes of spatial growth and change based on biological and electronic analogies. Buildings such as Candilis Josic and Wood's Berlin Free University and their proposal for Böchum, both dating from the mid-1960s, were highly influential. So were Hertzberger's office building in Apeldoorn of 1968 and John Andrew's Scarborough College in Canada at about the same time (Frampton 1980). Application of these ideas to the corporate office environment was probably inevitable given the central design problem of providing for expansion and modification.

As the building type evolved, systems complexes not only expressed architecturally inherent ideas about circulation patterns, activity areas, and expansion but also adopted a kind of mechanically organic language to symbolize these ideas. Thus building complexes in the guise of spines, stems, networks, and grids were superimposed on the land-

scape, sometimes even subordinating adjacent areas to the same architectural rhetoric. One advantage was that building modules within the overall system design, at least theoretically, could assume local functional peculiarities without the need for subordination under a single general planning framework.

A clear example of the type is the E. R. Squibb and Sons, Inc. World Headquarters in Lawrenceville, New Jersey, by Hellmuth, Obata and Kassabaum, with Dan Kiley as the landscape architect. Initially designed in 1969 and completed in 1972, the original complex, as depicted in figure 100, consisted of seven three-story buildings linked by a glassed-in pedestrian spine (Schmertz 1975). Each building was made up of one or more 90-foot square modules, comprising offices, laboratories, a library, or a dining hall. The parking arrangement allowed lateral expansion of the complex along the central pedestrian spine or by the addition of modules to the existing stemlike building structures (see figure 100). A ring road skirting the complex and two parallel bands of parking lots following the building on both flanks provided convenient access.

The architecture of the complex clearly expressed the modules and service cores that constituted each building (Joedicke 1975). A separation of functions, however, beyond categories of primary space and circulation was not pursued, thereby reinforcing the abstract systematic qualities of the overall formal organization. Today the facility has an articulated horizontal appearance, stretching out across the site. The landscape design of grassy berms, gently rolling topography, and clumps of trees complements the architecture and provides a rural atmosphere. A

large lake, situated between the entrance and the building complex, also gives the project an imposing yet informal quality.

Higher degrees of abstraction, as well as a clear superimposition of buildings on the landscape, were achieved by Kevin Roche John Dinkeloo and Associates in their design for the College Life Insurance Company of America Headquarters, completed between 1967 and 1971. Located just outside Indianapolis, the site is immediately adjacent to the junction of a major arterial road with a freeway. In plan, a systematic gridwork of nine separate buildings was placed on a trapezoidal platform, jutting out into an artificial lake (see figure 114). Three other adjoining trapezoidal platforms formed separate parking lots, with service roads and hedgerows in between. The buildings, of which only three were completed, were connected by both tunnels and bridges to ensure convenient horizontal access. Square office floor plates, roughly 120 feet on a side at the base, were placed against L-shaped walls, in plan, containing service cores, mechanical shafts, elevators, and stairs. Each additional floor of the eleven-story buildings became smaller, resulting in a pyramidal shape on three corners (Futugawa 1974, Dal Co 1985).

The pure abstract forms of the architecture were reinforced by the powerful planes of vertical concrete walls, as well as, elsewhere, by a sheer cladding of steel and glass. The landscape within the confines of each trapezoidal platform conformed precisely to its

geometry and to the grid of the building complex. The entire trapezoidal figure of the building footprint and the adjacent parking lots thus appears to have been superimposed on an otherwise naturalistic landscape. This gesture is perhaps most clearly visible along the sharp chamfered edges where the platform meets the lake. Here the geometry is uncompromising, as if impressed on the site from above. Overall there is a scaleless, surreal quality to the composition that transcends the mere investigation of a gridded network.

Another project by Kevin Roche Dinkeloo and Associates explored a different systematic form of office layout: a simple linear model of development. In their Richardson-Vicks, Inc. Headquarters, in Wilton, Connecticut, built from 1970 through 1974, vehicular movement and car parking became a central idea, effectively producing a "highway building" (Dal Co 1985). Essentially parking was placed inside the building on both the lower level and on the roof. Two floors of offices, for some 700 employees, were literally sandwiched in between, distributed on either side of a top-lit gallery, with views directly into adjacent woods. The environmental impact of the building was thus drastically minimized through a reduced footprint and support of the entire structure on columns above the ground (see figure 112). Three blocks of offices, each subdivided into five broad bays, were linked together under the rooftop parking lot, offering the possibility of simple linear expansion (Nakamura 1987).

The absence of a clear exterior image to the building and a strong focus on the surrounding site suggest a piece of infrastructure. Roche took up both

Figure 106   Enclosed atrium and winter garden: Codex World Headquarters, Canton, Massachusetts, by Koetter, Kim and Associates, 1983–1987

themes on a grander scale in the Union Carbide Corporation World Headquarters (1976–1982) (figure 107). Here an almost literal road building was created, which, in Roche's words, was like "a terminal to the highway" (Dal Co 1985, p. 64).

Incorporating a quarter-mile-long central block of structured parking for 2,850 automobiles with ramps at either end, the office complex was arranged in fifteen Y-shaped pods distributed along the perimeter. Each pod, in turn, embraced a fractal-like geometry of offices 13 feet, 5 inches square. At 1.3 million square feet, the complex is large, although it also occupies only a small percentage of its site. Together with Richardson-Vicks, Cummins Engine, and several other infrastructural projects, Union Carbide represents an almost complete evolution of the "systems complex" to a point where the systems relations themselves virtually become the building.

Hierarchical Configurations

A recently emerging type represents a strong hierarchical arrangement of spaces and building elements, usually in a symmetrical overall composition. Unlike the singular, closed form of the court building, or the multifaceted, open, and yet indeterminate form of the systems complexes, these offices are compositionally coherent, almost in a classical mode. Typically major and minor spaces are carefully organized and arranged in a supraordinate and subordinate manner. Sometimes, as at General Foods in Rye, New York, the architectural expression is classical in a distinctly historicist sense.

Invariably the surrounding landscape of the hierarchical office configurations is closely engaged with the buildings and organized by compositional principles that appear to emanate from within the buildings themselves. There is no direct superimposition or juxtaposition of buildings on the landscape. In this regard, the hierarchical configurations are similar to the earlier campus plans. If anything, there seems to be a relaxed acceptance of the larger visual frame of the landscape setting.

A clear example of the building type is the new General Foods Corporation Headquarters (1977–1982) in Rye, New York, by Kevin Roche John Dinkeloo and Associates. With the presence of a neo-Palladian villa, the formal symmetry of the building is both rigorous and grand (Miller 1980). At the center is a huge rotunda, entrance portico, and stairway that dominate the entire composition (figure 108). Within the rotunda, not unexpectedly, are primary public spaces, including a winter garden and a cafeteria. The wings of office space, flanking the rotunda equally on each side, are colonnaded, reinforcing the classical references of the building (Nakamura 1987). Entrance by car is made ceremoniously on a bridge across the lake and through the main portico. The lower three floors are dedicated to parking, forming a strong base to the building. The construction is faced with white aluminum shingles and ribbons of mirrored windows. Together with the deep colonnades, the resulting pattern tends to reduce the scale of the project, emphasizing its domestic origins (Miller 1980). The entire facility occupies a 54-acre site, near a major metropolitan highway, and consists of eight floors. The overall area is in excess of 1 million square feet, the employee population around 1,600. Other nonoffice facilities are also provided, such as shops and recreation areas (Miller 1980, Dal Co 1985).

The Pitney Bowes World Headquarters in Stamford, Connecticut, shares a number of organizational attributes with General Foods. Built between 1981 and 1987, the complex is largely symmetrical on two sides, with wings emanating from a prominent corner, near the entrance, around which were concentrated the public functions (see figure 118). In contrast to General Foods, however, the underlying model was of a public institutional building rather than a grand villa (Sachner 1988). The street front makes every attempt to enrich the public domain, with a 30-foot-high colonnade running the full length of the municipal roadway. The building literally attempts to take its place alongside others in the neighborhood. The overall site design, a collaborative effort between Henry Cobb of I. M. Pei and Partners and the landscape architects Hanna/Olin, used this urban strategy to further advantage by embracing the heavily wooded knoll of adjacent Kosciusko Park. The offices on the resulting 800-foot perimeter have

Figure 107   The merger of infrastructure and building: Union Carbide Corporation World Headquarters, Danbury, Connecticut, by Kevin Roche John Dinkeloo and Associates, 1976–1982

splendid views across the park toward Long Island Sound. A 1,000-car garage was recessed off to one side, away from the park, adding to the urban presence of the complex. By contrast, on the park side, two well-sculptured terraces lend a gardenlike amenity to the project (Olin 1988, Sachner 1988).

A hierarchical configuration need not be quite so figural, however, in either its civic or grand domestic references. The IBM World Trade Americas–Far East Corporation Headquarters (1975), by Edward Larabee Barnes Associates, is also highly symmetrical in its overall organization, with two identical wings flanking a central entrance (Global Architecture 1981). Nevertheless, the architecture is unabashedly abstract, minimal, and illusive, especially in the way in which it accentuates the surrounding landscape of a beautifully wooded site (Pile 1976).

Although it is comparatively modest in size at 380,000 square feet, a concerted effort was made to minimize disruption to the former Rockefeller family estate by reducing potentially long elevations of the complex, within a strong hierarchical plan (see figure 100). Other site work reflected the composed, symmetrical disposition of the facility. The roadway entrance, for instance, was placed on axis with the building's main space, thus establishing a biaxial symmetry with adjacent parking lots and landscaped areas. Placement of the building also divided the site in the other direction, roughly along its length. On the parking lot side, a geometric order was extended outward from the building. On the other side, the emergence of such an order was quickly suppressed by the gently sloping landscape of grassy areas, informal clumps of trees, and a pond. This immediate transi-

tion was reinforced by a precise narrow moat running the full length of the building and serving as a reflecting pool. The shape of this water body was immediately allowed to assume the naturalistic character of a small brook running on into the nearby pond (see figure 100). As one commentator aptly observed, "The project seems to suggest a delicate balance between the pride and grandeur of the corporate identity . . . and another, newer role for the corporation as . . . steward of things and places" (Pile 1976, p. 91).

DESIGN THEMES AND TRENDS

There are several other ways, in addition to a general morphological analysis, of discussing suburban corporate office complexes. Essentially they revolve around specific design issues, such as the way in which automobiles are accommodated within the complex, and around broader design themes, such as the symbolic expression of corporate identity. Among these design issues and themes, there are also discernible trends.

Accommodation of Automobiles

The relatively dispersed and sometimes remote location of many suburban office complexes has meant almost total dependence on the automobile as a means of getting to work. Consequently a fundamental part of the design of these complexes was the organization of internal roadways and parking areas, as well as access to buildings and offices. Generally a longitudinal trend can be clearly discerned, begin-

Figure 108   Corporate Headquarters as Neo-Palladian
villa in a suburban setting: General Foods Corporation
headquarters, Rye, New York, by Kevin Roche John
Dinkeloo and Associates, 1977–1982

ning with the straightforward placement of parking
lots beside office buildings and culminating with recent attempts to integrate and express vehicular
movement fully.

Almost without exception, early factory offices,
functional layouts, and campus plans provided on-
site, separate, grade-level parking lots immediately
adjacent to office buildings. Upon arrival employees
and visitors parked their cars in designated lots and
walked to nearby building entrances. Most lots were
landscaped with some tree cover and hedgerows, primarily as a visual screen from adjacent buildings and

public areas. Sometimes parking lots were removed
to less visible site locations—for instance at the
Youngstown Steel and Tube complex, where the major parking lot was located in the rear (see figure 102).

At these complexes, entry and egress, as well as
internal circulation, generally conformed to two sequences. First, visitors and some executive employees would arrive at a site by car through a well-
marked main entrance. They would then usually
move past this entrance into a nearby parking lot. The
rest of the trip would be made on foot, often under the
cover of an open breezeway. Even at relatively unas-

suming complexes, like Youngstown Steel and Tube, considerable attention was paid to this arrival sequence. There the roadway was ramped up around the expansive front lawn, providing entry to the building at its middle level.

The second sequence was for employees and may or may not have involved a prominent entrance. Often ring roads provided internal movement around a site and direct entrance to designated parking lots. In almost all cases, parking was subdivided into separate lots to reduce its visual impact and provide convenient access to various parts of large complexes.

In a further stage of development parking lots were structured and accommodated directly within building precincts. Often this was a method of reducing the impact of office development on the environmental amenity of a site. On other occasions it was dictated by the relative size of a site and the sheer magnitude of the parking requirements. At American Can, parking was structured directly below the offices, within the same building shell, in order to preserve the site's natural beauty. At Pitney Bowes, there was a similar motivation to structure the parking and also a space constraint.

Subsequent development toward an expressive integration of the movement system relied on further distinctions. At root, the difference between straightforward accommodation of parking within a building and true integration was largely a matter of design resolution and focus. A further distinction between integration and expressive integration extended this focus by requiring that vehicular movement and parking be a central and overt aspect of the architecture.

Movement and parking were clearly integrated within the building complex, for example, at the Texaco New York headquarters (figure 109) and at General Foods in Rye, New York (see figure 108). In both, these functions formed lower-level, or underground, bases for their respective buildings, and in both they were directly integrated within the internal movement system of the offices. At Texaco the grassed-over parking plinth created a giant forecourt of considerable architectural impact. At General Foods the horizontal base formed by the parking was completely consistent with and indeed required by the building's neo-Palladian concept. Finally, the expressively integrated movement system, or true highway building, emerged at Roche's Richardson-Vicks complex and was elaborated on at Union Carbide (figure 110).

Generally movement within nonhierarchical or open forms of spatial organization, like functional layouts, systems complexes, and campus plans, was less ritualistic and more expedient than for the other types. Clear exceptions were the special entry sequences for visitors. Monumentality in the entrance to office complexes usually followed the same kind of distinction among the types. Certainly the idea of control went with that of ritual. It can be argued, however, that the large-scale entrance to Union Carbide was merely an extension of the roadway and not overtly monumental (see figures 107 and 110). Nevertheless, since the 1950s there has been an increase in the consistent architectural articulation of movement within suburban corporate office complexes.

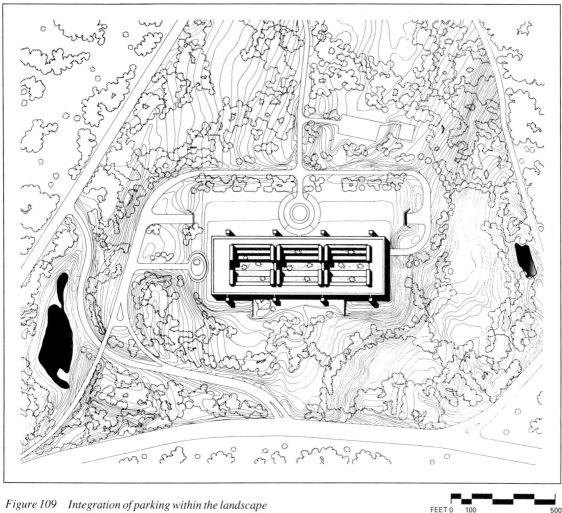

Figure 109   Integration of parking within the landscape of a building complex: Texaco Headquarters, Harrison, New York, by Skidmore, Owings and Merrill, 1978

FEET 0   100   500

Functional Integration

From the beginning, suburban offices have included other functions besides employee workspaces. An early sense of isolation and a need to provide attractive working environments for employees usually required inclusion of cafeteria and dining facilities, in addition to well-furnished common areas. Almost at once the well-landscaped site environs became a place for employee leisure-time activity. Without ready access to nearby commercial and service facilities typical of those found in a town, corporations

Figure 110   Complete integration of parking within a highway building: Union Carbide Corporation World Headquarters

were required to provide total working-day environments for their employees.

Today many corporate estates include an extensive range of functions and spaces to serve the needs of their employees: recreation and fitness centers, several restaurants offering a range of service, library, lounge, and so-called quiet areas, and jogging or bridle trails in the woods. The Codex headquarters provides all of these accommodations and is certainly not alone in this regard (Anderson 1987) (figure 111).

More and more, the builders of corporate estates appear to have conceptualized the working environment as something like a country club. Other much-needed facilities, like day care centers, are provided far less often.

Inclusion of bona fide civic functions has also figured in the development agendas of corporate estates. Extensive theater and display facilities, required periodically for business events, are routinely turned over to the public. Pitney Bowes, for example, has a gallery space used for the display of work by local artists, and Codex makes its large auditorium and lobby-exhibition area available to the township of Canton. For some corporate estates sheer isolation makes such arrangements impractical. Nevertheless, corporations appear generally to perceive that sharing and making facilities available to the public is either part of being a good neighbor or a price to be paid for their presence in a community.

Another aspect of the office environment that has undergone revision is the hierarchical spatial organization of workspace according to a worker's position on the corporate ladder. Early complexes, such as General Mills and Connecticut General Life, rather emphatically embodied the corporate management hierarchy. Consequently an executive suite was provided as a separate single building, linked with the main office complex. This practice has never entirely vanished, even within the most revisionist corporate schemes, but several efforts have been made to conceptualize the office environment in a functional non-hierarchical manner or from a social egalitarian viewpoint. The offices for Union Carbide might be the most extreme example. Each is dimensionally exactly the same—13 feet, 5 inches square—and all are arranged on the outside perimeter of the building,

Figure 111   Corporate office as country club: Codex World Headquarters

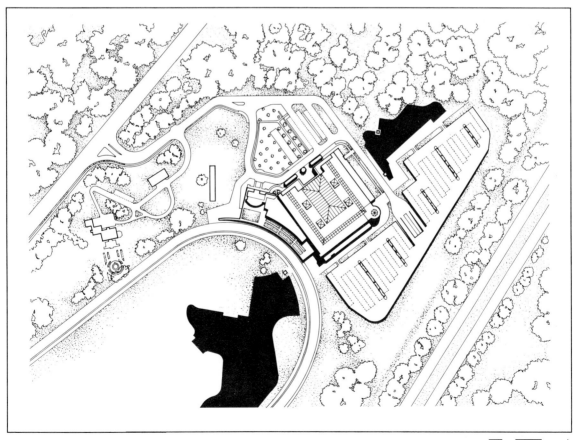

FEET 0   100   300

Figure 112   Juxtaposition and conservation while building in a naturalistic setting: Richardson-Vicks Inc. Headquarters, Wilton, Connecticut, by Kevin Roche John Dinkeloo and Associates, 1970–1974

with similar views of the surrounding woodlands (see figure 119). This spatial democracy is taken further by allowing employees to choose their own office furnishings, according to their own tastes, from among an extensive array of equally priced alternatives (Dal Co 1985). Other complexes also have a democratic air about them. At Texaco, for instance, the ample external terraces lining the exterior courtyards of the building are provided almost uniformly for use by employees. Furthermore, the common practice of providing private offices, for use on demand, adjacent to an open office landscape, is another way of functionally rather than hierarchically organizing the work environment.

Building and Landscape

At least four kinds of relationships are encountered between corporate office buildings and their landscapes. First is the building placed in a naturalistic setting where contrivance beyond the existing landscape conditions is kept to a minimum. Buildings and their environs are thus held in a certain tension, as illustrated in figure 112. The buildings appear as precise, machinelike artifacts, and their settings remain largely uncultivated and natural. The generic operational aspect of this relationship is clearly one of juxtaposition, if not superimposition. It is well illustrated by examples like Richardson-Vicks and American Can. The case of Union Carbide is only slightly more ambiguous, given the strong highway motif.

A second kind of relationship places buildings in a garden setting. Usually this involves considerable contrivance, and typically the chosen genre has been

from the English landscape tradition. The Arco complex, depicted in figure 113, with Hanna/Olin's skillful manipulation of existing site features, is a clear example. Meadows, wooded areas, hedgerows, and an orchard enhance the rolling countryside and clearly establish a pastoral image for the laboratories and offices. Landscapes at both the Squibb and Connecticut General Life headquarters are also pastoral in overall effect but with a clearer, open, fieldlike orientation (see figures 100 and 105). Generally a complementarity exists between buildings and the surrounding landscape, just as they do in a rural setting. The operational aspect of the relationship concerns placement and location rather than the tension produced by juxtaposition or superimposition. Often, in fact, attempts were made to mediate contrasts between buildings and the remainder of the landscape, again as we saw at Arco, with rural devices such as hedgerows and selective clearing.

Landscapes made in the manner of buildings, and vice versa, is a third kind of relationship. At the General Motors Technical Center, for instance, there was considerable reciprocity between the landscape architecture of Thomas Church and the building architecture of Saarinen and his associates. Especially in plan there appeared to be little difference in emphasis and mass between the clear rectilinear forms of buildings and the precise geometric arrangement of lawn areas and tree rows. Roche and Dinkeloo's College Life complex is another example, although here the buildings were concentrated on one quadrant of the site (figure 114). Nevertheless, the underlying geometry of both the offices and other components of the landscape is identical, conforming to a square trapezoid. The Johns Manville Complex outside Denver, by The Architects Collaborative, repeats this general approach. The building hovers above an elliptical sweep of parking in such a manner that the geometries of each facility become closely intertwined. At both corporate complexes, however, a clear tripartite arrangement is introduced by the presence of a larger setting: in the case of College Life an extensive pastoral landscape, and at Johns Manville a dramatic rocky hillside. Once again the generic operational features of the building-landscape relation-

Figure 113   The pastoral image of corporate building: Arco Research and Development Center, Newton Square, Pennsylvania, by Davis Brody, Llewelyn-Davies and Hanna/Olin, 1978–1981

ship, beyond the facilities themselves, are juxtaposition and superimposition.

Finally, the general landscape of an office complex can be rendered as a neutral field, offering only distance to the vantage points of passers-by and office occupants alike (figure 115). Overwhelmingly, the settings of many early factory offices and functional layouts had this quality. At both Youngstown Steel and at Searle, of the examples already described, relatively flat and featureless grassy areas surrounded the buildings. Other forms of landscape were kept to a minimum or to the perimeter of each site. The

building complexes were simply placed on the sites, and the tensions that might have arisen from this operation were completely ignored. Nevertheless, an abstract landscape just beyond such a neutral field can have an engaging effect. Gerald McCue's and Peter Walker's collaboration for the IBM complex at San Teresa, California, produced a surrealistic kaleidoscopic environment from abstract building planes and crisp, geometrically precise ground surfaces (Hoyt 1978, Walker 1989) (figure 116).

Among these four kinds of relationships between offices and landscapes, a trend is apparent. It started

Figure 114   Landscapes in the manner of buildings: College Life Insurance Company of America Headquarters, Indianapolis, Indiana, by Kevin Roche John Dinkeloo and Associates, 1967–1971

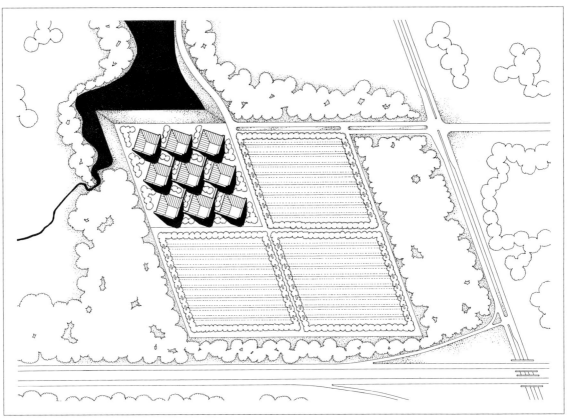

FEET 0   100   500

with the early placement of buildings in neutral fields and culminated with a strong contemporary reliance on buildings in naturalistic garden settings. Other alternatives, such as landscapes in the manner of accompanying buildings, or vice versa, were comparatively rare except in the category of campus plans.

Underlying this trend seems to be a rise in prominence of narrative forms of landscape design over those that are more strictly compositional or pictorial. Naturalistic garden settings have the advantage of quickly and unambiguously conveying stories about sites, replete with historical references and allusions to arcadian and pastoral ways of life. The stories surrounding formal gardens may be different but hardly less compelling or precise. They all quickly conjure up in the mind's eye a well-orchestrated web of images and illusions. Certainly an equation is well and truly struck between the corporate office environment and life on some earlier country estate. Abstract pictorial presentations are far more ambiguous and equivocable in the narrative power required to strike such an equation.

Identity and Symbolic Presentation

The matter of corporate identity, insofar as it can have a physical manifestation, appears to revolve around two central issues: the image of the company in the outside world and the esteem in which office workers hold their corporate employers. The first issue inherently pits the presentation of corporate power, wealth, and grandeur against the stewardship of natural resources, patronage of the arts, and institution-like contributions to civic circumstances. The second issue is concerned with overt presentation of the cor-

Figure 115   An office complex in a neutral field: Parker Pen, Jamesville, Wisconsin, by John J. Flad and Associates, 1954

porate managerial hierarchy in contrast to an egalitarian or democratic arrangement of the work environment. A response on one issue, however, does not necessarily foreshadow a similar response on the other. A corporation can appear financially successful and yet also seem to function as a nonauthoritarian employer.

Although the sheer size of most office complexes makes it difficult to dismiss allusions to corporate power completely, some are clearly more monumental than others, and in different ways. At the Texaco headquarters and even more literally at General Foods (figures 108 and 117), for example, the image of a huge villa or country mansion comes to mind. This domestic aspect to the allusion may well soften the corporate image, especially from the standpoint of a place to work, but it also clearly establishes each complex as a grand and special place. The use of

Figure 116   A surreal and kaleidoscopic environment: IBM Complex, San Teresa, California, by McCue Boone Tomsick and Peter Walker, 1977

strong historical references at both Codex and Conoco are to familiar environments and therefore serve to convey an air of familiarity and continuity. By contrast, the enormity and abstract character of the General Motors Technical Center, together with the equally if not more abstract formal quality of the College Life complex, exude a kind of technological, space-age, corporate competence.

On the side of the stewardship of natural resources, Arco and the IBM World Trade headquarters recede into their sites; the landscape and overall setting of both are the prevailing images being portrayed. A rural theme is pursued more vigorously at General Mills, Connecticut General Life, and Squibb, where office complexes of separate buildings merge with the surrounding farmland in the guise of modern country estates (see figures 100 and 105). Additionally, natural resource conservation is quite literally a theme at complexes like Richardson-Vicks and Union Carbide, where compact building forms and minimal ground contact preserve almost all of each site.

The merger of corporate identities with civic circumstances has already been discussed in some detail. The design of Pitney Bowes's Stamford headquarters (figure 118) expressly sought to convey an institutional image and programmatically incorporated civic functions. Similarly at Codex an arrangement for sharing facilities was made with the local municipal authority, and great care was taken in designing the complex to downplay an exclusive corporate image. The severe environmental constraints of the site were totally respected, and imagery from nineteenth-century rural mills substantially rectified the potential visual incongruity of the large complex against the backdrop of the Blue Hills Reservation. Much earlier projects, like the Searle laboratory complex, also clearly projected an institutional image by embracing the moderne architectural style of contemporary civic buildings.

In summary, although little apology was made for size, the manifestation of corporate wealth and power was usually partially disguised by the form of a villa, rural estate, or institution. Stewardship and responsibility toward the environment at large were projected by downplaying the presence of buildings in the landscape or by fostering an image of appropriate rural uses. Finally, direct contributions to civic life were provided largely by way of functional activities and the shared use of specific facilities.

Projection of an external corporate image also has ramifications for the presentation of the workplace to employees. Domestic allusions probably serve to downplay those impersonal, bureaucratic aspects of business life, and similarly an institutional presence and a civic involvement tend to blur some of the usual distinctions we often make between the public and private sectors of our lives. However, it is

Figure 117   Allusions of domesticity: General Foods Corporation Headquarters

Figure 118   A merger of corporate identity with civic circumstances: Pitney Bowes World headquarters, Stamford, Connecticut, by I.M. Pei and Partners with Hanna/Olin, 1981–1987. Copyright Stanley Jesudowich.

in the local presentation of the workplace, primarily through office layout and furnishing, that an internal image is most meaningfully established.

Here a distinction between two guiding policies is useful: offices and other spaces may be arranged functionally according to work needs, or the managerial style of a firm may be reflected in an office layout. Although neither policy reigns in the absence of the other, both dimensions are necessary to appreciate fully the arrangement of most workplaces.

The functional layout of office space is largely determined by physical parameters of work flow and communications. In locations where employees need to confer in groups, for instance, space is usually made available according to type of conference. Straightforward issues of privacy, as well as the ergonometric needs of a workplace, also clearly come into play. On the managerial side, the arrangement of offices and other workspaces may represent a corporate organizational hierarchy. Numerous references are made in everyday business to executives with corner offices and executive suites, as well as to the correspondence between corporate promotion and an increase in office size. Several of the corporate complexes under discussion, like General Mills and American Can, made strong hierarchical distinctions between company executives and the remainder of the work force. But such distinctions can be made more subtly or even almost entirely subordinated to a standardized view of office layout.

One issue that appears to be central to the physical arrangement of workplaces concerns control and employee self-determination. Characterizations of workplaces as democratic, egalitarian, or authoritarian are certainly used when speaking about office layout and architecture (figure 119). At Union Carbide, all offices are the same size and furnished by the occupant from a large range of choices (Dal Co 1985). An egalitarian attitude to space and considerable employee self-determination were clearly evident. The concept was also not without significant functional merit. By standardizing offices, the costs of accommodating newcomers and those promoted within the corporate hierarchy could be entirely avoided (Dal Co 1985). The egalitarian and democratic dimensions of underlying managerial philosophies, however, should not be necessarily comingled. Corporations may permit and even encourage democratic access to different kinds of accommodations without being in any way egalitarian.

SOCIETY AND THE CORPORATE IMAGE

A crucial aspect of the way in which corporations choose to present themselves publicly is the image and reputation they enjoy in society at large and the societal demands for them to act in accordance with prevailing ideas of public welfare. This role of the corporation in society has almost always been reflected in its architecture. From at least the post–Civil War period, when the office function rose in prominence, corporations have experienced periods of both public acceptance and public repudiation. This experience, in turn, has significantly affected the architectural expression and symbolic program of office buildings (Gibbs 1984). The modern era of this century is certainly not the only time at which business has been concerned with its public architectural image.

From the 1880s on, the controversy and criticism that surrounded business caused many corporations to revise their thinking about the scale and grandeur of their premises. The need for more office space inevitably meant increases in the sheer size of facilities. Moreover, size seemed to equate with effectiveness and success in business practice, a quality worthy of display. When they turned to the problem of architectural presentation, however, business leaders and their architects quickly strove to cloak this expression of power with a philanthropic, benevolent, and public-spirited image. Soon the idea of a business architecture "designed for the pleasure and edification of the observer" (Gibbs 1984, p. 93) emerged, together with the idea of businesses as solid institututions worthy of contemporary life. Dignity, grandeur, and the

Figure 119   Egalitarian disposition of office space:
Union Carbide Corporation world headquarters

City Beautiful were emphasized, with corporate office buildings often designed in the manner of Italianate civic monuments (Gibbs 1984, Scully 1988).

During the first decade of this century, criticism of business became rampant (Shannon 1969). At a time when the sociopolitical ideal was a unity of purpose over self-interest, the public remained largely unconvinced about business's philanthropy or claims to institutional status (Gibbs 1984). Interestingly, criticism directed at corporate architecture in the progressive era focused as much on the inner workings as on external appearance. Sullivan's moral tone, for example, directed against superfluous ornament, went as much to the internal integrity of a building as it did to its facade (Sullivan 1934).

In the early modern era, society placed considerable faith in technological progress and its inevitable benefits, and corporate architecture found it desirable to associate symbolically with this progressive impetus. To be overtly modern was to be forward looking, technically advanced, and organizationally efficient. The iconography of the moderne was quickly adopted, and since then the international style has almost become synonymous with all forms of business architecture.

Dwight D. Eisenhower's warning about the military-industrial complex and rising feeling against the anonymity of faceless corporations caused symbolic realignments in business architecture; technological monumentality and corporate grandeur were quickly disguised, or at least sufficiently equivocated, in order to offer alternative scenarios.

During this time, full advantage was taken of the expansiveness and natural amenity of many suburban office sites to introduce a landscape component more fully into the corporate image-making process. In turn, this strategy ultimately allowed different and more complex stories to be told about the role of corporations in the world, often through arcadian themes of social and environmental responsibility. Failing that, an aesthetic was certainly established, drawing on the inherent duality between the order of the built environment and the organic order of the surrounding landscape. In retrospect it was also an ensemble reminiscent of other bygone eras when we made great estates.

From its introduction at the end of last century, the automobile quickly won the hearts and minds of most Americans and dramatically changed metropolitan transportation. No longer were urban dwellers confined in their movements to the fixed routes and variable service of streetcars and trains. Now they could move almost literally at will through the metropolitan landscape. Wherever the roads went, so went the cars, and as the cars became more numerous and sophisticated, corresponding improvements occurred in the roads. Especially in suburban areas, it became difficult to imagine one without the other.

The relationship between the automobile and the road, however, was not always so direct or symbiotic. Private cars seem to have been produced and operated in increasing numbers in spite of poor roads (Flink 1970). In fact, it was only shortly after 1940 that 50 percent of America's roads had been improved with hard all-weather surfaces, up from a meager 6 percent in 1900. Meanwhile the automobile fleet had risen from a paltry 8,000 to well over 27 million vehicles during the same time period (Flink 1970, Rae 1971). Today the proportion of improved highway mileage stands close to 90 percent, and the automobile fleet has burgeoned to around 122 million vehicles, or slightly more than one car for every two people (Federal Highway Administration 1988). Overall, early automobile and roadway improvements appear to have followed a two-stage model of development. During the first stage there was a relative independence between cars and roadway improvements. Most roads were bad, but many cars operated with reliability. By contrast, during the second stage, as the number of vehicles and demands for good roads increased, the relationship between roadway improvements and automobile use approached the symbiotic qualities customarily presumed today (Flink 1970).

The rapid rise in popularity of the private automobile was due to several factors. First, vehicle operating costs plummeted from between 10 and 18 cents per mile traveled during the first decade of this century to slightly over 4 cents per mile during the 1930s (Owen 1949) as a result of declining costs in basic resources, such as gasoline, and dramatic improvements in vehicular durability and reliability. In 1925, for instance, the average private automobile traveled some 23 miles per service dollar, sharply increasing to 112 miles by 1945. Vastly improved rubber tires played a significant role in this performance, improving roughly threefold from 5,000 miles to 25,000 miles per tire over the same time period.

Overall average service life of an automobile increased from 22,000 miles in 1925 to around 81,000 by 1945 (Owen 1949).

A second factor in the automobile's popularity was its sheer affordability. Mass production techniques (figure 120) pioneered by Henry Ford before World War I were crucial to a decline in prices and then to a maintenance of those prices at relatively constant rates (Rae 1965). In the case of Ford's Model T, as the number increased the prices fell. Approximately 12,000 were produced in 1909 at a cost of $950 per vehicle. By 1916 production was over 577,000 vehicles at a unit cost of only $360 (DiBacco 1987). Overall, the wholesale price index for automobiles in 1940 was much the same as it had been two decades earlier in 1920 (Owen 1949). Vehicle production exploded, especially during the 1920s and the 1950s, both historical periods of reasonably stable prices and pent-up demand (Wilbur Smith and Associates 1961).

From the first appearance of the Duryea car in 1893 until the beginning of the postwar era, some 100 million cars were produced. During the boom period of the 1950s, another 100 million vehicles were produced—in the scant space of fifteen years (Rae 1965). The number of cars quickly grew disproportionately with respect to population, moving from a ratio of 1:13 in 1920 to 1:4.8 by 1940 to 1:2.3 in 1970, finally reaching less than two persons for every car by 1985 (Rae 1971, Federal Highway Administration 1988).

A third reason for the early rise to prominence of automobile transportation was the decline of streetcars. The period from roughly the 1880s to 1914 was

Figure 120   Automobile mass production brings a decline in price: Henry Ford's Assembly of Model T's, 1914

"the golden era of American electric tramways" (Foster 1981, p. 24). Between 1820 and 1920 trolley ridership grew about 700 percent, while the urban population rose by 150 percent. Nevertheless, the decline of trolley ridership was abrupt, increasing no further than the lines that were already in place by 1920 and capitulating almost entirely to automobiles by the 1930s (Ford 1981).

Several reasons lie behind the decline in the trolley industry. First, there was a gross lack of coordination among the various private lines that plied metropolitan areas. Consequently routes and schedules were inefficient. Second, most lines operated at a loss, concentrating their investment activities on land speculation. Third, partially as a consequence of these speculative activities, many trolley companies enjoyed unsavory public reputations, together with operating records of poor service. Finally, the automobile with its sense of independence, individuality, and privacy was a preferable form of transportation (Owen 1949, Foster 1981, Seeley 1987).

Behind the statistics and factual accounts of the automobile's rise to prominence in the United States was "a production achievement unparalleled in history . . . from which came drastic [economic and societal] transformations" (Rae 1965, p. 237). Of direct interest here are two major physical contributions to the American metropolitan landscape: the modern highway, particularly in the form of an expressway or freeway, and the street forms that serve the immediate transportation needs of local suburban subdevelopments. It is at these two scalar extremes, the one large and the other small, that we find the armatures around which the modern metropolis turns. The local scale serves the immediate transportation needs of various pieces of the metropolitan spatial mosaic, to return to an earlier description, whereas the regional highways hold them all together.

HIGHWAYS

Generally the development of highways in the United States during this century showed a shift in focus from rural, farm-to-market roads in the direction of interregional and interstate throughways. A corresponding shift in emphasis from rural roads to urban systems was also appreciable, especially as metropolitan areas expanded horizontally. Far from conforming to some instantaneous projection of the way the transportation system should be at some future time in history, highway development essentially followed an evolutionary process that kept pace with

various stages of public debate and governmental intervention (Miller 1950, Foster 1981, Seeley 1987). The process essentially started with the "good roads movement" around the turn of the century and the endorsement of state aid and federal government support for highway construction in 1903 and again in 1909 (Flink 1970). Apart from the amenity for recreation for groups such as the League of American Wheelmen (figure 121), it was proving prohibitively costly to haul goods any appreciable distance across bad roads (Rose and Rakeman 1976). In 1903, the cost to haul goods was about 25 cents per ton-mile versus 12 cents with better roadways in Europe (Flink 1970).

Some progress was made in 1916, with the Federal Road Act coordinating efforts to establish a comprehensive nationwide system of good roads, followed, in 1925, with the adoption of uniform signs and an emphasis on safety (Rose and Rakeman 1976). The Federal-Aid Highway Act of 1938 directed the Bureau of Public Roads to investigate the feasibility of building superhighways, a study completed in 1944, with the subsequent Federal-Aid Highway Act leading in the direction of an interregional system. It was not, however, until passage of the federal interstate highway enabling legislation of 1956 that the institutional framework for interregional and metropolitan-wide expressways was fully established (Rae 1965, Foster 1981, Seeley 1987).

Parkways and Other Early Beginnings

An early and strong influence on the process of metropolitan road construction was the parkway. Defined as a limited-access highway located through a park,

Figure 121   The "good roads movement" and federal efforts at highway improvement: touring in Virginia, 1904

the parkway originally combined recreational areas with the movement of passenger vehicles (Miller 1950, Zapatka 1987). Convinced of the need to guide the growth of cities, many planners conceived of parkway systems as a good way of giving orderly form to emerging metropolitan areas (Foster 1981). Two prominent planners believed that "parkways may become the framework for a new town-and-country community by providing a practical means for a better distribution of population" (Nolen and Hubbard 1937, p. xi).

The twin themes of traffic circulation and recreation were taken still further. First, there was the claim of reducing the strain of driving through good highway design. Second, there was evidence of a general long-run increase in land values accruing to neighboring properties (Nolen and Hubbard 1937). Overcoming the blight of unsightly signs and billboards

was also seen as a virtue (Moses 1957). Moreover, rapid or relatively uninterrupted traffic movement amid pleasant surroundings could only be a boon to commuting suburbanites.

The first efforts to build a parkway system occurred in Boston toward the end of the nineteenth century. Started on the advice of Frederick Law Olmsted, some 78 miles of parkway were constructed between 1877 and 1930, mainly under the Metropolitan District Commission (Nolen and Hubbard 1937, Rae 1971). Originally designed in the preautomobile era, the right-of-way appropriated for the parkways varied in width from as low as 116 feet to a more satisfactory dimension of 200 feet. Roadbed widths, such as those illustrated in figure 122, were reasonably generous, given the times, at 40 feet, remaining a standard for parkways well into the 1930s. Relatively smooth curves with a minimum radius of 700 to 800 feet were deployed to enhance the aesthetic experience of moving gently through a large public park. Roadways varied from two to four lanes, with the latter predominating. Traffic originally moved in both directions along each carriageway, a circulation pattern that quickly changed during the early automobile era into a system of one-way roads and loops. Bridle paths were also incorporated. The planting emphasized natural conditions, employing native species and conforming in design to the landscape tradition made popular by Olmsted and Vaux. To them a parkway "was simply a roadway that was wider and more richly furnished" (Newton 1971, p. 596). Along more urbanized links the landscape became more formal, befitting the more developed circumstances. The most notable of the parkways built in this manner were undoubtedly the Arborway and Riverway sections of Jamaicaway, moving out from the city of Boston to the southwest. And several others were constructed with considerable recreational amenity, such as the Mystic Valley Parkway (Nolen and Hubbard 1937, Newton 1971, Rae 1971, Zapatka 1987).

A number of other cities emulated Boston's parkway system. Kansas City saw almost contemporaneous developments, with the establishment of a Park Commission in 1893, as well as the planning

Figure 122   Emergence of an early parkway system: cross-section of the Boston parkways, including the Arborway and Jamaicaway

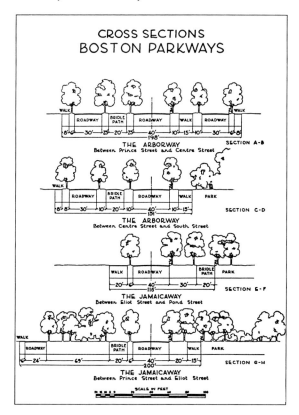

and construction of parkways, under the Department of Parks and Boulevards, as early as 1908. Again rights-of-way varied, largely according to surrounding circumstances of land use. Appropriations were as small as 100 feet, in the case of boulevards, and as high as 1,000 feet for full-fledged parkways. Grade separation of traffic, roadbed widths of 35 to 56 feet, bridle paths, and natural landscapes were all features of the Kansas City system (Kansas City Board of Park Commissioners 1905–1924, Nolen and Hubbard 1937).

The first modern parkway was the Bronx River Parkway, shown in cross-section in figure 123; planning began in 1906 under the newly formed Bronx River Parkway Commission (Rae 1971). The original aim of the project, however, was not to build a limited-access highway but to prevent further pollution of the Bronx River, thus reducing the death rate of animals in the Bronx Zoo and providing the area with better recreational opportunities. Construction was halted during World War I but resumed again in 1919. The 15-mile stretch of road, running north into Westchester County from New York City, was completed in 1923 under the auspices of the newly chartered Westchester Park Commission (Nolen and Hubbard 1937, Miller 1950, Newton 1971, Rae 1971).

In addition to the clean-up of the Bronx River and the recreational opportunities that it provided, the parkway formed a visually pleasing entry to New York City from the north. Gilmore D. Clarke, the project's landscape architect, in cooperation with Jay Downer, the chief engineer, set design standards that were extended and developed in the subsequent com-

Figure 123   Parkways in New York: typical cross-sections in the Westchester County parkway system

ponents of the 75-mile Westchester County Parkway System. The Hutchinson River Parkway (figure 124) was completed by 1928, followed by the Saw Mill River Parkway in 1929 and the Cross County Parkway in 1931. Overall the system incorporated more than 17,000 acres of parkland and 9 miles of beaches and shoreline (Newton 1971, and Rae 1971).

The principal design contribution of the Westchester Parkway system was the generosity with which both the roadways and the surrounding parklands were considered. Land rights-of-way were extensive, ranging from a minimum of 300 feet to about 1,500 or 1,800 feet. Consequently there was a complete separation of the parkway from abutting properties. The park landscape was harmonized with indigenous natural conditions, generally conforming to an English landscape tradition. Grade separation of crossing traffic was complete, with local streets bridging overhead. The highway itself consisted of four lanes, primarily with 40-foot carriageways running in each direction, separated by landscaped dividers and medians. Curves in the roadways were minimized in both the vertical and horizontal directions, and generous shoulders were provided for disabled cars (Nolen and Hubbard 1937, Clarke 1953).

In the New York metropolitan area, the Taconic Parkway, also by Clarke and later by Charles J. Baker, extended the Westchester Parkway system farther north. Robert Moses undertook the Long Island State Parkways in 1926 and 1927, with Clarke as a design consultant (Miller 1950, Clarke 1953). By 1940 Moses had completed the enormous task of building 153 miles of parkway and five bridges in the New York area. Under his leadership, New York was

Figure 124   Roads in park surrounded by metropolitan development: Hutchinson River Parkway, 1928, and Cross Country Parkway, 1931

the only city to build urban highways extensively during the 1930s, a period when national policy, guided primarily by McDonald from the Bureau of Public Roads, clearly subordinated highway building to the improvement of local and rural roads (Rae 1971, Seeley 1987).

Planning for the Merritt Parkway, linking New Haven and New York, began in 1926, and the road was constructed between 1934 and 1938 (figure 125). This 37-mile stretch of road was extended still farther northward, almost to Hartford, by the Wilbur Cross Parkway. The resulting divided highway, with complete grade separation and control of access, was the first long-distance, high-speed road in the United States and a forerunner of the later interstate highway system. So successful was this road that some ten years later, a journey that would have taken 109 minutes along conventional roads still took only 67 minutes. Therein lay much of the appeal of the limited-access highway system (Rae 1971).

The late 1930s saw a growing number of highways planned, under construction, or completed in various parts of the United States. Clarke finished the Mount Vernon Memorial Parkway along the Potomac River as early as 1932 (Clarke 1932). A report prepared in 1939 by the Los Angeles Regional Planning Commission proposed 300 miles of an eventual 600-mile highway system. A 1-mile section of the Arroyo Seco, or Pasadena Freeway, was completed in 1940, and through Cahuenga Pass, between Hollywood and the San Fernando Valley. Chicago experimented with an eight-lane divided highway around Lake Shore Drive in 1933, and Daniel Turner planned an extensive expressway system for Detroit in 1939, including the Davison Limited-Access Highway with three depressed lanes, separated and running in each direction. The first major highway system carrying mixed traffic (both cars and commercial vehicles) was the Pennsylvania Turnpike, although the Henry Hudson Parkway had carried some mixed traffic as early as 1931. Planned in 1935, the turnpike was financed in 1937, and approximately 160 miles were opened to the public by the end of 1940 (Miller 1950, Rae 1971, Seeley 1987).

How to recover the high cost of building highways prompted a hot debate over toll road or free road. In 1939, the Public Roads Administration reported to Congress that toll roads were wasteful and moreover, did not pay their way. Empirical evidence, though hardly conclusive because of imbalances in road mileage, showed that over 1 to 2 percent of the

Figure 125   Grade separation and controlled access: Merritt Parkway, 1934–1938

nation's traffic used toll roads, whereas only 12 percent journeyed along free roads (Seeley 1987). The report then argued that, because the road user pays anyway under either scenario, a tax should be instituted and the funds used to build freeways (Tyler 1957). The Bureau of Public Roads outlined a plan to construct 26,000 miles of free highways, connecting cities across the United States, paid for through gasoline taxes and other vehicular fees (Seeley 1987). The 1939 Master Plan for Free Highway Development succeeded in shifting the focus away from traditional rural roads toward urban areas, with priority for freeway construction (Seeley 1987). The stage was set for the rapid development of metropolitan expressways and interstate highways that took place after World War II.

Foreign Influences

Development of the high-speed highway in the United States was neither unique nor undertaken without reference to similar European efforts. Both the Italian *autostrade* and the German *Autobahnen* were comparatively early modern freeway systems. In 1924, Hillaire Belloc proposed that Britain construct major arterial roads as a comprehensive system linking major cities (Rae 1971). Construction of such a system, however, did not transpire until after World War II.

The Italian *autostrade* began as privately funded roads around the northern city of Milan, roughly between 1922 and 1930. Faltering through mismanagement, they were taken over by the Fascist government in 1933. Other links in what would later become a comprehensive system of free roads were constructed between Florence and Viareggio and between Genoa and Serravole. Most early examples of the *autostrade* were undivided and only two traffic lanes in width (Tunnard and Pushkarev 1963, Rae 1965, 1971).

The forerunner to the German *autobahnen* was the AVUS (Automobil-Verkerhrs-und-Übungs-strasse), constructed in Berlin between 1913 and 1919. Forward looking in conception, this 6-mile stretch of road through the Grünewald forest featured four lanes of totally divided, limited-access highway with no grade crossings (Tunnard and Pushkarev 1963). Moreover, the forested setting and division of directional traffic lanes foreshadowed the heavy landscaping and advanced engineering of later superhighways. Privately financed and built, the AVUS was occasionally used for motor races and to conduct speed trials.

In a manner not dissimilar from the good roads movement in the United States, agitation for a comprehensive system of improved roads began in Germany as early as the 1920s. Two motorways lobby groups, the Stufa and the Hafraba, were organized in 1924 and 1926, respectively. One result of their effort was 12 miles of undivided highway between Cologne and Bonn, constructed between 1930 and 1932 (Tunnard and Pushkarev 1963).

Almost from the outset, Hitler's National Socialists used highway construction as a method for relieving the disastrously high unemployment that occurred with the collapse of the Weimar Republic's economy. Once again there were parallels with the United States and the road-making provisions of the National Recovery Act of 1933 (Rae 1971, Rose and Rakeman 1976).

The first *Autobahn* was constructed in 1935, running from Frankfurt to Darmstadt (Zube 1935). By the end of 1941, some 2,326 miles of the system were in at least partial operation. Of this total, for 340 miles only one roadway was complete of the full two-road divided scheme, and about 1,400 miles were in various other stages of construction (Tunnard and Pushkarev 1963).

The German highways became influential because of their comparatively advanced design and engineering (figure 126). Constructed for medium-distance interurban movement, the *Autobahnen* had a maximum grade of just 4 degrees and a minimum curve radius of 6,500 feet. Engineer Hans Lorenz pioneered the long transition and spiral curves that were to become the hallmark of well-designed highways throughout the world. He was also responsible for the Aschaffenburg-Nuremberg *Autobahn*, considered one of the most beautifully designed high-speed roads (Tunnard and Pushkarev 1963). Interchange configurations of all roads were extremely well considered, featuring spiral on-and-off ramps and full cloverleaf intersections (Krüger 1937). (The latter was not a German invention; it is attributed instead to the French engineer Eugène Hernard in 1906, with an American patent going to Arthur Hale as early as 1916 [Rae 1965].) Nevertheless, "strong emphasis was placed [in Germany] on considering the freeway as a work of art and relating it positively to the surrounding landscape" (Tunnard and Pushkarev 1963, p. 165). Consequently highway aesthetics became a respectable topic among German highway engineers. No doubt a preoccupation with wilderness landscapes, mixed with the heroism of advanced engineering, also played well into prevailing Nazi cultural doctrines about the *Volk* and nationhood.

At the center of many of the German highway projects, especially in the later years, was the design doctrine of what Fritz Heller referred to as "internal *versus* external harmony" (Heller 1938, Tunnard and Pushkarev 1963). Generally internal harmony meant development of geometric configurations of roadways, including route locations and surface materials, that were as driveworthy as possible. The aim was to produce an almost effortless path along which high-speed automobile movement could take place. By contrast, external harmony referred to the situation of the roadway within the surrounding landscape. Here a contrast and complementarity of roadway with vegetative areas were sought. Together internal and external harmony epitomized a visually interesting, varied, and yet smooth, effortless journey by automobile from one urban area to another (Krüger 1937, Heller 1938).

Futurist Visions

The interwar period, in particular the 1930s, was a time in which better futures were imagined in positive technological terms. Happiness was often equated with the satisfaction of material needs, and technocratic know-how was seen to be omnipotent, quickly overcoming mundane problems of contemporary

Figure 126 Foreign influence: the German Autobahnen, *1935*

life, such as urban blight and traffic congestion (Akin 1977, Corn 1986). Generally an image of metropolitan life was projected in which people worked in positive office environments, often towering above park-like settings, and, lived in residential clusters nearby or in the countryside. Of paramount importance was the superbly efficient transportation system that linked everything together and, as one commentator put it, "enabled widely dispersed citizens to live and work wherever they might choose . . . [effectively] eliminating distance" (Segal 1986, p. 127).

One of the most optimistic and popular of the future visions in which the highway played a key role was Norman Bel Geddes's Futurama and Highways and Horizons exhibit at the 1939 New York World's Fair (Bel Geddes 1940, Kihlstedt 1986). Sponsored by General Motors, the realistic scale models and diorama portrayed American life in the year 1960 through a wide variety of geographic settings encompassing the metropolis, rural farms, and wilderness areas. The recurring image was Bel Geddes's "magic motorways," liberating commuters, day-tripper's, and vacationer's from traffic congestion and the ill will engendered by confinement to a monotonous roadway. He even proposed an automatic car control system that approached the concept of driverless movement.

Bel Geddes's scheme of motorways incorporated separated lanes of traffic, even in the same direction, total grade separation, and roads graduated by speed. For example, three roads might run between the same two points. Each alignment, however, would be separate and reflect, in its overall distance and number of curves, a different style of

motoring. The straightest and most direct route would be for speeds of 100 miles per hour; a curving, parkway-like road would be for travel at speeds of 50 miles per hour (Bel Geddes 1940).

The engineering of Bel Geddes's proposals was sketchy but favored multiple use of other public works, such as highways running along the tops of hydroelectric dams, or stacked one above the other on an existing roadway. For movement between high-speed highways at intersections, Bel Geddes proposed ramps that moved directly from one highway to the next (figure 127) without forcing any appreciable reduction of speed (Bel Geddes 1940). This form of intersection is not dissimilar from the so-called spaghetti of modern-day freeway interchanges. In fact, there is much about Bel Geddes's future vision that was simply an exaggeration of contemporary highway designs of the day. The general idea of high-speed, cross-country driving on limited-access high-

Figure 127 Future Motorways but without radical change: Bel Geddes's proposal for an interchange, 1940

ways, with bypasses around cities and towns, may have foreshadowed official postwar policies but was very much on the minds of many transportation planners. In other respects Bel Geddes borrowed and repackaged ideas from other contemporary visionaries. The presence of towers in a matrix of superhighways and parks was hardly novel and reflects, in content if not style, Le Corbusier's Plan Voisin of 1925 and Ville Radieuse of 1930. Furthermore, Bel Geddes's proposals for central city intersections closely emulate, again in content and not style, Corbett's 1927 "avenue of the future" (Kihlstedt 1986).

In keeping with the technological optimism of the times, Bel Geddes's proposals evinced an unshakable belief that technical progress equaled social progress. At times he went further, suggesting that machines could compensate for human failings. For instance, with regard to his automatic car control system, he stated that "these cars of 1960 and the highways on which they will drive will have in them devices which will correct the faults of human beings as drivers" (Bel Geddes 1940, p. 56). More important, his proposals captured the imagination of a great many Americans and strongly suggested that the contemporary efforts of highway engineers and transportation planners were headed in the right direction.

Other futuristic visions of metropolitan life also had highways and highly functional modern systems of movement as indispensable components. Ferriss's well-known Metropolis of Tomorrow of 1929 had multilevel roadways and interchanges (Ferriss 1929). Hilberseimer's 1944 proposal for an ideal city, as well as his plan for the redevelopment of portions of Chicago, relied heavily on superhighways, separated

movement systems, and all the technical paraphernalia of modern highway building (Hilberseimer 1955). Once again the path of functional separation and engineering refinement, already being followed by highway builders, was simply being projected forward. The role of the futurists was not so much one of charting bold new directions but extrapolating existing design concepts within an established technological paradigm. By so doing they not only contributed, however marginally, to the technical developments themselves but, more important, helped set public opinion firmly behind the highway program.

Expressways of America

The golden age of highway construction in the United States, which spans roughly 1945 to 1970, was effectively ushered in by the 1944 Federal-Aid Highway Act, first in the direction of a limited system of national highways, (figure 128) and then in the direction of metropolitan expressways as an integral part of that system. A plan totaling some 34,000 miles of freeway was recommended after due consideration of population centers, rates of metropolitan growth, motor vehicle density, the location of military establishments, farms, and so on (National Interregional Highway Committee 1944). Expressways were clearly seen as a practical means of rationalizing and dealing with traffic problems and city congestion. The watchwords among planners were to build roads in anticipation of growth, thereby exercising control (Kennedy 1944, Foster 1981).

In its finding of fact, the National Interregional Highway Committee described the need for metropolitan freeways in glowing terms: "The automobile

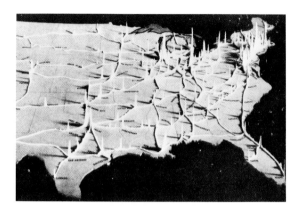

Figure 128   An early concept for an interregional expressway system: relief map of traffic densities along a comprehensive highway system proposed in 1944

has made partial escape from the undesirable state of affairs [of inner city blight] easy and pleasant for some of the population. . . . Suburban business centers have followed the clustering of suburban homes" (National Interregional Highway Committee 1944, p. 53). The inference was that we needed bigger and better metropolitan highways so that more people could partake of suburban life.

On passage of the 1956 Federal-Aid Highway Act, a nationwide system of toll-free superhighways and urban expressways was firmly established. A configuration of 41,000 miles of interstate and defense highways, including 5,000 miles of urban freeways, was to have been constructed, primarily at federal expense, using a cost recovery approach of excise taxes on fuel, tires, and so on (Rae 1965, 1971). In keeping with the basic reference-design philosophy established by the earlier Committees on Interregional Highways, bypass and urban loop roads were to be provided, in addition to expressways passing through central cities. The characteristic urban

spoked-wheel configuration was thus formed, incorporating outer circumferential loop roads and beltways crossing the urban sections of interstate highways moving from city center to city center. The first of these loop roads, Route 128, a distance of some 70 miles around Boston, was already under construction when the federal highway act passed. The land use response was dramatic. Across the country urban expressway systems provided better access for firms and residences, especially in outlying areas with adequate room for expansion.

In a design framework that rather closely paralleled earlier German principles of internal and external harmony, the principles of highway design that were officially espoused "rested upon landscape principles, as well as upon the more commonly recognized engineering principles. . . . A balanced agreement among the two sets of principles thus characterized the best design" (National Interregional Highway Committee 1944, p. 89). Flowing gradients and alignments, as well as spiraled curves, were preferred over linked configurations of straight and tangential roadway geometries. This design avoided the roller-coaster profiles that plagued earlier parkway designs. Slopes beside roadbeds were flattened to control erosion, and well-rounded road shoulders were provided. Roadside planting was regarded simultaneously as a matter of practicality (for controlling snow drifts or ease of maintenance, for example) and as a matter of enhancing aesthetic values. Dimensionally 12-foot lanes were recommended, with a maximum of 2 1/2 degrees of horizontal curvature to accommodate high-speed driving. Road rights-of-way on the order of 200 to 300 feet were required, depending on the presence of service roads. All roads were strictly grade-separated, with controlled access (figure 129) (Clarke 1950, 1953, Deakin 1951, 1952, 1953).

With these postwar advancements in basic highway design, landscape architects and engineers like Michael Rapuano, Clarence Coombs, Oliver Deakin, and Lawrence Hewes continued the parkway tradition into the construction of interstates and urban expressways. Rapuano, of the firm Clarke, Rapuano and Holleran, was instrumental in the design of the Garden State Parkway in New Jersey, as well as many sections of the New York State Thruway system (Newton 1971). Deakin served as the highly influential head of the Parkway Bureau of the New Jersey State Highway Department and was directly responsible, among others, for the splendid Route 4 installation (Deakin 1951). Coombs collaborated with Rapuano and others on the dramatic Palisades Parkway, outside New York City, and Hewes, as chief of the western headquarters of the Bureau of Public Roads, was influential on matters of design standards through his engineering manuals (Labatut and Lane 1950).

Under the auspices of the 1956 federal legislation, state highway departments assumed the major responsibility for constructing the interstate and urban expressway system. Design standards, based on both example and prior practice, generally were reached by a consensual process (Seeley 1987). Roadway alignments increasingly assumed utilitarian purposes as the economic dictates of rising construction costs and higher land prices tipped the balance away from landscape principles in favor of basic

Figure 129   Depression of urban freeways with controlled access: typical postwar expressway with off-ramp and multilane divided carriageways

engineering. Once the subject of considerable engineering pride and aesthetic appreciation, highways, particularly under urban conditions, could no longer cope with rising traffic congestion and became objects of urban blight.

In San Francisco in the early 1960s, freeway construction of the Embarcadero was halted by citizen protest, marking the beginning of the end of the urban freeway era. A 1962 amendment to the federal highway legislation required all future projects to make provision for "social and community values" (Rae 1965). Cutting swaths through socially coherent, inner-city neighborhoods was no longer tolerated in the name of better metropolitan-wide transportation service. In a full swing of the proverbial pendulum, the highway construction that had appeared to some critics early in the century as elitist, only to be seen during the 1930s as a democratic response to everyone's travel needs, once again seemed to favor privileged members of society. Why should inner-city neighborhoods suffer in order to improve the transportation accessibility of outlying metropolitan residents was the question that became asked.

To be sure, urban expressway projects continued through the 1970s and into the 1980s, and several are currently under construction. These, however, are largely projects long in planning. By the early 1970s the prolific era of new highway expansion was over.

SUBDIVISION STREET FORMS

In most respects, street patterns of early metropolitan subdivisions were logical extensions of roadway networks already in place from prior eras. Irregular rural and farm-to-market roads formed a basis for subdevelopment in the Northeast, and the survey system grid, dating from the late eighteenth century, formed the basis in many other parts of the country. At first the layout of streets and lots followed the earlier patterns, providing access to unimproved areas of land with a certain abstract consistency. Rectangular sections of land produced by the survey system, for instance, were further subdivided, in a like manner, to produce rectilinear residential subdivisions and commercial areas.

Later, however, layouts became far less general and abstract, conforming closely to the local topography and, above all, to functional distinctions that were made between various kinds of traffic. Pedestrian and vehicular movement often became separated, and the physical characteristics of roadways closely reflected specific design capacities and travel speeds. The role of the roadway network as a device for simply organizing land subdivision shifted toward the tangible provision of transportation service for specific sites and buildings.

Section Lines and Grids

An astute observer has commented that "the survey system adopted by the Continental Congress governed the settlement of America during the next century until the closing of the frontier. . . . America thus lives on a grand gridiron imposed on the natural landscape by the early surveyors carrying out the mandate of the Continental Congress, as expressed in the Land Ordinance of 1785" (Reps 1965, pp. 216–217). A regular rectangular network of survey lines was established with the fundamental unit of measurement being a square section, or simply a "section," 1 mile on a side. Theoretically sites for townships prior to sale were made up of thirty-six such sections, or an area of 6 miles square. According to the general provisions of the Land Ordinance, half the land was to be sold by township and the other half by section (Reps 1965).

As a matter of practicality many of the section lines laid out in advance of development became rural and town roads. Further regular subdivisions were routinely made into half and quarter sections, defining a further gridwork of roads and streets. During periods of rapid townsite speculation in the latter half of the nineteenth century in places like Kansas and Oklahoma, these land parcels virtually formed an independent medium of economic exchange. Typically the "New Babylons" of Kansas in the 1850s conformed to quarter sections, or 160-acre tracts, and half-sections, or 320-acre townsites. Similar practices were followed by the Boomers in Oklahoma during the 1870s and 1880s and in the West around the Los Angeles region at about the same time (Reps 1965).

Later the broad checkerboard pattern of land parcels was further subdivided into a comparatively regular array of rectangular blocks, roughly from 500 to 750 feet in length and 200 to 250 feet in width. Each block was separated on all sides by streets and composed of numerous building lots. Sometimes criticized for bringing uniformity and mediocrity to American cities, this almost ready-made rectangular pattern of lots, blocks, and streets certainly facilitated the nation's vast suburban expansion. The so-called super grids of arterial roads and collector streets help to establish a strong sense of order in many relatively featureless plains and also provided a crude functional hierarchy for automobile movement.

Growth and subdevelopment did not necessarily occur in a continuous accretive pattern. Rather, the pressure or even the mere indication of the imminent arrival of part of this super grid effectively enabled subdevelopers to be either responsive to other locational factors or simply to seek out speculative advantages slightly in advance of oncoming development. So-called leapfrog patterns of subdevelopment are clear examples of this form of gamesmanship.

Subdevelopment in the San Fernando Valley of the Los Angeles region, shown in figure 130, clearly followed this general process (City Planning Commission of Los Angeles 1946). A primary grid of arterial and collector streets, measuring 1 mile on each side, was overlaid across the landscape, conforming exactly to survey section lines. In areas of more intensive development, this pattern was subdivided further into a half-mile by half-mile secondary grid of streets. Subdivisions were then made either larger or smaller in scale than quarter-sections and yet continued to conform to a rectangular layout of residential streets. Sometimes subdivisions occurred next to each other within the same section. Others occurred in a less contiguous manner in more remote locations. During the 1940s parkways and expressways began to crisscross the area, although these routes rarely conformed to the original gridiron layout. The Whitehall Parkway, for instance, ran across the valley almost at a diagonal. The resulting roadway network and scheme of land parcels produced a four-level hierarchy: expressways, section-line arterial roads, quarter-section collectors, and subdivision plots of local residential streets. In fact, since World War II, this general scheme can be found throughout much of the metropolitan United States.

Functional Street Layouts

From about the 1930s on, developers began to encounter certain problems with the straightforward rectilinear gridiron layout of streets and blocks (Tunnard and Pushkarev 1963). First, in many well-developed areas of emerging metropolitan regions, regularly shaped parcels of flat land were becoming scarcer, often forcing subdevelopment into the more difficult terrain of surrounding hillsides. Second, a simple rectilinear street layout encouraged through traffic within a residential subdivision, diminishing public safety and providing a costly excess of street

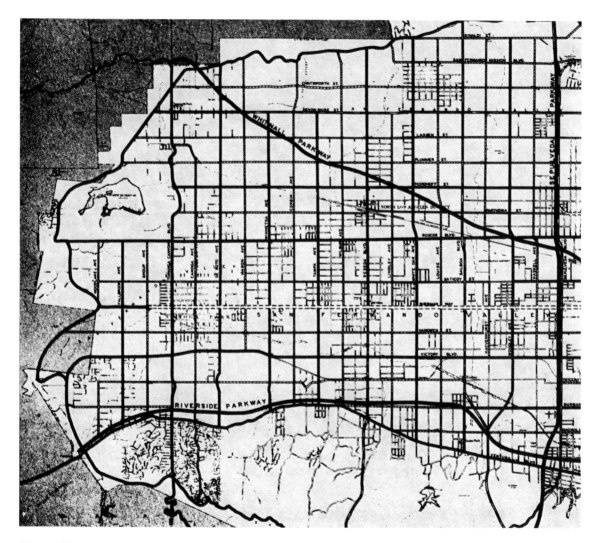

*Figure 130   Section lines, subdivisions, and local streets:
hierarchical subdevelopment of the San Fernando Valley
in the Los Angeles region during the 1940s*

capacity at low residential densities. Finally, subdivisions that remained large and undifferentiated in appearance often became regarded as overly uniform and monotonous. In response to these problems and increasing general demands to rationalize traffic movement, a search was undertaken for functional rather than merely geometric street patterns (Tunnard and Pushkarev 1963).

By the mid-1930s, design of residential subdivision layouts began to distinguish consistently among different types of vehicular movement, especially between local and through traffic, and in response streets were altered in both dimensions and landscape. Wide thoroughfares and boulevards became distinct from small-scale residential side streets and cul-de-sacs. Efforts were made to eliminate the number of control points presented at street intersections, favoring Y and T configurations over conventional four-way crossings. Privacy was secured within residential subdivisions by eliminating through streets almost entirely and replacing them by loop roads. Finally, a deliberate effort was made to reflect and even accentuate the topography of an area (Mott 1941, Tunnard and Pushkarev 1963).

Several forerunners to these functional street layouts were of a radical design. Stein and Wright's new community of Radburn, New Jersey, was a bold and ultimately influential attempt to deal rationally with various forms of vehicular traffic and an almost complete separation from pedestrian movement. Designed in 1928 and opened in 1930, Radburn featured motor courts leading from arterial and collector roads to relatively tightly organized clusters of single-family homes (figure 131). On the other side of the houses, an elaborate system of pedestrian pathways led past private lawns into a verdant commonly held corridor, which opened up to become an expansive park system running throughout the development. Major intersections between vehicular and pedestrian circulation were grade-separated, and every attempt was made to reduce any inherent traffic conflicts. Furthermore, the arrangement of collector roads and motor courts clearly minimized redundancy in the amount of roadway required (Stein 1966).

A consistent design concept that arose through the Greenbelt communities during the early 1930s

was the use of loop roads and cul-de-sacs, or motor courts, leading off major collector streets. Once again the nonresidential land between specific subdevelopments was freed from vehicular circulation and became a network of large parks. The plan for the community of Greenbrook, New Jersey (a project never completed), prepared under the direction of Rex Tugwell by Henry Wright and Allan Kamstra, clearly shows these principles (figure 132). In the design prepared for the Resettlement Administration in 1935, a hierarchical pattern of circulation is clear. Circumferential collector roads led from a major arterial, connecting the community to other parts of the region. Almost all residential development was then concentrated on a network of cul-de-sacs and loop streets radiating out into the surrounding park space from these circumferential collector roads. In a manner similar to Radburn, pedestrian movement was almost completely separated from the roadway network and largely confined to the park areas (Stein 1966). The concept of the superblock, which arose earlier in the urban context of garden apartment complexes by Thomas, as well as by Stein and Wright, was also fully deployed here and at Radburn (Stern 1980). This isolation of a broad residential precinct from any vehicular traffic effectively guaranteed an uninterrupted, sylvan, pedestrian recreational environment.

Other adaptations and examples of the same ideas began to appear in other parts of the country. In

Figure 131   Separation of vehicular and pedestrian movement: collector roads, motor courts, and footpaths at Radburn, New Jersey, by Stein and Wright, 1928–1930

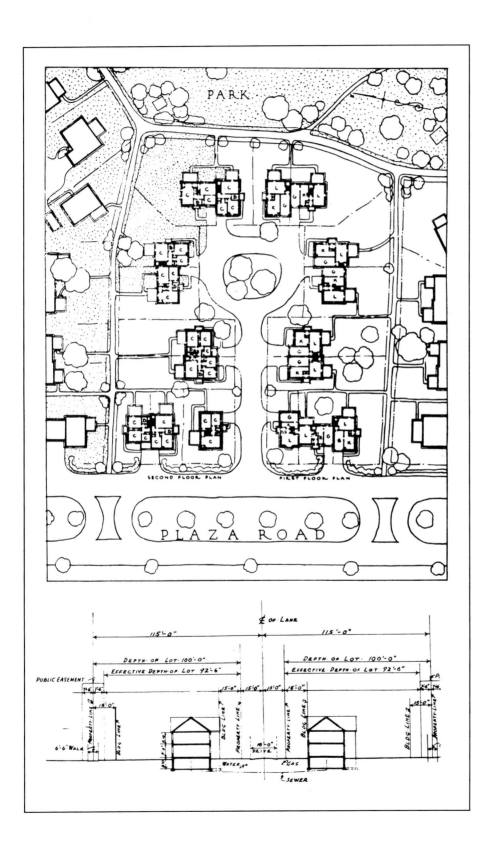

PARK

SECOND FLOOR PLAN   FIRST FLOOR PLAN

PLAZA ROAD

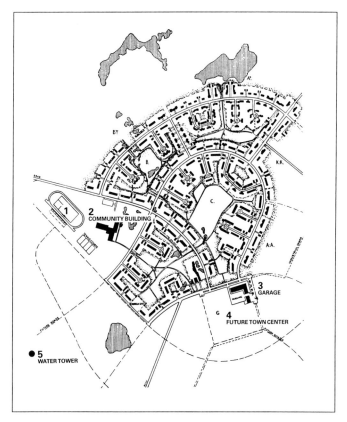

Figure 132 Hierarchical organization of specialized streets: Greenbrook, New Jersey, proposal, by Wright and Kamstra, 1935

1929, the Regional Planning Commission of the County of Los Angeles, for instance, proposed the idealized residential street design shown in figure 133, featuring a cul-de-sac arrangement for a motor court connecting to a larger street, off-street parking bays between two lots toward the center of the court, and a service alley along the backyard of the residences. In the words of the Planning Commission, "The park-like effect provides a pleasant prospect for the surrounding homes . . .the irregular shape of the lots makes possible greater individuality and changes

in planting, walks and garden features, and in the architecture of the home" (Regional Planning Commission, County of Los Angeles 1929, p. 29).

When the newly established Federal Housing Administration (FHA) embraced many of these design ideas in 1934, the dominance of straightforward, rectilinear, residential tract developments began to subside in earnest (Scott 1969). The FHA's Land Planning Division and its director, Seward Mott of the firm Pitkin and Mott, published several revisions to standard subdivision practice calling for explicit incorporation of common open recreational spaces within the subdivisions, an emphasis on T and Y intersections, and a sympathetic alignment of streets with prevailing topography and other natural features (Land Planning Division, Federal Housing Administration 1934). Minimum lot sizes were established for a range of housing types, such as the 5,000 square foot minimum for single-family detached housing (Twichell 1948).

In later deliberations by the Land Planning Division the concept of T and Y intersections was maintained, but the idea of superblocks and extensive areas of recreational green space near the center of subdivisions was abandoned because this "treatment with a multitude of cul-de-sacs protruding toward and entirely surrounding a central park area" did not prove practicable (Mott 1941, p. 160). Difficulties were encountered in providing adequate fire protection with long dead-end streets, higher costs per dwelling unit of service delivery were caused by the need to retrace movements constantly, and problems were encountered with the adequate and equitable maintenance of common park areas. On the other hand, standard roadway widths were adopted, following engineering practice, with most residential streets having a 50-foot right-of-way and a 24-foot-wide pavement. Furthermore, the idea of so-called long blocks of up to 1,000 to 1,200 feet, specifically located along major thoroughfares, was strongly advocated in order to reduce the number of intersections and to decrease the amount of through traffic in residential neighborhoods (Mott 1941).

These design principles, as well as earlier ideas about preserving the privacy of residential precincts, are apparent in the City of Los Angeles's proposal, shown in figure 134, for the redevelopment of a quarter section in one of its many suburbs (City Planning Commission of Los Angeles 1947). This example il-

lustrates the transition made from earlier rectilinear street layouts to more functional configurations. Here a double looping road system was used to minimize the number of entries into the subdivision and to allow for long blocks parallel to major thoroughfares at the perimeter. Street lengths and curvatures were varied to add visual interest to the overall layout, and a park with playground was incorporated at the center. Another feature of the redevelopment plan was the location of a strip commercial neighborhood shopping center at the intersection of two major streets on the corner of the subdivision, reflecting another recommendation from the Land Planning Division concerning the provision of retail stores at approximately 1 mile intervals or at each section line (Mott 1941).

The meticulous functional reasoning that lay behind many of these standards, as it had been at the turn of the century, was primarily based on principles for public health protection. When the 1940 census found that 7 million, or 23 percent, of the nation's 30 million nonfarm dwellings were substandard (Twichell 1948), government agencies quickly responded to provide the right kind of guidance; subdivision standards were one obvious way. The public health aspect of the standards included protection against hazardous accidents, provision of adequate daylight, sunshine, and ventilation, protection against atmospheric pollution, and provision of the possibility for reasonable aesthetic satisfaction. As for adequate daylight, sunshine, and ventilation, the mechanics of the functional reasoning process led to a standard minimum lot width of 50 feet for the single-family house, based on the preservation of a 20 foot by 30 foot sunny area in the backyard and sufficient width

Figure 133 Privacy, visual variety, and service: residential street design by the Regional Planning Commission of the County of Los Angeles, 1929

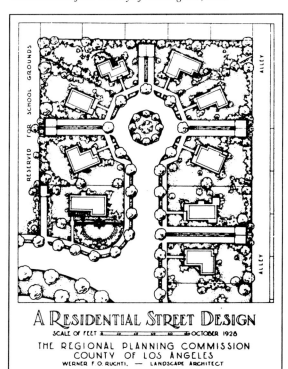

A RESIDENTIAL STREET DESIGN

SCALE OF FEET   OCTOBER 1928

THE REGIONAL PLANNING COMMISSION
COUNTY OF LOS ANGELES
WERNER F. O. RUCHTI. — LANDSCAPE ARCHITECT

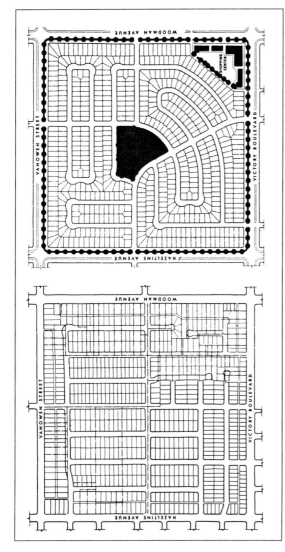

Figure 134   Redevelopment according to federal guidelines: City of Los Angeles proposal for the redevelopment of a typical suburban quarter section, 1947

to allow light into windows along the side of the house. Generally a 60-foot width was considered reasonable and 75 feet was desirable (Twichell 1948). Notions of public safety dictated a strict classification of street types, including standards about setbacks, and led to street patterns that minimized through traffic and reinforced the long block idea by providing a minimum distance of 800 feet between intersections along major streets (Twichell 1948).

Curvilinear Plans

Another outgrowth of revisions to subdivision planning practices during the early automobile era of the 1920s and 1930s was the curvilinear layout of streets —partially in direct response to the perceived uniformity and monotony of rectilinear plans and to a detailed functional consideration of suburban streets (Reps 1965). When coupled with any kind of topography, the concept of long blocks (to ensure privacy) together with the avoidance of four-way intersections (to reduce traffic conflict) quickly led to an organic, curvilinear street layout. Controlled closure of street vistas and the visual interest and variety introduced by curving streets in an otherwise identical alignment of houses were clearly considered advantageous and marketable (Regional Planning Commission, County of Los Angeles 1929).

The FHA's Land Planning Division strongly favored this approach for helping to reduce real estate market risk and for providing better dwellings (Tunnard and Pushkarev 1963). Their early brochures recommending standards and methods for subdivision development were replete with revisionist plans in a curvilinear mode (Land Planning Division, Federal Housing Administration 1935, 1938, and Scott 1969). In one example, illustrated in figure 135, a standard rectilinear grid of residential streets, abutting the curvature of a lake front, was entirely erased and replaced by a picturesque, gently curving arrangement with irregularly shaped lots. Neighborhood facilities were provided in one corner, and the lakefront was developed as a public park, with access provided from the streets between private lots.

The FHA's comprehensive subdivision review process helped enable broad adoption of these guidelines and models. Through the use of selected planning consultants, in conjunction with public planning agencies and civic groups, some 2,615 residential subdivisions in 1939 alone were reviewed and analyzed (Scott 1969). Containing 283,000 separate

Figure 135 A preference for organic, curvilinear street layouts: Federal Housing Administration proposal for redevelopment of a lakefront subdivision

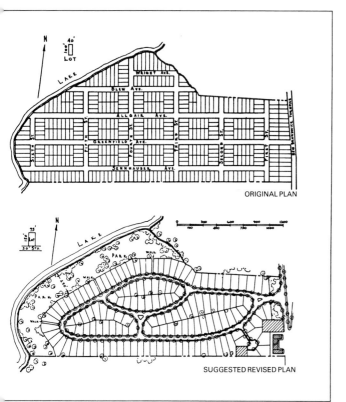

ORIGINAL PLAN

SUGGESTED REVISED PLAN

lots, this was well over 50 percent of the total volume of 515,000 housing starts for that year (U.S. Department of Commerce 1955).

Apart from assumptions about increased land value to be derived from good planning, Seward Mott and other members of the Land Planning Division were clearly emulating much earlier romantic and picturesque suburban schemes from Olmsted, Vaux, and Hanes (Mott 1941, Tunnard and Pushkarev 1963, Newton 1971). In particular, the similarity of the Land Planning Division's revisionist plans to Olmsted's and Vaux's Riverside of 1869, located 9 miles outside Chicago, was striking. The lozenge-shaped blocks with heavy landscaping along streets and in common areas were almost identical. The task of subdivision planning was also understood similarly. Privacy, public safety, and domestic tranquility were goals of the federal planners. In their report on Riverside, Olmsted and Vaux had recommended "the general adoption of gracefully-curved lines, generous spaces and the absence of sharp corners. The idea being to suggest and imply leisure, contemplativeness and happy tranquility" (Newton 1971, pp. 466–67).

Among the other subdivisions with similar sensibilities produced by Olmsted and Vaux were the 550-acre Roland Park in Maryland in 1891, where cul-de-sacs were liberally used in order to accommodate steep topography (Newton 1971). Forest Hills in New York, built between 1909 and 1912, as well as prominent contemporary projects, such as Draper's 1927 plan for Chicopee, Georgia, also probably influenced federal planners in the direction of picturesque, curvilinear subdivision layouts. By the beginning of the period after World War II, America's largest suburban projects, like Sharp's Oak Forest (1946) in Houston and the Levittowns of 1948 and 1950, incorporated curvilinear street patterns almost as a matter of routine (figure 136). Both practicality and aesthetic appeal provided convincing arguments.

Loops and Clusters

Subdivisions based on systems of loop roads were already being constructed during the 1930s, modeled after the Greenbelt communities and design principles espoused by the FHA. Loop roads, which reduced through traffic, were generally considered preferable to dead-end streets and motor courts for providing privacy to residential neighborhoods. By the mid- to late 1950s, loop roads, now in combination with housing clusters grouped around short cul-de-sacs, were applied to the design of a number of communities, especially those with a recreational focus. One clear advantage of this type of arrangement, in a low-density residential environment, was preservation of large amounts of open space, ideally suited for recreational facilities like golf courses. In more mundane applications the amount of outdoor space provided for each dwelling unit was concentrated in relatively large tracts. At least the perception of

available open space was enhanced by clustered concentrations of dwellings within a broader landscape. Other service and maintenance advantages also accrued to the overall arrangement through the lessening of required road length in comparison with stricter rectilinear schemes at similar densities (Urban Land Institute 1963, McKeever 1968).

During the 1960s, the concept of PUDs (planned unit developments) emerged, capturing the attention of many in the real estate industry. PUDs usually incorporate the idea of dwelling units grouped into clusters, allowing an appreciable amount of intervening land for open space (Huntoon 1971). Often housing is in the form of townhouses or apartments, or both, rather than confined to single-family detached residences. Not unexpectedly, the fundamentally different distribution of density, from traditional, uniform types of housing development, posed problems for conventional zoning codes and required special enabling legislation. In effect, gross residential densities replaced net densities, and much greater allowance was made in individual lot size to compensate for the larger expanses of nearby open space (Krasnowiecki and Babcock 1965).

During the late 1960s and 1970s the popularity of PUDs rose (Huntoon 1971). The concept allowed many older suburban areas to be redeveloped, usually at higher densities but without any loss of environmental amenity, with the by-product of a lower cost per individual unit; at minimum the cost of a unit could be maintained against rising construction and infrastructure costs. The Urban Land Institute found an almost 50 percent savings in service costs between comparable conventional and PUD subdivisions as a

Figure 136   Postwar infatuation with curvilinear street patterns: tract development in Nassau County, New York

result of benefits from reduced road lengths and widths allowable under loop and cluster arrangements with off-street parking (Huntoon 1971). The appeal of ecological preservation inherent in larger tracts of open space was a particularly compelling characteristic in the marketplace at a time when the broadly based American environmental movement was underway (figure 137).

While the trend of associating PUDs with recreational venues continued, many others used the concept simply to enhance the pastoral or arcadian qualities of their projects. Heritage Woods (1969), for example, by the Paparazzo Heritage Corporation in Avon, Connecticut, preserved most of a 347-acre

wooded site with an overall dwelling unit density that was only a little below standard practice for conventional suburban tract housing.

Traditional Neighborhoods and Pedestrian Pockets

Several recent efforts to overcome the single-use function of PUDs and the specialized qualities of many earlier subdivision layouts have attempted to recover the qualities of small towns. The first of these, sometimes referred to as traditional neighborhood development, was pioneered by Andres Duany and Elizabeth Plater-Zyberk in their 1983 design for the town of Seaside, Florida. Many similar projects

Figure 137   Recreational use of the planned unit development: Moss Creek Plantation, South Carolina, by Team Plan, Inc., 1972–1978

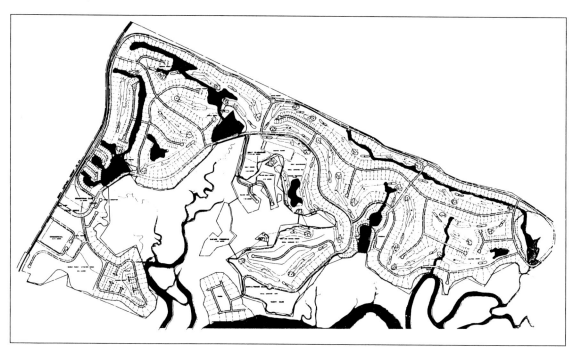

quickly followed primarily, like the early PUDs, as recreational projects (Abrams 1986, Boles 1989a).

In place of the highly particularized motor courts, off-street parking areas, and meandering loop roads, a multipurpose nonhierarchical street grid was proposed at Seaside that harkened back to the rectilinear street patterns of early, small, rural towns (figure 138). Instead of a highly determined movement system, traffic was allowed and even encouraged to filter slowly through neighborhoods. Extensive use was made of footpaths, in keeping with the model of a small southern town. According to the planners, this generalized network of roads, streets, and footpaths was not only more conducive to a mixture of adjacent land uses than the specialized systems of the functionalist tradition but also furthered their social agenda of encouraging social interaction (Abrams 1986). In a more recent project Alan Ward and Dennis Pieprz of Sasaka Associates were to apply similar principles to the redesign of a town center in Brambleton, Virginia (*Progressive Architecture* 1990).

The so-called pedestrian pocket, another recent development, is predominantly a mixed-use pedestrian environment where all residences and workplaces are within easy walking distance. The underlying model of a small, rural town is reinforced by notions of self-sufficiency and of being surrounded by a pastoral landscape (Boles 1989a). Although specific proposals by proponents like Calthorpe, Kelbaugh, Solomon, and Mack, vary in their assumptions about land use and host environments, nevertheless all envision a comparatively straightforward system of streets that have many of the same general qualities as traditional neighborhood devel-

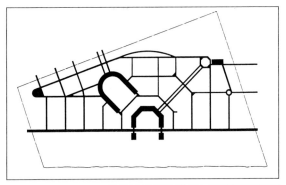

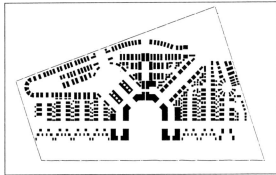

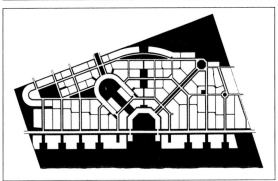

Figure 138   A multipurpose street grid: public places, buildings, and street network, Seaside, Florida, by Duany and Plater-Zyberk, 1983

opments. Once again emphasizing pedestrian movement, sidewalks and footpaths now become conspicuous elements (Boles 1989a).

With these recent developments in low-density community planning and subdivision practice, the pendulum once again seems to have made a full swing. The generalized street grid has returned once again after an interlude of functional planning and design in which street networks were increasingly more specialized and hierarchical. In the interim, however, social agendas also seem to have changed. Once the public's health, safety, and right to privacy were satisfied or became satiated by the controlled suburban idyll, there was, perhaps understandably, a certain longing for social interaction, chance encounter, and disorder.

SPATIAL DEVELOPMENTS AND VARIATIONS

Several spatial developments were evident during the evolution of the modern metropolitan highway and street system, each associated with a particular mode of design thinking and each in reaction to problems encountered during a previous period.

Geometric Transition and Change

Early roadway development was preoccupied with providing good, all-weather surfaces on existing alignments. Consequently road design was largely confined to experimenting with roadbed and surface materials under a variety of new load and speed conditions (Rose and Rakeman 1978). With the exception of the parkway, roadway sizes, alignments, and geometries varied little from those of the preautomobile era.

By the 1930s, however, dramatic shifts in design thinking began to occur as the functional requirements of high-speed and high-volume movement became central to roadway design. New design features that emerged included divided roadways for safety rather than aesthetic reasons, total grade separation of

crossing traffic, limited access, and the use of service roads with transition lanes. Above all, the design of major intersections employing spiral ramps, cloverleafs, and dramatic level changes introduced an entirely new artifact into the metropolitan environment (figure 139).

Once the modern highway was sketched out in broad strokes, a period of design refinement set in. From a geometric perspective, straight roadway links and tangential curves were replaced by smoother transitions and then by spiral curves in both horizontal and vertical directions. Standards were developed from practical experience for such design constraints as the radii of road curvature, grade changes, road shoulder design, and highway cross-sections. Uppermost in the minds of highway engineers, designers, and transportation planners was the path of least re-

Figure 139   Conceptualization of the modern, high-speed, high-volume roadway, replete with public amenities: proposal from the President's Report on Interregional Highways, 1944

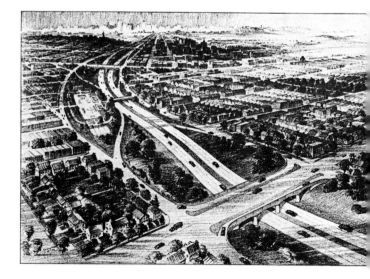

sistance that led to quick, smooth, stressless travel. Relations among various internal components of the highway were now understood as part of a complex moving body problem, and functional analysis and refinement became indispensable design tools. As construction costs increased, higher levels of engineering refinement were sought. As highways became more congested, higher levels of traffic control were developed. Nevertheless, once the general concept of the modern highway was established, these geometric and technical changes were largely matters of sustained continuous development.

A similar historical pattern can be discerned on the local street form of subdivisions. Once again there was an episodic quality to events. The general and somewhat abstract character of the section lines and corresponding roadway grid in most parts of the United States was simply reapplied to make sites for real estate development. Convenience in conveying land and expedience in providing access to that land were dominant concerns. Minimum lot sizes and practical street lengths, regardless of how they might be specifically used, provided constraints at one level of spatial resolution. At the other was the inherited geometry and partial development of the ubiquitous survey sections.

During the late 1920s and early 1930s, design attitudes changed quite sharply. The specific use and therefore physical layout of local street networks began to matter. Moreover, as more functional distinctions could be made among various types of movement, the hierarchy of different street types became deeper and broader (figure 140). An almost axiomatic separation occurred between pedestrian and vehicular movement. The cross-section of roads and streets varied according to speed and volume of movement. In short, street layouts were considered to be integrated functional networks.

Functional considerations of public safety and welfare initially led to several commonsense building practices that altered the geometry of streets. The need for privacy and safety from through traffic led to a more internalized street geometry within subdivisions and the use of long blocks. Over time an extensive hierarchy of streets developed from motor courts, cul-de-sacs, and low-speed residential streets to district neighborhood collectors and metropolitan arteries. Boredom with the monotony of rectilinear street patterns and an avoidance of four-way intersections produced curvilinear street geometries and a further differentiation of the overall hierarchy.

With matters of public safety and welfare largely met, later developments looked to the operating efficiencies of street networks. Functional minimization of road length, concentration of street frontage, and a more precise scaling of road sections to the speed and volume of traffic took place. Cost criteria for the

Figure 140   Functional distinction and hierarchical separation: postwar suburban area under development around the Meadowbrook Parkway, Long Island, New York

street system were quickly extended from capital costs to maintenance functions and the indirect economic impact on other community services. Consequently circularity and duplication of movement along road links were scrutinized more carefully for services like police patrols, garbage pickup, and street cleaning. Unworkable earlier assumptions about the practicality of large, common, open areas were revised. The cost accounting behind street layouts also became more inclusive, with more sensitive consideration of potential selling prices in conjunction with the perceived amenity of specific building lots. In PUDs loop and cluster arrangements facilitated higher local residential densities, with improvements in outdoor amenity.

Ironically, perhaps, recent developments in street layouts have returned to the generalized rectilinear grid, rejecting highly specialized and geometrically particular layouts. This apparent abandonment of functional design principles is less remarkable, however, when we realize the overall isolation and comparatively small size of the proposals concerned. The significance of traditional neighborhoods and pedestrian pockets lies in the fact that individual privacy and the likeness of surrounding land areas are no longer prized attributes.

Purpose and Layout

In the headlong rush to open up land for development and to solve rising problems of congestion and neighborhood safety, roads became pieces of urban infrastructure (rather than potentially positive social artifacts). The concept of roads and streets as multipurpose and well-integrated realms of the city gave way to streets as a subordinate installation supporting adjacent activities.

The various parts of the movement system were often separated as they multiplied. Walking and driving no longer occupied the same roadway alignment, a separation made necessary by increased vehicular speeds. The street layouts and highway corridors that emerged were internally coherent and separated from other adjacent parts of the city. This functional discimination inevitably led to the physical isolation of many land uses. For example, the street patterns that emerged produced residential enclaves that made good internal sense yet were found lacking because they discouraged social diversity and coherence (Boyer 1983). With this increased functional appreciation of system parts went a corresponding redirection of a roadway's relationship to the surrounding environment. Only functional solutions that satisfied internal movement conditions were adopted. Consequently the breadth of the design terms of reference was noticeably abridged between earlier and later expressway proposals. The depth of engineering design was, however, significantly greater. Even the futurists appear to have fallen into this way of thinking. Their extravagances also isolated problems of roadway design within the narrow realm of engineering.

The underlying emphasis on functional reasoning, born during the era of progressive reform around the turn of the century, was based on an implicit faith in the capabilities of apolitical technical experts (Akin 1977, Seeley 1987). An equation between technical progress and social progress was clearly struck as highway engineers, designers, and transportation planners took up the challenge of the new automotive technology and other forms of movement (figure 141). The setting of uniform standards consistent with this philosophy greatly broadened the immediate application of specific technical developments. Although these standards were always arrived at by consensus, they were, nevertheless, squarely in the bailiwick of technical experts (Seeley 1987).

Involvement of the federal government was both rapid and influential. With effectively nowhere else to turn, the good roads movement established a strong early federal role. The Bureau of Public Roads in highway design and the FHA in subdivision layout were instrumental in helping to establish new design paradigms. Although both declined in influence after World War II, the Bureau of Public Roads perhaps more than the FHA, their design guidelines were well in place.

Function and Imagery

In the early days of the automobile era, roads and streets were typically sand-covered rights-of-way that became rutted and muddy in rain or wind blown and dusty in the summer. Rarely more than two lanes in width, they either followed traditional trade routes or ran alongside survey lines. The proliferation of the automobile added pressure to the mounting clamor for better roads.

As the functional understanding of roadways became more precise and elaborate, two responses took place in their physical design and appearance. The first, perhaps the more understandable, took the form of crisp and well-made roadway alignments, directly reflecting the purposes they were to serve. Many freeway designs became engineering and functional

tour's-de-force, especially around major interchanges (figure 142). The visual appearance of these remarkable high-speed roadways seemed to be totally in keeping with the romance of the automobile—so much so that futurists made few alterations in their configuration.

The second response was in an opposite direction. As the functional specifications of the roads be-

Figure 141 Functional reasoning and the extreme objectification of transportation infrastructure: Dallas–Fort Worth Airport, by Hellmuth, Obata and Kassabaum, 1973

Figure 142 The rise of engineering precision and rationality: first American cloverleaf interchange, Woodbridge, New Jersey, 1928

Figure 143   Rational street layouts and romantic picturesque imagery: proposal for a modern residential cul-de-sac subdevelopment

came more precise, so did the tendency to temper a completely rational portrayal with romantic naturalistic imagery of the land (figure 143). Urban parkways, curvilinear subdivision layouts striving to project the image of quaint country lanes, and PUDs facilitated attempts to return to or to maintain and preserve preferred pastoral and arcadian qualities of the metropolitan living environment. One might even argue that many of the functional innovations that occurred in highway and street layout effectively allowed the design of roadway corridors and subdivisions to pursue other aesthetic agendas.

Not all, and perhaps not even most, highway and subdivision layouts in America conform to these aesthetic principles. Tract upon tract of suburban single-family housing, beside rectilinear uniform streets, can hardly be called romantic and picturesque, though the inclination may be there. Many urban expressways cut a swath through a jumble of different land uses and are lined by billboards instead of plying through verdant parklike settings. When functional reasoning became too narrowly defined or overwhelmed by economic expediency, issues of the surrounding roadway environment were never even broached. Results were a good deal better when "external harmony," to use Heller's term, was considered along with the immediate internal conditions of roadway building.

The urban arterial road network has been excluded from this discussion because it is not really an artifact of the modern era. Major grade-level throughfares have existed at most times and especially during the nineteenth-century expansion of American urban areas (Reps 1965). Today it is invariably along many of these roads that we find the strip-commercial development that is perhaps furthest removed from the arcadian suburban ideal.

A remarkable aspect of American land development and road building was a bold reliance on large conceptual frameworks. When the Enlightenment minds of founding fathers, for instance, first turned to matters of property, perhaps understandably they invoked Blackstone's rational if controversial notion of landownership. Through the Continental Congress they quickly followed with a broad, generally applicable gridded system of land sections. Both were universal blueprints for future specific actions. Similarly the nation's interstate highways reflect a comprehensive scheme. Interestingly, having made the rational leap forward in conceptual thinking, attention was then turned to making the results blend in and seem inevitably progressive. At precisely those moments, a romantic reaction often set in in an effort to temper any apparent excesses and to move subsequent developments into a comfortable middle ground.

PART THREE

Poetics and Making

The third part of this book addresses the making of a "middle landscape."
First a rural-urban synthesis is proposed between the age-old pastoral perspective and the
modern technical temperament, an attitude that ubiquitously manifests itself in a technological way of producing things, managing affairs, and interpreting the world. The resulting
philosophical equation of modern pastoralism is useful to the extent that each term can constructively qualify the other. For instance, the potential pandemonium of a technological onslaught on the environment can be restrained by moving toward arcadian simplicity, whereas
a rustic resistance to progress can be counteracted by creative technical reasoning. Along
the way, mythic images emerge within built landscapes that help mask inconsistencies and
inadequacies in the conduct of daily, metropolitan life. Modern pastoralism is a symbolic
construct that closely mirrors deeply seated pluralist-majoritarian tensions in contemporary
American society, as well as ingrained attitudes toward development.

The general task of locating the idea of modern pastoralism in the contemporary metropolitan landscape is portrayed largely as a matter of realigning and expanding
existing types of suburban development. Principally a richer, common residential landscape
must be invented, along with a more adequate commercial environment, and greater attention must be paid to a more comprehensively designed public infrastructure. Programmatically these tasks have little to do with buildings and land uses per se but are concerned with
the formal structure and functional adequacy of the spatial realms in between.

The issue of an appropriate aesthetic form, or "language," of expression
for the idea of modern pastoralism is broached. Here the verdict is largely in favor of the contemporary authenticity of modernism over historicism's claim to continuity. Finally, poetic
operations that might be employed in the realignment and expansion of suburban rhetoric are
identified and illustrated. They include juxtaposition, scaling, ordering, and typological
invention.

Abstract principles of social organization and conduct do not exist long in the world without homilies to explain them, stories to justify them and sing their praises, metaphors to give them enduring substance, and myths to reconcile their inconsistencies and inadequacies with actual practice. "Be kind to your fellows, regardless, and they shall be kind to you in return!" might be explained by the parable of the Good Samaritan, justified by an appeal to reason by way of the common good, enshrined by reference to saintliness, and mythologized through the idea of a serene life in the hereafter for those who deny self-interest. When appropriate, snippets from this extrapolated framework become part of daily banter—for example, "Alex, my son, came by today, such a nice boy. I'm sure I shall meet him in heaven." Much of the time, they are largely taken for granted. It is not at all clear that the principles come first and that the stories, metaphors, and myths follow thereafter. On the contrary, the principles may be formalizations of what is held to be customary.

In a democratic society like the United States, the conduct of that democracy according to principles of either majority self-rule or by protection of individual and minority rights can imply or even impress some spatial identity on its patterns of settlement. Certainly the inherent tension between these two

principles plays itself out in daily routines and community rituals. For instance, there is a dependence upon the common weal in metropolitan areas when it comes to the roadway alignments that allow us to get to work in the morning. Returning once again in the evening, we can symbolically reassert our individualism in similar yet personally distinctive abodes within what we would like to think of as unique neighborhoods. However, these social principles by themselves offer few clues to the shape and appearance of corresponding living and working environments. In fact, they probably seem decidedly disconnected from such matters; nevertheless they are at work. It is the separation of such analytical categories as the "look of things" from the "conduct of things" that masks the broader plots by which we seek to give coherent shape to our lives. It is, so to speak, the stories we live by and not the abstract principles. These narratives give us romance, a sense of adventure, and something to emulate.

In crucial aspects of our suburban metropolitan existence we may well behave according to democratic principles of pluralism and majoritarian rule. But our roles and, more important for us here, our settings are sympathetically shaped by different themes. On the one hand we fancy ourselves as being self-reliant individualists, in touch with our natural circumstances. We delight in our family homestead and the plot of land around it. Yet, we take pride in our technological and managerial progress. We seem to know more in specialized ways than we used to, and we have all manner of means at our disposal by which to shape our lives. In large measure we effect a rural-urban synthesis that ultimately combines and fuses two rather different ideas and viewpoints: a pastoral perspective and a modern technical orientation.

THE PASTORAL PERSPECTIVE

Pastoralism is an expansive and venerable topic. Basically it concerns rural life—its more rapturous aspects and its simple nobility (figure 144). Far from being a realistic portrayal of actual country life, pastoralism as an artistic and ideological motif seeks to transcend the ordinary by describing a far better world (Panofsky 1957, Preminger 1965).

As literary theme and literary form, pastoralism and the pastoral are firmly rooted in the Greco-Ro-

Figure 144   The simple nobility of rural life: reenactment of an early farmer with his plough

man tradition. Theocritus's Idylls date from the third century B.C. As Preminger put it, in their allegorical aspects they conjure up "the beautiful countryside of Sicily, so he, like the pastoral poets who followed him, was a city man longing for the country" (Preminger 1965, p. 603). Theocritus at the time was residing in Ptolemy's court in Alexandria, a majestic place then as it is today, but hardly pastoral. Moreover, this otherworldly aspect of the pastoral reflects not only its lack of realism but a certain longing for attainment as well. Later it was Virgil, through his *Eclogues*, who refined, consolidated, and popularized the conventions of pastoral poetry (Preminger 1965). In fact, it is his name that we probably most clearly associate with this literary form and its connection, in turn, with the Golden Age. Here again there was a deliberate intent to harken back to an earlier period of more honest values and what we might call roots and the faith of our fathers. In addition, there was certainly an outward expression of piety during a period of considerable internal upheaval and decadence. It can even be said that a literary gloss was provided on the new imperial order, thus helping to give it legitimacy. As we shall see, this appears to have been a rather constant and significant role for pastoralism.

Critical reception of the pastoral often centered on the issue of idealism versus reality (Empson 1950, Preminger 1965). For those of a romantic persuasion, pastoralism could be very much in accord with reality, especially given a predilection to look upon nature with heightened emotion and to imbue primitive life with benevolence. Seen this way, even the most effusive work might pass for straightforward description. This also serves to point up another close alignment with pastoralism, that of cultural primitivism (Marx 1964, Preminger 1965). Here it is not so much a case of being less civilized, in the normal chronological sense of the term *primitive*, but rather one of being in tune with nature to the extent of acquiring superior wisdom and insight.

During the eighteenth and early nineteenth centuries, the English countryside was literally transformed into idealized pastoral settings for both the establishment and the newly rich (figure 145). Yet again the pastoral design seems to have been chosen for its backward references and piety. Gardeners like Gilpin even referred to it as "moral gardening" (Hunt and Willis 1975). Nevertheless, it was also a way of masking the social realities of the industrial revolution and legitimizing the resulting individual accumulation of capital. Of greater relevance to us here, however, is the idea of pastoralism in American life and the strong attraction it has held for us there.

Leo Marx unequivocally states in the opening line of his classic work on the subject, "the pastoral ideal has been used to define the meaning of America ever since the age of discovery, and it has not yet lost its hold upon the native imagination" (Marx 1964, p. 3). He distinguishes two kinds of pastoralism, the first "popular and sentimental" and the second "imaginative and complex" (Marx 1964, pp. 12f.). The popular and sentimental version juxtaposes the ideal of rural life against the "moral vice and depravity of the city," to be found in depictions like figure 146. Those who are close to nature and retreat into "primitive self" are both better persons and happily insulated and sheltered from "big city life." Many popular versions of early rural life, the western frontier myth,

Figure 145   An opulent English country estate amid its pasotral setting: Claremont House, Surrey, by Capability Brown, 1770s

and even the communes of the counterculture reflect this sentiment (Smith 1950, O'Neill 1971). The most important aspect is pastoralism and dwelling in natural circumstances as an alternative to urbanism. The primitive hero retreats into the countryside and nature in order to "locate value as far as possible from organized society" (Marx 1964, p. 22).

Rather than presenting a clear alternative or an oppositional sentiment, imaginative and complex pastoralism strikes something of a dialectical relationship between the opposing forces of city and countryside. Like the Virgilian shepherd contemplating his arcadian landscape, there is an attempt to resolve any conflict between the different worlds of nature and art (Marx 1964, pp. 22f.). The more contemporary literary example Leo Marx uses to illuminate this concept is Nathaniel Hawthorne's "Sleepy Hollow," written in 1844. In this narrative set in the New England rural landscape, Hawthorne is meticulously observing and reflecting on his surrounding natural circumstances when his idyllic re-

Figure 146   Overcrowding, squalor, and city slums: Cliff Dwellers, *by George Wesley Bellows, 1913. The Los Angeles County Museum of Art, Los Angeles County Funds.*

velry is punctuated by the whistle of a railway train in the distance. This interruption has the rather immediate effect of causing a shift in attention from nature and self to the broader complex of nature, self, and the civilization of which both are now a part (Marx 1964, pp. 20f.). In this passage Hawthorne assigns to the train the role of qualifying the idyllic fantasy, thus grounding it in a contemporary reality, a motif commonly used by American landscape painters of the day. Overall it is a pastoral design in which the pastoral ideal, or metaphor, is exposed to the pressures that will change it most dramatically. In the hands of other nineteenth-century romantic writers like Wordsworth, Emerson, and Thoreau, the pastoral ideal became a form of semiprimitivism, located in, as Marx puts it, a middle ground, not entirely natural and not without the technological presence of civilization (Marx 1964, p. 23).

Ralph Waldo Emerson's tract "Nature" (1836) establishes and develops this theme. Not only are nature and romantic pastoralism a middle ground between opposing forces of civilization and nature, they are also in a preeminent relationship to those forces. "Nature is made to conspire with spirit to emancipate us," Emerson wrote (1836, p. 10). According to this transcendentalist manifesto, identity between people and their natural world is struck by constructive reflection on both circumstances. It seems to create a third term that is not entirely of humanity or of nature. Primary direction is still provided, however, though nature by the method of equating moral laws with natural laws (Czestochowski 1982). Emerson believed that man has immediate access to God, or the "Over Soul," as he put it, through nature. In short, the Over Soul was found in and throughout nature, finally rendering irrelevant differences, say, between hunter and hunted or between one idea and other ideas. All, in the end, were manifestations of the Over Soul (Miller 1956).

At this stage there may appear to be an unnecessary conflation of terms like wilderness, frontier, nature, and pastoralism, although all are certainly well distanced and in the same direction from the overtly man-made and from urbanism. The wilderness and frontier have been deliberately linked here with pastoralism to the extent that conquest of the wilderness on the frontier largely gave rise, in the American experience, to pastoral developments (Hart 1972). It is precisely this act of the conversion of the wilderness that seems to have resulted in a peculiarly American brand of pastoralism. It was also, according to historians like Turner, a process that profoundly promoted formation of a national character (Turner 1948, McGiffert 1970). The term nature, by contrast, is used far more comprehensively and loosely. Primarily it refers to nonartifactual environments.

The preoccupation of Americans with their natural circumstances is understandable given the relatively undeveloped state of their continent in the early years. The sheer fascination with the wilderness of the New World (Smith 1950, Nash 1982, Machor 1987) is nowhere more apparent than in the strong American tradition of landscape painting where an Edenic theme is constantly present, ranging from largely descriptive chronicles of nature's moods to the awesomely sublime (Czestochowski 1982). By the end of the first third of the nineteenth century, this interest in the wilderness landscape was closely aligned with the beginnings of an era of optimism that accompanied Andrew Jackson's election as president in 1828 and the so-called Jacksonian Revolution (Blum et al. 1963). In the affirmation of an American culture that was distinctly American, wilderness themes were a rather obvious recourse. As one chronicler wrote, "Wilderness landscape was valued for its Americanizing influence and its ability to transmit new energy to society" (Czestochowski 1982, p. 12).

The wilderness played a crucial role in the drama of nature versus civilization that was found in both the political and agrarian interests of Jackson and within intellectual circles of the time. As Perry Miller so aptly observed, "The most utilitarian conquest known to history had some how to be viewed not as a calculus of rising land values and investments, but . . . as an immense exertion of the spirit. . . . Those who made articulate the meaning of this drama found their frame of reference not in political economy but . . . in visions of sublimity." Paradoxically, "the more rapidly the primordial forest was filled, the more desperately [we] strove to identify the unique personality of this republic with the virtues . . . of 'romantic Nature'" (Miller 1956, p. 207).

Distinctively pastoral themes in landscape painting emerged strongly at this time, especially in works by Thomas Cole. Several of his major canvases juxtapose rural scenes and wilderness landscapes, suggesting not only two different points of view but a thematic transition as well. Not unlike Miller, Barbara Novak insightfully points out that the true wilderness was rapidly vanishing under the onslaught of development, raising a problem for "America's religion of God-in-nature" (Novak 1976, p. 45). Into the breach between reality and symbolic requirement fell pastoralism. What better way to endorse the "civilizing of the American wilderness in the name of progress" than by the transformation of the Edenic wilderness into a pastoral Garden of Eden, a rural paradise that humanized the impact of development (Novak 1976, pp. 45f.)?

Cole's *Expulsion from the Garden of Eden* (1827–1828) makes this distinction in artistic terms (figure 147). The scene is roughly divided into halves: on the right Eden represented as a pastoral scene; on the left a ravaged, unruly wilderness of gnarled trees and craggy rocks. Two figures stand at the threshold between these two domains, clearly passing from the Garden of Eden into the wilderness. On one level the painting is a straightforward biblical narrative that matches its title. On another level, it is a moral allegory about the human task of remaking the wilderness in the image of a pastoral setting (Novak 1976). A third related aspect of possible interpretation and one of historical import expands Novak's central point. Early settlers often came to the American wilderness from, at the best of times anyway, the productive and civilized influences of European rural landscapes. Cole's didactic point is one of inevitable transformation. Not only is it right and proper to transform the wilderness into a pastoral landscape but it is also an inevitable duty.

The same general argument appears in Cole's *The Oxbow* (1836), depicted in figure 148. Once again the scene within the painting is split roughly into two, although this time the dividing line runs approximately in a diagonal direction from top left to bottom right. The painting shows a view from a virgin forested hillside down and out over a verdant river valley, clearly under cultivation. The hillside already evidences a human presence; a few trees have been felled. Abandoning the Claudian frame of trees that dutifully embellishes the earlier pastoral setting, a thunderstorm appears over the forested area, while the rural landscape is bathed in bright sunlight (Czestochowski 1982, p. 15). The message of the picture clearly seems to be, "out of the wilderness toward civilization." This interpretation matches Cole's own in his "Essay" of 1836: "American associations are not so much of the past as they are of the present and

Figure 147   Wilderness and pastoral garden: Expulsion from the Garden of Eden, *1827–1828, by Thomas Cole. Gift of Mrs. Maxim Karolik for the Karolik collection of American Paintings, 1815–1865. Courtesy, Museum of Fine Arts, Boston.*

the future. . . . By looking over the yet uncultivated scene, the mind's eye may see far into futurity" (McCoubrey 1965, p. 102). The painting also has the potential for being a cautionary tale; the thunderstorm moving into the wilderness from the divide may bring not only the winds of change but a destructive wind as well, reflecting Cole's belief that the wilderness is the essential American landscape (McCoubrey 1965, pp. 101f.).

By midcentury landscape paintings showed an increasing tendency to depict agricultural settings.

James Hope's *Bird Mountain, Castleton, Vermont* (1855), for instance, seems to stress the benign coexistence of nature and human settlement in idyllic pastoral surroundings. Other paintings of the same period tend to dwell more on human enterprise, with the natural landscape receding into the background (Cantor 1976). George Inness's well-known *The Lackawanna Valley* (1854), probably the work most alluded to in this kind of discussion, seems to capture Hawthorne's theme from "Sleepy Hollow" (Marx 1964, p. 220). A young boy is portrayed sitting lean-

Figure 148   Out of the wilderness toward civilization:
The Oxbow *(The Connecticut River near Northampton),*
1836, by Thomas Cole. The Metropolitan Museum of Art,
gift of Mrs. Russell Sage, 1908.

ing against a tree on a small hill overlooking railroad lines, with a steam train moving out into a verdant countryside from a railroad terminal and turning shed. The same may be also said of Jasper Cropsey's *Starucca Viaduct* (1865), depicted in figure 149. The youthful observer ponders a pastoral scene already showing the affects of the industrial revolution. In this work the viewing point recedes further back in history, reflecting earlier conditions of wilderness.

Successive pictorial depictions move from the wilderness becoming pastoral to, finally, industrialization. Even today pastoral and pastoral devices persist, although the design often appears to have gone through another transformation. For instance, in

Rackstraw Downe's *The Coke Works of Clainton, Pa.* (1975), like the factory shown in figure 150, a rather romantic view of a sprawling coke works, running along a river bend near Pittsburgh, is presented, framed and even enveloped by a distinctly pastoral setting. Through luminous-colored smoke and stark figural outlines, the coke mill is made to appear intriguing and objectlike in its setting. The painting not only has the justifying effect on technological development that Novak pointed to earlier but seems to take another step in the historical progression of pastoral themes as well. We have been taken from wilderness, to rural landscape, to agriculture, to industry, and now back in the other direction. It is a complex pastoral image, to use Leo Marx's concept, but one in which the relative dominance of the terms is reversed. Nevertheless, it remains a hopeful presentation, optimistic about our ability to stem the industrial and technological tide by shifting it into a middle ground.

Robert Bechtle's *Agua Caliente Nova*, a piece of photorealism from the same year, is more cynical. In a direct reference to the nineteenth-century landscape painting of, say, the Hudson River School, we see a touring family and their car turning their backs on a pastoral view of Palm Springs. The pastoral design is

clearly complex and imaginative. It has a taut, slightly delirious quality, like the adventures in Pynchon's printed circuit megalopolis of "Telladyne," "the valley," and "pink flamingos."

James Machor has recently built on Leo Marx's conceptual framework, developing the concept of urban pastoralism (Machor 1987). He distinguishes it from the earlier simple and complex versions of pastoralism by emphasizing integration and differences in moral tone. For Machor, urban pastoralism is an urban-rural synthesis that is "more than an attempt to infuse into cities touches of greenery and rural virtue"

Figure 149   The wilderness, the pastoral, and the industrial: Starrucca Viaduct, Pennsylvania, *by Jasper Francis Cropsey, 1865. The Toledo Museum of Art: Gift of Florence Scott Libbey.*

Figure 150   A modern industrial-pastoral landscape

(Machor 1987, p. 14). Contrary to the Greco-Roman concept of pastoralism per se, the roots of urban pastoralism lie in biblical visions of a reconstituted city. The root metaphor is the Judeo-Christian concept of Isaiah's and St. John the Divine's New Jerusalem (Machor 1987). As such it carries with it both the mythic ideas of redemption and a paradise to be regained.

The change in moral tone or, as Machor puts it, "moral geography," is located by the difference between individualism and cooperative society. Whereas the pastoral idea connotes individual freedom in a landscape devoid of "corporate society," urban pastoralism emphasizes "personal fulfillment with a co-operative identity" (Machor 1987, p. 13). Machor uses Henry George's *Progress and Poverty* (1879) to illustrate this difference, stressing George's conclusion that "a rural urbanity [of] homes and gardens" would create a "great co-operative society . . .

in which government would be greatly simplified" (Machor 1987, p. 14). George was referring to the ultimate effects of his single tax idea, whereby wealth attributable to high land values, and not to production, would be severely taxed. George believed the government would require no other financial intervention into the lives of citizens, who, in turn, would dwell in an environment devoid of socioeconomic distinctions based on property ownership (George 1955). What is particularly interesting to us about this slant is that it begins to refer to the American corporate-government presence within the pastoral concept. It also associates a socialistically inclined form of majoritarianism as a political belief with pastoralism. All of this is not entirely happenstance either. Long before George, the popularity of pastoral artistic themes in the Jacksonian era coincided with the well-known rise of cooperative majoritarian party rule in American political life (Nelson 1982).

Pastoralism is a cornerstone of American intellectual and artistic experience, particularly when it comes to location of appropriate grounds for human settlement. Although there are certain naive and simpleminded applications of the concept as an escape from civilization and urbanity, pastoralism is essentially a complex formulation. Although it never denies the self-enlightening and moral benefits to be gained by a rural existence, it does not deny technological developments either. In its most sophisticated forms, pastoralism continues to serve as a critical lens through which to mark human progress and as an optimistic source for dealing with threats encroaching from either a natural or an urban wilderness. It also serves to remind us of basic, honest social values, particularly during the times of considerable change. America was and remains a great agricultural nation, rooted in the land.

THE MODERN TECHNICAL ORIENTATION

The modern technical orientation is sustained by three complementary ideas: a technological way of making things, a technocratic way of managing things, and, at root, a scientific way of interpreting people and their world. Unlike pastoralism with its overwhelming associations with a particular kind of place, the modern technical orientation and temperament is ubiquitous and primarily concerned with a mode of acting on the world.

By the end of the nineteenth century, the United States had surpassed its European rivals to become the largest manufacturing country in the world (Habakkuk 1962). This rapid rise from an agrarian economy a century earlier was due to the influence and progress made by mass production, or what was sometimes referred to as the American system of manufacture (Colton and Bruchey 1987, Sparke 1987). By as early as 1850 American industry had developed a generic kind of industrial production process that was structurally different from European counterparts, making far more advanced use of mechanization. Instead of relying on individual craftsmen to produce unique products, anonymous engineers within a mechanical production process designed and produced identical component parts, which were then assembled into products (Habakkuk 1962). This approach, once a commitment was made

to a particular product line, had the twin advantages of speed of manufacture and ease of later repair and maintenance. The key was standardization of product components and a fairly high level of interchangeability of those components to produce other, different products (Sparke 1987).

The rapid rise of industrial mass production in the United States was undoubtedly a complex phenomenon but one that in certain respects was born out of necessity (Habakkuk 1962, Bruner 1972, Sparke 1987). There was a relative lack of cheap, skilled labor to produce required goods; a burgeoning demand for products, under the pressure of very rapid population growth, that outstripped craft production; and a mechanization of complex crafts like gun manufacture, whereas in places like England mechanization was largely confined to simpler crafts like textiles (Giedion 1969, Sparke 1987). This reckoning with complexity paved the way for widespread early use of mass production. Finally, in a pragmatic spirit of basic utility in use first and decoration a long second, products could afford to be standardized and less involved simply with matters of taste. This last point may not entirely hold. Artifice was not lacking in many quarters. However, when faced with the larger issues of settlement and resource development, dalliance with style was deferred to a future period of calmer, stable prosperity. What is clear was the very early introduction of relatively unadorned factory products into the American domestic environment, as some of the very first examples of product design (Sparke 1987).

The broader social ramifications of widespread use and dependence on industrial technology were quite far reaching and part of the modern legacy. First, the system of manufacture required a highly organized division of labor. Even without achieving the pathetic heights of Charles Chaplin's *Modern Times* or the oppressive dronelike qualities of Fritz Lang's *Metropolis*, production tasks were narrowly defined and highly specialized. Furthermore, there was the constant tyranny of scheduling and production quotas to be met. All an industrialist, like Henry Ford, had to do was to increase the rate of the assembly line process (Nevins and Hill 1957, Hounshell 1985). Thus labor specialization and a dependence on some larger-order, abstractly conceived system of activities became commonplace.

Second, quantity production and product standardization brought with it requirements for high levels of capital investment in machines and manufacturing plants (figure 151). Accompanying this requirement were larger corporations and industrial conglomerates, which could effectively absorb the high initial costs. These large corporations, in turn, became a significant part of many Americans' daily lives. As we have seen, through a sort of paternalism and regimentation, ritual ways of doing things often emulated corporate procedures. Above all, scheduling and division of daily activities into discrete tasks gradually imposed a meter on our modern existence, dramatically changing its tempo.

Third, as Sparke points out, "the concept of a homogenous mass market was central to the idea of American mass production" (Sparke 1987, pp. 45f.). Probably nowhere was this concept more fully exploited than in the production of the Model T Ford automobile during the early 1920s. The uniformity was

Figure 151   Mass production in the manufacturing plant: General Motors assembly line in the 1960s

so total that it even inspired legendary statements by the car manufacturer to the effect that "you can buy any colored Ford that you want so long as you choose black!" (Nevins and Hill 1957, Hounshell 1985). Partial creation of mass markets undoubtedly followed from the ready availability of relatively inexpensive consumer products. However, expansion and perpetuation required sophisticated mass marketing, one of the effects of which was to sustain the production processes, at least during times of relative affluence (Galbraith 1958).

Necessity, opportunity, and technological know-how produced an American way of making things that centered on high capital investment, high division of labor, quantity production, variety within standardization, and mass marketing. Its appeal was (and probably remains) perceived improvements in the material quality of life and particularly broad access to that quality. By contrast, its romance and ability to capture the imagination are largely matters of a sense of conquest over the forces of nature (figure 152). To build a car that almost everyone could afford, to break the sound barrier, to put a person on the moon, and to perform thousands of complex calculations per second seemed magical. However—and this is perhaps why the romance continued—they were also feats that almost seemed inevitable. So ingrained had the prospect of technological progress become that there developed a tacit assumption that little was impossible.

Much of this optimism and a similar style of thinking carried over into the management of daily affairs. In addition to making things, performance of services, arrival at important decisions, and the direction of activities were all taken on as matters of the correct application of information and expertise. Performance in these pursuits became a dispassionate activity, with little room for immediate matters of the heart.

By the end of the first decade of this century, Frederick W. Taylor and others were devising and developing scientific principles for the control and management of seemingly even the simplest of tasks. In one of his classic early studies, Taylor sought to establish the optimum size, or load-carrying capacity, of a laborer's shovel. By performing empirical tests in which different-sized shovels were used to move sand from one place to another, he established a nonlinear relationship between shovel size and time to carry out the task. Similar so-called time-and-motion

Figure 152   The technological genie at work on the domestic environment

studies were performed for all manner of activities, ranging from the domestic environment of kitchens (figure 153) to industrial assembly lines. Corporations, smelling profits in the air, became fascinated by these exercises and predicated their production management procedures accordingly (Haber 1964).

Following World War II, special analytical techniques developed through branches of applied mathematics for better understanding and for being able to manipulate the behavior of complex arrangements of activities. Coordination of all the myriad number of tasks that went into the engineering and construction of a nuclear Polaris submarine, with varying schedules and attached levels of uncertainty, was probably the most celebrated case (Kaufmann 1968). Soon

corporations and government bureaucracies were making similar applications to a wide variety of enterprises. Quickly management became an arcane field for technical experts. Information, vital for their operations, became increasingly specialized, and unprecedented demands were placed on storage, collation, manipulation and dissemination of these data (La Patra 1973).

An underlying assumption in this technocratic way of doing things was that the world was subject to effective empirical description and, as a corollary, that performance could be measured (Catanese 1972, Dickey and Watts 1978). This manifests itself in terminology such as efficiency, optimality, and rationality, through which certain yardsticks can be con-

Figure 153   A result of Taylor's scientific management in the home: efficient versus inefficient kitchen layouts

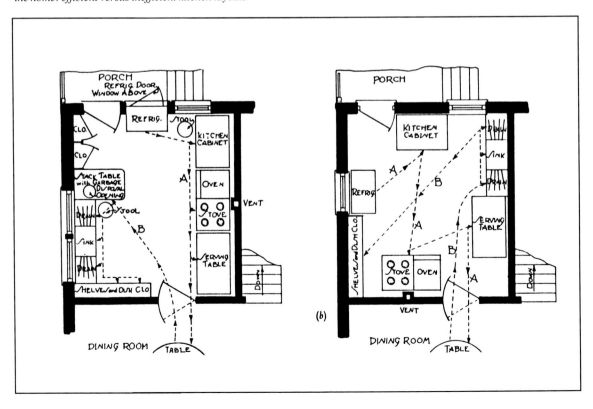

structed. Then, strategies can be developed for attaining a certain datum on a given yardstick. For instance, in the conduct of our business we might "maximize" our profits, "minimize" our losses, or even "maximize" our "minimum" losses—and we may do all of this with varying degrees of certainty as to the outcome of our business ventures. Soon a "science of decision making" was believed to have been fashioned and received widespread application in the affairs of both government and industry (Kaufmann 1968).

Soon after the turn of the century, the terrain of cities was subdivided, under the influence of so-called rational and comprehensive planning and zoning practices, along the lines of distinct and discrete patterns of use (Scott 1969, American Law Institute 1975, Krueckeberg 1983). The placement of transportation systems and their associated gradients of accessibility (figure 154) particularized land use distributions, both separating and concentrating functions across the metropolitan landscape (Clawson and Hall 1973). The home environment was just that—a residential area with support services such as schooling, shopping, and recreation provided nearby. Similarly places of work were aggregated together and serviced with their appropriate supporting functions. The emerging plans were deemed efficient, and the results provided a predictable and manipulable order ready to accommodate future development (Rowe 1987).

Quite apart from a specialized emphasis on objective categories and data in the worlds of business and governance, Americans throughout much of this century seem to have believed in facts. Furthermore,

Figure 154 Technocratic planning and the rational distribution of urban functions: development around the Central and Northwest Expressways, Dallas, Texas, 1985. Copyright Doug Tomlinson, 1985.

as Jean Baudrillard astutely put it, "Americans see statistics as an optimistic stimulus, as representing the dimension of their good fortune [and] their joyous membership of the majority" (Baudrillard 1988, p. 87). Score cannot only be kept, but life itself is perhaps best known through facts.

At the core of these technical ways of making things, doing things, and thinking about things is a firm belief in facts and a scientific interpretation of people and their world (Bernstein 1976, Rowe 1987). Not only is the natural world seen as validly subject to scientific analysis, but a science of human behavior is also possible, and the results of this science can be effectively used to create operational models, whereby abstract representations of phenomena, like transportation and housing choice, are created and then manipulated to predict patterns of human behavior under various controlling assumptions (Chadwick 1972,

Myths and Masks

Domencich and McFadden 1975). Real difficulties come, however, when moving from the realm of facts, by which this perspective is shaped, to those of value, by which it is not.

In spite of enthusiastic support and widespread use, there has been a concomitant questioning of the validity and comprehensiveness of this kind of scientific position in planning circles, largely on philosophical grounds (Krimerman 1969, Bernstein 1976). Whether there can be a full science of human behavior remains an open question, and with it the logical-empirical orthodoxy's a priori claims to validity and reliability. In the end this technical orientation can be set beside other interpretations of people and their world. For us the key difference is its pervasiveness as a fundamental part of our national temperament.

MODERN PASTORALISM

Conceptually the conjunction of pastoralism with a modern technical orientation brings with it several interesting asymmetries. Unlike Machor's urban pastoralism, where both terms relate to specific spatial domains like city and countryside, the geography of modern pastoralism is far less precise.

Pastoralism is strongly rooted in a particular kind of spatial domain. Even in its complex or urban pastoral forms it cannot be literally removed very far from the countryside or metaphorically from those special attributes the countryside has to offer—rusticity, a cultivated landscape, domestication of the wilderness, and so on. By contrast, modernism, es-

pecially in its technical aspects, is ubiquitous. It is a way of operating on the world and is not about place or a place in any particular sense. It is a temperament and an attitude that can just as easily exist in urban as in rural areas.

Another dimension along which the two terms seem to differ is the distinction that can be made between means and ends. The modern technical orientation is much more about means and ways of doing things than it is about ends, or the purposes to which the means are to be put. Pastoralism is the reverse, at least superficially. It prescribes a state of being in the world, an end, that is rather well defined.

A certain terminological slipperiness and equivocation arises, however, when we also realize that pastoralism, particularly in its sophisticated forms, is also about means. It is a way of understanding the world and, according to the romantic inclination, a way of transcending the immediate experience of both civilization and nature. In practice anyway, the logical-empirical orthodoxy at the core of technical modernism can suffer from a kind of means-ends conflation. Not infrequently government empirical surveys are conducted to identify social problems, the solution strategies for which are couched in the self-same empirical terms. For example, housing needs might well be assessed by enumerating for specific income groups the number of households compared to available units, from which it quickly follows that a particular number of units should be constructed or made available. This mode of decision making works until formulation of problems in this way either preserves distinctions inherent in the empirical model or precludes useful search for other kinds of solutions that reach well beyond the empirical orthodoxy (figure 155). Rather than being a case of personal shortsightedness, outcomes can be methodologically predetermined. Generally insisting so totally on empirical measurement and analysis limits the scope of problems that can be seriously entertained or, more important, speculated about. For instance, the symbolic realm of human experience is totally bypassed. The central issue is not whether planning models exhibit explanatory power or predictive accuracy. Rather it is that a limiting, dependent relationship can be struck between the possibility of formulating social goals and the technical exigencies of following through on empirical model development (Rowe 1987).

Apart from asymmetries, there is also a strict oppositional quality to the two terms in modern pastoralism in much the same way as Machor's urban pastoralism presents an inherent opposition (Machor 1987). As we saw, there is a certain organic oneness to the idea of knowing the world under pastoralism. It provides a framework through which, as Leo Marx put it, resolution can be achieved. The shepherd does not try to escape his immediate world to another place

Figure 155   Public housing tragically mired in an architecture of social difference: Robert Taylor Homes, Chicago, 1960.

but rather tries to resolve any inherent differences (Marx 1964, pp. 19f.). In complete contrast, knowing, according to the modern technical temperament, is a specialized and compartmentalized undertaking. There are different disciplines to be mastered, each with its own special language and technical accompaniment. Finally, organic knowing, at least in some versions of pastoralism, is of the senses, whereas the technical temperament is far more dispassionate and intellectual.

In its direct application to the interpretation of suburban metropolitan development, modern pastoralism also exhibits an asymmetrical arrangement of the two inherent concepts. For instance, in outward appearance anyway, the domestic environment of home and garden strongly favors the pastoral scene of a traditional cottage in a cultivated, bucolic landscape. In its period-style kitsch, it is often a naive and nostalgic pastoral presentation, as depicted in figure 156, although a more complex form can lurk below the surface. Generally, however, behind American suburban residential development has been a sort of moral superiority and sense of escape from the vice and depravity of the city (Warner 1962).

The modern office park usually presents a more complex pastoral form in which the two parts to the equation are more evenly balanced and therefore, at times, starkly contrasted. The garden setting is often landscaped in a naturalistic parklike manner reminiscent of eighteenth- and nineteenth-century English garden traditions. By contrast, the office buildings themselves usually bask resplendently in a highly abstract, well-engineered rational aesthetic. The resulting ensemble is very much a case of a machine in the

Figure 156   Naive and nostalgic pastoral presentation: a suburban house in Massachusetts

garden, to invoke Leo Marx's highly descriptive phrase.

The environment of commercial retail shopping centers pulls the equation still further in the techno-logical direction. Overtly these environments are ra-tionalized and functionally explicit. They are largely devoid of garden landscapes, except in rather pre-cious preserves. The pastoral perspective is almost entirely missing within the complexes themselves, becoming more apparent only in their larger setting. If we reserve judgment or concentrate on examples with highly articulated landscape architecture, the potential of striking a stronger balance between a technical orientation and the pastoral becomes apparent.

Roadways seem to fall somewhere in between corporate estates and retail centers. Certainly park-ways present a well-balanced formulation of the

modern pastoral equation where engineering neces-sity and refinement are well couched in bucolic, park-like settings. Similar remarks might also be made about the layout of numerous suburban subdivisions. Many urban expressways, however, are stark in their functional rationalism and as bereft of a pastoral pres-ence as many shopping areas (figure 154).

Modern pastoralism—that merger between the pastoral perspective and the modern technical orien-tation—is not evenly distributed in the modern met-ropolitan landscape. Different realms appear to have different emphases. The regional, spatial mosaic it-self remains ambiguous, belonging to both orienta-tions. From one point of view the specialization and separation of precincts of one kind from those of an-other make rational sense, fitting a sociotechnical perspective. From another vantage point, an agrarian model of spatial distribution is also well served.

HISTORICISM AND UTOPIANISM

Idealization of life in the countryside, one of the prin-cipal themes of suburban metropolitan development, points toward the future and provides a healthy alter-native to life in the allegedly dingy and decadent city. At first glance it has all the earmarks of being a uto-pian vision of human settlement. This aura is particu-larly evident in works like Ebenezer Howard's Gar-den City of 1898 and Frank Lloyd Wright's Broadacre City of 1935, or thereabouts, where ideal plans and social circumstances are proposed in the best tradition of at least nineteenth-century utopian planning (Benevolo 1971, Kostof 1985).

Howard's *Garden Cities of Tomorrow* proposed the vision of a new kind of a town, located out in the countryside, where the root causes of the dirt, grime, and confusion of industrial metropolises could be addressed beforehand (Kostof 1985). The town was to be laid out in concentric rings, moving from the town center and business area, via parks and tree-lined avenues, to houses in gardens and thence out into the countryside. Industry was located away on the periphery beside a railway, linked to other centers. The proposal was to house some 32,000 people on 1,000 acres of land, with an additional 5,000 acres of adjacent land set aside around the town for agriculture. Letchworth (figure 157), the first city based on these organizational principles, was established in 1902, about 80 miles northeast of London (Howard 1902). The Garden City movement—for that is what it became under the influential leadership of planners like Unwin and Parker—"drew strength from a deep English commitment to offset the gall of urbanization" (Kostof 1985, p. 680). Kostof ties it to the arts and crafts movement and luminaries like Morris and Ruskin, demonstrating an ancestry that has strong pastoral inclinations and an opposition to the despoiling effects of industrialization (Kostof 1985).

Wright began work on proposals for urban decentralization, the central theme of his Broadacre City proposal, in 1930 when the depression adversely

Figure 157   A garden city for tomorrow: Letchworth, England, 1902

affected his practice (Wright 1943). Elements of the proposal first appeared in the Kahn lecture he gave at Princeton University in 1930 and were subsequently pulled together in his *Autobiography* published in 1943 and in several earlier articles (Wright 1932, 1943). A partial proposal was also exhibited in model form at Rockefeller Center, New York, in 1935 (figure 158). Fundamentally, Broadacre City sets forth Wright's broad social ambitions for Usonia, a term he coined to refer to, as he put it," organic social welfare . . . and a reformed American society" (Wright 1943, Sergeant 1984). In a manner that refers directly to our prevalent suburban concepts of social organization," the Broadacre conclusion was to dig deeper, untangle and decentralize everything—except Government, to simplify and organize Government as a matter of the people's business directly" (Wright 1943, p. 20).

The proposal depicts a postscarcity society in which 1,400 families dwelled, with 1 acre of land each at their disposal. The community extensively employed technical and mechanical aids, such as high-speed highways, and a form of helicopter call the aerotor. They also lived in close touch with their agrarian circumstances, aiming at a kind of environmental self-sufficiency. Management of community affairs was largely the responsibility of technical experts, particularly those skilled in the study of structure, such as architects (Wright 1943, Sergeant 1984). In its use of technological and technocratic means within a clearly defined rural agrarian setting, Broadacre City has all the features of a modern pastoral. Given the future circumstance in which it is placed and the rhetoric that surrounds it, the proposal

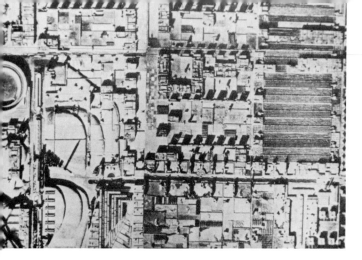

*Figure 158   A utopian postscarcity society: Broadacre
City, by Frank Lloyd Wright, 1935*

also has distinctly utopian overtones. Beyond appearances, however, the question still remains whether this and other proposals with strong pastoral inclinations should be considered utopian.

Mannheim, in his classic work on utopian thinking, defines the term utopia "by limiting [it] to that type of orientation which transcends reality and which at the same time breaks the bonds of the existing order" (Mannheim 1936, p. 192). Any direct link between now and the future, or indeed the past, is broken. Mannheim continued, "A distinction is thus set up between utopian and ideological states of mind," where "ideology" may transcend reality but without breaking the bonds of the existing order (Mannheim 1936, pp. 192–93). With these definitions, the utopian case for modern pastoralism and suburban metropolitan development becomes one about reference and history, for, as Bentmann and Müller point out, "utopia and history stand in the way of each other," by which they mean that the former must refer to the latter (Bentmann and Müller 1985, p. 84).

On the face of it, the inclination of pastoralism is toward the past. Its narrative is about a simpler age with more direct and sincere involvement with the basic circumstances and rhythms of living. The ref-

erences are thus historical, and therefore pastoralism may be ideological, but it is not strictly utopian (Bentmann and Müller 1985). Certainly if we focus the scope of this analysis on the domestic suburban realm, the symbolism of period styles of housing is blantantly historicizing, with direct references to specific eras in the American past. Moreover, there is a strong traditional pall hanging over everything. As we have already seen, according to Wood's study of suburban social organization and modes of government, past practices like the old New England form of town meeting are also preferred (Wood 1958).

While the present orientation of modern pastoralism in suburban metropolitan development is historicist rather than utopian, the question still remains whether pastoral and arcadian proposals are destined to remain that way. Is it possible to build in a country landscape in a manner that essentially breaks the bounds of the present order? The answer is largely affirmative. Orthodox architectural modernism and urbanistic proposals like Le Corbusier's Ville Radieuse go a long way in the utopian direction. The material composition and aesthetic inclination of the architecture make a strong break with the past (Le Corbusier 1964). The simple juxtaposition of buildings within a verdant, minimally cultivated landscape, sometimes in an alignment that seems to float free of the natural gorund plane, is also not traditional. Both aspects are well illustrated in the Chamberlain house (1940), designed by Walter Gropius and Marcel Breuer (figure 159). Nevertheless, amid all of this novelty, the thinking often reverts suddenly to the pastoral and arcadian aspirations from an earlier time. For instance, Le Corbusier made the following statement in obvious reference to Poissy and others of his villas: "I shall place this house on columns in a beautiful corner of the countryside; we shall have twenty houses rising above the long grass of a meadow where cattle will continue to graze," clearly establishing the agrarian pastoral motif. In the most telling passage he states" The dwellers in these houses, drawn hence through love of the countryside . . . their lives will be set within a Virgilian dream" (Le Corbusier 1930, p. 133). Suddenly utopia is transformed, or at the very least interpreted, as history.

Modern pastoralism's claim to being an ideology, in Mannheim's terms, is stronger and far less ambiguous. Many of the nineteenth-century formulations and uses of pastoral motifs conform closely to the essential structure of an ideology. The presence of a third term that transcends or resolves the natural and the technological progressive, found in complex forms of pastoralism, is of particular importance to this claim. Further, it suggests that naive and nostalgic forms do not have quite the same ideological

Figure 159 Orthodox modernism and the pastoral domestic landscape: Chamberlain House, by Gropius and Breuer, 1940

inclination, falling short, as they do, of the transcendental turn.

CRITICAL REALITY

Being rooted in both the past and present does not necessarily disable modern pastoralism from being a powerful and progressive critical ideology. Despite Bentmann and Müller's implications, the alternative to utopia is not necessarily socially regressive or dystopian (Bentmann and Müller 1985). Utopian thinking has a particular kind of positive social purpose but not the only one we might imagine (Mannheim 1936). By remaining disconnected from the current order of things, a utopian vision poses fresh, new social concepts. The upshot may be self-reflection, criticism, and ultimately striving in quite a different direction from the past. It is this distancing effect that gives utopian thinking its radical opportunity and, at times, its political acceptability.

The ideology of modern pastoralism may not be radical, but it can enjoy certain advantages from being connected with the present order. It becomes a practical kind of doctrine, one that can be used in the here and now. And it may not run quite the same risk of misunderstanding. For people like Americans with a strong pragmatic orientation and philosophical outlook, these advantages can be attractive.

This critical stance can work in the following reciprocal manner. First, the pastoral side of the ideological equation bounds the technical orientation by clearly establishing the terrain and many of the ends for urban development enterprises. Second, the modern technical orientation maintains productivity and prevents the pastoral from sliding into a useless wilderness. A more concrete example of this interplay is apparent in the use of conservancy to manage and redirect technological developments in, for example, energy and real estate industries. A benign semirural life can be promoted, in turn, by technological improvements to wild and remote areas. Admittedly, in this age of sophisticated technology, it is far more likely to be the case that the pastoral side of the ideology will have the more work to do. In fact, it is precisely for this function that modern pastoralism, as defined, holds out so much promise as the metaphorical context for contemporary metropolitan urban development.

Beyond processes of control and self-regulation, where one side of the ideological equation is made to work on the other, the true critical dimension comes from the insights and knowledge thus gained. Truly constructive and progressive ideologies must contain the basis for understanding their own limitations (Habermas 1971, 1975). Placing the pastoral perspective and the modern technical orientation in such a way that they can be used effectively in this manner provides a critical impetus to modern pastoralism.

Although neither American in outlook nor specifically pastoral in orientation, the contemporary radical architecture of groups like Superstudio and Archizoom Associati clearly and simply illustrates fundamentals of this critical ideological stance. In projects such as Superstudio's *Twelve Imaginary Cities* of 1971, for instance, as in work of the surrealists before them, we are immediately confronted, time and again, with images of commonplace objects ei-

ther enlarged or scaled down and either superimposed upon or displaced by the surrounding terrain. The work *Skyscraper with Rubber Plant Leaves* (1969), by Archizoom Associati, is almost self-explanatory in this regard. *Wind Town* by the same group from the same year is a little more enigmatic, although the image of something closely resembling a 1950s American automobile rear body fin, rising up amid the mesas of an Arizona landscape, has an immediacy about it that requires little explanation. Throughout, the principal narrative mechanism is a familiar object and a separate yet familiar context. Besides scaling, the poetic operations involved are usually juxtaposition and contextual shift. In short, familiar yet habitually separate objects and contexts of modern society are placed together in an unusual manner, generally though not exclusively for the purposes of qualifying and reordering the context.

The work in *Twelve Imaginary Cities* has been referred to as a "critical utopia" that "presented the existing world at a more advanced level of cognition" (Branzi 1984, p. 63). Utopian or not, it certainly presents a radical version of the present-day metropolis intended, in extremis, as an explanation of what already exists. By stretching the imagery to an almost ludicrous point of sheer madness, we are pushed to view these otherwise commonplace circumstances freshly. We are thus brought face to face with the idea of consumer culture and the practice of mass producing artifacts for popular consumption.

Clearly, here a strong debt is owed to the early avant-garde and, in particular, to movements like dada and surrealism (Jean 1980). Nevertheless, more contemporary concerns with both architecture and mass culture are also strongly in evidence. In fact, most of the urban-architectural ordering principles and images are concerned with postwar planning.

Tenth City: The City of Order (figure 160) is illustrative of this kind of approach, replete with pastoral overtones. In this work, a series of simple parallel planes rush into the perspectival scene from the foreground, disappearing toward the horizon against a distant backdrop of mountains. When making this trajectory, they seem to hover above a landscape enigmatically poised between being rural and a desert. The resulting image of human settlement is absolute and totally ordered in the most reduced possible way. Only the interval between the planes offers any kind of articulation. Both the shape and the superimposition of the urban form, as well as the inexorable drive across the countryside, immediately call

Figure 160   A comment on rational order: Superstudio's Tenth City: The City of Order, *1971*

attention to what the so-called order wrought by rational planning principles can really mean. By the same token, there is also a rather surreal beauty in the amplification and juxtaposition of these two landscape settings. Each works against the other in a confrontational yet finally complementary way.

SYMBOLIC FUNCTIONS

The twin themes of modern pastoralism can be found at work in the symbolic functioning of the cultural artifacts of the middle landscape. Moreover, the constant process of resolution under this ideological framework provides the landscape with its distinctive appearance. As yet modern pastoralism is rarely fully realized. Alas, what often occurs in its place is misrepresentation, vulgarity, and blight.

On the domestic front there is the constant pull toward modernity and progress, embracing the central ideological precept that through technology and technical planning the world can be made a better place. Conversely we also have the pull toward the traditional and the romantic. Continuity with the past, particularly a simpler rural existence where everyone is forthright and morally upstanding, can ameliorate the course of rapid growth and vast social change.

Architecturally both themes collude to produce the otherwise anachronistic artifact of the traditionally styled modern single-family house. Modernity found its way into the single-family home in its overall form and layout, although usually under heavy disguise. Tradition was the source of this disguise;

Myths and Masks _____

the shape and appearance of the house owed much to the colonial and frontier triumphs of the past, now reimagined in full pastoral splendor.

The potency of the combination drew, as much as anything else, on the disengagement of the form of the house from its figuration. Higher levels of functional efficiency, better layouts, real environmental comfort control, and longer-lasting appliances were difficult to argue with. The appearance of things, however, had other sociocultural requirements to fulfill. For several reasons it could not simply be an outcome of the fundamental tectonic makeup of the house, like the one shown in figure 159. First, such a full-blown commitment to modernity by way of technical progress, with all its connotations of mass production, flatly contradicted traditional notions of individualism, self-determination, and a simpler, rural way of life. Second, the machine aesthetic was diffi-

cult to understand and remained ambiguous and largely unexplored as a popular mode of symbolic expression. Traditional styling, by contrast, was more overtly figural and symbolically unambiguous. Furthermore, in its different variations, it could be used with much greater representational precision. The colonial of the eastern establishment, for example, could be easily deployed to mark respectability, economic stability, and conservative ease, as depicted in figure 161. It could also be used in conjunction with its surroundings to conjure up images reminiscent of the New England countryside. The western ranch could be used to mark other traditional yet no less valued sentiments of informality, openness, simplicity, and the out-of-doors. Here the surroundings tended to be more reflective of the Great Plains prairie landscape. Clearly both forms harken back to the past and both harken back to heroic moments in American his-

Figure 161   Symbol of respectability, economic stability, and ease: a suburban colonial revival house

Figure 162   Domestic realignment of the modern pastoral equation

tory—moments in which key ingredients of both intellectual and artistic pastoralism were apparent.

The poverty of current vernacular domestic architecture is not so much a matter of its incipient ideological underpinnings as it is a failure to live up to the potential of modern pastoralism. Among contemporary examples of these artifacts, what is most apparent is the use made of pastoral images as a form of disguise. The symbolic references are often used to mask the commodification that has clearly taken place, substantially undercutting the essence of the pastoral ideal being alluded to. By explicitly drawing on symbolic imagery that we historically associate with periods of egalitarian democracy, it also masks the socially regressive realities of segregation and economic elitism.

Apart from misuse, there have been few attempts in mass-produced single-family housing to harness the critical potential of modern pastoralism. Fundamentally the overwhelming use of kitschy period styling has not allowed complex versions of the ideology to be realized. The dominant reading remains one of escape to the country and into the past. With few exceptions, contemporary modern circumstances hardly register at all, let alone with sufficient presence, to pull the modern pastoral equation into a more productive symbolic alignment (figure 162).

In symbolically representing both major aspects of modern pastoralism, the contemporary suburban office park—and especially corporate headquarters—fare better than tracts of single-family houses. Here we are usually presented with a clear, often imaginatively articulated, parklike landscape into which is invariably placed an equally distinctive

building or architectural complex epitomizing modern technology. The entire ensemble usually exudes optimism, forward thinking, and reliability. Some of the examples discussed previously, like the Richardson-Vicks complex in a wooded Connecticut setting or the similar linear Union Carbide headquarters, are about as close as architecture can come to Marx's machine in the garden (figure 163). In a complex pastoral sense, movement between building and the surrounding landscape has such a direct thresholdlike quality to it that interruption and reflection on both realms seem unavoidable. Placement of high-tech offices literally within the trees could achieve the same contemplative response when office workers gaze out of the windows.

The darker side of this vision of work in a bucolic setting is the paternalistic interpretation that is often very apparent. Quite like grand English aristocratic manses, these corporate estates loom on the outskirts of many American urban areas. There is at once an exclusivity about them that sets them apart from neighboring development. Paradoxically perhaps, there is also a certain openness and egalitarian presentation to their architecture. Instead of the imposing, centrally composed facades of their earlier aristocratic counterparts, repetition of building modules seemingly expresses notions of system and function. Nevertheless, wrapped up in all of this is the strong signification of one's role in the corporation and the corporation's influence on the lives of its employees.

The stark contrast between the office building and its site's surroundings rather readily lends itself to another kind of interpretation. There is at once a sense of imposition of building on the landscape and a sense of disengagement. In a few cases, the buildings literally float across their sites. What seems to be very important is that the natural environment appears to be interrupted and impaired as little as possible. The landscape architecture complements the architecture, but both lead rather separate formal existences. Again, this combination bodes well for a machine in the garden. On the other hand, however, it may also be a piece of symbolic sleight of hand when the self-same corporation is heavily involved in resource extraction and development. The benign and progressive image being projected sometimes masks a far less benign reality.

Another in the assortment of interpretations of office building and landscape concerns corporate orientations toward the future. Here the message is one

Figure 163   A "machine in the garden": Richardson-Vicks complex in Connecticut

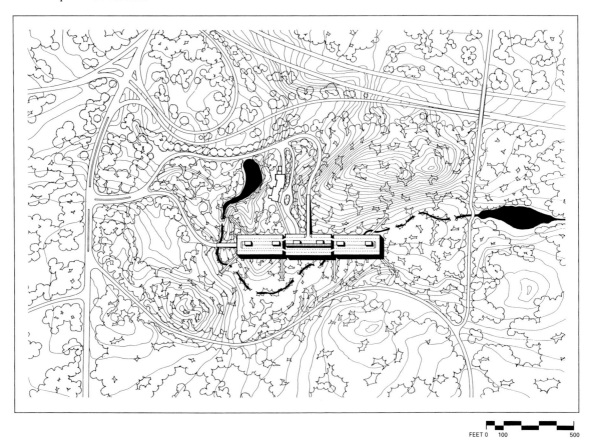

FEET 0   100   500

of faith and conviction in the abundant fruits of a technical temperament. Whether it is the idea of the release that modern technology provides to get up and go anywhere, or the capability modern information management gives to command empires, the ability to shape our environmental circumstances is strongly conveyed. It appeals to the mind rather than the senses, to the rational more than the organic. By remaining in an equivocal state, both the architecture and the landscape architecture can strike a sympathetic chord with modern pastoralism. Too often, however, the final interpretive result favors total human domination over natural circumstances.

The case to be made for modern pastoralism in contemporary suburban shopping realms is poorly defined and potentially something of a missed opportunity. Too often the commercial zone that bounds most metropolitan thoroughfares is a hodgepodge of different land uses and building types, bland-looking shopping malls, billboards, and desolate parking lots. Far from the civic distinction that traditional urban places of similar use have acquired over time, these areas have a decided lack of public identity. Many buildings have a temporary quality about them, and the spaces in between are frequently incomplete, uncared for, and inhospitable. There is little attempt for one building, or building complex, to reach beyond its site boundaries, even symbolically, to introduce visual coherence to the scene.

By the same token, sometimes there is also a graphic vibrance and excitement to the chaotic visual imagery of the commercial strip. Neon signs, billboards, and iconic symbols of all kinds vie with each other, clamoring for attention. Especially at night

there is often an atmosphere of sheer fantasy and spectacle (figure 164). The spirit of an otherwise mundane place can suddenly come alive in an immediate and visceral manner. For theorists like Venturi and Scott Brown these scenes are a source of popular iconography to be taken seriously in the representational imagery of contemporary architecture (Venturi and Scott Brown 1971, Venturi, Scott Brown, and Izenour 1972). To cultural commentators like Tom Wolfe, Saturday nights, "the strip," "low riders," and "funny cars" were part and parcel of a glorious episode of modern metropolitan life (Wolfe 1965).

To the extent that it is still tenable, the central equation of modern pastoralism in these contemporary commercial environments is skewed all the way over toward a highly rationalized system of land economics and functional engineering. The cacophony of signs and other related visual paraphernalia is largely a matter of labeling and packaging for mass market consumption. The inherent problem here is one of reduction. The buildings and surrounding landscape of roads, parking lots, and open spaces are usually designed according to only the most basic, least expensive requirements. Parking lots, for instance, offer little more guidance to traffic than white

Figure 164   Spectacle on the strip at night: entrance to the North Dallas Tollway, 1987

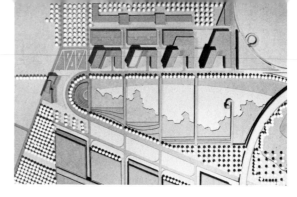

Figure 165   Integration and mixed use of the retail commercial landscape: proposal for a suburban commercial area by Ah-King Teo, 1987

lines on black macadam. This may be all that is needed to navigate a car from entrance to parking space, but the resulting walk across the lot toward the almost blank facade of the shopping mall can be inhospitable. To continue the disorientation, once inside you are artificially transported into another world over which you also have little or no control. The pity is that the reduced terms of reference for design probably need not exist, especially if we consider these commercial areas for what they are—significant portions of the public landscape where there is substantial opportunity for multiple use.

Under the stronger imprint of a more balanced formulation of modern pastoralism, it is possible to imagine parking lots as car parks, where elements of a vegetative and structured landscape perform far more than the single function of simply storing cars (figure 165). Furthermore, it seems possible to see landscape connections between adjacent shopping complexes other than through the wasteful means of driving from one lot to another. It also seems not so extraordinary to think of the whole terrain on which shopping complexes sit as artfully constructed landscapes fulfilling the local functions required of them but with the usual distinctive features subordinated to a larger, more coherent design. For instance, this could be a design that gives the terrain a distinct character of place, in much the same way that the entrepreneur Nichols did with his Country Club Estate in the teens and twenties or Watson and the Irvine Ranch did more recently. Rather than becoming overly contrived like these two examples through imported picturesque principles, design of the landscape setting might come directly from a functional

and representational enlargement of conditions at hand. In short, a poetic for the commercial middle landscape can be constructively fashioned according to principles inherent in the modern pastoral metaphor. The potential result is far less reduced and desolate and one that provides a more enduring sense of place.

PARADISE AND PANDEMONIUM

According to commonplace definitions, a myth is a story that expresses and symbolizes deep-seated and exemplary aspects of human existence. It usually sets out to allow reconciliation of two otherwise antithetical positions, thus moving beyond the scope of its immediate ideological underpinnings (Campbell 1959, Eliade 1959, 1960). To some scholars, a myth is simply a kind of perspective, not necessarily involved directly with storytelling; nevertheless, it remains a basic way of envisaging human experience (Cassirer 1955). To others, myth is an important mode of "collective thinking" (Eliade 1960). The importance of myth to the poetic mode of consciousness comes by way of the stable unifying framework it provides from which to interpret a given subject. This provision of stability and unification is particularly important in the modern era, when a broad, common understanding of mythic themes appears to be lacking or taken for granted (Preminger 1965).

At least four metaphors have been applied to the western city in various mythopoetic works (Sharp and Wallock 1987), all deriving directly from the Judeo-Christian tradition and representing different mythic concepts of human settlement: New Jerusalem, Babylon or Sodom and Gomorrah, the Infernal City of Dante, and the city of Babel. New Jerusalem symbolizes both human faith and aspirations. It is a heavenly city and a final state of "being with God" (Machor 1987). Babylon, the Infernal City, and Babel, by contrast, symbolize various kinds of dissolution of this heavenly ideal. Babylon is a depraved place of crime and vice; the Infernal City of Dante represents avarice and pollution; and Babel symbolizes confusion, noise, and a total lack of direction, in short, the "original urban chaos" (Sharp and Wallock 1987).

Each metaphor can also correspond to a particular historical stage of city development. For example, in one formulation by Carl Schorske, New Jerusalem is associated with the virtuous city of the Enlightenment, Babylon with the Victorian "city of vice," and Babel with the modern city: "a city of permanent transience" (Schorske 1963, pp. 95f). Clearly a mythic downward slide has occurred historically, resulting in a devaluation of the city over the past couple of hundred years. Schorske's hypothesis is that American urbanization has come to maturity during the last two metaphorical stages. Consequently there has been no positive guidance by which to shape an image of the city. This, in turn, has given rise to distinctly antiurban attitudes as people move toward what they regard as more positive (suburban) alternatives (Schorske 1963, Sharpe and Wallock 1987).

There is certainly evidence to support Schorske's interpretation, although not necessarily the implied decline of moral values. As a dominant form of settlement in America, the city held sway only from about 1820 until perhaps the 1920s or 1930s (Weber 1963). Before that period, the predominant form of settlement was small towns in rural areas and, after that period, suburban metropolitan development. Rather than pegging a particular metaphor to a specific era of urbanization, the four metaphors might also be used to symbolize different facets of contemporary life. To put it another way, the essential polarity between the concept of New Jerusalem and the other diabolical versions of human settlement can be posited as mythic orientations on either end of a moral continuum. One end is spiritually inclined toward paradise and the other toward purgatory and pandemonium. The most appropriate pairing for the modern metropolitan region would seem to be New Jerusalem in the paradisiac position and Babel or an Infernal Urban Wilderness, symbolizing pandemonium. In short, we are poised between a state of total chaos and entropy and one of naturalness, total fulfillment, and happiness.

Modern pastoralism certainly qualifies as a mythic concept by the earlier definitions and conflates these two spiritually inclined states of human existence into a single complex construct, potentially one with considerable mythopoetic power. In its orientation toward New Jerusalem, the pastoral perspective provides, for instance, a simplicity, a oneness and a coherence capable of quelling any flight toward pandemonium, when the "technical temperament" begins manically to pursue increasing levels of implosive specialization and fragmentation resulting in desolation. By contrast, it is precisely through the technical orientation that we can find our way clear to maintain a pastoral idyll and prevent it from sliding, from neglect, into a desolate wilderness. Conversely the pastoral side can be seen to constrain technical excesses toward explosive destruction, whereas exercise of the technical temperament may prevent an ultimate descent into the cultural desolation of nostalgic regression. Both terms in the construct interact, and neither is inherently stable. Furthermore, each carries the seeds of the other's destruction.

The image of New Jerusalem may take on different guises depending on the mode of expression; nevertheless, it is presumably a rapturous state in which people and nature are in accord, where communications go unabridged, and where life seems to be simple and easy yet simultaneously engaging and emancipated. The physical setting is a garden paradise, although conceptually it must also be a nonprimitive Eden and an arcadia without nostalgia. Above all, it is not simply a rustic escape.

On the darker side in this still rather abstract formulation, pandemonium can be represented by at least two versions of the city. In the first, communication has been obliterated, there is a complete lack of community, and the physical setting is something like an urban-industrial wilderness of disused, abused, and decaying building sites. An image that immediately comes to mind is the predatory small bands of outcasts in the industrial wilderness of the outer belt in the popular fiction *Max Headroom,* or

similar groups who have been forced away from once urban areas, as in *Mad Max.* (A totalitarian version of this fall from grace is unlikely, given the technical orientation's bureaucratic inclination toward special interests and fragmentation.)

The second version of pandemonium is probably more common and roughly coincides with existentialism's theme of alienation. Instead of a desolate urban-industrial wilderness or similar wasteland, the setting has the appearance of a paradise garden. The sun shines; the vegetation is lush, well watered, and well manicured. However, crisscrossing and winding through this arcadian landscape, we are all locked in our Tower of Babel, caught up in the endless pursuit of the constant dictates and imagined necessities emanating from life's printed circuit. In effect we are isolated from the arcadia outside. We are within sight but totally out of reach, and sooner or later we are no longer conscious of its presence. All the arcadian accoutrements are there, and yet, unlike in Thomas Cole's earlier paintings, there is no engaging human presence; therefore, the pastoral goes unrealized.

Our inclinations seem to be toward dystopian views of our possible future circumstances, or at least these are the starting points for many of our contemporary stories about the places we live, with mythic overtones. Heroes and heroines make their way out of the urban or holocaustic wilderness either through escape as in, say, the recent popular fiction *Bladerunner,* or by assisting those who are gradually restoring order, as in *Road Warrior* and *Mad Max.* Invariably, though, at journey's end they either find themselves, or imagine themselves, in an almost classic pastoral setting.

Modern pastoralism is a complex formulation, disinclined toward escape to the past or to simple solutions. It is the dialectic of the two inherent terms that gives it its power, as well as the possibility of staring straight at the dark side of one perspective from the temporary safety of the other. For example, from an arcadian retreat we are confronted with the prospect of Babel. It is this double vision that potentially provides the poetic with its critical faculty.

A connection can be made between modern pastoralism and the pluralist-majoritarian tension that resides in the social organization of contemporary suburban metropolitan areas. It is not a simple correspondence; the concepts are intertwined and mutable. For instance, Whyte's corporate organization man clearly embodies the modern technical temperament; he conforms and behaves largely according to the will of a majority. But so do Jefferson's noble husbandmen and Jackson's farmers in their pastoral existences (Whyte 1956, Marx 1964). By contrast, individualism and self-reliance are attributes that match well with a pastoral ideology, and yet they are also embodied in the political pluralism that is so highly protected by modern technical bureaucracies (Nelson 1982). Pastoralism does not simply equal pluralism; neither does the modern technical orientation. The same can be said for majoritarian self-rule and either pastoralism or technical modernism.

To go further and say that there is no relationship, however, is absurd. Pluralist-majoritarian social organization is visible in modern suburban metropolitan regions, and it does draw a substantial part of its spatial vision from urbanization with both a pastoral and a technical orientation—the concept of modern pastoralism. It is just not clear-cut, and therein lies the symbolic power. By being able to accommodate both sociopolitical views simultaneously, modern pastoralism resolves, or rather creatively maintains, the pluralist-majoritarian tension intact. In short, it is the mythic and metaphorical context for design in the American middle landscape. It is deeply rooted in the American past and has sufficient narrative sweep to continue to be of service in the future. What remains to be done is to press it fully into that service by developing a more comprehensive poetic for the middle landscape.

The most disconcerting physical characteristic of the middle landscape is the desolate and inhospitable space left between many buildings and building complexes. Commercial strips extend out into the surrounding countryside without any suggestion of a center or of termination. Bland residential subdivisions and office parks leapfrog over one another, leaving vacant land and unfinished subdevelopments in their wake. Many buildings have a temporary quality, suggesting that they might be here today and gone tomorrow. The surrounding landscape is pervaded by parking lots that offer little definition of their primary function, let alone an inviting environment. Entirely absent are characteristics of traditional city streets that graciously provide for public life.

What might be done to rid the middle landscape of its placelessness and inhospitality? What kind of design paradigms might be created to cope with these conditions of contemporary American metropolitan areas? More fundamentally, what kind of poetic might be established to guide design and provide a coherent source of inspiration? There are several approaches that merit serious consideration.

A POETIC OF THE MIDDLE LANDSCAPE

A poetic is a systematic theory, or doctrine, that specifies the forms and technical resources available for making or composing (Preminger 1965, pp. 636f.). Usually the term is applied to literature and specifically to theories of poetry, where it may concern properties of imitation, as in mimetic theories of poetry, techniques for achieving certain effects, as in stylistic theories, or the rules of internal organization to be found in objective theories about literary works. Since Aristotle the principles for ordering any art work can be discussed as poetics.

A poetic of the middle landscape is a way of making and composing within the physical conditions encountered amid contemporary suburban developments. It constitutes a number of important subordinate issues. First, there is the matter of thematic choice and whether we see the middle landscape as belonging essentially to the country, to the city, or to some other realm of existence. Second, there is the question of overall design within a thematic framework. How would we go about making a middle landscape in the manner of a traditional city, or, conversely, how might we introduce a greater sense of the countryside? Third are issues of symbolic scope and authenticity, particularly important if we are to be aesthetically consistent and meet contemporary societal needs. Finally, there are technical matters concerned with defining and elaborating specific ways of designing that might be most effectively used within a poetic framework.

Although they did not adhere precisely to this

framework, Tunnard and Pushkarev, in their classic work on the man-made American landscape, dealt explicitly with design and aesthetic issues (Tunnard and Pushkarev 1963). They diagnose aesthetic problems in six domains of interest and then carefully set out techniques and procedures for addressing them. The six domains coincide with major divisions in the landscape: the city center, the middle ground of older suburbs, suburbia, the urban-rural fringe, rural landscapes, and wilderness areas. The aesthetic concepts are divided into five groups: the urbanized landscape of the city proper; the "dwelling group" of low-density housing; the "paved ribbon," dealing mainly with freeway design; "monuments of technology," concerning the aesthetics of industry and commerce; and the "outlines of open space." Throughout, a principal concern is with suburbia and its undistinguished physical character. Tunnard and Pushkarev note that "the earlier settlement pattern (pre-suburban) which achieved an urban atmosphere in the town and a rural beauty of the countryside, has given way to an entropic form of growth the characteristics of which are chaos and sameness" (Tunnard and Pushkarev, 1963, p. 3).

Tunnard and Pushkarev's aesthetic attitude attempted to reflect the present-day realities of "man's relationship to nature [rather] than those which merely evoke a mood or a psychological reaction" (Tunnard and Pushkarev 1963, p.6). On this theme of mood and reaction, Tunnard was even more outspoken in an earlier work that criticized the contrivances of the picturesque in the name of modernism, attempting instead to find a rational, functional basis for landscape design (Tunnard 1938). In both works,

design principles such as "variety within unity," "articulation of groupings," "clustering," "rhythmic coordination," and "structural expression" form a consistent poetic framework based on careful articulation of man-made elements set against a uniform natural landscape, where material contrasts and spatial intervals play prominent roles. It is a poetic doctrine concerned with technological interventions within a rural field.

Modern pastoralism is a potentially progressive, critical ideology that can adequately form the mythopoetic context for design in a middle landscape. Care must be taken to frame the context so as to avoid ideological extremes that result in either social suppression or escapism. On the one hand, we have the powerful image of Pynchon's printed circuit crisscrossing a valley landscape and, on the other, we have Thoreau's "primitive hut" out in the wilderness. By avoiding such extremes we can establish a more complex and inherently interesting equation between pastoralism and the modern technical temperament, one that can be used to critical advantage. The machine must be able to qualify the garden, and vice versa. It is the emergent dialectical relationship that is of interest, not simply the terms themselves. However, the task still remains to put the machine in the garden, or, if we choose to come at it from the other direction, to put the "garden around the machine."

POETIC DESIGN

The general task of appropriately locating the idea of modern pastoralism within the conditions of contemporary metropolitan areas is a matter of reordering, realigning, and extending existing types of suburban development. A basic aspect of modern pastoralism's potential appeal as a legitimate, deeply seated cultural theme remains its incipient presence in the suburban landscape. It is not a concept that requires full-blown creation; nevertheless, the magnitude of the task should not be underestimated.

The crux of the realignment and extension of existing forms of development revolves around the way in which a new balance can be struck between the two terms of the modern pastoral equation. It is a balance that will likely vary from place to place and from one kind of development to the next. Currently, in some situations, the dominance of the pastoral design precludes any effective presence of the modern technical orientation. Suburban residential subdevelopments

Figure 166   Detachment of form and figure: Vissahickon Avenue Housing Project, by Venturi and Rauch, 1972

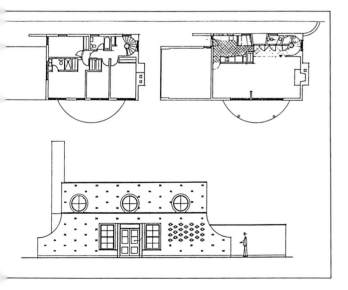

often run this risk by becoming whimsical and nostalgic. By contrast, the pastoral presence may be so reduced, as it is in many retail commercial developments, that we are left with nothing more than bland functionalism.

Toward a Common Residential Landscape

The cultural vitality of modern pastoralism within a suburban environment of houses and gardens depends on several considerations. First, socially defined figuration in the appearance of houses must be maintained. Architecturally this effectively means a conceptual detachment between the form of the house and its figural expression (Colquhoun 1978). A schematic symbolic approach might be taken without resorting to wholesale eclectic styling of highly functional and technically sophisticated modern layouts. In their unrealized Vissahickon Avenue project of 1972, Venturi and Rauch proposed a small estate of houses in which the architectural elements of doorways, windows, wall decoration, and facade outline showed strong inclinations toward Regency style (Stern 1981); however, there was no direct imitation, and the clean lines and modern plan clearly placed the work in the twentieth century (figure 166). The same firm's design in 1983 for the Park Regency Terrace residences in Houston employed a similar approach, although the cartoon character of the "cut-out" decorative motifs seemed to step over the bounds of seriousness into parody (Rowe 1987).

A second consideration in the constructive realignment of the residential modern pastoral equation is the establishment of a shared landscape—one that extends well beyond the front or backyard of an individual house. This could produce a heightened sense of community and civic identity, a frequently cited failure of suburban residential development, and also provide the site for local recreational and social amenities. The key is to enlarge the idea of the garden into something more than the residual spaces between houses and property lines. A more prominent civic presence is being sought in contrast to the ubiquitous patchwork regimen of privatization.

Pasadena's recent City of Gardens proposal presents a clear local resolution of this general idea, especially in the context of redevelopment. In order to preserve a valued traditional asset under threat of destruction, a zoning ordinance was developed with a primary focus on the continued development of private gardens in harmony with adjacent public, tree-lined streets. Together the gardens and the streets explicitly formed civic spaces of considerable grace and utility (Solomon and Haviland 1989).

Another way of accomplishing the same general task is to reverse the usual emphasis by developing the landscape ensemble of house and garden as a large garden with houses placed within it. Sharp's Oak Forest project (1946) is a commonplace example of this approach. Curvilinear streets and broad landscape easements at the rear of homes resulted in a dense wooded spine that always appears as a common backdrop to lines of single-family homes. The wooded spine is sufficiently dramatic to subordinate the idiosyncrasies of individual homes and gardens to a far more singular community identity. A similar end might be accomplished by clustering houses in groups, as Tunnard suggested. A fine example is the loose cul-de-sac arrangement of units surrounded by woodlands proposed for Coombe Hill, Surrey, in England, by Patrick Gwynne (Tunnard and Pushkarev 1963). The houses conform to a restricted palette of standard designs, heightening the thematic relationship between house and garden.

A similar formal approach, although with much more extensive results, can be found at Radburn, New Jersey, the 1928 landmark project of Clarence Stein and Henry Wright (figure 167). Together with the Greenbelt projects in the postdepression era and Baldwin Hills Village (1941) in the Los Angeles region, Radburn forged a new approach to suburban development (Wright 1935, Stern 1981, Schaffer 1982).

Although founded squarely within the Anglo-American Garden City tradition, these projects moved well beyond the picturesque coherence of other projects in the same tradition like Hogg, Potter and Kipps' 1923 River Oaks development in Houston. Significant structural changes were made to relationships among dwellings, streets, and open space, resulting in a more complex and potentially more coherent hierarchy of houses and gardens. With Radburn, the idea of separating pedestrian from vehicular traffic was introduced on a grand scale, accomplished by establishing clusterings of houses around motor courts in the form of cul-de-sacs onto which backed private houses. The front of the house was thus oriented toward a local common green space that resembled a linear park, through which pedestrian paths meandered. Each household could still maintain a private garden, but the dominant theme was community open space. A further realignment of common

Figure 167   A common landscape through functional separation: aerial view, Radburn, New Jersey, 1928, and a pedestrian underpass Greenbelt, Maryland, 1933

planning practice occurred in the grouping of housing clusters into so-called super blocks, each served by major internal streets and surrounded in the landscape by a more extensive common green space (figure 167).

The Greenbelt communities built by the federal government between 1935 and 1937 extended Radburn's planning concepts. In towns such as Greenbelt, Maryland, Greenhills, Ohio, and Greendale, Wisconsin, the idea of a protective greenbelt surrounding the development was devised, effectively preventing encroachment from adjacent subdevelopments. The concept was an elaboration of practical Garden Cities principles, much in the spirit of Howard's idea of towns within a broad rural landscape (Conkin 1959, and Stein 1966). Baldwin Hills went further by proposing a coherent formal garden instead of leaving open space simply as a wooded area (Stein 1966).

An even earlier American example of single-family housing clusters within an overall wooded landscape setting can be found in Walter Burley Griffin's Trier Center Neighborhood (1913) in Winnetka, Illinois (Brooks 1975). In many respects, this enclave of thirty-five small masonry houses was a direct precursor to Radburn (figure 168).

Returning to realignment of the modern pastoral equation, now rewritten as houses in a garden, the poetic appeal of this lineage of projects is twofold. It is not only the clear reading of dwellings within a larger shared landscape that is obtained but also the equally clear articulation of a civic hierarchy among houses, gardens, parks, and other community facilities. An important concern, nevertheless, is that the

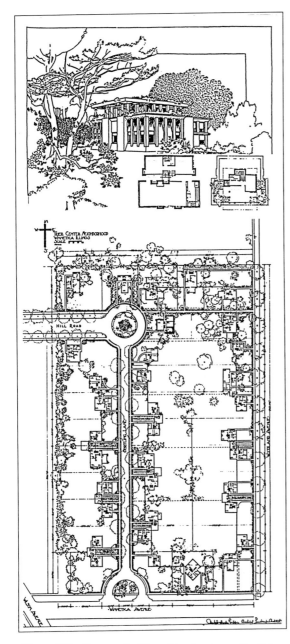

Figure 168   Community life amid natural amenity: Trier Center, Illinois, neighborhood and first house, by Walter Burley Griffin, 1913

public and shared space between residences and other facilities not merely remain a vegetated buffer but become an actively used community amenity with symbolic significance. Only through this increased richness and expressive potential can a viable version of modern pastoralism be maintained in something more than a simplistic form.

A third and important way of achieving or augmenting a common residential landscape is to enrich and embrace community services and facilities that constitute the necessary infrastructure for housing. Day care facilities, after-school centers, active recreational areas, health facilities, media centers, and communal truck gardens are in increasing demand by today's suburban residents. Life-style circumstances of families have changed, often quite radically, and household formation continues to diversify. Increased residential densities, produced by escalating land and site development costs, are making the multiple use of space within subdevelopments more necessary and the space around strictly residential precincts even more valuable as potential community assets. The concentration of populations is also making the provision of community services more practical within easy walking distance of residences. We must find ways to combine infrastructure within a common residential landscape so that opportunities for public life and community legibility are increased.

Dolores Hayden has admirably enumerated several experimental housing projects that seek to accommodate specific household types ill served by standard community patterns. Collective solutions are also prominent (Hayden 1984). For example, the

Mother's House project in Amsterdam (1980), by Van Eyck, helps to sustain the single-parent family in urban society by providing a living environment that includes facilities for group care of children. Far from being a novel idea, it follows from earlier collective housing projects like Nina West Homes in London (1972).

In suburban areas, Hayden describes practical strategies for retrofitting tract housing developments with back-lot communal spaces. Denise Scott Brown makes a similar kind of proposal that includes links joining home, institutions, and services (Brown 1983). In addition, Hayden suggests a gradual realignment of units on the street side to form more coherent clusters of units with a greater civic presence (Hayden 1984), a suggestion developed much earlier by Tunnard and Pushkarev who advocated varying setback alignments of houses along an otherwise linear street (Tunnard and Pushkarev 1963). A recent version is William Stern's Arlington Court project in Houston, shown in figure 169 (Taylor 1988). Developments in the housing of special populations, like congregate housing and especially housing for the elderly have also advanced ideas of suburban housing built around a coherent and intensively developed infrastructure of community facilities (Hoglund 1983, Building Diagnostics, Inc. 1985, AIA 1986). In all of these, the concepts of community attachment and protected independence play an important social role.

Emodi recently made an even more sweeping proposal, based primarily on Canadian suburban circumstances. He proposed guidelines and provided specific design proposals for redirecting what he saw as the inevitable redevelopment of existing suburban areas. The guidelines and proposals stressed the creation of a more varied building fabric; a greater emphasis on mixed use, including departure from traditional single-use zoning; and the strategic insertion of needed community facilities within underutilized parcels of development (Emodi 1989).

The design of almost all recent experimental residential prototypes for typical suburban situations rest on a new, or at least uncommon, relationship between private housing units and community spaces. The role of communal activities is increased over the typical suburban situation of individual self-sufficiency. In Hayden's words, a "neighborhood Strategy" can be proposed based on the "aesthetic models of . . . village and cloister . . . [where] private space to become a home, must be joined to a range of semi-private, semi-public and public spaces and linked to appropriate social and economic institutions assuring the continuity of human activity in these spaces" (Hayden 1984, p. 125). It seems possible to propose a common residential landscape for the suburbs that is both significant and well integrated into the surrounding neighborhood—something that can become an alternative form of community infrastructure (figure 170).

West and Leavitt's New American House proposal of 1984 incorporates many of these qualities (figure 171) (Sherman and Springs 1984, Nissen 1988). Attached houses, more or less like conventional townhouses, are lined up across suburban lots, with a single-story office in the front and family living quarters behind. The link between these two structures is formed by a kitchen and private garden court. The arrangement allows working parents to su-

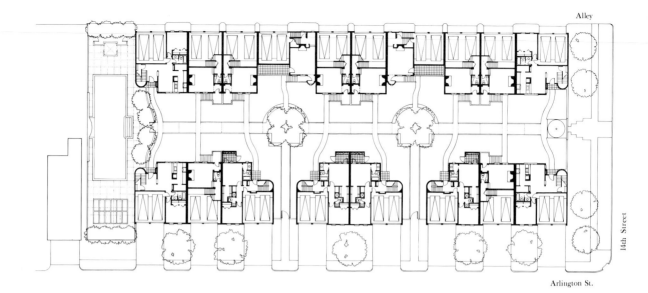

0   10   20   40

Figure 169   Retrofitting a suburban block: Arlington Court, Houston, Texas, by William F. Stern and Associates, 1983

Figure 170   Developing a community infrastructure: Neighborhood center at The Woodlands, Texas, by Mitchell Development Corporation, 1973

Figure 171   A new American house: award-winning proposal by Troy West and Jacqueline Leavitt, 1984

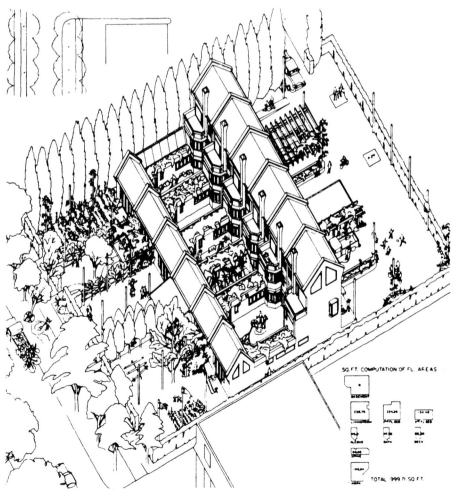

pervise children from the office area. The front yards are either gardens in the traditional sense or serve as vegetable plots. Upper-level decks augment the quality of outdoor space, and a common backyard area serves as garage entry and a hard surface area for children's play. The figural quality of individual homes is maintained by gabled roofs and other domestic architectural devices. In fact, the general housing configuration is basically a variant of zero-lot-line development with common areas between. A transformation of the design is scheduled to be built as a prototype (Nissen 1988).

More conventional mixtures of uses are contained within recent pedestrian pocket proposals. With the underlying model of a rural town firmly in mind, reliance is placed on creating a pedestrian environment to bring a diversity of living and working functions closer together. Higher levels of social service and self-sufficiency are also conspicuous characteristics of these proposals.

The multiple use and pronounced placement of commonplace features within the landscape itself, like fences, garden walls, and tree lines, can contribute to the apparent sense of common property within the residential landscape, as a counterpart to the current overwhelming presence of individual, distinctive dwellings.

A striking theoretical proposal in this regard is Peter Cook's Arcadian City (1976), shown in figure 172 (Sparke 1987, pp. 234–35). Cook envisioned dwellings composed of pristine glass and metal frame wall structures dividing the overall site, with ancillary pavilions attached. In some places these pavilions had a conventional appearance, whereas in oth-

Figure 172   Residential machines in the garden: Peter Cook's Arcadian City *proposal, 1976*

ers they were rendered as habitable walls in an abstract form of architectural expression along what would normally be fence lines. In still other places the land form itself is molded to cloak residential accommodations. Wooded areas, occasional water bodies, and fences of a more conventional kind traverse the site much as they would in a traditional suburban setting.

The pastoral design of Cook's proposal is at first glance a highly inventive though literal rendition of the machine in the garden. The natural setting is arcadian in every sense of the word, and the human imprint is unmistakably high-tech. Upon further analysis, the proposal assumes another guise: through the expressive treatment of boundaries as buildings, natural landscape as buildings, garden spaces in place of buildings, building-like surfaces in garden spaces, and so on, machine and garden begin to exchange their identities. Quite apart from the suggestion that neither might be quite so different as we first imagined, the reversal also suggests a much greater integration of land and building than we are accustomed to in conventional suburban settings. Aesthetically this work provides a constructively critical insight into contemporary problems of suburban settlement.

Reinvention of a Commercial Landscape

Manifestation of the idea of modern pastoralism within the commercial environment of highways, offices, and retail establishments suffers most from the absence of a coherent landscape. The equation between the two terms has become entirely overbalanced toward modernity and a basic functional pattern of land use. Unfettered exercise of the technological temperament has resulted in a mean and miserly artificiality that is inhospitable and entirely lacking in civic presence. The results are usually an experiential desert.

Programmatic reinvention of the space between buildings and building complexes is required to help divest suburban commercial zones of their placelessness. Opportunities for mixed use, shared use, and new use should be created and intensified. In this regard, increasing pressures for higher levels of cooperation among individual landowners should be recognized on matters of traffic congestion and the abatement of environmental impacts.

A necessary step in these directions might be to catalog the most deadening and inhospitable places within the commercial environment. Parking lots, and the termination of these lots along the blank facades of the buildings they surround are almost certainly at the top of this list. In addition, the lack of any recognizable division between public road and private lot underscores their general sense of placelessness. In the Framingham-Natick commercial center, for instance, the zone of feeder lanes, median strips, and parking lots between the Worcester Turnpike and any one of the adjacent shopping malls clearly illustrates this point. The same might be said of Sharpstown or any other suburban commercial area. A few curb cuts and driveways hardly conform to the dramatic scale of this highway environment. Once on the lot, motorists often become confused by the open expanse of unregulated space in which to drive or the mass of cars confronting them. It is only when they get inside a building that any sense of having arrived and of being somewhere is apparent. Even then they can be plunged easily into a fantasy realm of exotic atriums and mall concourses that is equally confounding; that, however, is another story.

The primary reason for such bleak and inconsequential exterior realms is the reduced terms of reference for their design. They are nothing more than expedient, barely functional, minimal solutions to car movement, temporary parking, and subsequent pedestrian access to buildings. Furthermore the public presentation of buildings is often reduced to the sheer bulk of the structure itself, looming at the edge of the parking lot with a sign tacked on the side announcing the firm that resides inside.

If we were to view this aspect of the middle landscape from the perspective of making movement a more pleasurable event and one that celebrates modern automobile use, then the terms of the design problem can be significantly enlarged. We might envisage, for instance, moments of anticipation and arrival being marked more emphatically by both the landscape and architecture of the place. We might also be reminded, at least once in a while, about the sheer individualistic exhilaration of moving through space that is allowed by modern modes of transportation. As we change mode and become pedestrians once again, there seems to be no reason for buildings and their grounds not to accommodate us more generously and graciously. On occasions in which our interests are largely focused on convenience, we should remember or be reminded that convenience need not be confused with a reduction in environmental quality or delight. Designers and their patrons of the past seem to have mastered both the expedient and the ritualistic aspects of going to and from places with scarcely more complicated ingredients of roads, gateways, courts, gardens, building entrances, and facades.

Under this alternative scenario, it now becomes reasonably easy to imagine parking lots, with the buildings they serve, as fully landscaped park settings and, in keeping with parks generally,ones in which other community uses might be accommodated (figure 173). A recent competition, sponsored by the city of Columbus and the Irwin Sweeney Miller Foundation illustrated this approach (Architecture, 1984, p. 36). Intermittent shared uses might be found, as they have in some parts of the Southwest, for environmental functions like the temporary storage of storm-water runoff. Other uses might be made of these landscapes as theaters for outdoor concerts, political rallies, and the like. A rectangular and flat field of asphalt is not the only conceivable, let

Figure 173   Parking lot as fully landscaped mixed-use theater of events: project by Riccardo Tossani, 1986

alone best, configuration for entering a site, leaving a site, and parking cars. Grading, tiering of parking stalls, and appropriate use of plant materials can radically transform the shape and use of parking lots. In addition, these areas might be regularly used for other temporary community events like circuses and craft fairs, again influencing their design within the primary functional requirements of a car park.

A recent international ideas competition for a suburban supermarket and adjacent parking area included several proposals that elaborated upon concepts of multiple use and the integration of buildings, parking lots, and landscape (*Architectural Review* 1987). In Taylor and Patel's proposal, like the project in figure 173, the usual relationship of building and lot was reversed. The supermarket formed part of a wall of activities that ceremoniously enclosed the site and the parking lot. This interior area was then made to appear as a garden. Parking bays were separated and surrounded by a high, thick hedge created by planting creepers over a steel mesh structure. The resulting form recalls the topiary hedge rows and separated parts of a classical partere garden, although the fluid curvilinear lines of the garden's outer edges, defining the roadway with the surrounding supermarket, clearly belong to the automobile age (*Architectural Review* 1987, pp. 76–78). Another entry, by Miszewski, van der Merwe, and Miszewski, took a different approach. In their proposal the main devices for ordering the parking lot were sculpturally displayed lines of billboards, unashamedly celebrating the commercial character of the supermarket. Garden elements were interspersed across the scheme in almost a random pattern, creating a tension with the otherwise systematic layout of site work (Architectural Review 1987, pp. 81–82). The overall image is in much the same key as some recent minimalist European public parks, such as those in Barcelona (Solà Morales 1986).

Successful implementation of such schemes requires focusing sufficient attention on the multiple uses of the site and organization of the interested parties to share development costs, obligations for liability, and continuing management. Without such arrangements, these landscaped areas could be prohibitively expensive for a single developer unless the opportunity is embraced as part of a relatively rare overall strategy to provide facilities at the high end of the real estate market.

Another outcome from a broad reconsideration of design in the commercial middle landscape is the possibility of a closer and architecturally organized engagement among roads, buildings, and surrounding siteworks. Rather than seeing only buildings as objects worthy of sustained design attention, as we do today, roads themselves can become pieces of architecture. This is especially important at the entry of building complexes and at interchanges, where roadways form distinctly three-dimensional features.

Greater design freedom could well be exercised in the name of capturing the dynamic and contemporary spirit of movement, bringing roadways into contact with and even through parts of the buildings they serve. Fanciful though this suggestion may seem, it has already been accomplished by, among others, Kevin Roche John Dinkeloo and Associates in several large-scale commercial complexes, like General Foods, Johnson-Vicks and the Union Carbide Headquarters. Moreover, this approach is all but routine at airport terminals, and, conceptually at least, it could be incorporated into a shopping mall and strip commercial environment, as shown in figure 174. One positive outcome of such a proposal is the possibility of creating viable public spaces both within the "highway-building" and next to adjacent developments.

Lecchini's Gasstop project (1988) provocatively incorporated many of these themes in a proposal to rehabilitate marginal land between a major metropolitan highway and an older rail yard. The basic program of functions for a gas station was expanded to include a wide variety of leisure-time uses, and architecturally elaborated into "a playground for the fuel injected, turbo-charged car culture" (Davies 1988, p. 68). An aesthetic that unabashedly celebrated the dynamism of modern-day movement was employed, with ramps, roadways, and buildings colliding and intertwining. Although proposed for a relatively dense urban setting, the independent virtual world of the program lends itself to reinterpretation along highways farther away form the city.

In a manner reminiscent of the great turnpike building era of the 1930s, wooded and open areas be-

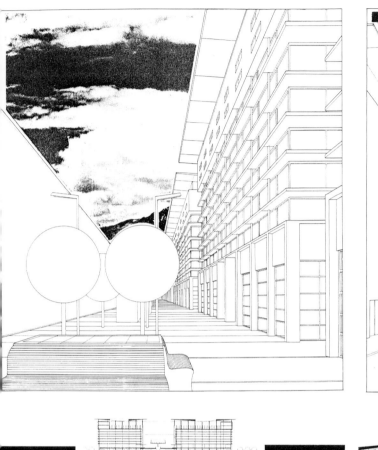

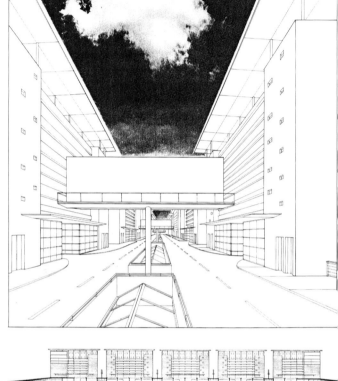

Figure 174   A highway-building and new public space in
the commercial strip, by Ramon Jurado, 1988

tween buildings and alongside roads could be incorporated as part of such a dynamic overall landscape
design rather than remaining as leftover space. For
example, the rough equivalence in physical mass between wooded areas and large, horizontal commercial buildings could be used effectively to construct
outdoor realms and provide an organized sense of enclosure and openness along roadways. The short-run
costs may be prohibitive, especially in circumstances

of existing buildings. However, given the ten- to fif-
teen-year economic life of many of these structures
and rising land costs, redevelopment will probably
become commonplace. Furthermore, greater competition for public attention and approval will likely
lead to demands for higher landscape quality.

This approach was taken in a proposal for the redevelopment of the Framingham-Natick commercial
center outside Boston. A rough equivalence was

struck between staggered floors of multistory parking flanking a regional mall and the terracing of parklands between buildings and across adjacent surface parking lots (figure 175). The usual strong distinction between building and landscape was almost completely blurred as both were subordinated to a common theme. Furthermore, the static earthbound and almost primal qualities of the resulting pyramidal forms were underscored by the dynamic presence of roadway ramps and overpasses threading through the complex. The modern pastoral theme was clearly established in a manner that suggests a new prototype for shopping centers and commercial strip developments.

Alternatively the transportation infrastructure itself might be objectified in the manner of buildings, again blurring commonplace distinctions and yet providing a greater clarity and positive presence to the public realm. The Alewife Garage and Station in suburban Cambridge, Massachusetts (1985), by Ellen-

Figure 175   Landscape as building and building as landscape: proposal for a retail commercial environment, by Vasilios Tsakalos, 1987

zweig and Moore, Associates, successfully pursues this idea (*Architectural Record* 1987). As depicted in figure 176, there is considerable engagement, both literally and metaphorically, between building and highway. Completion of the original off-ramp from Route 2, stopped for environmental reasons, would have reinforced this sense of engagement. Nevertheless, the stark contrast between the building and the adjoining conservation area heightens the legibility and presence of both public realms.

Several approaches can be taken to design the visually discordant and often functionally chaotic landscape of suburban and ex-urban commercial centers. By redefining their scope and creatively dealing with commonplace functions, events, and rituals that take place within this landscape, there is a promise of a newfound sense of place, one that is authentic to our time and could have considerable civic appeal. We should remember that places of civic pride and patronage tend to be those that are selected by acclamation because of their physical interest, convenience and commodity. Many of the plazas, squares, and open spaces that we now regard with considerable civic affection started as spaces between buildings or as isolated private precincts (Benevolo 1971).

POETIC EXPRESSION

In realigning the modern pastoral equation in various suburban metropolitan circumstances, how are we to judge the appropriateness of architectural expression? In pursuing this question, we immediately encounter two thorny issues. First is the matter of cul-

tural authenticity. Does a mode of expression meet modern-day circumstances in a genuine, constructive, yet liberating manner? Second, there are related questions of what might be called internal expressive logic. Does a mode of expression meet the ideological requirements of a philosophical construct like modern pastoralism?

This tripartite measure of cultural authenticity avoids unnecessarily time-bound concepts by suggesting that tradition and cultural enterprise are not mired in the past. *Genuine* means a mode of expression that is rooted in a place and maintains social validity. *Constructive* means that it is useful, practical, and intelligible. At least the mode of expression in context should offer guidance as to how we might make sense of it. And *liberating* places an additional qualifier on *cultural authenticity,* requiring the potential for progress, advancement, and continuation. In short, to be culturally authentic, a mode of expression must be socially valid, understandable, and allow room for progress.

The requirement for conformance between a mode of expression and the ideas of modern pastoralism ensures a consistency in genre and that the mode of expression incorporates a modern-pastoral design encompassing both the garden and the machine. It also focuses attention on how the mode of expression engages the modern pastoral ideal, regardless of other stylistic or symbolic attributions that might be involved.

Figure 176   Constructive engagement of buildings, infrastructure, and natural systems: Alewife Station and Garage, by Ellenzweig and Moore Associates, 1985

When we imagine urban and suburban land-scapes in the light of modern pastoralism, two modes of expression immediately come to mind. Each has already left its imprint on the American scene. First, there is expression in what we might call a historicist manner, where a deliberate attempt is made to engage the past and follow traditional building practices. Within this broad mode of expression are two princi-pal stylistic strains, reflecting between them a con-stant tension in American architecture over the past hundred years. They are classicism and romanticism. Within each strain a useful distinction can be made between vernacular forms of expression and those that are academic, with an eye to historical veracity and detail.

Projects that fit neatly into these characteriza-tions are sometimes difficult to find. Tyrone, New Mexico, a new town designed in 1915 by Goodhue for the Phelps-Dodge Corporation, was a notable combination of classical beaux-arts and romantic nat-uralist compositional principles (Stern 1981, Scully 1988). The town center was laid out according to beaux-arts and City Beautiful principles, and the hill-sides on either side conformed to a romantic natural-ist layout (figure 177). Similarly, the informal land-scapes of most other new towns and large subdevelopments in the Garden City tradition display distinct overtones of romantic naturalism. Neverthe-less, Howard's original diagram embodies beaux-arts planning principles in its axial and symmetrical plan-ning, as did Unwin and Parker's practical application in Letchworth (1904) (Scully 1988). Sometimes the line between vernacular and academic is also blurred. The town of Tyrone was an attempt to fit the local cir-

Figure 177   Mixed modes of expression: Tyrone, New Mexico, by Bertram Goodhue, 1915

cumstances of New Mexico but also included dis-tinctly European architectural references.

The second mode of expression is what we might call the modern manner, where there is no real at-tempt made to engage the past and, indeed, where there is even a reluctance to do so. Hallmarks of this expressive mode include a strong conformance be-tween function and form and an interest in the expres-sive capacity of modern technology. Again there are two principal versions: the "town country" merger of modern Garden Cities and the "tower or slab in the park" of orthodox architectural modernism. At first the former version might seem misplaced, in the light of the foregoing comments, and, indeed, the roman-tic inclinations of the Garden City movement are not-able. Nevertheless, outside the explicit context of style, the organization of this "town country" merger is modern. In the end, the historical and modern cate-gories are less a hard and fast distinction than they are a way of highlighting and usefully discussing the problem of poetic expression.

In a Historicist Manner

The application of classical compositional principles is a venerable tradition in American town planning. L'Enfant's grandiose eighteenth-century scheme for the nation's capital incorporated formal axial avenues radiating out from centers of government and national commemoration. Woodward's early 1807 plan for the city of Detroit employed similar devices, although the less important streets no longer conformed to a gridiron plan (Scully 1988, p. 76). Jefferson and Latrobe's extraordinary University of Virginia campus (1817–1826) is another instance, as are the Commonwealth Avenue and Back Bay developments in Boston around 1850.

By the end of the nineteenth century, use of these compositional principles had taken a distinctly academic turn (Scully 1988, p. 138). The World's Columbian Exposition of 1893 in Chicago, under the guidance of Daniel H. Burnham, epitomized the emerging City Beautiful movement (Kostof 1987, p. 184). Here could be found prolific use of axial symmetry, neobaroque articulation of space, and the deployment of historically exact statuary, obelisks, and other sculptural elements. The Grand Basin and Court of Honor were particularly conspicuous in these regards, together with McKim, Mead, and White's Triumphal Arch (Scully 1988, p. 138). In 1905 Burnham proposed an axial beaux-arts plan for San Francisco, followed by the better-known plan for Chicago of 1909 (Kostof 1987, Scully 1988). The latter proposal was particularly comprehensive, with

a grand axis running through the center of Chicago's gridiron of streets terminating out in Lake Michigan, where it was flanked by an enormous park containing important public buildings (Hines 1974). In the hands of others, like Bertram Goodhue, as well as Nolen, beaux-arts planning principles continued to be applied on both large and small projects well into the twentieth century (Stern 1981). The overall plan for Mariemont, Ohio, of 1918 by Nolen, for instance, had an explicitly classical form, much in keeping with a historicist tradition (Mariemont Company 1925). Nevertheless, like Tyrone before it, the architecture and many detailed planning considerations followed a distinctly romantic agenda (see figures 143 and 178).

The romantic tradition in American architecture and urbanism is also deeply rooted and time honored. Toward the end of the eighteenth century and during the first half of the nineteenth century, romantic revivalism and eclecticism were on the rise. The use of historical references in the construction of public buildings allowed the young American nation symbolically to associate government with the free republics of antiquity. This tendency was epitomized

Figure 178   A plan in the beaux-arts tradition: Mariemont, Ohio, by Nolen, 1918

by Thomas Jefferson's proposal to build the state capital building in Virginia as a replica of the Maison Carée at Nîmes (Early 1965, pp. 13f., 35). Additionally, emotion and sentiment began to replace logic and rationality in architecture as the aesthetic doctrine of associationism began to take hold. The influential American landscape architect Andrew Jackson Downing, for instance, read and propagated Alison's associationist treatise *Essays on the Nature and Principles of Taste* of 1790 (Jellicoe et al. 1986). According to this aesthetic doctrine, forms are not beautiful per se but because of the thoughts they raise in the minds of spectators. Thus an emotional response could be solicited through historical suggestiveness (Early 1965, pp. 35f.). Finally, the broadening of American democracy, and, with it, an emphasis on egalitarian individualism, began to disintegrate the hegemony of particular academic tastes. As one historian put it, "The older sense of community under the influence of a refined minority was sacrificed to the democratic belief in the taste of every man" (Early, p. 30).

By about mid-century, again under Downing's and others' powerful influence, romantic naturalism and the picturesque emerged as a national style for creating urban and rural landscapes. In his *Theory and Practice of Landscape Gardening* (1841), and *Architecture of Country Houses* (1850), Downing offered an approach to the central question: "Does it [the landscape] make a good picture?" Essentially he argued for design principles that would fuse buildings with their natural surroundings in the manner of paintings by Claude, Poussin, and Dughet (Early 1965, p. 60). Later his two principal protégés, Calvert Vaux and Frederick Law Olmsted, applied and then extended this doctrine in some of the great American parks of the nineteenth century: Central Park (1858), Prospect Park, Boston's so-called Emerald Necklace, and the Capitol Grounds in Washington, D.C. (Jellicoe et al. 1986, pp. 408–9). Even later suburban developments, such as Cook's Beverly Hills (1906) and Kipp's River Oaks (1923), depicted in figure 179, followed in this tradition, as did many other examples of the Garden City movement (Stern 1981 and Stern 1986b).

A good contemporary example of both of these historicist modes of expression is the town of Seaside in northwest Florida (see figures 51, 63, and 138), planned in 1980 by Duany and Plater-Zyberk for a local developer, Robert S. Davis. It is situated on 80 acres of land with 2,300 feet of ocean frontage along the Gulf of Mexico. The master plan calls for eventual development of 350 dwelling units, 100 to 200 additional units of lodging, and a variety of commercial and public uses concentrated around a town center (*Progressive Architecture* 1984, Boles 1985).

The dominant characteristic of Seaside is a conscious return to traditional American architectural and formal planning practices of the nineteenth century. One critic called it a "hybrid of traditional European and American models" (Boles 1985, p. 112). Nevertheless, it is a figure in the beaux-arts manner, especially where it becomes centered on the waterfront, employing a well-balanced compositional layout of concentric vehicular streets radiating out from a central public area within which a park is honorifically placed (see figure 138). Larger streets and avenues terminate in traffic circles, and the overall net-

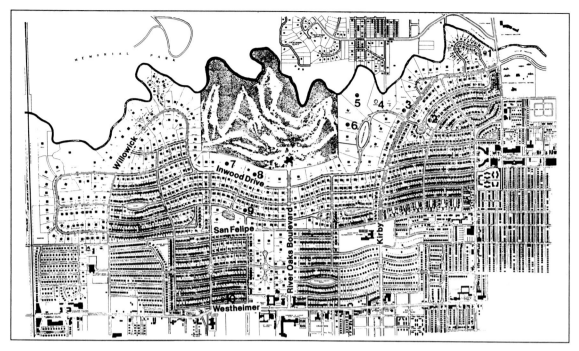

Figure 179   A plan in a picturesque tradition: River Oaks, Houston, Texas, by Kipp, 1923

work of streets is clearly organized in a strong hierarchical manner. The immediate typological reference is to small southern American towns built prior to World War II, although, as several critics have suggested, influences reach into a broader classical repertoire (Boles 1985, Scully 1988, Langdon 1988).

Residential and commercial architecture within the overall master plan is similarly inclined toward the nineteenth century, presenting an eclectic and romantic array of styles. One complex, Rosewalk Cottages, by Orr and Taylor, is distinctly Victorian in the use of decorative fretwork on gables, porches, picket fences, and pergolas (see figures 51 and 63). Shuttered windows, an occasional cupola, and the pervasive southern stick style of the architecture further recall the late nineteenth century. Other residences, like the proposed Greek revival house (1985) by Leon

Krier, are no less thematic (Boles 1985). The town of Seaside is not unique; there are a rising number of contemporary condominium developments and vacation resorts cropping up across the country with similar stylistic appearances (Langdon 1988).

Coherent layout and architectural formality are appealing in the order and clarity they bring to a community like Seaside. Moreover, the direct invocation of traditional small town values, intimate scale of development, and a simple life immediately create a link with country villages and pastoralism. By implication, so does the prospect of eventual democratic self-rule when the Seaside Corporation becomes a public town authority. However, there is also something paradoxical about the fact that, as one commentator put it, "the newest idea in development is the nineteenth-century town" (Langdon 1988, p. 1). Such a deliberate backward expressive turn is also difficult to equate satisfactorily with the inherent ideas of modern pastoralism.

The symbolism of places like Seaside is inescapable: we are almost literally taken back to the nineteenth century. In an otherwise well worked out scheme, such an orientation might be dismissed as a decorative exercise in nostalgia; however, it seems more deliberate than that and therefore raises serious questions about symbols, the control of closely associated references, and their modern applicability—that is, the problem of cultural authenticity.

There can be little doubt that the references are culturally genuine. We know from both the results and accounts of the design process for Seaside that considerable effort was spent on couching the project in southern American and other period-style references (figure 180). In fact the authors of many other postmodern projects in a historicist manner seem to delight in academic accuracy and connoisseurship (Jencks 1980). We might also conclude that the symbolic frame of reference chosen for the project is socially constructive by making a direct connection to small rural town values and by capturing a national mood that leans heavily in the direction of historical eclectic taste. As we have already seen, questions of identity and feelings of alienation are modern dilemmas in our growing metropolitan areas; when a sense of cultural community is threatened, stylistic eclecticism often results.

The constructive nature of the symbolic exercise should also be qualified. While certainly democratic, the nineteenth century in America and, in particular, the laissez-faire doctrines of the Victorian era hardly coincide with contemporary ideas of social progress,

except perhaps of a most conservative kind. Moreover, the sense of liberation and forward thinking that was claimed as an important dimension of cultural authenticity is also poorly served. By its very nature, too literal a use of historicism quickly closes down the symbolic frame of reference to a particular time, place, and set of sociocultural associations.

The use of historicism as an expressive mode for the ideas of modern pastoralism encounters similar problems. Once again, a link can be clearly made to the pastoral side of the equation. In fact, following Bentmann and Müller's (1988) argument, perpetuation of pastoralism requires a backward turn and use of appropriate historical references. In this case, however, historicist forms of urban-architectural expression do not allow the ideological hold of pastoralism to be broken in a critical and progressive manner. In short, the "modern" aspect of the modern pastoral equation is damagingly precluded.

A more positive case can be made if we regard historicist proposals for creating a middle landscape,

Figure 180   A return to the vernacular small town: Seaside, Florida, by Duany and Plater-Zyberk, 1983, with houses by Orr and Taylor. Copyright Mick Hales, 1985.

such as Seaside, as vernacular rather than academic forms of expression. Largely by references to traditional ways of building, enduring qualities of a place are effectively engaged. Unless we are willing to argue that continual development of a vernacular tradition is not culturally authentic, there could be little objection to such an approach. Moreover, modern continuation and development of a tradition, along with a sense of small town regionalism, could very well comply with the idea of modern pastoralism.

At least two issues, however, can upset such a straightforward vernacular interpretation. First, the traditional form of building cannot be entirely imitative of past practices; there must be some demonstrably modern ingredient. Second, care must be taken to gauge what counts as being vernacular in this day and age rather than in some bygone ear. Regionalism, for instance, is a relative and geographically slippery term. What was once a region due to a particular conjunction of social, economic, and environmental circumstances may no longer be so clearly defined. On the contrary, some urban theorists have argued that essential differences in the contemporary way by which we construct settlements are more a matter of time and era than of place (Lynch 1972).

On both these points, Stern's Subway Suburb proposal of 1976 (figure 181) appears to be reasonably successful. The project, prepared for the Venice Biennale, was a theoretical demonstration of the way in which blighted inner-suburban residential areas of American metropolitan regions could be improved. After accepting the functional and real estate requirements of moderate-priced suburban housing, the exercise confined its attention to the realm of shape and

symbol (Stern 1981, p. 112). Small, freestanding cottages, reminiscent of those built at the beginning of this century, were lined up in rows of lots fronting onto suburban streets. A central figure was introduced into the symmetrical plan in the form of an oval, or crescent, with clear allusions to eighteenth- and nineteenth-century precedents. In many ways the project was traditional, well within the vernacular tradition of subdevelopments like Mairemont in Ohio. Nevertheless, the basic terms of reference for the proposal and the specific rational manner in which it was detailed expanded the project well beyond traditional means. The project also opens the door to a kind of radical vernacular where any imitative pretense is immediately set aside in favor of a more critical and fruitful agenda that deliberately fashions new meanings out of well-known urban-architectural references.

Extensive use of historicist planning and design principles within mixed commercial environments of the middle landscape introduces similar problems. Although we might like the idea of parks, visual axes, and avenues introduced by such approaches, we might also quickly object to such a vision on the grounds that it is both inappropriate and inauthentic. Is it, for instance, appropriate to monumentalize rather humdrum office and retail commercial establishments in this manner? It is one thing to use grand avenues and visual axes connecting important buildings in the design of a nation's capital, and quite another to use the same organizational devices in suburban office and shopping complexes, thereby according them much the same status. By closely equating consumerism and governance, such a phys-

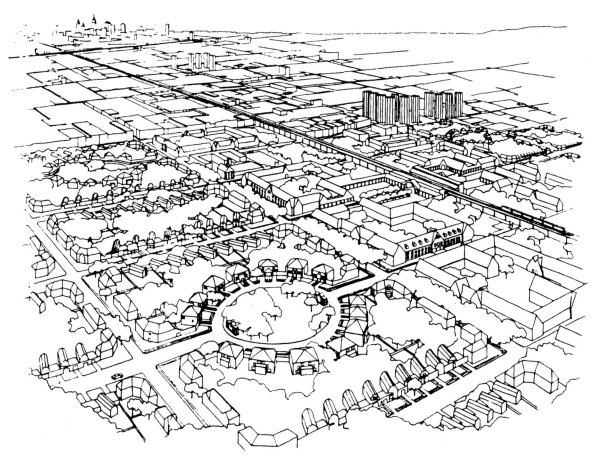

*Figure 181   Vernacular and historical precedent: Robert
A.M. Stern's* Subway Suburbs *proposal, 1976*

ical arrangement raises serious questions about society's priorities and their manifestation. Furthermore,
the overall legibility of metropolitan areas may suffer, particularly when we cannot easily distinguish
specific functions and building types.

This is certainly not a new objection. Proponents
of Gothic revivalism, in the nineteenth century had
similar reactions. To them the classical treatment of
domestic architecture, especially Greek revival,
could be confused too easily with public and religious

functions (Gowans 1986). Nevertheless, the issue of
appropriateness remains. The matter of authenticity
also stems not only from how we see shopping, office
services, and other functions in the overall scheme of
our lives but from how these functions are expressed.
Essential aesthetic features of the commercial strip,
for instance, are bound up with the modern romance
of the automobile, individual freedom of movement,
and, more generally, a lively popular culture. Clearly
these features and the popular activities that they sup-

port—among them "cruising" and "hanging out"—represent almost the antithesis of the formality or pictorial contrivance found today in traditional urban landscapes.

In a Modern Manner

Two modern modes of expression are clearly evident in the contemporary middle landscape. First is a version of Howard's "town country" merger that is both an inevitable result of land subdivision and an application of some Garden City planning principles (see figures 131, 132, and 157). Most recent subdivisions incorporate a relatively even distribution of buildings across a naturalistic garden landscape, commodiously subdivided according to function and serviced by modern roadways and utilities.

The second mode is the "tower or slab in the park," the result of certain proposals of the modern movement in architecture, like Le Corbusier's Ville Radieuse, and of the modern pressures of real estate development. Here large, separate, multistory buildings, such as office parks and some high-rise residential condominium developments, are placed within a naturalistic landscape setting.

A significant feature of both modes of modern expression is the tendency toward repetitious placement of uniform buildings in a naturalistically cultivated context. Another characteristic is the presumed universality of such proposals, regardless of local conditions and cultural heritage. Moreover, there is little, if any, continuity established with past building practices, either local or otherwise. Finally, few attempts are made to disguise the direct outward expression of the technology used to build the settle-

ment. In other words, both the technology and its use can become a source of expressive content.

The mass production of contemporary residential tract developments clearly illustrates these characteristics. It is only the overt imprint of technology in the building architecture that is absent. For this we can turn to Hilberseimer and Neutra and their modern highway cities of slab blocks set in a green field (figure 182). Neutra's Rush City (1928), for example, is a utopian proposal for Los Angeles in which tower slabs, roads, and other facilities are simply imprinted on the host environment (Hilberseimer 1955, Hines 1982). Another clear illustration of these characteristics is Tunnard's 1938 proposal for the redevelopment of an estate outside London as a "modern dormitory" (Tunnard 1938). In all three schemes, the population was to be housed in multistory slab

Figure 182   "Slabs in the Park" : Neutra's Rush City, 1928 and Hilberseimer's city proposal, 1955

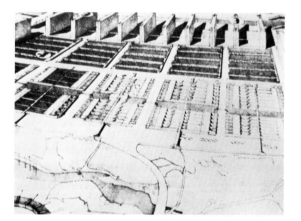

blocks, repetitively aligned in a bucolic parkland setting. Each household was to have a garden allotment on the ground near the tower slabs of apartments, together with play areas and other community facilities. As far as possible, at least in Hilberseimer's and Tunnard's proposals, an informal picturesque garden setting was to remain untouched by the new tower buildings and other facilities. In fact, the placement of the towers and other buildings, in all three schemes, on pilotis, floating, it seemed, above the ground plane, symbolically reinforced a sense of detachment of buildings from their surrounding naturalistic circumstances.

In these modern proposals a major shortcoming from the idea of modern pastoralism occurs in the separation of the two implicit realms of landscape and building. Pastoralism is clearly symbolized by an informal and naturalistic landscape setting, especially one that includes both open cultivated expanses and denser outdoor wooded areas, as in Hilberseimer's and Tunnard's proposals. The modern technical temperament is just as clearly symbolized by a functionalist modern architecture. However, the relationship between the two realms, and hence the two terms in the modern-pastoral idea, usually remains at a basic, simple level. A relationship is struck because of proximity and not much else. Alternatively there is a presumption that placement of a "machine in the garden" alone is enough to bring the two sides of the modern-pastoral equation together. More often than not, however, the landscape merely becomes a backdrop for the building and therefore not a particularly active element in the design. Furthermore, the modern technocratic tendency of regarding the landscape

simply as green space, or biological function, implies an undifferentiated universality of substance that denies special articulation. Consequently the landscape aspect always seems to remain generic, with no capacity for any further cultural identity.

Even in the absence of a naturalistic landscape, the same sort of universal tendency can also be observed. The space between buildings in the form of parking lots, roadways, and vacant lots is rhetorically reduced to a bland generic level, with little capacity for further cultural identity except in the chaotic symbolism of buildings, billboards, and neon signs. No doubt visual vitality, dynamism, and a kind of cultural authenticity can be found. Moreover, this kind of pop environment has served as the inspiration for contemporary architecture that attempts to use popular imagery and symbolism within its aesthetic repertoire (Venturi, Scott Brown, and Izenour 1972). However, the range of applications is clearly limited. For instance, there is usually a generic quality to such settings that restrains their rhetorical usefulness other than for rather obvious and mundane commercial functions. Unlike classical rules of formal composition, which in a manner similar to a language apply to a wide range of conditions, the architectural realm of pop culture is as yet far more circumscribed.

Modernism, when adopted so often as the mode of expression for corporate headquarters and other facilities of big business, can symbolically convey other messages. If not universal, multinational corporations are certainly widespread, and the repetition of their architectural expression is no longer simply a matter of sameness. It can also become one of indifference to indigenous circumstances and bear the imprint of economic control from afar (Frampton 1987).

Modern expressions in the form of contemporary suburban mergers of the image of town and country, usually suffer from a slightly different shortcoming. Certainly they are widespread and sameness can signify indifference; however, symbolic emphasis on modernity typically recedes well into the background. By contrast, there is an overwhelming preference exhibited for small town and pastoral images. As we have seen on a number of occasions, the suburban residential environment is deliberately made not to appear modern.

What, then, are the most promising expressive approaches to the middle landscape? How might we best go about representing modern pastoralism in making a middle landscape? Clearly historicism can quickly lead to nostalgia, sentimentality, and symbols of social irrelevance. Almost by definition, in its romantic inclinations it embraces the pastoral side of the equation but largely precludes expression of the modern technical temperament. But expression in a modern manner, through the town country merger, can suffer from the same drawback. By contrast, modernism in an orthodox architectural form can emphasize both sides of the modern-pastoral equation, but there is no real engagement between the two. Instead separate and axiomatic relationships are usually struck between "building" and "modernity" and between "landscape" and at least a very general idea of "pastoralism." Reconciliation or resolution is much rarer.

The most promising expressive approach still seems to lie in a modern direction. Like much of this broad cultural framework, design of the middle landscape remains an unfinished project. Today it has usually been specialized and separated along rigid functional lines. In some places, like commercial retail areas, the functional terms of reference are often extremely reduced and monolithic, whereas in other environments, like corporate office parks, they are not. Both buildings and landscapes are usually prominent though infrequently integrated into larger, coherent frameworks. In short, the most important and persistent problem with modern expression is to find a way of appropriately amplifying the functional terms of reference for design and of more effectively encompassing buildings in landscapes.

POETIC OPERATIONS

It is clear from Neutra's, Hilberseimer's, and Tunnard's examples of slabs in the park that a principal reason for the almost absolute separation of building from landscape and the modern from natural derived from modern architecture's relatively closed symbolic frame of reference. Form followed environmental and technological functions—and that was about all. Conversely there was an impoverishment of such functions when it came to the landscape, other than stipulations of separation from other buildings. If we are to move in a modern direction, we must find the means of engaging the machine with the garden and vice versa.

We have explored a number of programmatic interventions such as shared uses and common landscapes. Now it remains to discuss appropriate poetic operations once those programmatic adjustments have been made. Of particular interest are poetic operations concerned with the placement and engagement of objects in a larger context, such as juxtaposition, scaling, and ordering. Also of interest are operations that accomplish higher levels of engagement through the alteration of object and context, such as various forms of typological invention.

Juxtaposition

Minimalism involves some of the most striking forms of juxtaposition, especially in the large outdoor earthworks of Michael Heizer, Robert Smithson, and Walter De Maria. Invariably these works, such as Heizer's *Complex One* (1972–1976) and De Maria's *Lightning Field* (1974–1976) present the very antithesis of the free organic shapes of their natural surroundings in their sheer size and concern for real space. The resonance of the works largely comes through the marks of rational, arbitrary, and man-made order interposed in nature. Nevertheless, the works also enjoy an ambiguous relationship with the land they occupy. As one critic put it, "They are not involved with landscape in any pictorial sense: rather they stem from self-reflexive sculptural sensibilities preoccupied with structure, materials and scale" (Baker 1976, p. 93). As such, the land becomes a strong countertheme to a work's formal rather than scenic properties. By refusing to be programmatically involved with the landscape, the works enhance this focus on formal properties. One possible exception is De Maria's *Lightning Field,* where there is a certain logical narrative connection between lightning rods and a desert landscape (Baker 1976). In summary, the minimalism of contemporary artworks is essentially nonrepresentational, nonprogrammatic, and nonscenic. By contrast, especially in work like Robert Irwin's Coreten Steel installation in Dallas's Library Plaza (figure 183), it is a concern with formal properties of material and space. Through careful juxtaposition of man-made objects in naturalistic circumstances, these qualities are expressed and explored.

A similar minimalist mode of expression can be found in the recent work of architects like Pinon and Viaplana (Solá Morales 1986). Their Plaza de Sants project in Barcelona (1983) transforms the vast ground-level concrete deck over the main railway station into a thought-provoking sculptural landscape. The program was sparse, mainly involved with traffic movement, and nonrepresentational. Instead spatial movement and surface, on an unusually large scale for a dense urban area, became the themes.

Surrealist works like Méret Oppenheim's *Luncheon Service* (1936) show other forms of juxtaposition. Here a furry cup, saucer, and spoon break the normal conventions surrounding a tea service and invite us to reexperience chinaware in a new way (Herder and Breisgau 1979). The poetic operations involved, however, are more ones of material transformation than of juxtaposition.

This use of juxtaposition can be effective in the effort to create a heightened sense of engagement between building and landscape within a modern pastoral ideological design, but it needs careful control so that the inherent properties of theme and countertheme can be fully exploited. First, the relative size and expansiveness of buildings and their setting

*Figure 183   Juxtaposition and the self-reflexive
sculptural sensibilities of artworks: Robert Irwin's
installation, Library Plaza, Dallas*

should be of a scale that facilitates a clear reading of object and context. In many suburban commercial environments, buildings and remaining elements of the surrounding landscape are of comparable size and presence, severely undercutting the clear perception of objects in a more or less continuous field. Usually the remedy lies in creating a far more cohesive context—for example, by maximizing the extent of surrounding natural landscape. Alternatively the arrangement of roads, parking lots, and open spaces could be made into a well-ordered and yet distinctively singular pattern.

Second, formal and figural expression should be controlled in both building and field in the direction of the spatial and material properties of interest, such as displacement of space by the building, the extensiveness of the field, and the texture of both building and field. Also, in situations where the landscape as a readily identifiable or imaginable entity does not clearly exist, the buildings can be used to re-present a particular place. For example, through De Maria's extensive line of lightning rods, we come to appreciate better the expansive qualities of a desert landscape (Baker 1976, p. 93). An upshot of the necessity for controlled figural expression is elimination of any extraneous forms of symbolic representation. Within

commonplace circumstances of most commercial strips this means further emphasis on the relative scale of signs, buildings, and the surrounding landscape.

Finally, placement and articulation of building and landscape elements should emphasize inherent tensions within the modern-pastoral equation. For instance, although functional in all respects, an otherwise abstract and arbitrary organizational scheme might be juxtaposed usefully with one that is rural and organic.

A plan for the redevelopment of the Framingham-Natick commercial area takes this kind of approach (figure 184). Wherever possible the relatively extensive presence of wooded area on the site was expanded and buildings proposed at much higher densities. The connection between the network of roads and the buildings they serve was intensified, creating a distinction between built form and the remainder of the site. Finally, the layout of building complexes was imposed according to highly regular geometries. The resulting ensemble of buildings and landscape brought the spatial orders of both into sharp focus in rich and complex ways. Moreover, the less dispersed forms of building were concentrated in such a way that the potential for adverse environmental impact was substantially mitigated.

There is, however, one key distinction between minimalism per se and the use of juxtaposition as a way of rendering modern pastoralism within a suburban metropolitan landscape. Minimalist works deliberately set out to suppress any narrative and programmatic content. A modern-pastoral rendition of juxtaposition, by contrast, must remain thematically

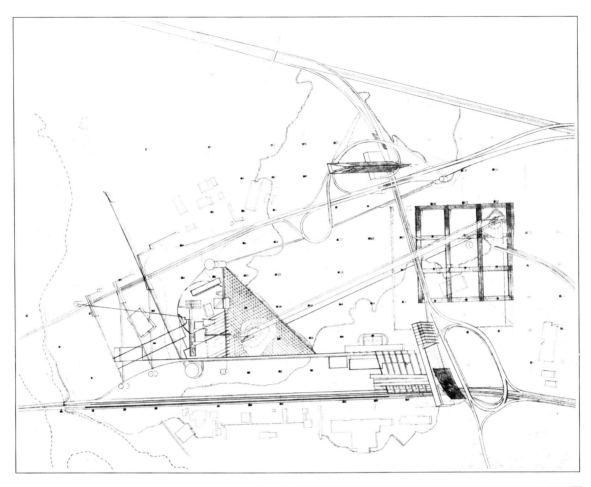

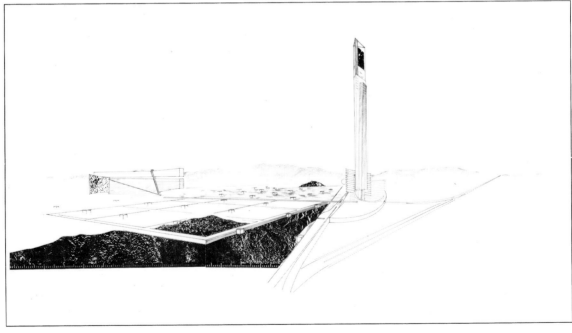

faithful to both pastoralism and a modern technical orientation. The landscape must appear cultivated and not simply as a wilderness or an urban scene. Nevertheless, the relationship between building and landscape should be neither pictorial nor representational. Instead attention should remain focused on essential spatial, tactile and tectonic properties.

This kind of distinction raises the question of those formal properties around which both the modern and the pastoral seem to turn. In other words, along what aesthetic dimensions should we seek to exploit a relationship constructively? Where would modernity and pastoralism lie along those dimensions?

The first dimension might concern patterns of spatial distribution among elements within buildings or the landscape. For example, construction systems within buildings and the way trees are planted can establish spatial patterns. Modernity might turn toward constructed, open systems, whereas pastoralism might be inclined toward repetitious, cultivated, and closed spatial arrangements (figure 185). Both would be essentially geometric, as the disciplines of construction and cultivation tend in that direction.

Along a second dimension, of form and function, modernity would stress technical-structural considerations and pastoralism would similarly center on environmental pragmatism. Both would be strongly influenced by use and function. For instance, modern buildings emerge from the materials of which they are made, the functions they perform,

Figure 184   Exploiting the tension between building and landscape: plan and perspective of a project, by Guy Perry, 1986

and the systems of construction that are used, and cultivated lands depend on economy and ecological balance.

A third dimension of tectonic order would probably be arranged between abstract and organic, with pastoralism in the latter position. Finally, in the symbolic realm pastoralism inclines toward romanticism and the vernacular, whereas modernity tends to focus on technical, functional, and abstract imagery.

Scaling

Scaling is another operation for constructively establishing a relationship between building and landscape. The essential feature involves enlargement and amplification of commonplace elements or the

Figure 185   Editing an urban landscape: Hilberseimer's proposal for South Chicago, 1953

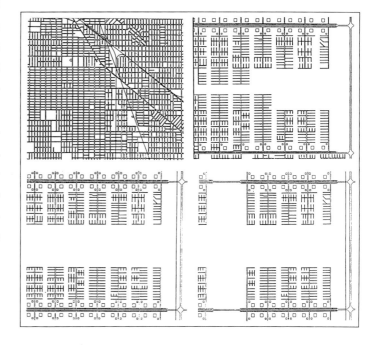

reverse, reduction and diminution, as in Peter Cook's
Arcadian City (1976). Along with a certain amount of
typological invention, a gridiron pattern of regular
land subdivision was emphasized by amplifying
fence lines, greenbelts, and roadway alignments.

This example also illustrates another important
characteristic of the scaling operation. The elements
that are either enlarged or diminished remain in their
usual locations. The aim is to emphasize an underlying pattern or spatial arrangement inherent in a typical suburban environment, not to invent a new one.

More generally scaling is an important operation
for developing the spatial presence of the common
residential landscape (figure 186). It is also a way of
enlarging the design frame of reference within many
retail commercial environments. Here, such commonplace elements as lane markers on parking lots,
entry portals, light stanchions, and landscaped
fringes can be amplified and coherently designed in
order to give a heightened sense of place to an otherwise bland environment.

Scaling can also be used with juxtaposition.
Both operations are at the heart of pop realism. Archizoom Associati's provocative *Wind Town* (1969)
first enlarges the form of an automobile tail fin to the
scale of a high-rise building and then places the building complex in the relatively uninhabitable environment of desert mesas (Branzi 1984, p. 62). SITE's
projects for Best Stores (figure 94) and several other
corporate suburban building complexes of the 1970s
use both operations to comment on the tectonic order
of such buildings and satirize a consumer society in
the process. Organic forces and the ravages of time
seem to have invaded parking lots and the buildings

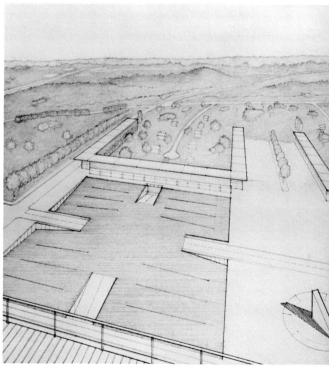

*Figure 186   Rescaling the suburban landscape: proposal
for Burlington, Massachusetts, by Nader Tehrani, 1989*

themselves, leaving behind crumbled walls, over-grown structures, and ghostly outlines of half-inundated automobiles (Klotz 1988, p. 410f). Raimund Abraham's *Nine Houses* triptychon of 1976 turns away from technological utopianism in the direction of an earthbound organic portrayal of settlement (Klotz 1988, pp. 405–10). Here scaling is primarily employed as a means of blurring distinctions between buildings and their surroundings.

Finally, scaling in conjunction with popular and vernacular symbolism has been a theme consistently explored by Venturi and Scott Brown. Their theoretical work, *Learning from Las Vegas* (1972), presented a vision of the contemporary American landscape where billboards are the most important architectural elements, and buildings recede into the background. Rather than condemning this visual reality as abhorrent, they saw it as inspirational. After all, they asked rhetorically, wasn't the facade of a Gothic cathedral one single giant billboard (Venturi, Scott Brown, and Izenour 1972)?

The architectural work that followed took up this theme, exploiting the vitality of contemporary commercial symbols. Billboards and commercial streets-capes were proposed for Philadelphia in 1973 and later for Miami (Klotz 1988, pp. 161f.). However, it is in the architecture of the Best and Basco supermarkets that the scaling of popular symbolism is most evident. The Basco supermarket project in Philadelphia (1976) is a pared-down, quintessential decorated shed (figure 187). Sign and building are located in an ordinary manner, but the scale relationship is dramatically altered. A line of two-story-high, freestanding red letters, spelling B A S C O, stands in front of a well-proportioned, unadorned blue single-story building. In oblique views, the scale and proportions of the letters can be appreciated less literally and become simply bold sculptural elements in a commercial landscape.

A similar approach was followed, in the collaboration of Frank O. Gehry and Associates with the Office of Peter Walker and Martha Schwartz, for the Herman Miller Western Regional Facility in Rockland, California, in 1983 (figure 178). Instead of letters, usually found on a building, forming a land-

Figure 187   Scaling and a redefinition of the commercial landscape: Basco Supermarket, Philadelphia, by Venturi, Rauch and Scott Brown, 1976, together with the Herman Miller Western Regional Facility, Rockland, California, by Frank O. Gehry and Associates with the Office of Peter Walker and Martha Schwartz, 1983

scape, boulders and riprap were skillfully deployed in both the building and the parking lot to scale up essential qualities of the site (Boles 1989b). It is precisely this capacity for double reading that makes both projects provocative and useful models for design in a middle landscape.

Ordering

Ordering is the third fundamental way of constructively modifying relationships among building and landscape elements found in the middle landscape. At a rudimentary level this operation involves changing the interval or spacing between elements in a field. As Smithson points out, the concept of interval strongly pervades American urbanism as a major organizing device (Smithson 1981). It is the space between buildings and the perceptual rhythms that are thereby established, as much as the buildings themselves, that gives the American suburban landscape its identity. Tunnard and Pushkarev had recognized

Figure 188   A reintergration of parts: proposal in a suburban context, by Sahel Al-Hiyari, 1988

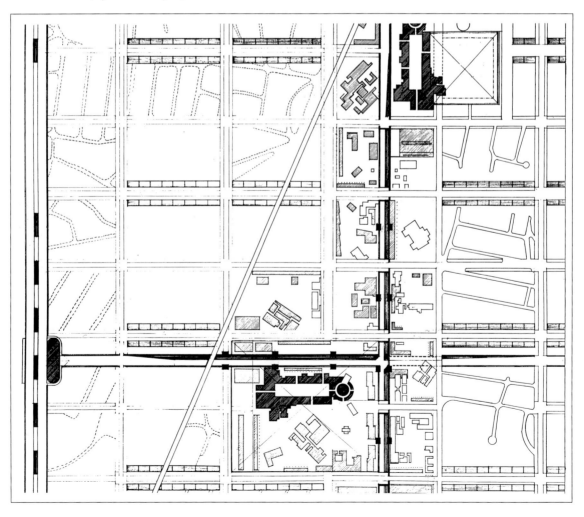

this concept in their proposals for reordering the arrangement of buildings within the dwelling group in order to achieve higher levels of visual coherence and civic order. Drawing on visual principles that exploited variety within the essential unity of a linear distribution of buildings, they sought to increase the hierarchical order of suburban residential environments. Further articulation of the resulting groupings of buildings could then be used to create smaller community clusters of houses, still within a basic linear street network (Tunnard and Pushkarev 1963, pp. 98f.).

The general point of these and other similar operations concerns the systematic differentiation and integration of building parts within an overall contextual whole, constructively demonstrated by the project in figure 188. The aim is at least twofold: to make the visual aspect of an otherwise monotonous or chaotic environment more coherent and memorable and to increase the hierarchy of building program and spatial order inherent in the environment, thus offering higher levels of functional choice for day-to-day activities. For example, setbacks along a residential street can be manipulated to produce semienclosed common areas that are more conducive to neighborly activities and children's play than typical linear arrangements. At least the spatial frame of reference within the street is enlarged beyond the singular function of conveying traffic.

A second and more complex form of ordering is to break present patterns of development and redistribute various components according to a new order. A good example of this operation is provided by yet another scheme for the redevelopment of the Fra-

mingham-Natick commercial area, the general aim of which was to bring a greater public presence to the suburbs (Schuyler 1986). The proposal began by asserting the primacy and inevitability of automobile transportation and by devising a highly rational roadway system for the area. Instead of a normal arrangement, however, curvilinear streets were used as major arterials, thus creating less perfunctory public spaces in front of major buildings (figure 189). A second form of reordering occurred with the inversion of the conventional retail shopping mall from a singular building complex surrounded by an expanse of parking lot to an annular configuration that surrounds a public parking area. In spirit, this arrangement was much like Taylor and Patel's proposal for the suburban supermarket already described. A third kind of reordering occurred, as shown in figure 189, with the dispersion of suburban office buildings away from the usual arrangement in isolated enclaves or districts. Instead these facilities were redistributed to take better advantage of transportation accessibility and to overcome the usual sense of separation from other buildings and land uses. The reordering of single-family residential units at a local level took the opposite tack in the direction of aggregation. By self-consciously grouping houses amid a common space centered on the street (figure 189), the urban scale of residential development was enhanced in a manner that could be related more effectively with the scale of neighboring shops and offices. Finally, civic institutions were concentrated in a regular pattern of tall buildings, thus reordering the usual suburban hierarchy of structures to clearly symbolize a public presence. Throughout the proposal, little alteration was

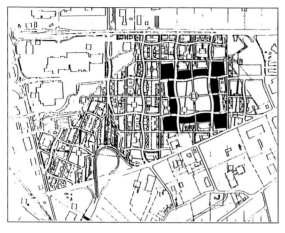

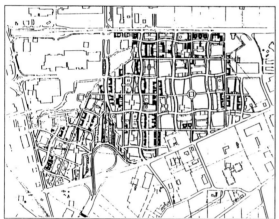
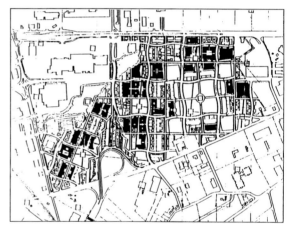

Figure 189   Reordering the middle landscape: project for Framingham-Natick, Massachusetts, by John Schuyler, 1986

made to typical building types. Rather, the exercise was a bricolage according to new ordering principles of distribution and arrangement.

A third type of reordering can occur in existing circumstances or habitual patterns of development by introducing a new level of order into a typical spatial hierarchy, generally by monumentalizing a functional component of the suburban environment. For example, it can be established by imposing a highly integrated rational order on a commercial strip, based primarily on vehicular movement (figure 190). As a consequence, the cross-section of roadways and parking lots can be changed radically. Instead of the usual flat expanse of parking between a row of buildings and a relatively undifferentiated roadway, an articulated concave cross-section can be developed that alleviates traffic congestion and enhances a driver's sense of direction and destination. The resulting

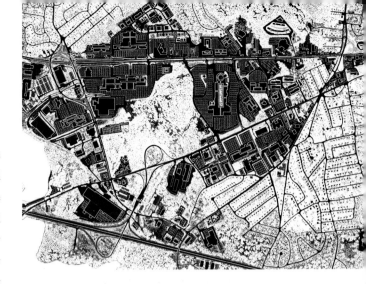

proposition is a relatively finite and closed landscape that bounds a prevalent and chaotic tendency toward unnecessary extension out into the countryside. The resulting monumentality and compositionally closed character of the commercial strip can be enhanced by a dominant central facility, such as a major highway interchange or a similar public transportation facility (see figure 190).

Typological Invention

In addition to operations that change the perception of essentially existing elements in response to new programs of use, the elements themselves can be changed. Desirable opportunities for more mixed use and higher integration of uses within a typical middle landscape have already been discussed in detail. There also seems to be room in the direction of new suburban building and landscape types—that is, new machines and new gardens.

One approach toward a new landscape focuses attention on large-scale elements such as roadways, building complexes, parking areas, and open spaces and deliberately sets out to structure them as parts of a singular landscaped entity. This idea is clearly explored in Emilio Ambasz's Lucille Halsell Conservatory in San Antonio (1987), shown in figure 191. It is also an underlying theme in the same designer's proposal for the Schlumberger Research Laboratories in Austin, Texas of the same year (Ambasz 1988).

In essence, the strategy relies on exploiting two characteristics. The first is the rough equivalence in potential scale of these elements. For instance, the bulk or footprints of building complexes, parking lots, highway interchanges, and conservation areas

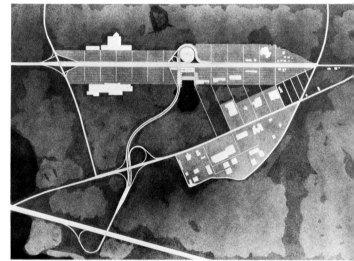

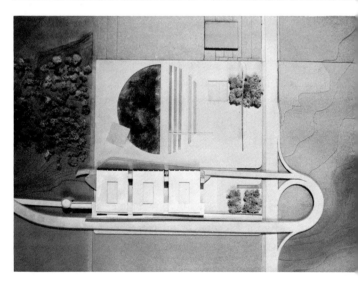

Figure 190   Bringing a monumental order to the suburban strip: proposal by Donna Paley, 1987

are often similar in size. The second is the dynamic qualities that can be captured by moving through and between separate realms. For example, movement through conservation areas and beside building complexes (figure 192) can be facilitated by a more deliberate and dramatic orchestration of the connection between the roadway and the surrounding environment. Parking lots and other neglected surfaces within the overall landscape can also be viewed as potentially positive features with sculptural qualities of their own. The results, illustrated in figure 192, can be a compositional merger between the dynamics of automobile movement set within a highly diversified ensemble of intersecting planar elements, each with its own spatial qualities and, therefore, more complete modulation of the experience of movement.

A perceptual problem facing attempts to compose a coherent landscape at this scale is the absence of viewing points from which to appreciate the whole scene. Unlike a piece of art, even a large earthwork, pieces of the landscape have to be constructed mentally in the manner of something like a cinematic experience. This perceptual difficulty places special emphasis on the ritualization of movement within the landscape. Through the control of entry and egress, such a ritual can be orchestrated, at least according to a few major sequences.

Another perceptual problem with this kind of landscape is the ability to appreciate bounded figures of such expansive planar proportions. Parking lots rendered as abstract folded plates and artfully intersecting planes escape appreciation in the manner of garden art because of their sheer size and reduced figural quality. This effect might be counteracted

through movement and by intensifying a pedestrian's spatial experience at the edges or at certain lines along the sculptural parking plates. Sudden changes in grade from one parking area to another might be developed as a covered pedestrian pathway leading into a building complex. Thus by dramatically changing the perceptual experience of someone who is walking from a car to a building, the abstract qualities of planes, lines, and surfaces that underlie such a compositional strategy can be appreciated.

The rituals of movement are exploited in a second kind of typological invention, one that involves new building prototypes. So far, with few exceptions, suburban commercial buildings have been designed in the same way that they might have been in a conventional urban context of streets and blocks. In other words, design attention has been focused on housing the primary accommodations, almost to the exclusion of other necessary subsidiary facilities and site works not typically found in strictly urban contexts. By according more of an equal role to the subsidiary facilities, especially those associated with arrival, circulation, parking, and entry into the building proper, a new prototype begins to emerge, characterized by the complete integration of circulation, parking, and entry into the public sequence of spaces within the building complex.

Several provocative examples of this approach toward typological development have been proposed by Machado and Silvetti (Machado 1983, 1988). In almost all cases, the sequence and ritual of automobile movement was the organizing armature around which the design proposal was formally developed. Moreover, a conscious attempt was made to integrate

Figure 191   Typological invention of a landscape setting: Lucille Halsell Conservatory, San Antonio, Texas, by Emilio Ambasz, 1987

Figure 192   Reinvention of a middle landscape: proposal for a mixed-use suburban area, by Garth Paterson, 1987

building complexes with the street instead of the typical practice of separating them across an expanse of parking or garden landscape. This gesture allowed the equivalent of a public foyer to be provided to the building complex in a manner analogous to public entries in traditional urban settings. Another feature of these examples was penetration of the traditional building envelope by automobile entry ramps and other elements of circulation. Instead of isolating the major space within, say, an office building according to normal practice, it was now located at the intersection of the automobile entry, car parking, and office space. In other schemes, grade-level parking lots were populated with building elements and deliberately transformed into formal, gardenlike settings. Again habitual arrangements of building program were abandoned in favor of a more coherent overall approach that openly embraced the needs of automobile movement.

A project that convincingly portrays Machado and Silvetti's typological inventiveness and their concern for civic function and automobile movement is La Porta Meridionale (1987) in Palermo, Sicily (Rowe 1989). Although it is not American, the proposal explicitly addresses a highway environment on an urban fringe. Of particular note for us here is the conversion of a highway interchange into a monumental gateway to the city. Framed by walls and incorporating parking areas within cylinders created by highway ramps (figure 193), the cloverleaf becomes a freestanding "building" in the surrounding landscape. Also noteworthy is the termination of a major street in a building complex housing a bus station, a garage, office facilities, and residential development.

The formation of a tower and public viewing platforms, an integral part of this complex, seems to collide with the mountainside and perceptually and metaphorically extends the roadway from below monumentally into the mountainous landscape above (Rowe 1989).

The conjunction of office parks and related functions around highway interchanges might be similarly reconsidered (figure 194). Effectively a public infrastructure of roadways, utilities, and fully serviced building plots could be established to facilitate and lend civic credence to ensuing commercial development. Needed community facilities for neighboring residential developments could be integreted as part of the same infrastructure, functionally recreating the equivalent of a town center. In its overall planning, the project is reminiscent of Stirling's project for Siemens AG (1969) in Munich, without, however, quite the same monumentality and megastructural presence (*Architectural Design* 1980).

No doubt there are other examples of typological invention. Certainly some of the pioneering and visionary schemes from the Russian constructivists of the 1920s embraced the opportunity of vehicular movement systems as an integral part of a new urban landscape. Tikhonov's Nikitski Boulevard proposal for Moscow was a powerfully imaginative design for defining a freeway that moved well beyond a basic engineering frame of reference (Khan-Magomedov 1983, pp. 316–17). Kocar's scheme for a commercial center incorporated novel forms directly associated with automobile movement, such as cylindrical parking ramps doubling as entry gates to the complex (De Feo 1963, p. 96). Melnikov's Commune House

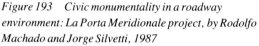

Figure 193   Civic monumentality in a roadway
environment: La Porta Meridionale project, by Rodolfo
Machado and Jorge Silvetti, 1987

project of 1922–1923 fully integrated high-speed
movement, housing, parking and public facilities
into a rational yet lyrical ensemble (Khan-Magomedov 1983, pl. 895). None of these proposals was fully
realized, so we have no way of appreciating the
results. Nevertheless, they remain powerful testa-
ments to the poetic opportunities and promise of radical design thinking in contemporary metropolitan
circumstances.

MAKING A MIDDLE LANDSCAPE

There seems to have been a social logic and an inevitability behind the emerging spatial mosaic of modern
American metropolitan development. Flight from the
city of Dante's Inferno at the end of the nineteenth
century resulted in a conflation of the customary distinctions between town and country. The middle
landscape that emerged was neither one nor the other.

It incorporated the functional specialization, diversity, and social heterogeneity of the traditional city
with dispersed, disurban, and almost rural patterns of
small-town, country life. The inherent tension that
persisted also strongly reflected analogous tensions in
American society that have culminated in the emergence of special interests and the rise of social
pluralism.

Fundamentally American metropolitan development has been a story of technical planning, scientific
management, and mass production. In the building
artifacts that were produced, an inherent tension appeared to exist. Especially during periods of introduction, the rational excesses of tract housing, shopping centers, office parks, and expressways were
often cloaked in romantic imagery. Furthermore, the
respective root metaphors of cottage, marketplace,
country estate, and parkland all had pastoral origins.

By simultaneously embracing two major underlying cultural themes in contemporary American so-

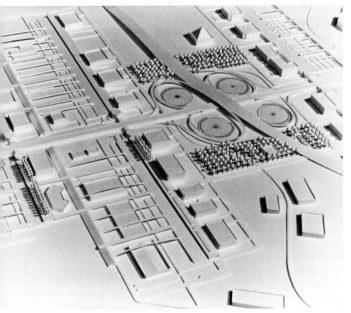

Figure 194   Reconsideration of the public infrastructure around a highway interchange: proposal for the New Jersey Turnpike, by Antonio Fiol-Silva, 1989

ciety, the inherent idea of modern pastoralism forms a mythopoetic context for suburban metropolitan development. More specifically the modern technical temperament with its technological optimism, technocratic style of management, and reliance on the world of facts is engaged with complementary attitudes of individual self-reliance, traditional small-town values, and dwelling close to nature. As a dialectic this relationship can form a critical and progressive ideology that deliberately used one set of proclivities to qualify the other. Thus any tendency toward conservatism, nostalgia, and sentimentality on the part of pastoralism is immediately curbed by the modern technical temperament's drive toward productivity and new development. Conversely, the pastoral side of the equation establishes the essential terrain and ends for the modern technical orientation. Beyond self-regulation, the constructive engagement of these two very different ideas leads to critical insights and knowledge about contemporary prospects for the middle landscape.

Several tasks must be undertaken in order to realize the poetic dimensions of modern pastoralism as a way of making the middle landscape. First, extensive realignment and invention must occur in the design program of suburban metropolitan development. In general terms, a common residential landscape must be devised that creates a greater sense of civic identity, recognizes the rapidly changing needs of households, and provides a higher level of convenient social service. As Mumford wrote some time ago, fundamentally the middle landscape is "a collective effort to live a private life" (Mumford 1938). The terms of reference for development and design of commercial landscapes must be significantly amplified beyond singular and basic functional requirements to promote higher levels of mixed use, greater expressive latitude, and a heightened sense of common property resource.

Second, modes of expression must be found that are appropriate to the task of adequately rendering modern pastoralism. Historicism brings continuity with the past and the symbolic restoration of traditional values, but the modern technical temperament is barely acknowledged and the positive dynamic circumstances of daily life all but ignored. Modernism, estranges us from the past and, more important, bifurcates the middle landscape in a manner that disengages the modern technical temperament from the pastoral perspective. The machine and the garden have become two exclusive realms.

To remedy this problem, more engaging ways must be found of placing the machine in the garden or the garden around the machine. To this end bold design proposals that make use of available poetic operations of placement such as juxtaposition, scaling, and ordering must be actively explored and elaborated. There seems to be ample room for typological invention whereby ideas of function and form, as well as building and landscape, can be reconsidered fundamentally. It is only by recognizing the middle landscape as a real locus of growth and innovation in our society, rather than trying to make it in the manner of somewhere else, that progress will be made. It is not too late. The middle landscape is still very much under development in both a physical and cultural sense. Like the city and the country beforehand, which were constantly being made and remade, the initial outlines of the middle landscape are now in need of thoughtful elaboration.

Figures 2, 3, 6, 7, and 29: Courtesy of the Frances Loeb Library, Harvard University.

Figures 4, 5, 43, 45, 47, 49, 50, 53, 54, 100, 104, 109, 111, 114, and 163: Drawn by Vasilios Tsakalos.

Figures 8 and 135: Scott 1969, pp. 461 and 351 respectively.

Figure 9: Photograph by Carolyn Leaman, 1986. Reproduced with permission.

Figure 10: Courtesy of the Planning Department, Township of Framingham.

Figure 11: Drawn by Nancy Hadley.

Figure 12: Texas Highway Department Traffic Survey 1953, p. 3.

Figure 14: Courtesy of Fondren Library, Rice University.

Figures 18, 21, and 99: Courtesy of the Astrocard Company, Inc., Houston, Texas.

Figures 22, 96, 136, 140, and 142: Tunnard and Pushkarev 1963, pp. 20, 333, 100, 254, and 163 respectively. Courtesy of Aero Service Corporation, Geoffrey Baker, Fairchild Aerial Surveys, Fairchild Aerial Surveys, and the New Jersey State Highway Department, respectively. Reproduced with permission of Yale University Press.

Figure 24: Winningham 1986, p. 99. Reproduced with permission of Rice University Press.

Figure 26: Kennedy 1944, p. 2.

Figures 28 and 82: Photographs by Bill McIlroy, 1987. Reproduced with permission.

Figures 31 and 95: Gruen and Smith 1960, pp. 258 and 26 respectively. Photographs by Anthony Lane and Warren Reynolds respectively. Reproduced with permission on Van Nostrand Reinhold.

Figure 33: From a photograph by Bill Harris.

Figure 34: Photograph by Tom McHugh Photo Researchers, Inc.

Figure 35: Photograph by Emil Reynolds. *Time Magazine*. Reproduced with permission.

Figure 36: Photograph by Bernard Hoffman, *Life Magazine*, Copyright Time, Inc. Reproduced with permission.

Figure 37: Copyright David Hockney, 1967. Reproduced with permission.

Figure 39: Rae 1965, p. 119. Courtesy of Sears Roebuck and Company.

Figures 40 and 160: Branzi 1984, pp. 67 and 160 respectively (MIT Press).

Figure 41: Courtesy of the Museum of the City of New York.

Figure 42: Courtesy of Landslides of Boston.

Figure 44: Architects Small House Service Bureau 1929, p. 23.

Figure 51, 63, 180: Courtesy of Orr and Taylor. Copyright Mick Hales 1985.

Figures 56a, 131, 132, 167a, and 167b: Stein 1966, pp. 58, 42 and 56, 182, 70 and 140 respectively. Photographs by Gretchen van Tassel, Washington, D.C. (MIT Press).

Figure 58: McCoy 1960, p. 123.

Figure 59: Jones and Emmons 1957, p. 58. Photograph by Julius Shulman. Reproduced with permission of Van Nostrand Reinhold.

Figures 60 and 84: *Architectural Forum,* January 1938, p. 29, and December 1951, p. 180, respectively.

Figure 64: May 1958, p. 79.

Figure 69: Bender 1973, p. 35 upper. Courtesy of SENCO Products, Inc. Reproduced with permission of Van Nostrand Reinhold.

Figure 70: Courtesy of Ryland Homes.

Figures 72, 74, 75, and 90: Baker and Funaro 1951, pp. 185, 113, 271, and 223. Reproduced with permission of Van Nostrand Reinhold.

Figures 79 and 81: Baker and Funaro 1951, pp. 90 and 95. Photographs by Aerial Photoservice and Dick Whittington, respectively. Reproduced with permission of Van Nostrand Reinhold.

Figures 73, 80, 83, and 85: Drawn by Riccardo Tossani.

Figure 86: Gillette 1985, p. 452. Courtesy of Gruen Associates.

Figures 91 and 124: Labatut and Lane 1950, pp. 143 and 399 respectively.

Figures 92 and 93: Courtesy of *The Progressive Grocer.*

Figure 97: Langdon 1986, p. 57. Courtesy of Martin Cable, photograph by Edwin Schober.

Figures 101 and 115: Goble 1957, pp. 187 and 163 respectively. Reproduced with permission of McGraw-Hill Publishing Company.

Figures 102: *Progressive Architecture* 1959, June, p. 158.

Figure 103: Holleman and Gallagher 1978, p. 151. Reproduced with permission of Wayne State University Press.

Figure 105: Reinhold Hohl, *Office Buildings: An International Survey* (Praeger Publishers, New York, 1968), p. 11. Reprinted with permission.

Figures 107, 108, 110, and 119: Courtesy of Kevin Roche John Dinkeloo and Associates.

Figure 112: Courtesy of Kevin Boche John Dinkeloo and Associates. Photograph by Anthony Esposito, Bethany, Connecticut.

Figure 113: Courtesy of Hanna/Olin Ltd.

Figure 116: Hoyt 1978, p. 71. Reproduced with permission of McGraw-Hill Publishing Company.

Figure 118: Reproduced with permission of Stanley Jesudowich, 1988.

Figure 120: Rae 1965, p. 49. Courtesy of the Ford Motor Company.

Figure 121: Flink 1970, p. 206. Courtesy of the Smithsonian Institution, Washington, D.C.

Figure 122: Reprinted by permission of Harvard University Press from *Parkways and Land Values* by John Nolen and Henry Hubbard, copyright 1937 by Henry Vincent Hubbard.

Figure 123: Nolen and Hubbard 1937, p. 79. Courtesy of the Westchester County Park Commission, White Plains, New York.

Figure 125: *Highway,* 1952, cover.

Figure 126: Krüger 1937, p. 94.

Figure 127: Bel Geddes 1940, p. 48.

Figures 128 and 139: National Interregional Highway Commission 1944, p. 42 and pl. x respectively.

Figures 130 and 134: City of Los Angeles 1946, pp. 13 and 38 respectively.

Figure 133: Regional Planning Commission, County of Los Angeles 1929, p. 29.

Figure 137: Courtesy of Team Plan, Inc.

Figure 138: Abrams 1986, pp. 16 and 17. Reproduced with permission of Edizioni Electa.

Figure 141: Courtesy of H.S. Crocker International.

Figures 143 and 178: The Mariemont Company 1925, pp. 11 and 3 respectively.

Figure 145: From an engraving by W. Watts after Geo Barrett, R.A. 1779, in Clark 1980, pl. 42.

Figure 151: Rae 1965, p. 118. Courtesy of General Motors Corporation.

Figure 152: Gilles 1946, p. 64.

Figure 153: Christine Frederick, *Scientific Management in the Home: Household Engineering* (1970), and Forty 1986, p. 217.

Figure 155: Bowly 1978, p. 125.

Figure 157: Benevolo 1985, p. 929 (MIT Press).

Figure 158: Ciucci, Dal Co, Manieri-Elia, and Tafuri 1973, p. 356 (MIT Press).

Figure 159: Mock 1944, p. 37 (MIT Press).

Figures 165, 173, 174, 175, 184, 186, 188, 189, 190, 192, and 194: Courtesy of Ah-King Teo, Riccardo Tossani, Ramon Jurado, Vasilios Tsakalos, Guy Perry, Nader Tehrani, Sahel Al-Hiyari, John Schuyler, Donna Paley, Garth Paterson, and Antonio Fiol-Silva respectively. All work was completed in the Urban Design Program at the Graduate School of Design at Harvard University between 1986 and 1989.

Figure 168: *The Western Architect,* August 1913, p. 68 (plan) and p. 69 (house).

Figure 169: Courtesy of William F. Stern and Associates.

Figure 171: Nissen 1988, p. 13 (MIT Press).

Figure 172 Sparke 1987, p. 234. Courtesy Architectural Association Slide Library.

Figure 177: *Architectural Forum,* April 1918, p. 130.

Figure 179: Papademetriou 1972, p. 85. Reproduced with permission.

Figures 166 and 181: Courtesy of Architectural Design Magazine, London.

Figure 182: Courtesy of the Smithsonian Institution, Washington, D.C.; Hilberseimer 1955, p. 201.

Figure 185: Hilberseimer 1955, p. 241.

Figure 187: Klotz 1988, p. 157 (MIT Press); Boles 1989b, p. 58, photograph by David Walker.

Figure 190: Plan drawn by Glenn Forley.

Figure 191: Photograph by Vasilios Tsakalos, 1988. Reproduced with permission.

Figure 193: Courtesy of Rodolfo Machado and Jorge Silvetti.

References

Abbott, Carl. 1981. *The New Urban America: Growth and Politics in Sunbelt Cities*. Chapel Hill: University of North Carolina Press.

Abbott, Carl. 1987. "The Suburban Sunbelt." *Journal of Urban History* 13, no. 3, pp. 275–301.

Abrams, Janet. 1986. "The Form of the American City: Two Projects by Andreas Duany and Elizabeth Plater-Zyberk." *Lotus International*, no. 50, pp. 7–29.

Adams, John S. 1970. "Residential Structure of Midwestern Cities." *Annals of the Association of American Geographers*, no. 60, pp. 37–62.

Akin, William E. 1977. *Technocracy and the American Dream: The Technocratic Movement, 1900–1941*. Berkeley: University of California Press.

Ambasz, Emilio. 1988. *Emilio Ambasz: The Poetics of the Pragmatic*. New York: Rizzoli.

American Institute of Architects. 1986. *Design for Aging: An Architectural Guide*. Washington, D.C.: American Institute of Architects.

American Law Institute. 1975. *A Model Land Development Code: Complete Text*. Washington, D.C.: American Law Institute.

Anderson, Grace. 1987. "A Corporate Villa." *Architectural Record* (November): 25–29.

Archer, John. 1987. *Building a Nation: A History of the Australian House*. Sydney: William Collins, Pty., Ltd.

Architects Small House Service Bureau. 1929. *House Designs*. Boston: Architects Small House Service Bureau of New England.

Architectural Design. 1980. "A.D. Profile: Stirling Gold." *Architectural Design* 50, nos. 7–8.

Architectural Forum. 1936. *The 1936 Book of Small Houses*. New York: Simon and Schuster.

Architectural Forum. 1938. "Frank Lloyd Wright's Wiley House." *Architectural Forum* (January): 27–31.

Architectural Forum. 1951. "Shoppers World." *Architectural Forum* (December): 180–199.

Architectural Forum. 1953. "New Thinking on Shopping Centers." *Architectural Forum* (March): 122–144.

Architectural Forum. 1954. "Northland: A New Yardstick for Shopping Center Planning." *Architectural Forum* (June): 102–145.

Architectural Record. 1951. "Administration Buildings." In *Office Buildings*, pp. 116–117. New York: F. W. Dodge Corp.

Architectural Record. 1986. "Small Pleasures." *Architectural Record* (April): 90–97.

Architectural Record. 1987. "Interfacing Cars and Trains." *Architectural Record* (January): 72–75.

Architectural Review. 1971. "Pastoral Palazzo." *Architectural Review* 149 (January–June): 137–146.

Architectural Review. 1987. "Ideas for a Supermarket: Competition Results." *Architectural Review* 181 (June): 75–86.

Architecture. 1984. "City of Columbus Parking Lot Competition." *Architecture* (June): 36–37.

Architecture and Urbanism. 1986. "Alewife Station and Garage." *Architecture and Urbanism* 195 (December): 47–54.

Arquitectonica. 1984. "Hadden Town Houses, Houston." *Architectural Record* (August): 87–91.

Babcock, Richard F. 1966. *The Zoning Game*. Madison: University of Wisconsin Press.

Baker, Elizabeth C. 1976. "Artworks on the Land." *Art in America* (January–February): 92–96.

Baker, Geoffrey, and Bruno Funaro. 1951. *Shopping Centers: Design and Operation*. New York: Reinhold.

Baldassare, Mark. 1986. *Trouble in Paradise: The Suburban Transformation in America*. New York: Columbia University Press.

Banham, Reyner. 1971. *Los Angeles: The Architecture of Four Ecologies*. New York: Penguin.

Bank of Southwest. 1971. *Key to the City: Houston, Texas*. Houston: Bank of the Southwest.

Banker and Tradesman. 1986. May, p. 11.

Barna, Joel W. 1989. "Solana in the Sun." *Progressive Architecture* (April): 65–73.

Bassett, Edward M. 1931. *Buildings: Their Uses and the Spaces about Them*. New York: F. W. Dodge.

Baudrillard, Jean. 1988. *America*. New York: Verso.

Beardsley, John. 1984. *Earthworks and Beyond: Contemporary Art in the Landscape*. New York: Abbeville Press.

Beddington, Nadine. 1981. *Design for Shopping Centres*. London: Butterworth Scientific.

Bel Geddes, Norman. 1940. *Magic Motorways*. New York: Random House.

Bender, Richard. 1973. *A Crack in the Rear-View Mirror: A View of Industrialized Building*. New York: Van Nostrand Reinhold.

Benevolo, Leonardo. 1971. *The Origins of Modern Town Planning*. Cambridge, Mass.: MIT Press.

Benevolo, Leonardo. 1985. *The History of the City*. Cambridge, Mass.: MIT Press.

Bentmann, Reinhard, and Michael Müller. 1985. "The Villa as Architecture of Domination." *9H*, no. 7, pp. 83–104.

Berger, Bennett M. 1960. *Working-Class Suburbs: A Study of Auto Workers in Suburbia*. Berkeley: University of California Press.

Berger, Bennett M. 1971. *Looking for America: Essays on Youth, Suburbia and Other American Obsessions*. Englewood Cliffs, N.J.: Prentice-Hall.

Bernstein, Richard L. 1976. *The Restructuring of Social and Political Theory*. New York: Harcourt Brace Jovanovich.

Berry, Brian J. L. 1975. "The Decline of the Aging Metropolis: Cultural Bases and Social Process." In George Sternlieb and James W. Hughes (eds.), *Post-Industrial America: Metropolitan Decline and Inter-Regional Job Shifts*. New Brunswick, N.J.: Center for Urban Policy Research.

Birch, D. L. 1970. *The Economic Future of City and Suburb*. New York: Committee for Economic Development.

Birmingham, Stephen. 1978. *The Golden Dream: Suburbia in the 1970s*. New York: Harper & Row.

Blake, Peter. 1964. *God's Own Junkyard*. New York: Holt, Rinehart and Winston.

Blum, John M. et al. 1963. *The National Experience*. New York: Harcourt, Brace and World.

Boles, Daralice D. 1985. "Robert Davis Small Town Entrepreneur." *Progressive Architecture* (July): 111–118.

Boles, Daralice D. 1989a. "Re-Ordering the Suburbs." *Progressive Arthicture* (May): 78–91.

Boles, Daralice D. 1989b. "P/A Pofile: Peter Walker and Martha Schwartz." *Progressive Architecture* (July): 56–61.

Bone, A. J., and Martin Wohl. 1959. "Massachusetts Route 128 Impact Study." *Highways and Economic Development,* bulletin 227.

Boston Globe. 1989. "Top 50 Employers." *Boston Globe,* June 13, p. C3.

Boston Redevelopment Authority. 1982. *City of Boston Population Projections: A Summary*. Boston: BRA Research Department, February.

Bowly, Devereaux, Jr. 1978. *The Poorhouse: Subsidized Housing in Chicago, 1895–1976*. London: Feffer and Simons.

Boyer, Christine. 1983. *Dreaming the Rational City*. Cambridge, Mass.: MIT Press.

Branzi, Andrea. 1984. *The Hot House: Italian New Wave Design*. Cambridge, Mass.: MIT Press.

Brenner, David. 1987. "Interfacing Cars and Trains." *Architectural Record* 175 (January): 72–75.

Brenner, Douglas. 1982. "The Meadows: A Sylvan Campus for Arco." *Architectural Record* 170 (April): 108–115.

Brooks, H. Allen (ed.). 1975. *Prairie School Architecture*. New York: Van Nostrand Reinhold.

Brown, Denise Scott. 1983. "Changing Family Forms." *Journal of the American Planning Association* 49, no. 2 (Spring): 135–143.

Brownell, Blaine A. (ed.). 1987. "Suburbanization." *Journal of Urban History* 13, no. 3 (May).

Bruce-Briggs, Barry. 1977. *The War against the Automobile*. New York: Dutton.

Bruner, James E., Jr. 1972. *Industrialism: The American Experience*. New York: Benziger.

Builder. 1983–1986. "Home Buyer Surveys."

Building Diagnostics. 1985. *Independence through Interdependence: Congregate Living for Older People*. Boston: Building Diagnostics.

Burdick, Eugene. 1956. *The Ninth Wave*. Boston: Little, Brown.

Bureau of Economic Analysis. 1981. *BEA Regional Projections Massachusetts*. Washington, D.C.: U.S. Department of Commerce.

Bush-Brown, Albert. 1983. *Skidmore, Owings and Merrill: Architecture and Urbanism*. New York: Van Nostrand Reinhold.

Byron, Joseph. 1985. *New York Life at the Turn of the Century*. New York: Dover.

Campbell, Joseph. 1959. *The Masks of God*. New York: Dover.

Camus, Albert. 1955. *The Myth of Sisyphus and Other Essays*. New York: Vintage Books.

Cantor, Jay E. 1976. "The New England Landscape of Change." *Art in America* (January–February): 51–54.

Cassens, Alwin, Jr. 1953. *Ranch Houses for Today*. New York: Archway Press, Inc.

Cassens, Alwin, Jr. 1955. *Favorite Ranch House Plans*. New York: Archway Press, Inc.

Cassirer, Ernst. 1955. *The Philosophy of Symbolic Forms, I–III*. New Haven: Yale University Press.

Catanese, Anthony J. 1972. *Scientific Methods of Urban Analysis*. Urbana: University of Illinois Press.

Cavitt, L. C., Jr. 1947. *Ranch Type Houses*. Culver City, Calif.: Murray & Gee, Inc.

Chadwick, George. 1972. *A Systems View of Planning*. New York: Pergamon Press.

Chermayeff, Serge, and Christopher Alexander. 1963. *Community and Privacy: Toward a New Architecture of Humanism*. Garden City, N.Y.: Doubleday.

Chinitz, Benjamin (ed.). 1964. *City and Suburb: The Economics of Metropolitan Growth*. Englewood-Cliffs, N.J.: Prentice-Hall.

City Planning Commission of Los Angeles. 1946. *Year Book*. Los Angeles: City of Los Angeles.

City Planning Commission of Los Angeles. 1947. *Year Book*. Los Angeles: City of Los Angeles.

Ciucci, Giorgio, Francesco Dal Co, Mario Manieri-Elia, and Manfredo Tafuri. 1973. *The American City: From the Civil War to the New Deal*. Cambridge: MIT Press.

Clark, Clifford Edward, Jr. 1986. *The American Family Home, 1800–1960*. Chapel Hill: University of North Carolina Press.

Clark, H. F. 1980. *The English Landscape Garden*. London: Alan Sutton.

Clark, Thomas A. 1979. *Blacks in Suburbs: A National Perspective*. New Brunswick, N.J.: Center for Urban Policy Research.

Clarke, Gilmore D. 1932. "Our Highway Problem." *American Magazine of Art* (November).

Clarke, Gilmore D. 1936. "Some Views on Highway Design." *Association of Highway Officials of the North Atlantic States (February)*.

Clarke, Gilmore D. 1950. "The Design of Motorways." In Jean Labatut and Wheaton J. Lane (eds.), *Highways in Our National Life*, pp. 164–167. Princeton: Princeton University Press.

Clarke, Gilmore D. 1953. "History and Growth of Expressways and Parkways in Metropolitan Areas." In J. Carter Hanes and Charles H. Connors, *Landscape Design and Its Relation to the Modern Highway*, pp. 1–10. New Brunswick, N.J.: Rutgers University.

Clausen, Meredith L. 1948. "Northgate Regional Shopping Center—Paradigm from the Provinces." *Journal of the Society of Architectural Historians* 32, no. 2, pp. 144–161.

Clawson, Marion. 1971. *Suburban Land Conversion in the United States*. Baltimore: John Hopkins University Press.

Clawson, Marion, and Peter Hall. 1973. *Planning and Urban Growth: An Anglo-American Comparison*. Baltimore: John Hopkins University Press.

Cleveland Chapter AIA. 1958. *Cleveland Architecture. 1796–1958*. Cleveland: AIA Chapter.

Cohn, Jan. 1979. *The Palace or the Poorhouse: The American House as a Cultural Symbol*. East Lansing: Michigan State University Press.

Cole, Thomas. 1835. "Essay on American Scenery." In John W. McCoubrey, *American Art, 1700–1960,* pp. 98–109. Englewood Cliffs, N.J.: Prentice-Hall, 1965.

Colquhoun, Alan. 1978. "Form and Figure." *Oppositions 12* (Spring): 29–37.

Colton, Joel and Stuart Bruchey. 1987. *Technology, The Economy and Society: The American Experience.* New York: Columbia University Press.

Conkin, Paul K. 1959. *Tomorrow a New World: The New Deal Community Program.* Ithaca, N.Y.: Cornell University Press.

Conrads, Ulrich. 1964. *Programs and Manfestos on 20th Century Architecture.* Translated by Michael Bullock. Cambridge, Mass.: MIT Press.

Converse, Paul D. 1946. *Retail Trade Areas in Illinois.* Urbana: University of Illinois Press.

Cook, Peter. 1970. *Experimental Architecture.* New York: Universe Books.

Corn, Joseph J. 1984. *Yesterday's Tomorrow: Past Visions of the American Future.* New York: Summit Books.

Corn, Joseph J. (ed.). 1986. *Imaging Tomorrow: History, Technology, and the American Future.* Cambridge, Mass.: MIT Press.

Cowan, Ruth Schwartz. 1982. "The Industrial Revolution in the Home: Household Technology and Social Change in the Twentieth Century." In Thomas J. Schlereth (ed.), *Material Culture Studies in America,* pp. 222–397. Nashville, Tenn.: The American Association for State and Local History.

Craig, Lois. 1986. "Suburbs." *Design Quarterly* 132.

Czestochowski, Joseph S. 1982. *The American Landscape Tradition: A Study and Gallery of Paintings.* New York: E. P. Dutton.

Dal Co, Francesco. 1985. *Kevin Roche.* New York: Rizzoli International Publications.

Davey, Peter. 1988. "Collegiate Corporation." *Architectural Review* (August): 52–57.

Davidoff, Paul, Linda Davidoff, and Neil H. Gold. 1971. "The Suburbs Have to Open Their Gates." *New York Times Magazine,* November 7.

Davies, Colin. 1988. "Gasstop." *Architectural Review* 184, no. 1097 (July): 67–86.

Davis, Allen J., and Robert P. Schubert. 1976. *Alternative Natural Energy Sources in Building Design.* New York: Van Nostrand Reinhold.

Davis, John L. 1982. *Houston: A Historical Portrait.* Austin, Tex.: Encino Press.

de Monchaux, John. 1988. "Getting Things Done in Messy Cities." *Places* 5, no. 4, pp. 3–6.

Deakin, Oliver A. 1951. "A Complete Modern Highway." *Contractors and Engineers Monthly* (March): 47–50.

Deakin, Oliver A. 1952. "Landscaping the Modern Highway." *Highway Magazine* 43 (February): 29–32.

Deakin, Oliver A. 1953. "Geometric Standards as Related to Alignment and Safety." In J. Carter Hanes and Charles A. Connors, *Landscape Design and Its Relation to the Modern Highway,* pp. 21–37. New Brunswick, N.J.: Rutgers University.

De Feo, Vittorio. 1963. *URSS: Architettura, 1917–1936.* Rome: Editori Riuniti.

DiBacco, Thomas V. 1987. *Made in the U.S.A.: The History of American Business.* New York: Harper & Row.

Dickey, John W., and Thomas M. Watts. 1978. *Analytical Techniques in Urban and Regional Planning.* New York: McGraw-Hill.

Dietz, Albert G. H., and Lawrence S. Cutler. 1971. *Industrial Building Systems for Housing.* Cambridge, Mass.: MIT Press.

Dipman, Carl W. (ed.). 1935. *Modern Food Stores.* New York: Progressive Grocer.

Dobriner, William M., ed. 1958. *The Suburban Community.* New York: G. P. Putnam's Sons.

Dobriner, William. 1963. *Class in Suburbia.* Englewood Cliffs, N.J.: Prentice-Hall.

Dolce, Philip C. (ed.). 1976. *Suburbia: The American Dream and Dilemma.* Garden City, N.Y.: Anchor Press.

Domencich, Thomas A., and Daniel McFadden. 1975. *Urban Travel Demand: A Behavioral Analysis.* New York: North-Holland.

Donaldson, Scott. 1969. *The Suburban Myth*. New York: Columbia University Press.

Doolittle, Fred C., George S. Masnick, Phillip L. Clay, and Gregory A. Jackson. 1982. *Future Boston: Patterns and Perspectives*. Cambridge, Mass.: Joint Center for Urban Studies of MIT and Harvard University.

Douglass, Harlan Paul. 1925. *The Suburban Trend*. New York: Arno Press. Reprint ed., 1970.

Downs, Anthony. 1970. "Alternative Forms of Future Urban Growth in the U.S." *Journal of the American Institute of Planners,* 36, pp. 1–11.

Downs, Anthony. 1973. *Opening up the Suburbs: An Urban Strategy for America*. New Haven: Yale University Press.

Dunbar, Clarence Peckham, and William Hunter Dillard. 1936. *Houston 1836–1936: Chronology and Review*. Houston: Business Research and Publications Service.

Early, James. 1965. *Romanticism and American Architecture*. New York: A. S. Barnes and Co.

Eichler, Ned. 1982. *The Merchant Builders*. Cambridge, Mass.: MIT Press.

Eliade, Mircea. 1959. *The Sacred and the Profane*. New York: Harper & Row.

Eliade, Mircea. 1960. *Myths, Dreams, and Mysteries*. New York: Harper & Row.

Ellis, John. 1988. "U.S. Codes and Controls." *Architectural Review* 184, no. 1101 (November): 79–85.

Emodi, Tom. 1989. "Piazza Canadian Tire: Emerging Urban Spaces in the Suburbs." In Detlef Mertins (ed.), *Metropolitan Mutations: The Architecture of Emerging Public Spaces,* pp. 201–208. Boston: Little, Brown.

Empson, William. 1950. *Some Versions of Pastoral*. New York: New Directions.

Federal Highway Administration. 1988. *Highway Statistics*. Washington, D.C.: U.S. Department of Transportation.

Feldman, Saul D., and Gerald W. Thielbor (eds.). 1975. *Life Styles: Diversity in American Society*. Boston: Little, Brown.

Ferriss, Hugh. 1929. *The Metropolis of Tomorrow*. New York: Ives Washburn.

Fischer, Claude S. 1976. "The Suburban Experience." In *The Urban Experience,* pp. 204–233. New York: Harcourt Brace Jovanovich.

Fish, Gertrude S. (ed.). 1979. *The Story of Housing*. New York: Macmillan.

Fisher, Leonard Everett. 1985. *Masterpieces of American Painting*. New York: Exeter Books.

Fisher, Thomas. 1988. "Remaking Malls." *Progressive Architecture* (November): 96–101.

Fishman, Robert. 1987. *Bourgeois Utopias: The Rise and Fall of Suburbia*. New York: Basic Books.

Flink, James J. 1970. *American Adopts the Automobile, 1895–1910*. Cambridge, Mass.: MIT Press.

Ford, James, and Katherine Morrow Ford. 1940. *The Modern House in America*. New York: Architectural Book Publishing Company.

Forty, Adrian. 1986. *Objects of Desire: Design and Society from Wedgewood to IBM*. New York: Pantheon Books.

Foster, Mark S. 1981. *From Streetcar to Superhighway: American City Planners and Urban Transportation, 1900–1940*. Philadelphia: Temple University Press.

Frampton, Kenneth. 1980. *Modern Architecture: A Critical History*. New York: Oxford University Press.

Frampton, Kenneth. 1987. "Ten Points on an Architecture of Regionalism: A Provisional Polemic." *Center* 3, pp. 20–27.

Funaro, Bruno, and Geoffrey Baker. 1949. "Shopping Centers." *Architectural Record* 106, no. 2, pp. 110–135.

Futugawa, Y. 1974. "College Life Insurance Headquarters." *Global Architecture,* no. 29.

Gakenheimer, Ralph (ed.). 1978. *The Automobile and the Environment: An International Perspective*. Cambridge, Mass.: MIT Press.

Galbraith, John Kenneth. 1958. *The Affluent Society*. London: Pelican.

Gans, Herbert J. 1967. *The Levittowners: Ways of Life and Politics in a New Suburban Community*. New York: Pantheon.

George, Henry. 1955. *Progress and Poverty*. New York: Robert Schalkenbach Foundation.

Gibbs, Kenneth Turney. 1984. *Business Architectural Imagery in America, 1870–1930*. Ann Arbor, Mich.: UMI Research Press.

Giedion, Sigfried. 1969. *Mechanization Takes Command*. New York: Prager Books.

Gilles, Mary Davis (ed.). 1946. *Let's Plan a Home*. Toledo, Ohio: Surface Combustion Corporation.

Gillette, Howard, Jr. 1985. "The Evolution of the Planned Shopping Center in Suburb and City." *Journal of the American Planning Association* 51, no. 4, pp. 449–460.

Glaab, C. N., and A. T. Brown. 1967. *A History of Urban America*. London: Macmillan.

Gleason, David King. 1985. *Over Boston*. Baton Rouge: Louisiana State University Press.

Global Architecture. 1981. *G.A. Document, Special Issue 1970–1980*. Tokyo: Ada Edita.

Goble, Emerson (ed.). 1957. *Buildings for Industry*. New York: F. W. Dodge Corp.

Godfrey, Tony. 1986. *The New Image: Paintings in the 1980s*. New York: Abbeville Press.

Gowans, Alan. 1964. *Images of American Living*. New York: J. B. Lippincott.

Gowans, Alan. 1986. *The Comfortable House: North American Suburban Architecture, 1890–1930*. Cambridge, Mass.: MIT Press.

Greenhouse, Linda. 1974. "Isolation in Suburbia." In Louis H. Masotti and Jeffrey K. Hadden (eds.), *Suburbia in Transition,* pp. 32–35. New York: New York Times.

Gries, John M., and James Ford (eds.). 1932. *Home Finance and Taxation*. Washington, D.C.: National Capital Press.

Gruen, Victor. 1973. *Centers for the Urban Environment*. New York: Van Nostrand Reinhold Company.

Gruen, Victor, and Larry Smith. 1952. "Shopping Centers: The New Building Type." *Progressive Architecture* 33, no. 6, pp. 67–94.

Gruen, Victor, and Larry Smith. 1960. *Shopping Towns USA: The Planning of Shopping Centers*. New York: Reinhold Winston.

Haar, Charles M. (ed.). 1972. *The End of Innocence: A Suburban Reader*. Glenview, Ill.: Scott, Foresman.

Habakkuk, H. J. 1962. *American and British Technology in the Nineteenth Century*. Cambridge, Mass.: MIT Press.

Haber, S. 1964. *Efficiency and Uplift: Scientific Management in the Progressive Era, 1890–1920*. Chicago: University of Chicago Press.

Habermas, Jürgen. 1971. *Knowledge and Human Interests*. Translated by Jeremy J. Shapiro. Boston: Beacon Press.

Habermas, Jürgen. 1975. *Legitimation Crisis*. Translated by Thomas McCarthy. Boston: Beacon Press.

Habermas, Jürgen. 1987. *The Philosophical Discourse of Modernism: Twelve Lectures*. Cambridge, Mass.: MIT Press.

Hadley, Nancy. 1983. "Morphological Trends in the Uncontrolled City: Houston, Texas." Unpublished paper. School of Architecture, Rice University.

Hall, Peter. 1968. "The Urban Culture and the Suburban Culture." In R. Eells and C. Watson (eds.), *Man in the City of the Future: A Symposium of Urban Philosophers,* pp. 99–145. London: Macmillan.

Handlin, Oscar, and John Burchard. 1963. *The Historian and the City*. Cambridge, Mass.: Harvard University Press.

Hanes, J. Carter, and Charles H. Connors (eds.). 1953. *Landscape Design and Its Relation to the Modern Highway*. New Brunswick, N.J.: Rutgers University.

Harris, Curtis C. 1966. *Suburban Development as a Stochastic Process*. Berkeley: University of California Center for Real Estate and Urban Economics.

Harrison, Henry S. 1973. *Houses: The Illustrated Guide to Construction, Design and Systems*. Chicago: National Association of Realtors.

Hart, John Fraser (ed.). 1972. *Regions of the United States*. New York: Harper & Row.

Hayden, Dolores. 1982. *The Grand Domestic Revolution: A History of Feminist Designs for American Homes, Neighborhoods and Cities*. Cambridge, Mass.: MIT Press.

Hayden, Dolores. 1984. *Redesigning the American Dream: The Future of Housing, Work and Family Life*. New York: W. W. Norton and Co.

Heller, Fritz. 1938. *Die Strasse*. Berlin: Volk and Reich Verlag.

Hemingway, Peter. 1986. "The Joy of Kitsch." *Canadian Architect* (March): 32–35.

Herbert, Gilbert. 1984. *The Dream of the Factory-Made House: Walter Gropius and Konrad Wachsmann*. Cambridge, Mass.: MIT Press.

Herder, Verlag, and Freiburg Breisgau. 1979. *Surrealism and Dadaism*. Oxford: Phaidon Press, Ltd.

Herrera, Philip. 1967. "The Manhattan Exodus." *Fortune* 75 (June): 106–109, 144, 147.

Hess, Alan. 1983. "California Coffee Houses." *Arts and Architecture* 2, pp. 42–51.

Hilberseimer, Ludwig. 1955. *The Nature of Cities: Origin, Growth and Decline, Pattern and Form, Planning Problems*. Chicago: Paul Theobald and Co.

Hill, David R. 1985. "Lewis Mumford's Ideas on the City." *Journal of the American Planning Association* 51, no. 4, pp. 407–422.

Hillier, Bevis. 1975. *The Decorative Arts of the Forties and Fifties: Austerity to Binge*. New York: Clarkson N. Potter.

Hillier, Bevis. 1983. *The Style of the Century: 1900–1980*. New York: E. P. Dutton.

Hines, Thomas. 1974. *Burnham of Chicago*. New York: Oxford University Press.

Hines, Thomas S. 1982. *Richard Neutra and the Search for Modern Architecture*. New York: Oxford University Press.

Hirschman, Albert O. 1958. *The Strategy of Economic Development*. New Haven: Yale University Press.

Hoglund, J. David. 1983. *The Intangible Qualities of Housing*. New York: Gruzen Partnership.

Hohl, Reinhold. 1968. *Office Buildings: An International Survey*. New York: Praeger.

Holden, Bob R. 1960. *The Structure of a Retail Market and Market Behavior of Retail Units*. Englewood Cliffs, N.J.: Prentice-Hall.

Holleman, Thomas J., and James P. Gallagher. 1978. *Smith, Hinchman and Grylls: 1853–1978*. Detroit: Wayne State University Press.

Hounshell, David, 1985. *From the American System to Mass Production*. Baltimore: Johns Hopkins University Press.

House and Home. 1954. "Post-Beam-Plank Construction." vol. 5, no. 6, pp. 98–115.

House and Home. 1967–1977. "Home Buyer Surveys."

Housing. 1978–1982. "Home Buyer Surveys."

Houston City Planning Commission. 1940. *Annual Report of the City Planning Commission, Houston, Texas*. Houston: City of Houston.

Houston City Planning Commission. 1942. *The Major Street Plan for Houston and Vicinity*. Houston: City of Houston.

Houston City Planning Department. 1980. *Houston Downtown Data Book: 1980 Update*. Houston: Houston City Planning Department.

Houston-Galveston Area Council. 1981. *1980 Person and Housing Unit Counts*. Houston: Houston-Galveston Area Council.

Howard Ebenezer. 1902 (1898). *Garden Cities of Tomorrow*. Paternoster Square, England: Sonnen Schien & Co.

Hoyt, Charles King (ed.). 1978. *Buildings for Commerce and Industry*. New York: McGraw-Hill.

Hoyt, Homer. 1960. "The Status of Shopping Centers in the United States." *Urban Land* 19, no. 5, pp. 4–16.

Hughes, Robert. 1988. "Discontents of the White Tribe." *Time*, May 30, p. 71.

Hunt, John Dixon, and Peter Willis. 1975. *The Genius of the Place: The English Landscape Garden, 1620–1820*. New York: Harper & Row.

Hunt, William Dudley, Jr. (ed.). 1961. *Office Buildings*. New York: F. W. Dodge Corp.

Huntoon, Maxwell C., Jr. 1971. *PUD: A Better Way for the Suburbs*. Washington, D.C.: Urban Land Institute.

Hutton, Jim, and Jim Henderson. 1976. *Houston: A History of a Giant*. Tulsa, Okla.: Continental Heritage.

Iovine, Julie V. 1987. "The Elusive Model." *Metropolis* 7, no. 5 (December): 48–53, 71.

Jackson, Kenneth T. 1985. *The Crabgrass Frontier: The Suburbanization of the United States*. New York: Oxford University Press.

Jackson, Kenneth T., and Stanley K. Schultz (eds.). 1972. *Cities in American History*. New York: Columbia University Press.

Jean, Marcel (ed.). 1980. *The Autobiography of Surrealism*. New York: Viking Press.

Jellicoe, Geoffrey, Susan Jellicoe, Patrick Goode, and Michael Lancaster (eds.). 1986. *The Oxford Companion to Gardens*. New York: Oxford University Press.

Jencks, Charles (ed.). 1980. *Post-Modern Classicism*. London: Garden House Press.

Joedicke, Jürgen von. 1962. *Office Buildings*. New York: Praeger.

Joedicke, Jürgen von. 1975. *Office and Administration Buildings*. Stuttgart: Karl Krämer Verlag.

Johnson, Jory. 1988. "Regionalism and Invention: Codex World Headquarters." *Landscape Architecture* (Arpil–May): 58–63.

Jones, A. Quincy, and Frederick E. Emmons. 1957. *Builder's Homes for Better Living*. New York: Reinhold Publishing Corporation.

Jones, Robert T. 1929 (1987). *Authentic Small Houses of the Twenties*. New York: Dover.

Jones, Victor. 1942. *Metropolitan Government*. Chicago: University of Chicago Press.

Kansas City Board of Park Commissioners. 1925. *Reports: 1905–1924*. Kansas City, Mo.: The Board.

Kansas City Chapter of the AIA. 1979. *Kansas City*. Kansas City, Mo.: Kansas City Chapter of the AIA.

Kaplan, Samuel. 1976. *The Dream Reformed: People, Politics and Planning in Suburbia*. New York.

Kassler, Elizabeth B. 1984. *Modern Gardens and the Landscape*. New York: Museum of Modern Art.

Kaufmann, Arnold. 1968. *The Science of Decision-Making*. New York: McGraw-Hill.

Keats, John. 1957. *The Crack in the Picture Window*. Boston: Little, Brown.

Kennedy, G. Donald. 1944. *Here's How You Can Help Redevelop Your City with Modern Highways*. Washington, D.C.: Chamber of Commerce of the United States.

Khan-Magomedov, Selim O. 1983. *Pioniere der Sowjetischen Architektur*. Berlin: Locker Verlag.

Kierkegaard, Søren. 1962. *The Present Age*. New York: Harper and Row.

Kihlstedt, Folke T. 1986. "Utopia Realized: The World's Fairs of the 1930's." In Joseph J. Corn (ed.), *Imagining Tomorrow: History, Technology and the American Future*. Cambridge, Mass.: MIT Press.

King, A. D. 1984. *The Bungalow*. London: Butterworth.

King, Jonathan, and William Cannady. 1973. "Galleria." *Architectural Design* (November): 695–697.

Klotz, Heinrich. 1988. *The History of Postmodern Architectue*. Cambridge, Mass.: MIT Press.

Knight, Carelton, III. 1984. "Return to Columbus." *Architecture* (June): 36.

Knight, Carelton, III. 1986. "Serene Pavilions Traversing a Lake: Conoco Inc. Headquarters, Houston." *Architecture* 75, no. 12 (December 1986): 56–61.

Knight, Christopher. 1988. "Composite Views: Themes and Motifs in Hockney's Art." In Maurice Tuchman and Stephanie Barron, *David Hockney: A Retrospective*. New York: Harry N. Abrams.

Knobel, Lance. 1986. "A Tale of Two Cities." *Designers Journal* (November): 37–41.

Koetter, Fred. 1987. "The Corporate Villa." *Design Quarterly* 135, pp. 31–40.

Kostof, Spiro. 1985. *A History of Architecture: Settings and Rituals*. New York: Oxford University Press.

Kostof, Spiro. 1987. *America by Design*. New York: Oxford University Press.

Kramer, John (ed.). 1972. *North American Suburbs: Politics, Diversity, and Change*. Berkeley, Calif: Glendessary Press.

Krasnowiecki, Jan Z., and Richard F. Babcock. 1965. "Legal Aspects of Planned Unit Residential Development: With Suggested Legislation." *Urban Land Institute Technical Bulletin* 52 (May).

Krieger, Alex. 1987. "The American City: Ideal and Mythic Aspects of Reinvented Urbanism." *Assemblage* 3, pp. 38–59.

Krimerman, Leonard I. 1969. *The Nature and Scope of Social Science: A Critical Anthology*. New York: Appleton-Century-Crofts.

Krinsky, Carol Hirselle. 1988. *Gordon Bunshaft of Skidmore, Owings and Merrill*. Cambridge, Mass.: MIT Press.

Kroc, Ray. 1977. *Grinding It Out: The Making of McDonalds*. Chicago: Henry Regnery.

Krueckeberg, Donald A. (ed.). 1983. *Introduction to Planning History in the United States*. New Brunswick, N.J.: Center for Urban Policy Research.

Krüger, Karl. 1937. *Die Strassen der Welt: Eine Strassengeographie*. Berlin: Volk und Reich Verlag.

Labatut, Jean, and Wheaton J. Lane (eds.). 1950. *Highways in Our National Life*. Princeton: Princeton University Press.

Lake, Robert W. 1981. *The New Suburbanites: Race and Housing in the Suburbs*. New Brunswick, N.J.: Center for Urban Policy Research, Rutgers University.

Lampard, Eric E. 1983. "The Nature of Urbanization." In Derek Fraser and Anthony Sutcliffe (eds.), *The Pursuit of Urban History*. London: Edward Arnold.

Lancaster, Clay. 1985. *The American Bungalow, 1880–1930*. New York: Abbeville Press.

Lancaster, Clay. 1986. "The American Bungalow." In Del Upton and John Michael Vlech (eds.), *Common Places: Readings in American Vernacular Architecture*. Athens: University of Georgia Press.

Land Planning Division of the Federal Housing Administration. 1934. *Planning Neighborhoods for Small Houses*. Washington, D.C.: Federal Housing Administration.

Land Planning Division of the Federal Housing Administration. 1938. *Planning Profitable Neighborhoods*. Washington, D.C.: Federal Housing Administration.

Langdon, Philip. 1984. "The American House: What We're Building and Buying." *Atlantic* (September): 45–77.

Langdon, Philip. 1986. *Orange Roofs, Golden Arches: The Architecture of American Chain Restaurants*. New York: Alfred A. Knopf.

Langdon, Philip. 1987. *American Houses*. New York: Stewart, Tabori & Chang.

Langdon, Philip. 1988. "A Good Place to Live." *Atlantic* vol. 261, no. 3 (March): 39–70.

La Patra, J. W. 1973. *Applying the Systems Approach to Urban Development*. Stroudsburg, Penn.: Dowden, Hutchinson and Ross.

Leavitt, Zetta R., and Martha E. Ryder. 1947. *The Coming of the First White Settlers to Framingham, 1647–1672*. September 26.

Le Corbusier. 1930. *Precisions sur un état présent de l'architecture et de l'urbanisme*. Paris: Editions G. Crès et Cie.

Le Corbusier. 1964 (1933). *The Radiant City*. New York: Orion Press.

Leinberger, Christopher B., and Charles Lockwood. 1986. "How Business Is Reshaping America." *Atlantic* (October): 43–63.

Lemann, Nicholas. 1989. "Naperville: Stressed Out in Suburbia." *Atlantic* 264, no. 5 (November): 34–47.

Levitt and Sons, Inc. 1951. "Background Memorandum on Levittown, Pennsylvania." Mimeographed. Frances Loeb Library, Havard University.

Liebs. Chester H. 1985. *Main Street To Miracle Mile: American Roadside Architecture*. Boston: Little, Brown.

Long, John F. 1981. *Population Decentralization in the United States*. Washington, D.C.: U.S. Bureau of the Census.

Lynch, Kevin. 1972. *What Time Is This Place?* Cambridge, Mass.: MIT Press.

McAlester, Virginia, and Lee McAlester. 1986. *A Field Guide to American Houses*. New York: Alfred A. Knopf.

McComb, David G. 1981. *Houston: A History*. Austin: University of Texas Press.

McCoubrey, John W. (ed.). 1965. *American Art, 1700–1960*. Englewood Cliffs, N.J.: Prentice-Hall.

McCoy, Esther (ed.). 1960. *Five California Architects*. New York: Whitney.

McCoy, Esther. 1977. *Case Study Houses, 1945–1962*. Los Angeles: Hennessey and Ingalls.

McGiffert, Michael (ed.). 1970. *The Character of Americans: A Book of Readings*. Homewood, Ill.: Dorsey Press.

Machado, Rodolfo. 1983. "Domains of Architecture." *New Art Examiner* (June): 9.

Machado, Rodolfo. 1988. "Public Places for American Cities." *Assemblage*, no. 6 (June): 98–113.

Machor, James L. 1987. *Pastoral Cities: Urban Ideals and the Symbolic Landscape of America.* Madison: University of Wisconsin Press.

McKeever, Ross J. (ed.). 1968. *Community Builder's Handbook.* Washington, D.C.: Urban Land Institute.

McKeever, Ross J., and Nathaniel M. Griffin. 1977. *Shopping Center Development Handbook.* Washington, D.C.: Urban Land Institute.

McKeever, Ross J., and Nathaniel Griffin. 1985. *Shopping Center Development Handbook: Second Edition.* Washington, D.C.: Urban Land Institute.

McKenzie, R. D. 1933. *The Metropolitan Community.* New York:

Makinson, Randall L. 1974. *A Guide to the Work of Greene and Greene.* Santa Barbara, Calif.: Peregrine Smith.

Manasseh, Leonard, and Roger Cunliffe. 1962. *Office Buildings.* New York: Reinhold.

Mandelker, Daniel R. 1971. *The Zoning Dilemma.* Indianapolis: Bobbs-Merrill.

Mannheim, Karl. 1936. *Ideology and Utopia.* New York: Harcourt, Brace and World.

Marcus, Clare Cooper, Carolyn Francis, and Colette Meunier. 1980. "Mixed Messages in Suburbia: Reading the Suburban Model Home." *Places* 4, no. 1, pp. 24–37.

Mariemont Company. 1925. *Mariemont: The New Town, A National Exemplar.* Cincinnati, Ohio: Mariemont Co.

Martin, Ralph G. 1950. "Life in the New Suburbia." *New York Times Magazine,* January 15.

Marx, Leo. 1964. *The Machine in the Garden: Technology and the Pastoral Ideal in America.* New York: Oxford University Press.

Maslow, Abraham H. 1968. *Towards a Psychology of Being.* New York: Van Nostrand Reinhold.

Masnick, George, and Mary Jo Bane. 1980. *The Nation's Families: 1960–1990.* Cambridge, Mass.: Joint Center for Urban Studies of MIT and Harvard University.

Mason, Joseph B. 1938. "Scientific Methods Reduce Home Costs." *Big Value Homes,* pp. 24–27.

Mason, Joseph B. 1982. *History of Housing in the United States: 1930–1981.* Houston: Gulf Publishing Company.

Masotti, Louis H. (guest ed.). 1975. "The Suburban Seventies." *Annals of the American Academy of Political and Social Science* 422, pp. vii–151.

Masotti, Louis H., and Jeffrey K. Hadden (eds.). 1973. *The Urbanization of the Suburbs.* Beverly Hills, Calif.: Sage.

Masotti, Louis H., and Jeffrey K. Hadden (eds.). 1974. *Suburbia in Transition.* New York: New Viewpoints.

May, Cliff. 1946. *Sunset Western Ranch Houses.* San Francisco, Calif.: Lane Publishing Co.

May, Cliff. 1958. *Western Ranch Houses.* Menlo Park, Calif.: Lane Publishing Company.

Meikle, Jeffrey L. 1979. *Twentieth Century Limited-Industrial Design in America, 1925–1939.* Philadelphia: Temple University Press.

Meinig, Donald W. (ed.). 1979. *The Interpretation of Ordinary Landscapes.* New York: Oxford University Press.

Meltzer, Jack. 1984. *Metropolis to Metroplex: The Social and Spatial Planning of Cities.* Baltimore: Johns Hopkins University Press.

Merriam, John M. 1948. *The Hills of Framingham.* Framingham, Mass.: Lakeview Press.

Merrill, Lynch, Fenner and Smith. 1982. *Housing Industry: A M-L Basic Report,* January.

Metropolitan Area Planning Council. 1982. *Regional Decline or Revival: An Interim Population Forecast for the Boston Metropolitan Area, 1980–2010.* Boston: Metropolitan Area Planning Council.

Metropolitan Area Planning Council. 1985a. *Metrowest Growth Impacts Study.* Boston: Metropolitan Area Planning Council.

Metropolitan Area Planning Council. 1985b. *State of the Region 1985.* Boston: Metropolitan Area Planning Council.

Metropolitan Transit Authority of Harris County. 1981. *Regional Transit Program: Southwest/Westpark Corridor.* Houston: Metropolitan Transit Authority of Harris County.

Meyrowitz, Joshua. 1985. *No Sense of Place: The Impact of Electronic Media on Social Behavior.* New York: Oxford University Press.

Mieskowski, Peter, and Mahlon Straszheim. 1979. *Current Issues in Urban Economics*. Baltimore: Johns Hopkins University Press.

Miller, Henry. 1945. *The Air-Conditioned Nightmare*. New York: New Directions.

Miller, Nory. 1980. "General Foods Corporation Headquarters." *GA Document* 2, pp. 88–91.

Miller, Perry. 1956. *Errand into the Wilderness*. Cambridge, Mass.: Belknap Press of Harvard University Press.

Miller, Spenser, Jr. 1950. "History of the Modern Highway in the United States," In Jean Labatut and Wheaton J. Lane (eds.), *Highways in Our National Life,* pp. 88–119. Princeton: Princeton University Press.

Mock, Elizabeth (ed.). 1944. *Built in the USA, 1932–1944*. New York: Museum of Modern Art.

Moore, Charles W, et al. 1983. *Home Sweet Home: American Domestic Vernacular Architecture*. New York: Rizzoli International Publications.

Moore, Charles W., and Richard B. Oliver (eds.). 1977. "Building Types Study 500: Forty Years of American Architecture." *Architectural Record* (April): 117ff.

Morrison, Peter A. 1979. "The Shifting Regional Balance." *American Demographics* 1, no. 5 (May: 9–15).

Moses, Robert. 1956. "The New Super-Highways: Blessing or Blight?" *Harpers Magazine* 213 (December): 27–31.

Mott, Seward H. 1941. "Neighborhood Planning." In *American Society of Planning Officials National Conference on Planning,* pp. 156–162. Chicago: American Society of Planning Officials.

Muller, Peter O. 1978. *The Suburbanization of Corporate Headquarters*. Englewood Cliffs, N.J.: Prentice-Hall.

Muller, Peter O. 1981. *Contemporary Suburban America*. Englewood Cliffs, N.J.: Prentice-Hall.

Mumford, Lewis. 1938. *The Culture of Cities*. New York: Harcourt, Brace and Co.

Mumford, Lewis. 1961. *The City in History*. New York: Harcourt, Brace and World.

Myrdal, Gunnar. 1957. *Economic Theory and Underdeveloped Regions*. London: G. Duckworth and Co.

Nakamura Toshio (ed.). 1987. *Kevin Roche: Kevin Roche, John Dinkerloo and Associates*. Tokyo: A&U Extra Edition.

Nash, Roderick. 1982. *Wilderness and the American Mind*. New Haven: Yale University Press.

National Commission on Urban Problems. 1968. *Building the American City*. Washington, D.C.: U.S. Government Printing Office.

National Interregional Highway Committee: 1944. *Interregional Highways*. Washington, D.C.: U.S. Government Printing Office.

National Research Bureau. 1985. *Directory of Shopping Centers in the United States, Eastern States*. Washington, D.C.: The Bureau.

Nelson, William E. 1982. *The Roots of American Bureaucracy, 1830–1900*. Cambridge, Mass.: Harvard University Press.

Nevins, A., and E. F. Hill. 1957. *Ford*. 2 vols. New York: Scribners.

Newsweek. 1955. "Blooming Prairie: Sharpstown." *Newsweek,* March 21, pp. 88–90.

Newton, Norman T. 1971. *Design on the Land: The Development of Landscape Architecture*. Cambridge, Mass.: Belknap Press of Harvard University Press.

Nichols Company, J. C. 1983. *Seventy-five Years: A Commemorative Publication*. Kansas City, Mo.: J. C. Nichols Co.

Nissen, Anne D. 1988. "Beyond the Frontier 1." *Places* 5, pp. 8–14.

Nolen, John, and Henry V. Hubbard. 1937. *Parkways and Land Values*. Cambridge, Mass.: Harvard University Press.

Norberg-Schulz, Christian. 1965. *Intentions in Architecture*. Cambridge, Mass.: MIT Press.

Norberg-Schultz, Christian. 1971. *Existence, Space and Architecture*. New York: Praeger Books.

Norberg-Schulz, Christian. 1980. *Genius Loci*. New York: Rizzoli International Publications.

Novak, Barbara. 1976. "The Double-Edged Ax." *Art In America* (January–February): 44–50.

Ochsner, Jeffrey Karl. 1982. *H. H. Richardson: Complete Architectural Works*. Cambridge, Mass.: MIT Press.

Olin, Laurie. 1988. Personal interview. December.

O'Neill, William L. 1971. *Coming Apart: An Informal History of America in the 1960s,* Chicago: Quadrangle Books.

Owen, Wilfred. 1949. *Automotive Transportation: Trends and Problems*. Washington, D.C.: Brookings Institute.

Owens, Bill. 1973. *Suburbia*. San Francisco: Straight Arrow Books.

Panofsky, Erwin. 1957. *Meaning in the Visual Arts: Papers in and on Art History*. New York:

Papademetriou, Peter C. (ed.). 1972. *Houston: An Architectural Guide*. Houston: Houston Chapter, American Institute of Architects.

Park, Robert E., and Ernest W. Burgess. 1967 (1925). *The City*. Chicago: University of Chicago Press.

Paul, Jeffrey. 1980. *Suburban Industrial/Office Park Reconnaissance Report*. Boston: Central Transportation Planning Staff.

Perin, Constance. 1977. *Everything in Its Place: Social Order and Land Use in America*. Princeton, N.J.: Princeton University Press.

Phillips, Kevin, 1978. *"The Balkanization of America." Harpers* (May): 37–47.

Pickering, Ernest. 1951. *The Homes of America*. New York: Thomas Y. Crowell.

Pile, John. 1976. *Interiors Third Book of Offices*. New York: Watson-Guptill.

Preminger, Alex (ed.). 1965. *Princeton Encyclopedia of Poetry and Poetics*. Princeton, N.J.: Princeton University Press.

Progressive Architecture. 1959. "Youngstown Steel and Tube Company: Boardman, Ohio." *Progressive Architecture* (June): 158–161.

Progressive Architecture. 1984. "The Town of Seaside." *Progressive Architecture* (January): 138–139.

Progressive Architecture. 1990. "Urban Design Citation: Brambleton." *Progressive Architecture* (January): 118–119.

Pynchon, Thomas. 1966. *The Crying of Lot 49*. New York: Bantam Books.

Rae, John B. 1965. *The American Automobile: A Brief History*. Chicago: University of Chicago Press.

Rae, John B. 1971. *The Road and the Car in American Life*. Cambridge, Mass.: MIT Press.

Rainwater, Lee. 1975. "Post-1984 America." In Helen I. Safa and Gloria Levitas (eds.), *Social Problems in Corporate America,* pp. 371–378. New York: Harper & Row.

Rathbun, Robert Davis (ed.). 1986. *Shopping Centers and Malls*. New York: Retail Reporting Corporation.

Real Estate Research Corporation. 1974. *The Costs of Sprawl*. Washington, D.C.: Council on Environmental Quality.

Regional Planning Commission of the County of Los Angeles. 1929. *Landscape Design*. Los Angeles: County of Los Angeles.

Relph, Edward. 1976. *Place and Placelessness*. London: Pion, Ltd.

Relph, Edward. 1987. *The Modern Urban Landscape*. Baltimore: Johns Hopkins University Press.

Reps, John, 1965. *The Making of Urban America: A History of City Planning in the United States*. Princeton: Princeton University Press.

Restany, Pierre, and Bruno Zevi. 1980. *SITE: Architecture as Art*. London: Academy Editions.

Rice Center for Community Design and Research. 1978a. *Downtown Fact Book: Technical Report*. Houston: Rice Center for Community Design and Research.

Rice Center for Community Design and Research. 1978b. *Growth Options for Houston*. Houston: Rice Center for Community Design and Research.

Rice Center for Community Design and Research. 1978c. *The 30 Percent Rule: Costs and Benefits*. Houston: Rice Center for Community Design and Research.

Rice Center for Community Design and Research. 1979. *Research Brief 2: Employee Distribution and Access, Office Location Issues in Houston*. Houston: Rice Center for Community Design and Research.

Rice Center for Community Design and Research. 1980. *Flood Control in Houston*. Houston: Rice Center for Community Design and Research.

Richardson, Walter J. 1988. "Designing High-Density Single-Family Housing: Variations on the Zero-Lot-Line Theme." *Urban Land* (February): 15–20.

Riesman, David. 1950. *The Lonely Crowd*. New Haven: Yale University Press.

Rogers, Kate Ellen. 1962. *The Modern House, USA: Its Design and Decoration*. New York: Harper and Brothers.

Rose, Albert C., and Carl Rakeman. 1976. *Historic American Roads: From Frontier Trails to Superhighways*. New York: Crown Publishers.

Rothblatt, Donald M., and Daniel J. Garr. 1986. *Suburbia: An International Assessment*. London: Croom and Helm.

Row, Albert T., Louis P. Dolbeare, and Judith Tannenbaum (eds.). 1948. *Framingham: Your Town, Your Problem*. Cambridge, Mass.: Harvard Graduate School of Design.

Rowe, Peter G. 1972. "A Question of Architecture, a Matter of Style." *Architectural Design* (August): 466ff.

Rowe, Peter G. (et al.) 1978. *Principles for Local Environmental Management*. Cambridge, Mass.: Ballinger Publishing Company.

Rowe, Peter G. 1987. *Design Thinking*. Cambridge Mass.: MIT Press.

Rowe, Peter G. 1989. "Modern Pastoralism and the Middle Landscape." *Oz* 11, pp. 4–9.

Rowe, Peter G. (ed.). 1989. *Rodolfo Machado and Jorge Silvetti: Buildings for Cities*. New York: Rizzoli.

Rowe, Peter G., and John Michael Desmond. 1986. *The Shape and Appearance of the Modern American Single-Family House*. Cambridge, Mass.: Joint Center for Housing Studies of MIT and Harvard University.

Rubin, Lilian Breslow. 1967. *Worlds of Pain: Life in the Working Class Family*. New York: Basic Books.

Russell, Cheryl. 1981. "Inside the Shrinking Household." *American Demographics* 3, no. 9 (October): 28–33.

Sachner, Paul M. 1988. "Pillar to Post." *Architectural Record* (June): 122–127.

Safa, Helen I., and Gloria Levitas (eds.). 1975. *Social Problems in Corporate America*. New York: Harper & Row.

Schaeffer, K. H., and Elliot Sclar. 1975. *Access for All: Transportation and Urban Growth*. Baltimore: Johns Hopkins University Press.

Schaffer, Daniel. 1982. *Garden Cities of America*. Philadelphia: Temple University Press.

Schlesinger, Peter Alan. 1983. "Civilizing the Suburb: Creating a Contemporary American Suburban Civic Place." Thesis report, Harvard University.

Schmertz, J. 1975. *Office Building Design*. New York: McGraw-Hill.

Schmitt, Peter. 1969. *Back to Nature: The Arcadian Myth in Urban America*. New York:

Schodek, Daniel L. 1975. "Operation Breakthrough: The Changing Image." *Industrialization Forum* 6, no. 1, pp. 6–15.

Schorske, C. 1963. "The Idea of the City in European Thought: Voltaire to Spengler." In Oscar Handlin and John Buchard (eds.), *The Historian and the City,* pp. 95–114. Cambridge, Mass.: Harvard University Press.

Schuyler, John Anthony. 1986. "An Architecture Which Facilitates the Development of Our Self-Consceptions." Master's thesis, Harvard University.

Schwartz, Barry (ed.). 1976. *The Changing Face of the Suburbs*. Chicago: University of Chicago Press.

Scott, Mel. 1969. *American City Planning since 1890*. Berkeley: University of California Press.

Scully, Vincent. 1988. *American Architecture and Urbanism*. New rev. ed. New York: Henry Holt and Company.

Seeley, Bruce E. 1987. *Building the American Highway System*. Philadelphia, Pennsylvania: Temple University Press.

Segal, Howard P. 1986. "The Technological Utopians." In Joseph J. Corn (ed.), *Imagining Tomorrow: History, Technology and the American Future*. Cambridge, Mass.: MIT Press.

Sennett, Richard. 1977. *The Fall of Public Man*. New York: Alfred Knopf.

Sergeant, John. 1984. *Frank Lloyd Wright's Usonian Houses: Designs for Moderate Cost One-Family Homes*. New York: Whitney Library of Design.

Shannon, David. 1969. *Twentieth Century America*. Vol. 1: *The Progressive Era*. Chicago: Rand McNally and Company.

Sharpe, William, and Leonard Wallock (eds.). 1987. *Visions of the Modern City: Essays in History, Art and Literature*. Baltimore: Johns Hopkins University Press.

Sherman, Harvey, and Elizabeth Springs (eds.). 1984. *A New American House, Architectural Design Competition, 1984: Catalogue of Winning and Selected Designs*. Minneapolis: Minneapolis College of Art and Design.

Shopping Center World. 1985. *Biennial Census of Shopping Centers*. Washington, D.C.: Shopping Center World.

Siegan, Bernard H. 1972. *Land Use without Zoning*. Lexington, Mass.: Lexington Books.

Smith, Henry Nash. 1950. *Virgin Land: The American West as Symbol and Myth*. New York: Vintage Books.

Smith, Norris Kelly. 1966. *Frank Lloyd Wright: A Study in Architectural Content*. Englewood Cliffs, N.J.: Prentice-Hall.

Smithson, Peter. 1981. "Space Is the American Mediator." *Harvard Architectural Review* 2 (Spring): 106–115.

Solà Morales, Ignasi de. 1986. *Minimal Architecture in Barcelona*. Milan: Electa.

Solomon, Daniel, and Susan Haviland. 1989. "The Emerald City." *Oz* 11, pp. 42–45.

Sparke, Penny. 1987. *Design in Context*. Secaucus, N.J.: Quatro Publishing.

Stein, Clarence. 1957 and 1966. *Towards New Towns for America*. Cambridge, Mass.: MIT Press.

Stein, Clarence S., and Catherine Bauer. 1934. "Store Building and Neighborhood Shopping Centers." *Architectural Record* 75, no. 2, pp. 175–187.

Stern, Robert A. M. 1980. "Without Rhetoric: The New York Apartment." *Via IV,* pp. 78–111.

Stern, Robert A. M. (ed.). 1981. *The Anglo-American Suburb*. London: Architectural Design Profile.

Stern, Robert A. M. (ed.). 1986a. "Suburbs." *Design Quarterly,* no. 132.

Stern, Robert A. M. 1986b. *Pride of Place: Building the American Dream*. Boston: Houghton Mifflin.

Sternlieb, George S. 1971. *The Affluent Suburb: Princeton*. New Brunswick, N.J.: Center for Public Policy Research.

Sternlieb, George, and James W. Hughes. 1981. *Shopping Centers: USA*. New Brunswick, N.J.: Center for Urban Policy Research.

Stickley, Gustav. 1909. *Craftsman Homes*. New York: Craftsman Publishing Co.

Stilgoe, John R. 1988. *Borderland: Origins of the American Suburb, 1820–1939*. New Haven: Yale University Press.

Sullivan, Louis H. 1934. *Kindergarten Chats*. Chicago: Scarab Fraternity Press.

Sumichrast, Michael, and Robert Enzel. 1974. *Housing Component Costs*. Washington, D.C.: National Home Builders Association, September.

Sutcliffe, Anthony. 1984. *Metropolis, 1890–1940*. London: Mansell.

Tableman, Betty. 1951. *Governmental Organization in Metropolitan Areas*. Ann Arbor: University of Michigan Press.

Taylor, David. 1983. *Framingham Center*. Cambridge, Mass.: Community Assistance Program, Harvard University.

Taylor, Frederick W. 1911. *Principles of Scientific Management*. New York: John Wiley.

Taylor, Rives T. 1988. "Beyond the Frontier II." *Places* 5, no. 3, pp. 15–26.

Teaford, Jon C. 1979. *City and Suburb: The Political Fragmentation of Metropolitan America. 1850–1970*. Baltimore: Johns Hopkins University Press.

Teaford, Jon C. 1986. *The Twentieth-Century American City: Problem, Promise and Reality*. Baltimore: Johns Hopkins University Press.

Texas Highway Department Traffic Survey. 1953. *Houston*. Austin: Texas State Highway Department.

Toll, Seymour I. 1969. *Zoned America*. New York: Grossman Publishers.

Tomlinson, Doug, and David Dillon. 1985. *Dallas Architecture, 1936–1986*. Austin: Texas Montly Press.

Traylor, David. 1983. "Framingham Center." Unpublished monograph, Graduate School of Design, Harvard University.

Tuchman, Maurice, and Stephanie Barron. 1988. *David Hockney: A Retrospective*. New York: Harry N. Abrams.

Tunnard, Christopher. 1938. *Gardens in the Modern Landscape*. London: Architectural Press.

Tunnard, Christopher, and Boris Pushkarev. 1963. *Man-Made America: Chaos or Control, An Inquiry into Selected Problems of Design in the Urbanized Landscape*. New Haven: Yale University Press.

Turner, Frederick Jackson. 1948. *The Frontier in American History*. New York: Holt Rinehart and Winston.

Twichell, Allan A. (ed.). 1948. *Planning the Neighborhood: Standards for Healthful Housing*. Chicago: Public Administration Service.

Tyler, Poyntz (ed.). 1957. *American Highways Today*. New York: H. W. Wilson Company.

Ullmann, John E. 1977. *The Suburban Economic Network: Economic Activity, Resource Use and the Great Sprawl*. New York: Praeger.

U.S. Bureau of the Census. 1923. *Mortgages on Homes*. Washington, D.C.: U.S. Department of Commerce.

U.S. Bureau of the Census. 1975. "Social and Economic Characteristics of the Metropolitan and Nonmetropolitan Population: 1970 and 1974." *Current Population Reports*. Series P-23, no. 55. September.

U.S. Bureau of the Census. 1900–1980. *Censuses of Population*. Washington, D.C.: U.S. Department of Commerce.

U.S. Bureau of the Census. 1930–1980a. *Censuses of Population: Boston Massachusetts SMSA and Adjacent Areas*. Washington, D.C.: U.S. Department of Commerce.

U.S.Bureau of the Census. 1930–1980b. *Censuses of Population: Houston Texas SMSA and Adjacent Areas*. Washington D.C.: U.S. Department of Commerce.

U.S. Bureau of the Census. 1983. *Place of Work*. Washington, D.C.: U.S. Department of Commerce.

U.S. Bureau of the Census. 1984a *County Business Patterns 1983, Massachusetts*. Washington, D.C.: U.S. Department of Commerce.

U.S. Bureau of the Census. 1984b. *Local Population Estimates, Massachusetts*. Washington, D.C.: U.S. Department of Commerce, September.

U.S. Bureau of the Census. 1985. *Census of Retail Trade, Massachusetts—Geographic Area Services*. Washington, D.C.: U.S. Department of Commerce.

U.S. Bureau of Public Roads. 1985. *Motor Vehicle Registrations*. Washington, D.C.: U.S. Department of Commerce.

U.S. Department of Commerce. 1955. "Construction Volume and Costs, 1915–54." In *Construction Review Statistical Supplement*. Washington, D.C.: U.S. Department of Commerce.

U.S. Department of Commerce. 1955–1987. "Construction Volume and Costs." In *Construction Review Statistical Supplement*. Washington, D.C.: U.S. Department of Commerce.

U.S. Geological Survey. 1950. *Quadrangle Maps, State of Massachusetts*. Washington, D.C.: United States Department of the Interior.

U. S. Geological Survey. 1975. *Eastern Massachusetts Land Use Map*. Boston: U.S. Geological Survey.

Urban Land Institute. 1963. "Land-Use Intensity Rating: A New Approach to Residential Development." *Urban Land* (October): 1–9.

Urban Land Institute. 1985. *Shopping Center Development Handbook, Second Edition*. Washington, D.C.: Urban Land Institute.

Urban Land Institute. 1987. *Development Trends*. Washington, D.C.: Urban Land Institute, November.

Vance, James E., Jr. 1962. "Emerging Patterns of Commercial Structure in American Cities." In Knut Norborg (ed.), *Proceedings of the IGU Symposium in Urban Geography,* pp. 485–518. Lund, 1960.

Vance, James E., Jr. 1977. *This Scene of Man: The Role and Structure of the City in the Geography of Western Civilization*. New York: Harpers College Press.

Venturi, Robert, and Denise Scott Brown. 1968. "A Significance for A&P Parking Lots, or Learning from Las Vegas." *Architectural Forum* (March): 37–43.

Venturi, Robert, and Denise Scott Brown. 1971. "Ugly and Ordinary Architecture, or the Decorated Shed (Parts 1 and 2)." *Architectural Forum* (November): 64–67, (December): 48–53.

Venturi, Robert, Denise Scott Brown, and Steven Izenour. 1972. *Learning from Las Vegas*. Cambridge, Mass.: MIT Press.

Visitor Guide. 1987. *Boston; Business Map*. Boston: Visitor Guide Publishing.

Vogel, Carol. 1987. "Clustered for Leisure: The Changing Home." *New York Times Magazine,* June 28.

Walker, Lester. 1981. *American Shelter: An Illustrated Encyclopedia of the American Home*. Woodstock, N.Y.: Overlook Press.

Walker, Peter. 1989. Public lecture. Graduate School of Design, April.

Warner, Sam Bass, Jr. 1962. *Streetcar Suburbs: The Process of Growth in Boston (1870–1900)*. Cambridge, Mass.: Harvard University Press.

Warner, Sam Bass, Jr. 1968. *The Private City: Philadelphia in Three Periods of Its Growth*. Philadelphia: University of Pennsylvania Press.

Weber, Adna Ferrin. 1963 (1898). *The Growth of Cities in the Nineteenth Century: A Study in Statistics*. Ithaca, N.Y.: Cornell University Press.

Weber, Max. 1952. "The Presuppositions and Causes of Bureaucracy." In Robert K. Merton (ed.), *Reader In Bureaucracy,* pp. 60–68. Glencoe, Ill.: Free Press,

Webber, Melvin M. 1964a. "The Urban Place and the Nonplace Urban Realm." In Melvin M. Webber et al. (eds.), *Explorations in Urban Structure,* pp. 116ff. Philadelphia: Pennsylvania: University of Pennsylvania Press.

Webber, Melvin M. 1964b. "Order in Diversity: Community without Propinquity." In Lowdon Wingo (ed.), *Cities and Space*. Baltimore: Johns Hopkins University Press.

Webber, Melvin M. et al. 1964. *Explorations into Urban Structure*. Philadelphia: University of Pennsylvania Press.

Weiss, Marc A. 1986. *Community Builders*. New York: Columbia University Press.

Weiss, Marc A. 1987. *Own Your Own Home: The American Real Estate Industry and National Housing Policy*. New York: Columbia University Press.

Wells, H. G. 1902. *Anticipations*. London.

Wentling, James W., and Lloyd W. Bookout (eds.). 1988. *Density by Design*. Washington, D.C.: Urban Land Institute.

Whitney, David (ed.). 1988. *Eric Fischl*. New York: Stewart, Tabori and Chang.

Whitney, Frank L. 1957. "Newer Trends in Industrial Buildings." In Emerson Goble, *Buildings for Industry,* pp. 1–5. New york: F. W. Dodge Corporation.

Whyte, William H., Jr. 1956. *The Organization Man*. New York: Simon and Schuster.

Whyte, William H., Jr. 1968. *The Last Landscape*. New York: Doubleday.

Wilbur Smith and Associates. 1961. *Future Highways and Urban Growth*. New Haven: Wilbur Smith and Associates.

Wilson, Sloan, 1955. *The Man in the Gray Flannel Suit*. New York: Viking.

Windsor, Duane. 1979. *Fiscal Zoning in Suburban Communities*. Lexington, Mass.: Lexington Books.

Winningham, Geoff. 1986. *A Place of Dreams: Houston, an American City*. Houston: Rice University Press.

Wolfe, Tom. 1965. *The Kandy-Kolored Tangerine-Flake Streamline Baby*. London: Mayflower.

Wood, Robert C. 1958. *Suburbia: Its People and Their Politics*. Boston: Houghton Mifflin.

Woods, Robert A., and Albert J. Kennedy. 1962. *The Zone of Emergence*. Cambridge, Mass.: Harvard University Press.

Wright, Frank Lloyd. 1901. "A House in a Prairie Town." *Ladies Home Journal* (February).

Wright, Frank Lloyd. 1932. "Broadacre City: An Architect's Vision." *New York Times Magazine,* March 20, pp. 8–9.

Wright, Frank Lloyd. 1938. "The Raymond Griffith's Ranch." *Architectual Forum* (February).

Wright, Frank Lloyd. 1943. "An Autobiography, Book Six: Broadacre City." Mimeographed. Francis Loeb Library, Harvard University.

Wright, Gwendolyn. 1981. *Building the Dream: A Social History of Housing in America*. Cambridge, Mass.: MIT Press.

Wright, Henry. 1935. *Rehousing Urban America*. New York: Columbia University Press.

Wright, Henry N., and George Nelson. 1943. "Houses for Human Beings: Give People Better Engineered Housing and Let Style Take Care of Itself." *Fortune* (April): 100–104, 152–160.

Young, Mahonri Sharp. 1973. *The Paintings of George Bellows*. New York: Watson Guptil.

Zapatka, Christian. 1987. "The American Parkways: Origins and Evolution of the Park-road." *Lotus International* 56, pp. 97–128.

Zeidler, Eberhard H. 1983. *Multi-Use Architecture in the Urban Context*. New York: Van Nostrand Reinhold.

Zimmerman, M. M. 1955. *The Super Market: A Revolution in Distribution*. New York: McGraw-Hill.

Zube, E. 1935. "Germany Builds Express Highways." *Roads and Streets*, no. 78 (June): 187–190.

Index